SIBERIA

ITS CONQUEST AND DEVELOPMENT

Inside the Arctic Circle. The quest for valuable furs was one of the earliest incentives to the colonization of inhospitable Siberia.

SIBERIA
Its Conquest and Development

YURI SEMYONOV

Translated from the German by

J. R. FOSTER

HELICON PRESS

BALTIMORE

Helicon Press, Inc.
1120 N. Calvert Street
Baltimore 2, Md.

Library of Congress Catalog Card Number: 63-15003

First published in English language 1963

Translated from the original text "Sibirien"
published in the German language by Verlag Ullstein G.m.b.H.,
Frankfurt/Main – Berlin, 1954

Printed and bound in Great Britain for
Helicon Press, Inc.
by Cox & Wyman Ltd, Reading
Set in Monotype Imprint

CONTENTS

Contents

Contents

ILLUSTRATIONS

MAPS

*Maps originally drawn by Elisabeth Armgardt, Ilse Eckart and
Willi Leetz and redrawn for this edition by Leo Vernon.*

GLOSSARY

Artel   an association or guild formed by Siberian colonizers.

Baidarka   a kind of boat used by Aleutian Islanders.

Boyar   Russian baron. A *Boyar's* son did not necessarily acquire the rank of *boyar* but enjoyed a distinct status of his own.

Gospoda   a District Authority.

Hetman (ataman)   Cossack leader.

Kocha   Cossacks' flat-bottomed boat.

Kotik   same as *sivuch*.

Lodsha   a kind of boat.

Mir   a village community.

Odinetz   a prize pelt.

Ostrog   fortified settlement built by Siberian colonizers.

Otkupchik   monopolist in the distilling and sale of vodka.

Pestzy   a kind of fox found on Bering Island.

Posadnik   chief town magistrate.

Prikastshik   supervisor of government trading post.

Pud   old measure of weight, about 35 lb.

Shitik   a kind of boat.

Sivuch   a species of seal found on Bering Island.

Streltzy   a detachment from a rifle regiment.

Taiga   coniferous forest lands of northern Siberia.

Veche   town assembly.

Verst   measure of distance, about two-thirds of a mile.

Voivode   military commander of a district.

Vsyatka   colloquial word for bribe.

Yassak   tribute of furs paid to the government.

A NOTE ON DATING

Dates of events in Russia and Siberia are normally given according to the Old Russian (Julian) calendar, which was ten days behind the European (Gregorian) calendar in the seventeenth century, eleven days behind in the eighteenth, twelve days behind in the nineteenth and thirteen days in the twentieth. Events of European importance in the nineteenth and twentieth centuries, such as wars, diplomatic negotiations and Nordenskiöld's voyage, are given their 'European' date. If two dates are given, the first refers to the Russian calendar, the second to the European: e.g. 19 February (3 March) 1861.

TRANSLATOR'S PREFACE

THIS BOOK is a history of that vast area extending from the Urals eastward to the Chinese border and the Pacific, from which Russia now draws so much of her economic strength. It tells the story of the exploration, conquest and development of Siberia, from the rise of Moscow and the first eastward trips of the traders of Novgorod in the Middle Ages to the construction of the Trans-Siberian railway, the Russo-Japanese War and the enormous economic progress of the last forty years.

Its author, Yuri Semyonov, is a Russian who left his native country after the Revolution, lived for many years in Germany and is now Lecturer at the Slavonic Institute of Uppsala University in Sweden. Personal acquaintance with Siberia, where he travelled as a young man, together with an easy mastery of the considerable literature on the subject, has enabled him to bring his narrative to life with a wealth of picturesque but pertinent detail. Yet it never lags; with five hundred years and five thousand miles to cover, it scarcely has time to. The background of the story ranges from Murmansk to Hawaii; its actors include priests like St Stephen, first bishop of Perm, Cossack freebooters like Yermak, merchant venturers like Shelikhov, explorers like Bering and Nordenskiöld, colonial governors like Baranov, the veritable patriarch of Russian America, princely proconsuls like Muravyev and statesmen like Witte, who built the Trans-Siberian railway and might even have saved the Tsarist régime from destruction if he had been allowed to introduce the reforms which he saw to be necessary.

The book is an expansion and modernization of an earlier *Conquest of Siberia* published in 1937. Both the present book and its predecessor originally appeared in Germany, and it was partly German interest in Siberia – the result of the forced sojourn there of large numbers of prisoners in the Second World War – which stimulated the author to produce a new version of his earlier book.

Apart from the intrinsic interest of the story (in which many Englishmen have figured, from Chancellor and the Muscovy Company to the enterprising Captain Wiggins in the nineteenth century), it is useful to be reminded of the Russian achievement in subduing this vast and inhospitable land. For it was indeed an achievement, carried out largely by enterprising individuals with very little government support. We have grown so used to laughing (often unjustifiably) at Russian claims to have discovered or invented almost everything that we are in some danger of forgetting their very real accomplishments in other fields besides that of missiles. History may teach no lessons (so at least we have been assured by one eminent contemporary English historian) and understanding your opponent may not remove the reasons for differing from him, but knowledge can nevertheless remove misconceptions and force us to revise preconceived opinions. It is valuable as well as amusing to be reminded that in the nineteenth century Russia regarded America as her best ally against Britain and that the North was grateful for Russian support during the Civil War; hence the sale of Alaska to the United States.

It only remains to say that in the transliteration of Russian names I have aimed at consistency but rather doubt whether I have achieved it. I can only hope that they appear in forms which are recognizable – and not too irritating to Russian scholars.

J. R. F.

I

DRIVING FORCES

———◆◆◆◆———

THE IRON GATE

AT THE beginning of the twelfth century the Russian lands
absorbed the Mongol wave that had piled up in the east to
crash down on Europe. So huge was this wave that parts of it
swept on as far as central Europe, but the bulk of it broke in
the great Eurasian plain and took two and a half centuries to
disperse.

The brilliant political, economic and cultural developments
which had begun on the banks of the Dnieper were halted. Prosperous, thickly populated districts were transformed into a waste-
land. All who could fled to the north, to the forests. The Russian
Mesopotamia, the land between the rivers Volga and Oka,
acquired its population. When the Asiatic horde passed on, there
were people enough there; they only needed to be united and
organized. This was done by Moscow.

One after the other, like nocturnal shadows on the walls of the
Kremlin, the figures of old Moscow flit past us. First there is Ivan,
nicknamed 'Money-bags', an arid old miser, a pious usurer, who
bought out his fellow-princes with 'wise humility'.

There is his oldest son, Simeon, who continued his work. He
inherited his father's wisdom, but not his humility. He passed into
history as 'the proud'.

There is 'Money-bags' ' great-grandson, Dimitri, described by
a chronicler as 'strong, brave and divinely beautiful'; at the age of
twelve he mounted a charger, waged war against the Lithuanians,
Tver, Ryazan and the Tartars and at twenty-nine, at the head of
the Russian host, defeated Khan Mamai at the battle of Kulikovo.

There is Dimitri's grandson, Vasily the Dark, the severely
tested Job of Moscow, who waged war for nearly twenty years on
all fronts, was defeated more than once, ruined, taken prisoner and
finally blinded; wrapped in eternal darkness, he went on with his

collecting and collected more than his fortunate father or his legendary, heroic grandfather.

There is Ivan III, the first ruler of Moscow to call himself 'Tsar'. The word 'Tsar' comes from 'Caesar'; the greatness and glory of the Roman Empire already hovered before the eyes of this Muscovite prince.

Ivan III was one of the most successful Tsars. He ended the payment of tribute to the Tartars and shook off the Tartar yoke once for all. He invited artists and scholars from Europe to Moscow. Moreover in 1472 he took as his second wife Sophia, the niece of the last Byzantine emperor. Byzantium was the heir of Rome, Moscow the heir of Byzantium. Moscow was the third Rome; there was to be no fourth.

Ivan III now felt himself the real Tsar of all the Russians. However, the Russian lands had still to be united. A path into the outside world had still to be found. To the south it was barred by the Turks, to the east by the Tartars, and to the west by the Poles and Lithuanians. There remained only the path to the north and north-west, the path to the Baltic and the White Sea, and this was blocked by Novgorod.

The spirit of freedom had flourished at Novgorod since olden times. The people of Novgorod were merchants, and merchants like freedom because it helps trade. The great conqueror Tamerlaine had once said that, and it was also the view of that enlightened ruler Catherine II.

All Novgorod's supplies were brought to it from a distance. It obtained its corn and every other kind of food from the east, from the Volga and the Oka. But the people of Novgorod had nothing to give in exchange; they could only obtain what their corn-suppliers wanted – cloth, arms, ironmongery and glassware – from the west, from Dutch merchants at first and later from the Hansa towns. But the Hansa towns did not give things away for nothing either; in exchange they wanted the products of the forests and seas of the north: furs, honey, wax, tar, potash, blubber and walrus teeth. The people of Novgorod took charge of the barter-trade between east and west; and after they had handed out furs and wax in one direction and cloth and axes in the other, a considerable number of gold and silver ducats, florins, dollars and roubles remained behind in Novgorod.

It is profitable to sell other people's goods, but even more profitable to sell your own. So active young citizens of Novgorod climbed aboard their boats and sailed down the River Volkhov to Lake Ladoga, and from there down the Svir to Lake Onega. Other rivers and lakes took them farther north and east. When they could not sail any farther they pulled their boats overland; when they came to water again they launched their boats once more, and finally reached the Dvina and the White Sea.

The path to the north-east had already been opened up by the Varangers. As early as the ninth century they had pushed on to the Perm region, to Biarmia, which was supposed to conceal legendary treasures, and for two centuries they had sent expeditions there. The little town of Cherdyn, on the Vichera, a tributary of the Kama, was at that time a centre of trade and the capital of rich Biarmia. Crowds of Persian, Arabian and Armenian merchants assembled there.

The men of Novgorod started the colonization of the north, where they appeared as civilizers and missionaries. They founded the town of Khlynov, later known as Vyatka and today as Kirov, at the end of a successful campaign in which God never left their side; he even indicated the site on which Khlynov was to be built. As the men of Novgorod were preparing wood for the construction of the town on the banks of the Khlynov, the water rose and carried all the wood to another spot.

Wherever the men of Novgorod went on their expeditions to the north-east they bought furs which had come from regions still farther to the north-east. Beyond these lay the 'great rock', and the road was barred by the 'iron gate'. This was how the men of Novgorod described the Urals, beyond which an unknown world began.

Its inhabitants – the men of Novgorod called them 'Yugrians' – were 'impure', that is, heathen, and also extremely warlike. In 1032 the *voivode* (or military commander) Uleb marched through the iron gate and returned with booty. In 1079 Prince Glyeb Svyatoslavovich set out with a great expedition and still greater hopes, but neither the prince himself nor any of his followers returned. In 1169 an expedition once again met with success. In 1187 another, undertaken by the nobles of Novgorod, who were joined by a hundred *boyars*' sons, returned without booty or *boyars*' sons.

Again and again the men of Novgorod marched into these

15

remote lands. Again and again they met disaster, and the impression which they formed of the region was not a very favourable one. On his campaigns through the world, so the people of Novgorod used to say, Alexander the Great crossed the 'great rock' (the Urals) to Yugria and the icy sea. He saw the inhabitants of the land. They ate carrion and corpses and all kinds of filth, prayed to idols and knew nothing of Christianity. So Alexander prayed to God to free the world from such monsters. God heard his prayer and bade the great rock close round these impure tribes; he left one single copper gate in the ring of rock and this gate he locked and bolted. Only at the Last Judgement would this gate be opened again.

The 'disciple', that is, the employee, of one Gyurata, who was sent 'on business' to Yugria in 1096, brought this story back to his master. Gyurata passed it on to the chroniclers. Two points in it deserve attention. First, the gate is described as being made not of iron but of copper. The 'disciple' had obviously discovered that the Urals were rich in copper as well as iron-ore. Second, although he mentions many things in his vivid picture of the impure tribes, there is one thing that he does not mention: namely, that in that land, as well as the 'impure', there were also beavers, sables, red foxes, black foxes and polar bears; that millions of walruses crawled up the icy shores and mammoth-tusks – ivory – were buried in the earth.

This story is one of the oldest, and Gyurata's expedition one of the earliest. Very little was known about Yugria in Novgorod at that time, but the cunning Gyurata knew how to keep business secrets.

THE NOVGOROD BARRIER IS FORCED

As the Muscovite state grew, the lands in the north and north-east began to give rise to disputes. Moscow asserted that the local chieftains had sworn allegiance to her; Novgorod, on the other hand, treated these territories as her own.

The chancelleries went on quarrelling but in fact the men of Novgorod were on the spot and continued to exert their 'influence'. They pumped everything they needed out of these lands: furs, honey, wax and gems from the Urals, tar and salt from the regions of Vyatka and Perm, river-pearls, walrus teeth and blubber from Pechora, the Dvina and the White Sea. Trade flourished. The Hanseatic merchants were always in Novgorod and close attention was paid to their advice about the sort of goods in demand.

The line of 'colonies', 'mandates', 'protectorates', 'spheres of influence', or whatever you like to call them, ran from Great Novgorod to Pechora and the northern slopes of the Urals. This huge bow was held by the slender thread of Novgorod settlements, the nodal points formed by the scattered towns and the monasteries. Below this bow, cut off by it from the Baltic and all the legendary lands of the north, lay double-dealing Moscow, now strong and self-confident. It was only a question of time before it sprang the bow.

In the first half of the fourteenth century, together with the tribute-gatherers and river-pirates of Novgorod, the first large-scale colonial entrepreneur had arrived in the Perm region, an industrial pioneer with capital, a man who could wield a spade as well as the sword: his name was Svoyesemtzev. He was successful in the biggest enterprises and was the first to build salt works in that region. Towards the end of the century Svoyesemtzev was the richest man in Novgorod and all Russia.

Soon other famous Novgorod families made their mark as owners of businesses: the Ananyins, the Lochinskys and others. In the old lands nearer to Novgorod other respected *boyar* families reigned: the Akinfiyevs, the Boretskys. When Martha, the daughter of the *boyar* Lochinsky, married Isaac Boretsky, two 'spheres of influence' were combined: Perm joined hands with the White Sea, and colonial enterprises were united to ancestral lands.

The 'high finance' of Novgorod also contributed to the alliance. Martha's first husband had been the *boyar* Philip, a financier, cosmopolitan and, naturally, a 'westernizer'. The marriage had been unlucky; the husband died very soon after it. Some years later Martha married the chief magistrate or *posadnik* of the city, Isaac Boretsky; when he died in 1460 his wife became not only the richest but also the most powerful woman in Novgorod. In her house matters were decided before they were brought before the *veche* or town assembly. People with complaints came to her. She appointed and dismissed officials.

But storm-clouds were already gathering over Novgorod. Martha and her friends knew that Moscow wanted to swallow them up.

They knew that Moscow was stronger than they were. They knew that if Moscow cut off Novgorod's corn supply the great city would have to be fed on German gingerbread and Indian pepper. This eventuality had long been foreseen at the meetings in Martha's house. A secret pact had been concluded with Casimir IV, king of Poland and Lithuania. The watchword was 'great Novgorod's ruler and protector: the king of Poland'.

Moscow knew all this; for it had its friends in Novgorod. The Novgorod clergy did not want the protection of a Catholic king. The metropolitan of Moscow demanded decisive action.

It was not difficult to find an excuse, and the war began in 1471. The two armies met on the banks of the River Shelon. The men of Novgorod fought bravely; twelve thousand of them fell and only seventeen hundred were taken prisoner, among them their commander, Martha's son, Dimitri Boretsky and his whole staff.

Novgorod's will to fight was broken. After a short siege the city confessed that it had been guilty of 'rebellion' against the grand prince. Its ambassadors begged Ivan on their knees for forgiveness and the archbishop called for it in the name of God.

Ivan forgave Novgorod. He even gave it back the Dvina territory, which in the meantime had been occupied by Muscovite troops, and kept only the rest for himself. He was content with a payment of 80 *puds* of silver, but the foreign policy and military affairs of the free city were henceforward directed by Moscow.

Martha tried to retrieve the city's shattered fortunes. Blind with rage, actuated only by the desire for revenge, she was no longer capable of judging a situation correctly. Her last son, Fyodor, was quite useless; good-natured, almost soft, he was known in Novgorod as Fyodor the Booby. Martha appointed this booby chief magistrate (*posadnik*). Naturally he was a bad governor and allowed all kinds of illegal occurrences. When the Grand Prince Ivan visited Novgorod shortly afterwards he was besieged with complaints. Fyodor and his friends were dismissed from office, put in chains and banished to remote monasteries. Fyodor became a monk and died a year later.

The struggle seemed to be over, but there were still a number of details to be settled. For example, Novgorod 'democracy' still existed and, what was more important, so did the trade with the Hanseatic League and the Novgorod 'spheres of influence'.

An end had to be made to all this, and it soon was. At a reception at Moscow the ambassadors of Novgorod failed to use the right verbal formula, and the city's excuses were declared unsatisfactory. In 1478 the Grand Prince's troops arrived in front of the free city. They did not even have to fight. The people of Novgorod tried to negotiate, but in vain. When the capitulation had been signed the Grand Prince entered the city. This time the final closure was applied. The symbol of Novgorod's freedom, the bell that summoned the people to the assembly, was taken down and shipped off to Moscow. Martha and many others went into exile. With her little grandchild, Fyodor the Booby's son, she was banished to a convent near Nishni-Novgorod and ended her life there as a nun.

HOLY AND UNHOLY PATHS

After Perm, Moscow swallowed up Vyatka (Khlynov). The people of Khlynov rejoiced at the fall of Novgorod. They had eagerly joined Moscow and helped it to defeat the men of Novgorod on the Dvina and the Shelon. It did not occur to them that they were undermining their own freedom.

They continued to do what they had often done before: they made attacks on the Muscovite town of Ustyug and the Muscovite colonists in Perm. But their neighbours were only waiting to teach the 'thieves' a lesson.

When the Muscovite troops appeared before the gates of Khlynov the 'thieves' tried to offer resistance, but soon had to surrender.

Time marched on. The merchants of Novgorod faced ruin. But the Hansa merchants were ruined too. For two and a half centuries they had pioneered the road to the east. They had not only held court at Novgorod; they had penetrated far into Novgorod territory. After the final subjection of Novgorod trade with the Hanseatic League was immediately forbidden. Nine years later it was allowed again. Then the trade was alternately allowed and prohibited. For a time the Hansa merchants were even given the right to trade through the White Sea as well as through Novgorod. But by that time the Dutch and the English were appearing in north Russia, and the Hansa merchants had to trade on the same footing as these newcomers. Their earlier privileges were a thing of the past.

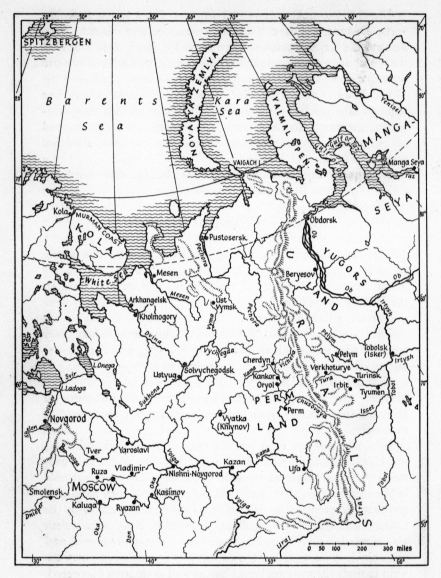

The Grand Princedom of Moscow down to the year 1600,
with Perm, the Urals and Mangaseya.

After Moscow had removed all vestiges of independence in the north the road was open for its merchants to trade to the White Sea and the Urals. But it was not only to help their merchants that the Muscovite forces were compelled to advance into the far north. Moscow also wanted to protect its colonists.

The bases or strong-points of this first colonization were the monasteries. The links between religion and trade are proved by the monasteries which were built with the merchants' money and by the centres of trade which still stand where monasteries stood earlier.

The Muscovite settlements on the River Sukhona, a tributary of the Dvina, cut like a wedge into the Novgorod colonies. Here lay the town of Ustyug. It was rich, for it lay at the junction of the roads from Moscow and Novgorod to the Urals. The inhabitants were Russian, and so there was a church; the church had a priest, a deacon and a sacristan; and in 1345 a son was born to the sacristan. This son was christened Stephen; later on he played a tremendous rôle in the history of north Russia and was canonized by the Orthodox Church.

Like all the boys in Ustyug, Stephen used to roam about the streets; he was particularly fond of loitering in the market. There he made the acquaintance of the Zyrians and learned their language. There, too, he came to know his future flock.

Soon he had overtaken his father and become deacon at the church where his father was sacristan. Then he entered a monastery in north Russia. There he spent ten hard, ascetic years and received the higher clerical education, studying Greek among other subjects. A splendid career was open to the talented young priest. His companions went off to Moscow to angle for a good benefice, but Stephen preferred to go his own way.

He returned to his native town of Ustyug and proceeded to perform his great act of faith. He had decided to set about the conversion of the Zyrians, those poor inhabitants of the Perm region whom, as a boy, he had despised because of their 'impurity'. Like the people of Perm, they used to bring skins, poultry and wild honey to Ustyug market. They were just as grey and bright-eyed as the people of Perm, but they were smaller in stature. Beside them, the big Russian farmers looked like giants.

Attempts had already been made earlier on to convert these pagans and 'knaves' to the true faith by violent methods. Stephen was the first to talk to them. He compiled a Zyrian grammar and translated the scriptures into Zyrian. He explained the Word of God to these pagans in a language that they could understand. This was in the fourteenth century.

He did not stay put in his native Ustyug. He travelled to the north-east, crossed the Dvina and sailed up the Vychegda and its tributary the Vyma. The sources of the Vyma lie near Pechora. This was the Zyrians' native land, and the town and monastery of Ust-Vymsk, which Stephen founded there, became the centre of Christian civilization in this forgotten wilderness of forest. From here Stephen journeyed out to preach. He challenged the Zyrian magicians to theological disputations. He defeated them by his words and the force of his personality. He burned down the temples of their idols before the eyes of the Zyrians, who saw with amazement the powerlessness of their gods and priests before this little monk. Challenged by a Zyrian priest, he submitted himself to trial by fire and water. According to the legend, he was not harmed by either element, but the magician disappeared at the last moment and was seen no more.

In place of the miserable little temples that had been burnt down he erected churches, modest buildings of wood. To the savages these chapels seemed the height of splendour; they were dazzled by the pictures of the saints and mesmerized by the sound of the bells. They saw that Stephen had no interest in furs and demanded no tribute from them; he promised them happiness in heaven, and even on earth he healed their diseases and gave them bread.

Stephen built one church after another, pushing on continually farther north, nearer to Pechora, and the 'rock'. Russian colonists settled round the churches. Ten years went by on work of this kind. The tasks which Stephen saw before him grew continually wider. In his town of Ust-Vymsk lived monks, warriors, craftsmen and scholars. Moscow grasped the significance of this holy colonization; Stephen was made a bishop.

Moscow's *voivodes* had orders to give every assistance to the Bishop of Perm. He made use of this assistance only to a limited degree, but his reputation grew greater and greater among Russians, Zyrians and the people of Perm. Native princes and ordinary folk, too, turned to him for help when the Muscovite authorities pressed them too hard. He had become the mediator between them and the Grand Princes of Moscow. He was always on the move and sometimes went on business to Moscow, too. He died on one of these journeys at the early age of fifty-one.

Nevertheless he had succeeded in laying a firm foundation and a whole series of successors continued his work. The bishopric of Perm became a mighty spiritual principality, owning monasteries, whole villages and very extensive lands. Its political influence was immense. Even before Siberia was subdued, the prince-bishops of Perm were acting as arbitrators between the native princes on the far side of the Urals.

The course of the River Vyma, which Stephen had chosen for his heroic spiritual conquests, formed at that time the most important road to Pechora and the northern Urals. In 1499 a great expedition from Moscow entered the land of the Yugors by this path. At its head was Prince Semyon Kurbsky.

His army consisted of four thousand men. This host crossed the Pechora in winter and reached the Ob on the far side of the Urals, but Kurbsky was unable to stay there.

The *voivodes* travelled across the tundra with the help of reindeer, the common soldiers with the help of dogs; so says the chronicler. It is difficult to imagine four thousand men on sledges pulled by dogs; there were not enough dogs for that in the whole of the tundra. All the same, the expedition as a whole was a grandiose conception. Although he lost some of his men, Kurbsky returned with a thousand prisoners and a considerable number of furs. But on the whole his trip across the tundra was not a success. It was clear that St Stephen's path was of little value for military or political excursions into Siberia. It thus remained the preserve of private enterprise for the time being, and was only later to play an important part, in the sixteenth and seventeenth centuries. It was a difficult and dangerous road, and for this reason there were persistent attempts to find a more convenient link with Siberia. This was discovered when the saints and *voivodes* were succeeded in the task by the traders.

THE CHOICE OF ORIENTATION

In the heroic days of Dimitri Donskoy, when the Russian princes were harnessing their last resources in the attempt to resist the

Mongolian hordes of Mamai, the will and energy of Novgorod were focused on economic expansion. Bold pioneers travelled out to new regions. The dangers were no less than those of the struggle against the Tartars; the gains to be won were considerably greater. Among these pioneers was a citizen of Novgorod called Spiridon. He was not of particularly distinguished birth; there is no record of his having served the state in any capacity. He went to the Dvina region and engaged there in trade; he bought and exchanged raw materials, took them to Novgorod, sold them to the Hansa merchants and returned home with fresh wares to exchange.

This Spiridon was the first Stroganov about whom we have reliable historical information.

He died in 1395, leaving behind him numerous children. His oldest son, Kosma, continued his father's work; he built his own warehouses for his goods and gained the reputation of being a sound and reliable merchant.

The stormy fifteenth century rolled on. Side growths branched out in many directions, but the family grew stronger and stronger. Kosma's son Luka was a great man in the Dvina region. He continued to expand the family's trading activities. Like his father and grandfather he sent furs and raw materials to Novgorod. But he also set out on a fresh tack, and so altered the destiny of the whole Stroganov clan.

The Grand Prince of Moscow also had possessions on the Dvina. But their owner was a long way off and the income they brought him was small. Luka rented a large number of these possessions; he collected taxes from them, retained a fixed proportion for himself and sent the rest to Moscow.

In this way he forged a link with Novgorod's great enemy. However, he did not break off relations with the free city. He did not forget to send gifts to the churches of Novgorod and he employed Novgorod men in his business. The longest economic perspectives opened up in the direction of Moscow, and this fact became clearer and clearer to the far-sighted merchant. Luka sent his Hanseatic and Novgorod goods, as well as the taxes for the Prince, via Ustyug to Moscow.

When Luka had realized the value of the 'Moscow orientation' he drew all the logical conclusions. One of his actions shows how a line of profit-making generations can suddenly throw up a man who becomes a historical figure. This action is connected with the fate of the most tragic of the Moscow 'collectors', Grand Prince Vasily the Dark. The Tartars were involved in the internal disputes of the Russian princes. Vasily had fallen into the hands of the Khan of Kazan. From Kazan a demand for ransom arrived at Moscow.

We do not know exactly how much the Tartars asked for him. The chroniclers mention various sums, ranging from twenty-nine thousand to two hundred thousand roubles. The second figure is hardly credible; at that time even twenty-nine thousand roubles constituted a fabulous sum. In any case, Vasily had to pay an enormous sum for his release and there was no money to be had at that time in ruined Moscow.

Luka Stroganov gave the money. Whether he gave all of it or only a part is not important. What is important is that he indubitably had to convert a large part of his fortune into ready money for the purpose, and that he sacrificed this money without any guarantee that Vasily would still remain Grand Prince when he returned from captivity. The fate of the house of Stroganov was already linked to the fate of the princes of Moscow. Luka could only carry out his plans, which he kept to himself, in conjunction with Moscow. He sent the money without hesitation, and without any strings attached to it.

This deed was not forgotten in Moscow. In the charter granted by the Tsar to Luka's descendants a hundred and fifty years later we read: 'In times of difficulty *boyars* and merchants gave the state money, but they demanded pearls, furs, precious vessels and the revenues of taxes as security; the Stroganovs, on the other hand, took no securities and sought no advantage for themselves.'

ANIKA STROGANOV

The Stroganovs did not find a spot that suited them right away. Luka had settled on the Dvina, but his son Fyodor felt cramped there. He moved his house from the Dvina to the Vychegda and settled down in the remote township of Solvychegodsk. 'Sol' is the Russian for 'salt'. The new situation meant new work; it transformed the Stroganovs from merchants into industrialists.

Fyodor preserved the reputation of the Stroganovs as a God-fearing family. All through his life he maintained good relations with the Church and at the end of his days, when he was an old man, he finally devoted himself to God: he entered a monastery as a monk, under the name of Theodosius. Two years earlier, when the old man was already being measured for his monk's cowl, so to speak, another son – his fourth – was born to him. This late-comer, Anika, grew up to become the most important and powerful pillar of the house of Stroganov.

It should be emphasized that at Fyodor's death the sons divided the estate and as a result Anika began not with the great fortune in land left by his father but with only a quarter of it. His brothers claimed the estates in the various parts of the Ustyug region; Anika stayed in Solvychegodsk.

He was seventeen when he became the master of the house. His education was already complete; he could read and write, knew by heart all the requisite prayers and could have celebrated Mass as well as any pope.

When Fyodor chose the site for his house, he did not pick a spot next to the fairly big settlements at Solvychegodsk but one seven *versts* away from them, a forsaken place in a barren region. A forest had first to be rooted up and a marsh drained; nearby there was a salt lake.

At seventeen young men tend to dream, some of love, others of distant seas and unknown lands. No doubt Anika dreamed of love, too, but he did not need to dream of unknown lands; they lay just outside the gates of his house. As for unknown seas, he made up his mind to gain control of the salt lake at his feet. Anika's father had begun to boil salt in this region and other local residents did it as well. They had built their primitive little factories all round the lake. The equipment used was simple. A deep well was dug, a wheel was erected over it, and salt water flowed down con-duits into the salt-pan, which was heated by a wood fire. The water turned into steam and the salt was left in the pan. There was a layer of rock salt under the surface; the spring water was satur-ated with it. Anika began to swallow up first his neighbours, then those farther off. If the reader asks where a seventeen-year-old boy got an appetite like this from, the answer is perhaps that it is an example of inherited knowledge: the newly-hatched duck makes for the water, the young spider sets about catching flies.

At the end of ten years most of the salt-works were in Anika's hands. The head of the enterprise was not lazy and it grew steadily.

Methods of production were improved and rationalized, and the most difficult part of the business – disposal – was organized on a big scale. The salt floated down the Vychegda and the Dvina in boats, up the Sukhona to Ustyug and on to Moscow. The story of Luka indicates why it took this direction. There is no salt round Moscow or in central Russia. The Hansa merchants once brought salt from Bruges to Novgorod, and the traders of Novgorod carried it onward to the Volga. Moscow obtained its salt from the Crimea; it was carried right across the great Russian plain by the producers, who had to pay taxes and customs-dues everywhere and were constantly threatened by Tartar arrows and Cossack sabres. Hence Moscow's never-changing friendliness to the Stroganovs.

Another ten years went by and Anika's sons were already beginning to help their father. In twenty years of marriage his wife Mavra had given him eight children, and concern for their health and welfare had even caused him to engage a personal doctor. He brought him back from Kola, where many foreigners came for the fur trade. The doctor is described as 'German, a doctor and apothecary'. We know something about him because he found river-pearls in the little River Iksa, and Anika made him head of the pearl business. These river-pearls were mostly small and angular, but nevertheless they were real pearls and had always been popular in Russia as ornaments for women's dresses and pictures of saints.

Meanwhile Anika had developed into a vigorous man. He was stern, dry and realistic, and possessed a commanding personality. These qualities were not usual ones and legends grew up round his person. That he was a capitalist and 'bourgeois', that he worked to amass money, and that he amassed money in order to be able to widen the field of his activities, was incomprehensible to most men. There are many stories about the fantastic treasures that Anika was supposed to have buried in the 'Stroganov hill'. In reality he left no 'treasures' when he died. Everything is listed in his will: silver cups, ornaments, precious icons, embroidered cloth. Every reasonably comfortable Moscow *boyar* possessed as much. On the other hand, the value of the enterprises that Anika left behind him was inestimable. All his factories were working at full blast. His whole capital was usefully employed. There was gold only on his icons, and there, too, it earned him interest, even if it was only payable in the next world.

Anika did not confine himself to the salt industry. He expanded his activities in every possible direction, sending his young sons out to travel round buying and selling. But he always kept his attention mainly on Moscow. To Moscow, via Ustyug, he sent every conceivable kind of goods from the north. From the mouth of the Pechora fishermen brought him caviare, and salted, smoked and frozen fish. From the distant tundra he obtained reindeer skins, and from the nearby forests feathers, down and wax, not to mention furs.

These things brought him not only big profits but also access to the highest circles, including the court of the Tsar. Anika's generosity and affability won him useful friends, and this helped him in his business deals.

He soon became the regular court supplier. Whatever was needed at court was provided by Anika. He became indispensable. If the Tsar wanted to give a present to his 'beloved brother' the Emperor Maximilian or his 'beloved sister' Queen Elizabeth, Anika delivered valuable furs. When Ivan's wife's bed was too hard, Anika provided down. If the Tsar wanted to go hunting, Anika provided hawks; if he wanted amusement, Anika provided bears. It goes without saying that he supplied fish and game for the Tsar's table. All this was quite natural, but what bordered on the magical was that he also supplied wares from overseas, things that simply did not exist on the Vychegda. He sent Italian wines to Moscow for the Tsar's table. Where did Anika get them from? His furs and salt procured them. At this time he sent salt not only to all the towns of Russia, but also to Lithuania, and Lithuania was Europe. At Kola fair, too, he obtained foreign goods in exchange for his furs.

Anika equipped an expedition of ten men and sent it over the Urals to trade in the land of the Yugors, which he naturally knew by hearsay. Anika's men did no one any harm on their way, no one did them any harm, and they returned laden with furs.

In the following year he sent out another band of men, providing them with still more goods to barter. According to Dutch reports it was mainly cheap stuff: little bells, worthless ornaments and suchlike, 'because of his enormous greed', add the reports. The Dutch were very sensitive about this question of greed; they themselves had come to Moscow from purely idealistic motives, of course.

From now on Anika sent out an expedition every year. He required his envoys to investigate everything on the spot: what kind of people lived there, how they lived and what sort of roads there were. He collected information and furs at the same time, making a good profit out of the latter. A splendid stone church was built at Solvychegodsk; out of sable and ermine, you might say.

Sable also contributed to the development of the salt industry, for Anika used his income from trade to enlarge his salt-works. He was up to his ears in business, so much so that he himself could no longer attend to all the details. Three sons assisted him. His first wife, Mavra, had died. How could Anika live without a wife to look after his house? He was not old yet; only fifty-one.

Sophia was twenty years younger than he was. She was carefree; but age is cautious and looks round suspiciously. When Sophia moved into the house, Anika immediately sent his only unmarried son, Semyon, to his distant salt-works.

His businesses were numerous. Their scope grew continually wider. The expeditions across the Urals opened up a gold mine. They followed in the footsteps of St Stephen: from the Vychegda to the Vyma, from the latter to the Pechora and up its tributaries through the 'iron gate' into the land of the Yugors. Anika's employees knew the local languages; there were natives of the region among them. He thus received precise information about everything.

In Moscow legends circulated about his vast store of furs, his secret relations with unknown princes who delivered furs to him, about a whole great land that Anika was supposed to have subdued and kept hidden from Moscow. It was at this time that the name of the land appeared for the first time. It was called Mangaseya. Where this name came from is not known – it may be derived from 'Mokaseya', the name of a mythical ruler, or from 'Mokasse', the name of an old tribe on the other side of the Urals – but in any case the new word created a myth and stimulated men's imaginations.

In this land lived the Mangaseyans. They ate reindeer flesh and fish, and occasionally each other; this practice of cannibalism earned for them the name *samoyeds*, from *sam* – self, *yede* – eater. The Muscovites believed that the Samoyeds were small in stature, with flat faces and small noses; they were supposed to be excellent runners and bowmen, and to drive teams of reindeer and dogs; if a guest arrived among them, they knifed their own children and served them up to the guest; if he could not cope with this diet and died from it, they did not bury him but ate him, too; they were also supposed to devour their own dead.

Again, there were other tribes which kept the black sables in herds for meat; in that region, thick white clouds floated in the sky; sometimes they sank right down to earth and little squirrels and baby deer jumped out of them. . . .

The legendary Mangaseya lay in reality far away, farther than the land of the Yugors, beyond the mouth of the River Ob and the basin of the Taz. Even at that time there were in fact people who knew something about Mangaseya, but they lived far from Moscow, on the White Sea and the Pechora. In their flat-bottomed sailing-boats they sailed to the Yamal peninsula, up the rivers, dragged their boats over the watersheds, and floated down the rivers on the other side. Thus they arrived in the basin of the Ob and finally reached Mangaseya. How they managed all this we simply cannot imagine today, and nor could the English and Dutch in the sixteenth century. They did it, all the same. We possess an imaginative record of it, a document that also contains the legends about the 'impure Samoyeds'. It is entitled 'The saga of the unknown peoples' and was probably compiled at the very end of the fifteenth century. Anika Stroganov certainly knew of this route, but it was too remote for him; its immense difficulties must also have been known to him. It was not until after Anika's death that his sons struck out towards Mangaseya across the Arctic Ocean.

The sagas and legends interested Anika very little. But when the story-tellers began to describe how he, Anika Stroganov, had subdued all these peoples and forced them to pay tribute, he thought to himself that his silence might cause displeasure at the Kremlin. Accordingly in 1557 he appeared in Moscow with his sons, bowed respectfully to all the right people – not with empty hands, either, as was only right – and presented the Tsar himself with costly gifts; but, above all, he took the opportunity to give a detailed report on Mangaseya.

The old man was given a friendly reception. He was known and respected in Moscow. The metropolitan of Moscow was his friend, for Anika had never been mean about presents to the Church and even the Tsar recognized his theological knowledge.

The booksellers of Moscow, too, knew that he would pay any price they liked to ask for a beautiful 'sacred' book. In this way he had assembled a library of two hundred and six of the rarest and most valuable volumes.

But it would not be right to depict Anika as a saint. At home his clerks groaned under his rod, and his second wife bore him one child after another. Ten great salt-works worked day and night for him. Carts laden with goods of every kind creaked over the rough roads, heavily loaded ships sat deep in the water. At that time he had over six hundred workmen and clerks.

Anika gave the Tsar a sober account of Mangaseya. He explained that it would be difficult for the time being to take the land by force, and that he could obtain more furs for the Tsar by quiet friendliness than the *voivodes* could with their clumsy artillery. He told the Tsar what kind of a road it was that led there: through regions where there were no animals or birds, where a giant mountain stood which one of his employees had spent seventeen days in climbing without reaching the top. 'You cannot take this land of Mangaseya, Tsar, until you have opened up another way to it. The road through the land of Perm. There the earth is desolate and empty; no men live there. Give me this land . . .'

Anika spoke convincingly, and his words were not lost on the Tsar. After a century and a half of 'collecting', the occupants of the Kremlin understood very well what frontier territories and trade routes meant. Anika did not conceal what attracted him to Perm. There was virgin ground there, and salt. You could grow corn. There were minerals.

Anika needed all these things for his business. It cost him too much to feed his people on imported wheat. He had no iron for his salt-works. There was no waterway leading direct from Solvyche-godsk to Moscow; the salt had to be unloaded from the boats on to carts, and then back on to boats again. By the time the salt arrived in Moscow half of it had been lost, the rest was damp, and the price was tripled. Moscow had to be prepared almost every year for a shortage of salt. And on top of all this Perm lay there fallow!

Such were Anika's words to the Tsar. He thought he was doing a business deal; in reality he was making history. He was the first to awaken Moscow's interest in Siberia. He explained the economic importance of Mangaseya and indicated the necessity of a more convenient means of access farther to the south.

It can hardly be supposed that Anika had in mind the conquest and colonization of Siberia. He wanted the land of Perm; his proposal meant no more than the colonization of this region, and he offered to head the work of colonization himself. However, the final result of his suggestion was a Russian Siberia and a frontier on the Pacific Ocean. Never in the whole history of Russia was a more far-sighted and realistic programme mapped out. Few colonial enterprises have been based on such bold, creative ideas and carried out so splendidly as Stroganov's Perm project.

A year later a letter from the Tsar was handed to Anika's eldest son, Grigory. It was fastened down with a big seal of red wax, which meant that it contained good news. When a document of this sort was sealed in black, people in Moscow usually had Masses for the dead sung, but red wax was the signal for prayers of thanksgiving.

According to this charter of 4 April 1558 all uncultivated land that lay on the tributaries of the Kama from their mouths to their sources – that is, on the Inva, Obva, Yaiva and Usolka – passed into the possession of Grigory Stroganov for a period of twenty years. In these regions Grigory was allowed to build towns, keep his own bodyguard and cast cannon. He could till the soil there, build salt-works, boil salt, fish in the rivers and lakes and look for mineral ore. Discoveries of silver, copper and tin he had to report to Moscow immediately, nor was he allowed to smelt them himself. Permission to smelt iron ore had already been granted to Anika himself earlier on.

It was emphasized several times in the charter that the Stroganovs had the right to settle these wildernesses, but not with fugitive peasants; they were also strictly forbidden to welcome thieves and vagabonds who had fled from military service, or *boyars'* sons who had avoided service to the state, otherwise 'the charter was no longer valid'.

In these new territories the Stroganovs and their dependents were released completely for a period of twenty years from all taxes, contributions and obligations to the state. They could trade with foreign merchants without paying any customs dues. If the Tsar's ambassadors travelled through their territory to or from Siberia or other regions, the Stroganovs did not have to provide food and shelter or give them horses for nothing; everything had to be paid for at the full price.

As a final touch to this charter of Stroganov privileges, they and their people were released from any control by the local authorities; they were subject only to the Tsar's court in Moscow.

All in all, the charter formed in effect the constitution of a new state on the borders of the Muscovite realm between the latter and unknown Siberia. 'Wildernesses' had been leased to people before and were again, but no one had ever been granted such rights before. The Kremlin realized that Anika was proposing something of unparalleled importance. In this respect the little phrase about ambassadors 'travelling to or from Siberia' was very significant. All the land north of the Volga and Kama right to the Arctic Ocean had already fallen, in fact or in name, into the hands of the Tsar of Russia. All these territories had been inherited from Novgorod. One after the other the separate pieces of the Tartar empire were added to them. Five years before Anika's successful interview with the Tsar the kingdom of Kazan had been finally subdued. Three years earlier Astrakhan had fallen. The whole course of the Volga was in Russian hands. Moscow had advanced almost to the Urals. The inhabitants of Siberia drew their own conclusions. Two years before Anika's interview ambassadors from Siberia appeared for the first time at the court of the Tsar. They handed over gifts, brought greetings from their sultan, Etiger, congratulated the Tsar on the conquest of Kazan and Astrakhan, and expressed the hope that the Russian Tsar 'would assure the peace and security of their land', in return for which they promised eternal loyalty and friendship.

Ivan felt very flattered and graciously accepted the gifts, which consisted of sable and squirrel skins. The ambassadors promised to bring a fixed number of similar gifts every year: a thousand sables and a thousand squirrels. In other words, the gifts formed a tribute, and the Tsar added a further title to the many he possessed already: that of 'Commander of all Siberia', as he described himself in a letter to King Edward VI of England.

In reality, this title anticipated events to some extent. But that was normal in those days. A little later on Charles II of England called himself ruler of Canada although he owned far less of it than Ivan did of Siberia. It should be pointed out, too, that at this time the name 'Siberia' covered regions this side of the Urals as well as beyond them. Mangaseya was Siberia, and so was the land of the Yugors, whose little princes had sworn allegiance to Ivan III,

Ivan the Terrible's grandfather. But now payments of tribute were coming from the real Siberia; from the lands where the Tartars, Turks and Mongols lived.

In 1558 Anika was seventy years old. That explains why the charter was made out in the name of his son Grigory. Of the thirteen children whom Anika had begotten with two wives, five had died in childhood. Of the eight surviving children only three were sons: Grigory, Yakov (Jacob) and Semyon, who were all children of the first wife. Semyon was still young, but his two elder brothers were already married themselves and seasoned merchants.

The land made over to Grigory comprised an area of more than five and a half million acres. The 'wildernesses' were covered with primitive forest, through which deep rivers ran. The ground contained salt and mineral ores. The forests were full of birds and animals, and the rivers were swarming with fish. People lived on the edge of the forest, on the banks of the rivers, in wide clearings and even in the forest itself. There were already small Russian settlements there, the cells of holy men and 'hermitages', little private monasteries in which men sought to preserve their souls from sin and their bodies from the loving chastisements of the authorities. Finally, there were also whole villages of natives – Permans, Votyaks, Zyrians and Cheremisses.

The ore had first to be found, but Anika already knew all about the salt deposits and the settlements. Only bureaucrats in Moscow could imagine that it was possible to settle and develop an area of twelve thousand square miles in the course of a few years exclusively with people brought in from outside. Anika knew that a country without native inhabitants is of no use to anyone.

At the end of a year Anika and his two elder sons moved to the Perm region. Semyon, the youngest, stayed in Solvychegodsk and carried on the business. On the Kama the blows of axes resounded and the sky was bright with the glare of forests being burnt down. Anika arrived with a whole troop of men. The men were equipped not only with arms but also with axes, saws and ploughshares. Anika rolled up his sleeves and seized hold of an axe.

At a 'secure spot', where the little River Kankora flows into the Kama, the little town of Kankor was built as Anika's residence. This town, which has now disappeared, was the base from which all the other towns of Perm were founded. These towns all sprang up later; the capital, Perm, was founded in the time of Peter the Great, on the site of a farm which one of the Stroganovs' tenants had built himself. In Anika's time, only his residence of Kankor existed. Salt-works soon sprang up all round it, together with houses for the employees and warehouses for supplies. Boats were moored on the river. At the same time as the town was founded Anika laid the foundation stone of a monastery close by. It was officially dedicated to Tsar Ivan, and the monks had to pray for their benevolent ruler, but old Anika was really thinking of himself; he was building his last dwelling on earth.

This tireless pioneering work lasted another five years, during which period Anika became a real patriarch. His power and influence were boundless. His realm grew ceaselessly before his eyes. His turnover rose to an enormous figure. His salt was to be found literally on every plate in Moscow. According to Russian sources the yearly salt production of the Stroganovs at the end of the sixteenth century amounted to nearly nine thousand tons. The Englishman Fletcher recorded that ten thousand men were employed by the Stroganovs in the production and transport of salt and wood, and another five thousand serfs had to till their land. In their service they had 'their own doctors, surgeons, apothecaries, and all kinds of craftsmen from Holland and other foreign countries'. Quite apart from cattle, land and other property of this sort, they possessed a capital of 300,000 roubles and paid the government every year 23,000 roubles in taxes, indubitably the greatest single contribution received by the Russian exchequer in those days.

Anika soon made use of the privilege granted by the charter of smelting iron in Perm. The ore was discovered, and Anika obtained special permission to build blast furnaces and to cut down wood for them. The ore was extracted from marshland and the iron at first produced in a primitive way with hand-driven bellows. But soon employees of the English concessionaire Randolph appeared in the district and built far more sensible factories. Anika was commissioned to watch their activities on behalf of the Russian treasury and in doing so learnt how to build smelting-furnaces after the English pattern.

By this time no one round Anika remembered the conditions of the imperial charter: 'No fugitives, no thieves, no vagabonds'. His sons remembered them least of all. They worked with great ardour, building and exploring. Grigory looked mainly for minerals. He found iron for himself, but no copper for the Tsar, although he must have walked over it in dozens of places. His methods were too primitive. It is also possible that he had no desire to discover copper and to see the Tsar's supervisors and foremen in Perm. At any rate, eighty years later the first copper-smelting works was opened on the very spot where Kankor stood.

Anika was pleased with his sons. They were quick to learn, and grew shrewder and shrewder. But they showed no mercy to their old father and sent him off to Moscow once more. Anika travelled to the capital with presents for their Moscow friends and returned home again with smaller gifts. For his sons he brought three million acres of fresh land, wrapped up in the charter of 2 January 1564.

The sons needed them. For a long time they had been playing a game that required a lot of space. They were building towns and factories, harbours and fortresses. Their summons echoed out on the Kama, the Volga, the Oka and even the Don. All kinds of people heard and answered it; they did not show the Tsar's charter to everyone of them, nor did they ask awkward questions. They were not inquisitive. People streamed to their new work-places where everyone could start a new life. Once Russia had fled before the Tartars and their chiefs to Moscow; now people were leaving Moscow and crossing the Kama. Later they were going to strike out over the Urals.

Honest men and thieves, peace-lovers and highwaymen, religious cranks and murderers, they all streamed to Grigory and Yakov. It was perfectly comprehensible: 'They promised industry its fruits, and boldness its booty,' as the great historian Karamsin puts it so expressively.

There was no time to lose; it was not men that were needed but labour. From now on the land belonged to the Stroganovs and their word was law. If a site for a salt-works was needed, the Mordvins or Permans had to make way for it. If a piece of land was to be brought under cultivation, the pasture of the Cheremisses was ploughed up. The Stroganovs did not behave like gangsters. They did not ruin people for fun. Especially during Anika's lifetime they observed the principle which the expedition to the land of the Yugors had taught him: you can get more by kindness than by force. Robbing people of all they possessed meant losing

36

them, and without them the new land could not be opened up. Anika's sons followed this Stroganov tradition. But they were realistic, and realism taught that a certain proletarianization of the native peoples was in the direct interest of the Stroganov economy.

The 'natives' did not understand this properly. They thought that the wicked Russians were simply driving them away from their ancestral lands and robbing them of part of their already scanty incomes, and when they found an opportunity they gave expression to their displeasure. Not every hunter came back from the hunt; fishermen returning to their nets sometimes found neither nets nor fish; and crops were burnt down before the harvest.

The trouble was that the natives had relatives outside the Stroganov frontiers. This covered their rear and gave them a base. There was even political agitation from this quarter, for there were still remnants of the great Mongol empire there, Nogai Tartars and small Vogul princes. Worst of all, these natives were not all complete savages. There were men among them who grasped the situation and were both energetic and bold; otherwise it would have been difficult to explain how they succeeded several times in sending envoys with complaints to Moscow.

But how could these poor pagans fight successfully in orthodox Moscow against two brothers who had the support of Anika, friend both of the Tsar and of the Metropolitan!

Anika answered these complaints personally in Moscow with still more serious complaints of his own. He spoke of continual raids, rustled cattle, murdered colonists, and profaned churches. At the same time he told of the tireless explorations which his sons were undertaking in honour of the Tsar; it was true that they had discovered neither silver nor copper, but they had reliable information that these things were to be found farther off, in the Urals. It might well be that they would have already been successful in their search were they not continually interrupted by 'robbers and traitors', the Cheremisses, the Voguls and the Tartars. His son Yakov had again discovered salt deposits in a fresh wilderness. It lay farther to the east, on the River Chusovaya; the land there belonged to no one; there was nothing but dark forests, wild rivers and desolate islands.

The envoys trudged off home, their letters of complaint unread, through the slush of the March roads. They had had the legal position explained to them. They were told not to appear again at Moscow with their grumbles; in a big economic enterprise disagreements were bound to arise, and they should take their complaints to their masters, the Stroganovs.

Anika and his son Yakov hurried to get home before the thaw in their warm, covered sleigh. This sleigh can still be seen, as far as I know, in the town museum at Solvychegodsk. It is not big, and not particularly comfortable by our standards; one would be considerably better off with a third-class railway ticket. Still, there was enough room in it for father and son in big furs and for the further one and a half million acres which they took with them, in the form of the third charter, granted this time to Yakov Stroganov and dated 25 March 1568.

Far away from the envoys and also from Anika lay, where it belonged, the River Chusovaya, its tail curled round the Urals, its head stuck into the Kama; it looked livid but powerless in its strait-jacket of ice. On each side of it, covered in forest and snow, lay Yakov's acres. Anika knew that the brothers were friends, but he also knew their greed; Grigory had got enough already, and Yakov must not be hurt, especially as it was he who had discovered and explored the new land.

This imperial charter was Anika's last *coup*. He had pulled it off with all his old skill, but he knew that his energies were declining. Before the journey to Moscow he had buried his second wife, Sophia; he was seventy-eight and now it was his turn. When the spring floods subsided he went off to his son Semyon at Solvychegodsk. He wanted to see his old house once again.

But he found no peace there. Perhaps he was disturbed by the restless energy of the thirty-year-old Semyon, the same inherited Stroganov energy that a whole life long was his blessing and his torment. After three months he returned to the Kama, not to his town of Kantor, but to his monastery. He was clothed as a monk under the name of Joasaph. He lived another two years in the monastery, following all the rules of the order and missing not a single Mass. Then suddenly he grew restless. Once again he travelled back to Semyon at Solvychegodsk. According to the story, the young monk who served him found him sitting dead in his armchair. On his knees lay a map of Perm. The Kama wound round in a great curve; the Chusovaya clung to it like a leech.

With their arms the two rivers embraced the 'fallow land' round Anika's burial mound.

THE SONS

Anika's powerful biblical personality was shared among his three sons – and each of them got enough of it. They were made of the same stuff, but they were not patriarchs; Anika was the last of the series. They were duller and more rugged. The eldest, Grigory, had inherited his father's love of book-learning; Yakov was a huntsman, a doctor and a collector of herbs and medicines; and Semyon, the youngest, was an amateur of holy pictures and a patron of artists. To him can be traced the origin of the famous Stroganov school of icon-painters. But in business, as we know from commercial documents which have been preserved, he was just as wily as Anika had once been as a young man.

However, he had apparently not inherited his father's flexibility in dealing with other people, for in 1586, sixteen years after Anika's death, he was murdered in his own house at Solvychegodsk by the rebellious Russian inhabitants, who were all his own subjects.

When Anika was still alive and Yakov happened to be staying in Moscow, a dreadful deed took place there under Ivan's rule. During a quarrel the Tsar struck his own son with a stick which had an iron ferrule. Boris Godunov, who was present, tried to hold the Tsar back and himself received a number of blows.

Afterwards the Tsar was overcome, as usual, by terrible remorse, and lay stretched on his face day and night in his chapel. Godunov was at home in bed looking after his wounds. His doctor was the 'experienced healer' Yakov Stroganov.

Godunov was of Tartar descent and although he was a declared 'westernizer' he was very interested in everything to do with the east. When he later became Tsar himself the Russian drive to Siberia received a fresh impetus. Godunov's own son, his unlucky successor on the throne, Fyodor, drew a map of Russia which reflects the contemporary knowledge of Siberia. On it appears the whole basin of the Ob, which had in fact been occupied by the end of the sixteenth century.

After Anika's death the brothers quarrelled. Yakov and Grigory stuck together and Semyon opposed them. We do not know the cause of the quarrel; probably it was over their inheritance. Semyon may have wanted to share in the Perm enterprise instead of just staying at home by the salt-works.

The Tsar in person acted as judge between the brothers. It is quite understandable, in view of Yakov's friendship with Godunov, that the decision went in favour of Yakov and Grigory; Semyon was delivered completely into their hands. The two brothers behaved like true Stroganovs; they did not destroy Semyon or even drive him from his home. But they would not let him come to Perm; he had to stay in Solvychegodsk.

The expansion went on swiftly; the two brothers did not waste a moment. They had such reliable support behind them in Moscow that they felt no hesitation or doubts. The boundaries of their domain had been pointed out to them on the map by the Tsar, but how much real meaning could these boundaries have when the map had about as much resemblance to reality as a child's drawing to a real horse? According to the map they had to halt at certain mountains and river, which in reality lay in quite a different spot. They were indisputably situated in regions which the Stroganovs had not yet reached. And the Stroganovs went on farther. It is impossible to say exactly how much land they took over beyond what had been leased to them. Two hundred years later, when really precise maps, not just primitive sketches, were finally compared with the original charters, the government felt like tearing its hair out. At the end of the eighteenth century the Russian treasury had to go to law to recover from Anika's descendants the difference between what had been granted to them and what they had taken for themselves. The difference amounted to over three and a half million acres.

Grigory and Yakov were their father's sons all right, yet they were different as well. When Anika died they endowed his beloved monastery of Pyskor on a regal scale. To pay for Masses for their parents' souls they gave the monastery everything round it: salt-works, mills, granaries, fields, beehives and fishponds. The monastery stood on the defence-line which the Stroganovs had built on the Kama and pushed forward to the Chusovaya. On the distant Kola peninsula, on that tail of the 'Scandinavian tiger' which hangs down into the White Sea, there was another monastery by the side of the Stroganov salt-works. This one, too, received all the Stroganov salt-works as a gift, likewise in return for Masses for the parents' souls. The only thing was that before the brothers handed over the works to the monks they removed the most valuable part of the equipment – the salt-pans.

The fact was that the brothers wanted to have nothing to do with Kola. Their interests lay on the Kama. The area of their sovereignty grew and so did the number of their subjects, but these subjects were not always willing to recognize the authority of the Stroganovs. The Ostyaks paid their tribute quietly, but the Cheremisses and the Tartars were restless. The main reason for this was their kinship with Siberian tribes, and so a rebellious Siberian core was formed in the Stroganov realm.

The brothers understood this very well. Immediately after Anika's death they moved their quarters. Ten miles from Kankor, farther down the Kama, they built the new fortress township of Oryol. They surrounded it with a moat and a stockade. Behind these they posted cannon, and in the centre of the town they built good, solid houses for soldiers and stone magazines for powder and supplies.

Tsar Ivan was very interested in Siberia, and so was his adviser Godunov. It may be recalled how, two years before Anika's historic interview with Ivan, the Siberian sultan Etiger (or Yadiger) had asked Moscow for its friendship. The reply had been that, like a cloak, friendship only gave warmth when it was lined with fur.

Afterwards the tribute did actually arrive, if not regularly. Its regularity was impaired by the circumstance that a struggle for the hegemony of Siberia was in progress. What Etiger feared was a war on two fronts. From the south he was being pressed by Khan Kuchum, who wandered about with his hordes between the Caspian and the River Amu Darya (Oxus) and would have liked better-watered pasture on the middle Ob. On the steppes, water means wealth; so Kuchum wanted to obtain control of this region, and his court historians provided him with an unassailable claim to the Siberian throne. According to these historians, Sheiban, the grandson of Jenghiz Khan and lord of all the lands to the north of the Amu Darya, begat Batur Khan, Batur Khan begat Chuchi Khan, Chuchi Khan begat Badakul, Badakul begat Manga Timur, Manga Timur begat Bekondi, Bekondi begat Ali Oglan, Ali Oglan begat Hadsim Mahomet, Hadsim Mahomet begat Mamudak

Murtasa, and Murtasa, who was Khan of Bukhara, begat Kuchum.

This official genealogy indicates the long tradition of sovereignty that Kuchum had behind him. No less weighty was the fact that Kuchum's authority rested on a religious and cultural tradition. Kuchum was a Mohammedan, and it is to him that Islam is mainly indebted for the conversion of the Siberian Tartars. He represented a religious mission, while his opponent, the Siberian sultan Etiger (Yadiger) was no more than an empty-headed pagan. Even before Kuchum appeared on the Ob, the way had been prepared for him by Muslim propaganda.

So Kuchum subdued the Tartars to the west of the Ob and Irtysh, demanded regular tribute from the Voguls and Ostyaks who lived farther to the north, murdered Etiger and his brother Seid Akhmat, and took over their capital of Isker or Sibir, the remains of which lie nine miles from the present town of Tobolsk.

This descendant of Jenghiz Khan now called himself Tsar of Siberia and ruled 'in great luxury, pleasure and joy', as the chronicle puts it. He was certainly rich, especially in horses.

Now that Kuchum had succeeded Etiger on the throne of Siberia he ought to have taken over Etiger's obligations. At any rate, that is how the lawyers of Moscow saw the situation; they had pointed out from the start that Kuchum had attacked a vassal of Moscow who enjoyed the protection of the Russian Tsar. When the news of the upheaval in Siberia reached Moscow in 1563 there was a Siberian delegation in the city. Its members were immediately sent to the new sultan to remind him about the sables and squirrels.

Although Kuchum proclaimed himself the lawful ruler of Siberia he was not yet confident of his position. He still had a dangerous opponent, Etiger's nephew, son of Seid Akhmat, who had been murdered at the same time as Etiger (see above). Kuchum therefore considered it prudent to agree at first to send the annual 'presents' to Moscow. However, this 'policy of appeasement' did not last long. Like many others before and after him who regarded themselves as the descendants of Jenghiz Khan, Kuchum was more inclined by nature to take than to give. So he soon forgot Moscow.

But Moscow did not forget Siberia. By capturing the two main Tartar fortresses of Kazan and Astrakhan, Ivan had opened up the whole course of the Volga for trade with Bukhara and Persia.

It was known in Russia that farther to the east beyond these lands lay India and China. As early as 1466 a merchant from Tver called Afanasy Nikitin had tried to use the Volga route to open trade relations with India. He succeeded in reaching India, but no trading took place because he had already been robbed of all his goods on the Volga by the Astrakhan Tartars. All he brought home in 1472 was the story of his journey. Almost a century had gone by since then and Moscow was once more reminded of India and China. In 1557, Anthony Jenkinson, the representative of the newly-founded English company for trade with Russia, appeared in Moscow. He was a well-educated merchant, sailor and diplomat, who had already travelled half-way round the world and was better informed than anyone else at that time on the question of economic geography. He had an interview with Ivan. With the Tsar's approval he tried to reach China, first via Bukhara and then through Russia. The Volga route was already open by this time, and Jenkinson reached Bukhara in 1558 and Persia in 1562, not without adventures, it is true, but at any rate without being harmed or robbed. However, he did not manage to get any farther, and therefore returned to Moscow.

All this was very illuminating and was bound to increase Moscow's interest in Kuchum's realm. It can therefore be understood that when Kuchum replied to the reminder about tribute with a 'note' to Moscow, which he not only failed to accompany with gifts but also sent in the custody of an ordinary Vogul called Iwak instead of in that of an ambassador, the Tsar flew into a rage. Even the tone of the note seemed intolerable.

'God is great,' wrote Kuchum. 'The free and independent Tsar Kuchum writes to the great prince, the white Tsar!

'We have heard that you are both great and just. Your father made peace with our father, and ambassadors travelled to and fro, because your land is near. Our peoples lived in peace and there was no hostility between them.

'I have not written to you before today because I was waging war against my enemy, but now we have captured him. With anyone who wishes peace, we shall make peace, but against anyone who wants war we shall fight.

'I send you an ambassador and friendly guests; let us conclude peace! Free those of our people who are prisoner in your land. Whoever was friendly with the father, to him shall the son also show friendship. We recognize you as our elder brother – if you want peace.'

The note ended with these dignified sentences: 'Send a messenger on horseback as quickly as possible. Tsar Kuchum presents his compliments with this letter.'

The white Tsar did not reply to the 'free and independent Tsar's' note.

The Stroganov brothers were informed of all these happenings. To them, the connection between the revolts in their territories and the new tone of the Siberian envoy was clear. If letters like this came from beyond the frontier, it was not surprising that there were bands of rebels on this side of it. This 'resistance movement' was no longer satisfied with defence; it started making attacks itself.

With Kuchum's accession the nature of these attacks did in fact change. Fairly large bands began attacking the Stroganov dependents. The latter could deal with small gangs themselves, but two years after Kuchum's message, in the middle of July 1573, when work in the Stroganov fields was in full swing, a horde of Cheremisses, Tartars and Ostyaks fell on a Stroganov squadron, robbed it, killed the men and set fire to the neighbouring settlements.

Winter went by and summer arrived again. It started off very hot and dry. There was no more rain after May. And then, when work pressed and every pair of hands was needed, a fire destroyed a considerable portion of the Stroganov forest with everything in it: settlements, beehives, game-preserves and huge piles of wood ready for use in the salt-works.

They were still fighting the fire when fresh crowds of fugitives appeared. Whole families which had abandoned their houses, farms and ripening crops streamed towards Kankor and Oryol. They were retreating before a danger far worse than fire: a whole army was coming from Siberia. On the way its number was swollen by Voguls, Ostyaks, Cheremisses and Tartars; and it burnt, murdered, plundered and took prisoners. At its head rode the Siberian prince Mahmetkul, nephew of Tsar Kuchum!

Mahmetkul pressed on to the Kama, and halted only three miles from Oryol. His attempt to take the town failed, and he did not repeat it. He knew that he would have to lay siege to it; a siege demanded time, and time meant the arrival of the *voivodes* of Perm with their troops.

The Sons

Mahmetkul confined himself to laying waste the surrounding district and to taking as many prisoners as possible with a view to asking a ransom for them later. On one of his forages he met Chebukov, an ambassador of the Tsar, who was on his way to the Kirghiz. Chebukov would not surrender himself alive. He and his companions tried to defend themselves and were all killed.

This time Grigory and Yakov did not let the enemy get away with things so easily as the previous year. When Mahmetkul's assault had rebounded from their fortifications and the Tartars had turned their horses homeward, the Stroganovs set out in pursuit. They harried the intruders and forced them to release a number of their prisoners, but did not dare to venture too far from their base. What they did do was to send a detailed account of the episode to the Tsar, and they laid particular emphasis on the slaughter of his ambassador. At the end of their report, where the Tsar would be impatiently expecting a description of the trophies and an enumeration of the prisoners, they informed him that they did not dare to carry the war any farther into Siberia without his specific permission.

It was curious that Grigory and Yakov, who paid so little attention to the Tsar's charters when it was a question of transforming free natives into their own subjects or taking possession of other people's land, should not dare to pursue the Siberian hordes without Moscow's assent.

In reality the brothers were afraid of nothing; but they realized that the stakes were growing bigger. Kuchum and Mahmetkul were not inferior in strength to Grigory and Yakov. The struggle could only be pursued successfully in alliance with the Tsar.

The skill and persistence with which the brothers continued the policy begun by their great-grandfather and confirmed by their grandfather is amazing. The great-grandfather, Luka, had once found support in Moscow. From then onwards the family's economic interests swing round like the jib of a huge crane, describing an arc from Novgorod to Isker, from the Volkhov to the Irtysh: Kola, Dvina, Solvychegodsk, Perm, Mangaseya, Siberia.

Moscow understood what the Stroganovs had in mind. The answer to their report was a fresh charter, granted in the next year, 1574. The Tsar leased to the brothers the 'Siberian Ukraine', the land behind the great rock, that is, Mangaseya, and the land on the banks of the Tobol, its tributaries and lakes – the region where

Kuchum raised his armies. The Stroganovs were given the right to wage war on the Ostyaks, Voguls, Yugrians, Samoyeds, Tartars and Nogai; and also to build fortresses, to garrison them, to build farms, cut down woods, put land under the plough, run estates, catch fish and introduce settlers. They were permitted not only to produce iron in Siberia, but also to mine copper, zinc, lead and 'inflammable sulphur'.

The lease ran for twenty years, until 1594. Thus Tsar Ivan rented Siberia to the Stroganovs, although it did not yet belong to him. He recognized the annexation in advance; the charter was in effect an invitation to march out and conquer Siberia.

Moscow's support was now assured. The Stroganovs had never suffered from short-sightedness; now their horizon widened in an unprecedented way. And such changes were in progress in the world that the Siberian question was in fact a burning one.

THE BIRTH OF A GREAT IDEA

It was the sixteenth century. Moscow lay far away from the main roads of history, and the Stroganov's realm still farther, but from the events which were occurring in foreign countries of which they knew nothing invisible vibrations reached even them.

This was the century in which the Europeans discovered the world and divided it up among themselves. They even divided up parts of it which they had not yet discovered, just as the Stroganovs hastened to secure their title to the 'wilderness'. Pope Alexander VI treated the New World in the same way as Ivan the Terrible treated Siberia; with the aid of a defective map he gave away territories which did not belong to him. As early as 1493, not a year after the discovery of America, he shared out 'spheres of influence' to the Spaniards and Portuguese and entrusted them with the task of planting Christianity and commerce in these areas. They proceeded to do this, and afterwards both Spaniards and Portuguese refused to allow any other countries to trade with their new possessions. To safeguard their monopoly they used their navies. It is understandable that the English and Dutch, who for the time being had been left behind, should have begun to think of unknown regions and untravelled routes. Above all they were looking for a new way to India and China, neither of which had yet been seized by the Spaniards or Portuguese. Since Columbus's experience everyone knew that in such a search you might stumble on something quite unexpected. Sebastian Cabot knew this particularly well. He remembered how he and his father had once sought the north-west passage to China and had discovered Newfoundland instead. They were looking for gold and spices, and found cod. Later Cabot tried to find a different, south-western way to India and discovered the River Plate. Looking for gold and silver, he found the brazil nut. What would one find if one sailed along the north coast of Europe towards the east?

If everything had been known in advance, nothing would have been discovered. Sebastian probably said that to the sons of the merchants who half a century earlier had equipped his father's expedition. In 1551 these merchants' sons founded the 'Mistery and Company of Merchant Adventurers' for the discovery of 'Regions, Dominions, Islands and places unknown'; they bought three ships, and had them carefully converted for their purpose.

Sebastian Cabot – Cabota, as he was called in England at the time – was an Italian. His suggestion was based on an idea which had spread from Italy throughout Europe. The history of this idea is not without importance, for it led to one of the most glorious geographical enterprises of the new age, an enterprise which even today has not reached its conclusion.

In 1519 the Genoese merchant Paolo Centurione arrived in Moscow. On the authority of Ptolemy and Strabo, Centurione assumed that the old Oxus (Amu Darya) still flowed into the Caspian, and he wanted to reach India by way of the Volga, the Caspian and the Oxus. He brought a letter of recommendation from Pope Leo X and received a friendly reception in Moscow. However, he did not get the passport he wanted for the rest of his journey and returned home without achieving his aim.

Six years later he appeared in Moscow again, this time with a letter from Clement VII. The Grand Prince Vasily attached a great deal of importance to good relations with Rome, so instead of sending Centurione to India he sent him back to Italy, and with him he sent an ambassador to the pope, Dimitri Gerasimov.

Gerasimov was a diplomat of high rank. He spoke fluent Latin and German and was well versed in international politics and economics. He had previously led important missions to Sweden,

47

Denmark, Prussia and Austria. In addition, he had a good knowledge of theology, which was very convenient for an ambassador to the Holy See. In Rome he devoted his leisure to the study of Italian art and music. He was probably small in stature and cheerful by nature, for at Moscow he was nicknamed 'Mitya Maly', that is, 'little Dimitri'. Nevertheless he knew how to behave in a dignified way, and according to the Catholic historian Pierling 'he did credit to the Muscovites while he was at Rome'. It was particularly noticed that although he was a good talker he also knew when to keep silence.

His appearance at Rome in September 1525 caused a stir and he met many highly-placed people. A man whom he saw very often was the writer and historian Paolo Giovio, the friend of Vasari. The result of Gerasimov's conversations with Giovio was a book by the latter which appeared at Rome in the same year, 1525: '*Pauli Jovii Novocomensis libellus de legatione Basilii Magni Principis Moschoviae.*' Giovio says himself that it was based on his conversations with Gerasimov, and Gerasimov was the source of its most important passage, which runs as follows:

'Swollen by innumerable tributaries, the Northern Dvina flows fiercely towards the north, where the sea is so vast that by turning right and sailing along the coast one can very probably reach Cathay (China), unless there should be any land in between.'

Giovio's little book was immediately translated into a number of languages, and the north-east passage to China became a universal theme of conversation. Nor did the matter rest at conversations. Only two years after the appearance of Giovio's book the Bristol merchant Robert Thom handed to the English ambassador at Seville a memorandum for Henry VIII on the route 'to Molucca by the North'. The king of Sweden, Gustav Vasa, was probably thinking of a similar expedition. This idea, which was, so to speak, in the air, was appropriated and made his own by Sebastian Cabot. Cabot did not have to persuade the British merchants, for they had long been familiar with the idea and were only waiting for 'good old Master Cabot' to get things moving. They all knew that the northern route to China lay through lands full of sable, beaver and ermine. Who owned these lands they apparently did not know; at any rate, the letters of recommendation given to the captains by Edward VI were addressed in general terms to 'all kings, princes, rulers and commanders in all countries under the sun'.

How vague conceptions of the north-eastern sea-route to China were even a century later can be seen from the passage in Book X of *Paradise Lost*, where Milton speaks of

> Mountains of ice, that stop the imagined way
> Beyond Petsora eastward to the rich Cathaian coast.

But Sebastian was well-informed about the furs, and English merchants were even better informed. For centuries the fur trade had been a monopoly of the Hanseatic League, but now the Hansa was in a bad way and very few furs were arriving by that route. As a result, prices were rising steadily.

The expedition equipped on Sebastian's advice awoke unusual interest in England, and considerable sums were invested in it. The risk was great, but the possible profit was still greater, and the merchants felt certain that something would be discovered. Twenty-six years earlier Cabot's good friend, Robert Thom, had written in his memorandum: 'No land is uninhabitable, no sea unnavigable.'

When the *Bona Esperanza*, the *Edward Bonaventure* and the *Bona Confidentia* set sail from Ratcliffe near London in May 1553 they were seen off by a crowd of many thousands. The three ships had a combined displacement of three hundred and seventy tons; their crews totalled ninety-seven men, and they had eleven merchants on board as passengers.

The leader of the expedition was Sir Hugh Willoughby, an erstwhile cavalry officer who had taken to the sea in 1550 and thus had only three years' experience as a sailor.

By the middle of August the expedition had reached the Lofoten Islands. From then on things went wrong. The ships were scattered by a storm and lost touch with each other. After waiting seven days at the prearranged rendezvous, Richard Chancellor, the captain of the *Bonaventure*, steered his ship into the White Sea and after a week dropped anchor in the Dvina, by the monastery of St Nicholas, in the harbour of Kholmogory, above the present city of Archangel.

Meanwhile Willoughby was struggling with the difficulties of the seaman's calling. They turned out to be insuperable. The leader of the expedition not only had no idea of pilotage; he could not even navigate.

After some time the *Esperanza* and the *Confidentia* reached the

Murman coast. They anchored in a little bay at the mouth of the River Varzina and decided to winter there, although it was only the middle of September. Their food supplies were almost exhausted and scurvy was raging. Lapp hunters came upon the ships early in the next spring; they were wooden cemeteries. Willoughby himself was sitting in a hut over his log-book, still gripping the pen in his lifeless, frozen hand. His notes show that he was still alive in the middle of January 1554.

Meanwhile Chancellor had received a friendly welcome from the authorities in Kholmogory. They provided him with free supplies while messengers hastened to Moscow. Orders were received to take the guests to the Tsar.

Ivan the Terrible was clever and also, by the way, not yet 'terrible'. He realized that by forbidding the Hansa merchants to trade in Russia he had harmed himself as much as the Germans. Here were unsolicited competitors who were also consumers into the bargain; they could provide Moscow with a direct link with Europe.

The Englishmen dined with the Tsar in the Golden Hall. Over a hundred guests were present. The tables were covered with golden dishes, and the hundred and fifty servants put on clean livery three times during the course of the meal; which is not surprising seeing that the meal lasted many hours. Not only the *boyars'* clothes, but those of the servants as well, glittered with gold. The Englishmen spoke later in London of the 'incomparable splendour' of the Tsar's court.

In February 1554, Chancellor set out on the return journey with an extremely friendly letter from Ivan to Edward VI. But in the meantime Edward had died. Queen Mary received Chancellor, who handed over Ivan's letter. The captain who had discovered a new land was fêted and Sebastian Cabot, too, was congratulated from all sides. The 'Merchant Adventurers' were rechristened the 'Muscovy Company'. In 1555 Queen Mary gave the new company its first charter, which conferred on it the exclusive right to trade with Russia and with other countries by way of Russia. The Muscovy Company was the first of those great colonial companies which later opened up both the New and the Old World for Europe. It served as a model for the English and Dutch East India Companies, which were not founded until fifty years later. The Muscovy Company itself sent out a whole series of expeditions both eastward and westward; Baffin and Hudson were among its captains.

In the same year, 1555, Chancellor arrived again in Kholmogory. This time he brought four ships with him, laden mainly with cloth and sugar. These wares were intended for the trade with Moscow. But the dream of 'unknown lands' had not been abandoned. Captain Borough set sail at the same time as Chancellor, to find the way not to China but only to Mangaseya; the English liked 'first-hand' trade as well, and the first hands for furs were on the other side of the Urals, in Siberia.

Borough had learnt of the sea-route to Mangaseya from fur-dealers in the Dvina region, who sailed there in their wretched little boats. He reached Novaya Zemlya and the island of Vaigach, but although it was August the stern sentinels of the iron gate – fog, storms and towering icebergs – prevented him going any farther.

Chancellor set course for London with his ships fully laden. He had paid twenty-six thousand pounds for the wax, blubber, tallow, furs, felt and hemp stowed away in the *Edward Bonaventure* and *Bona Esperanza*. What was more important, on board his flagship, the *Edward Bonaventure*, he had the Tsar's ambassador, his retinue of sixteen, and a trading agreement with Moscow as well. This charter made up for the failure to find a route to China; it gave the Englishmen the right to trade without paying customs dues in all the towns and provinces of Russia. They also received a number of other privileges, but not the one they would have liked most of all: a trade monopoly. Ivan banked on other guests following the English; then it would be possible to talk to the English in different terms. In the event, everything turned out precisely as he wished.

But poor Chancellor had no luck. On the voyage back to England one of his ships was wrecked on the Norwegian coast, another disappeared and the *Bonaventure* was wrecked on the cliffs of Scotland. Chancellor himself was drowned, together with his son, most of the crew and seven Russians. But the ambassador from Moscow, who had never seen the sea before, not only swam ashore but also saved the Tsar's letter. He delivered it safely; as for the gifts which he was supposed to hand over to the queen, only the inventory remained. The gifts themselves were scattered on the shore with part of the cargo and carefully gathered up by the local inhabitants. Considerable efforts were made to recover them from the Scots, but without success.

The Russian ambassador, Ossip Grigorievich Nepeya, was certainly an able man; unlike Willoughby, he did not belong to the aristocracy, and to make a career for himself he must have had other attributes. He displayed his ability not only by his performance as a swimmer but also by the skilful execution of his mission. He gained an extremely good reputation in England.

His reception in England corresponded to the hopes that people then set on the idea of trading with Russia. Nepeya was loaded with gifts. Eighty 'Adventurers' in ceremonial dress, with golden chains hanging on their chests and a throng of servants behind them, met him twelve miles outside London. He was welcomed by the Lord Mayor and later received in audience by Queen Mary and King Philip. All his expenses in England were paid by the Muscovy Company.

This promising start was followed by a regular traffic between England and Russia via the White Sea. English merchants erected warehouses in Kholmogory, built houses and began trading. Moscow was glad to see the guests from overseas. The establishment of trade relations with the English was an important matter to Ivan. It made economic sense of Moscow's seventy-five-year-old hostility to the Hanseatic League and justified the whole struggle with Novgorod. Ivan was frightened of scaring the English away, but at the same time he did not want to put himself entirely in their hands. What he needed was an energetic, diplomatic and trustworthy agent to supervise their activities, a man who was not afraid of any responsibility.

After Ivan had weighed all these points, he sent a messenger to Anika Stroganov. Anika was commissioned to see that the Englishmen fulfilled all their obligations, did the Russians no wrong and suffered none themselves. Anika was to inspect all their wares before anyone else and to buy anything the Tsar's court needed.

One can imagine what power and esteem this appointment conferred on Anika and what sums were continually passing through his till. It was a business with fat profits in it. Anika was not interested in small gains. He returned presents from the Englishmen with interest. He was paying them for what he was learning from them. Through them, he saw not only weapons and tools of novel design, pocket watches and compasses; he also saw new horizons and, beyond them, new markets. It was only when he met the English that he realized his own stature, his wealth and the significance of the support he was receiving.

Just once he travelled over to see them himself; after that he sent his sons. Grigory and Yakov understood just as clearly as their father what the arrival of the English meant. These Englishmen were trying to reach Mangaseya, the Mangaseya to which Anika's men had long been travelling. With the furs of Mangaseya these proud sailors, their ships and their compasses could all be bought.

The years that followed confirmed this conviction. Mangaseya remained a secret treasure, the keys to which lay in the hands of Anika and his sons. Moscow held the same view, so did the English and the Dutch who came after them. The Stroganovs knew that the keys possessed a value only for him who could reach the gate. The sea-route from the Dvina to the Ob was so difficult and dangerous that it was not a practical proposition. The northern land-route, St Stephen's route by way of the Vyma to the Pechora, was not much better.

There was a third way. It led through Perm, up the Chusovaya, over the Urals and on to the River Tobol. By this route you could reach Mangaseya, and perhaps even China, by water. But astride this route sat Kuchum, the Tsar of Siberia.

Sensitively the Stroganovs listened to the voices of the sixteenth century. Genoa, Lisbon, Amsterdam and Bristol had sent the dream of China out into the world. Sebastian Cabot in London was thinking of the route to China. Ivan the Terrible in Moscow was thinking of it. Anika Stroganov was doing the same in Kankor. To him this route was nearer and more concrete than it was to Sebastian and Ivan. It was bound up with the route to Mangaseya, and Mangaseya was his own land.

After the English the Dutch appeared in Kholmogory. Tsar Ivan was pleased. There was fierce competition between the two sets of foreigners and each tried to trip up the other. In 1565 a Dutch ship arrived at the mouth of the Dvina. Among the merchants on board her there was a certain Oliver Brunel, a man from Brussels who was in Dutch employment. When he arrived in Kholmogory the first thing he did was to find a teacher and start to learn Russian. He was eager to find out as much as he could about Russian life, travelled about the surrounding region and very soon opened a trading office in which he welcomed Russian merchants and officials with a great show of friendliness.

There were a fair number of Englishmen in Kholmogory at the time and they were not at all pleased by Brunel's activities. Brunel was soon arrested on suspicion of spying for Sweden and taken to Yaroslavl. There he was caught up in the plans of the Stroganovs. The Stroganovs needed men who knew something about foreign countries and could speak their languages. As a result of the endless wars with Sweden, Lithuania and Livonia there were many foreign prisoners in Russia, and the Stroganovs' agents were always on the look-out for educated men with commercial experience among them.

Brunel was just their man. It was true that he was a political suspect, not an ordinary prisoner-of-war, but this was no obstacle for the two all-powerful brothers. So in 1570 Brunel entered their service.

Precisely what his function was is not certain; but we know that he made trips to Europe and sold furs for the Stroganovs in Holland and Paris. 1581 saw him abroad again. On the island of Ösel he met the Dutch merchant Johann Balak, the friend of the famous geographer Mercator, and informed him that the Stroganovs had already built two ships on the Dvina for an expedition to China; two Swedish shipbuilders had been specially brought in to supervise the work. Brunel was to recruit two experienced sea-captains in Holland. It went without saying that he would be chosen as the leader of the expedition, for he had already been to Mangaseya twice; once through 'Siberia and the land of the Samoyeds' and on the other occasion by sea.

This story, which Balak passed on to Mercator, established the fame of Brunel as the first western European to have reached the Ob by water; he was the pioneer of the north-east passage! Everyone believed this: Balak, Mercator, Russian historians and even A. E. Nordenskiöld. No one thought of subjecting Brunel's claim to a careful examination. When they eventually did, it turned out that Brunel had a vague second-hand notion of the Ob, but none at all of a sea-route to it. It is also difficult to believe that the Stroganovs had sent him to Mangaseya; they naturally needed such a man, with his command of foreign languages, for their business in Europe. It is doubtful whether he had ever set eyes on the Ob.

However, this did not prevent him from continuing to help with the preparations for the expedition. He negotiated with the Prince of Orange about the latter's financial participation. The only thing was that he forgot about the Stroganovs' share in the project, and the expedition finally took place without them. The generous Nordenskiöld thought that Brunel 'wanted to secure the fame of this enterprise for his own country alone'. Perhaps it was not so much the fame as the profit that he had in mind; this explanation would at any rate correspond better with the Dutch commercial mentality. But whatever the truth was, the expedition was a failure. Brunel only got as far as the island of Vaigach, and on the return voyage his ship was wrecked at the mouth of the Pechora. Brunel himself escaped with his life, returned to Europe, later entered Danish service and organized an expedition to Greenland. That is the last we hear of him.

Even if Brunel himself was only an adventurer, his propaganda was by no means ineffectual. His plans were well known to his fellow-countryman, Peter Plancius, who lived in Holland and was the founder of the school of navigation at Amsterdam. William Barents was trained at this school about this time. Later Barents led three Dutch expeditions 'to China'. He explored that part of the Arctic Ocean which lies between Spitzbergen, the Murman coast and Novaya Zemlya, and which is now known as the Barents Sea; in 1596 he discovered Spitzbergen; and he sailed round the north of Novaya Zemlya, losing his life on its east coast.

It is not difficult to discover why the Stroganovs gave up the project. By this time they were already waging continual war against Kuchum. Kuchum's nephew had already appeared before the gates of Oryol and the brothers had received their mandate over Siberia from the Tsar. In the ten years during which Brunel was in the service of the Stroganovs the personnel of the watch on the Kama had changed twice; Anika had died in 1570, and the brothers Grigory and Yakov followed him between 1575 and 1579. These ten years had been spent in ceaseless fighting. The Stroganovs had realized that for them all roads led through Siberia; but both the road to China and the road to Mangaseya were barred by Kuchum.

In 1581, the year in which Brunel was negotiating with the

Prince of Orange, Yermak Timofeyevich led his army over the Urals.

COSSACKS

The story of Yermak's life is as obscure as the circumstances which preceded his expedition. There is no lack of records, but they are full of contradictions. In the modern Russian school of historiography, which has no time for anecdotes, it had become the fashion round the turn of the century to devote only a passing reference to the 'Yermak adventure' or 'Yermak episode'.

We know the rôle played by the Stroganovs in the struggle for access to Siberia. Tsar Ivan had not only leased Siberia to them; he had expressly commanded them to build fortresses on the River Tobol. In other words, he had laid it down that they should fight their way into Siberia. In spite of this he put no forces at their disposal. The Stroganovs were to arm their own men.

The Stroganovs grasped the difficulties of this situation better than the strategists in Moscow. The bureaucrats of the capital found it perfectly easy to share out other people's land and to deal with foreign rulers. But on the Kama and the Chusovaya it was realized that protection from Kuchum and Mahmetkul would have to be found before there could be any question of taking the field against them. The Stroganovs were not just adventurers. They had behind them two hundred years' experience of colonization and opening up new territories.

They had enough money to mount a campaign against Siberia; but no men to spare for it. They needed their own men to guard their frontiers. On the other hand they were aware of the existence of an abundant reserve of manpower which could produce all the bold fellows you wanted for any enterprise you might like to name.

This reserve consisted of men who had settled on the lower reaches of the Volga, the Don and the Dnieper. They were men who, for one reason or another, had come into conflict with the laws of Moscow. Their own name for themselves was 'Cossacks'; the people called them 'free people', and in government documents they were described as thieves, robbers, vagabonds and escaped peasants. It was these peasants who made up the majority of the 'free people', and they formed the core of the free economic colonization of the Don region. Owing to its geographical situation this region commanded the trade routes between Moscow and the Black and Caspian seas, and there was a powerful temptation for the enterprising to take part in this trade in their own way. In practice it was not always easy to decide where the Cossack stopped and the robber began. At home on the Don the Cossacks were citizens of a military republic. If they set sail on the Sea of Azov or the Black Sea, they became combatants waging a legitimate war against the Turks. On the Volga and the Caspian they turned into pirates, robbing both Russian and Persian merchants.

About the time when the Stroganovs were repulsing Mahmet-kul's attack, Don Cossacks sailed up the Don, landed where it flows near the Volga, then sailed down the Volga and across the Caspian Sea to the mouth of the Ural, sailed about thirty miles up the Ural and sacked Saraichik, the capital of the Nogai Khans. The town lay on an island, and possessed mosques and wealthy shops; trade between Bukhara and Moscow passed through it.

The leader of the raiding party was *hetman* Ivan Kolzo, a capable and experienced man. His chief assistants were three *hetmeni* called Barbosh, Mitya Britusov and Ivan Yuryev. They were obviously well-known specialists in their trade, for when the Nogai Khan complained to Ivan the Terrible the latter sent a punitive expedition to the Volga with orders to capture and string up these three in particular.

News went out from the Don to the Cossacks that it would be as well if they did not show their faces there; people had no desire to be involved in a war with the Tsar because of a private enterprise of Kolzo and his comrades.

This made the Cossacks think. The only direction in which there was any point in advancing was towards the north and the River Kama, and there they duly turned up in 1580, headed this time by Yermak Timofeyevich.

Where had Yermak been until then? Chronicle, legend and folk-song assert unanimously that this hero of the invasion of Siberia was robbing and plundering with Kolzo and four other *hetmeni* on the Volga, and that he first won fame there. But the truth seems to be that while Kolzo and his friends were dealing with Saraichik, Yermak and his band were fighting on the Livonian front. That is why Yermak is not mentioned in the Tsar's decree condemning the robber-chiefs and *hetmeni* to death, although all the rest, including relatively unimportant men, are described in detail. Christian names as well as surnames being quoted.

There is no doubt that at some time or another Yermak was on the Don. He was all too familiar with Cossack tricks; he was 'one of them'. All bold, 'free' men took the road to the Don at that time. According to tradition, Yermak's grandfather was a coachman in the Murom forest; he drove honest people as well as the robbers for which this forest was notorious. On the orders of the *voivode* he and his passengers were thrown into the town gaol at Vladimir. He succeeded in escaping and went off with his wife and children to settle far away on the Volga. His children set up house still farther off, on the Chusovaya, where no officials from Moscow could lay hands on them. It was there that the hero of Siberia was born.

As a young man he had great physical strength and a ready tongue. Both were needed in his profession: he was a porter, and later a river-sailor. However, he had no desire to spend his life dragging Stroganov salt about and went off to the Don.

He did not achieve much success on the Don; his name is never mentioned in connection with any particular incident there. Only an established Don Cossack – men like Kolzo, Britusov or Yuryev – could make a name on the Don. Yermak was a son of the north; his home was on the upper Volga near the Kama or the Chusovaya.

For a long time Yermak plied his trade on the Volga, too. Probably he did not bother much whether what he did was strictly legal or not. He was a Russian peasant; a Cossack by calling, a thief from necessity and a loyal subject of the Tsar at a safe distance. There have been men like that in Russia both before and since.

GENTLEMEN'S AGREEMENT

The Livonian War brought Yermak nothing but disappointment. Instead of capturing enemy towns the Russians had to surrender some of their own. Yermak returned to the Volga and there met Kolzo and his companions. After the attack on Saraichik they had gone north to escape the Tsar's troops. To the Cossacks Yermak appeared like an angel from Heaven. He knew more about geography than they did and did not lose his way in the damp, impenetrable forest which oppressed and frightened the south-erners from the Don.

Yermak may have already been in touch with the Stroganovs' agents, who were looking all over Russia for the men they needed. At any rate, Yermak led his troop straight to the Stroganovs.

The Stroganovs had Yermak to thank for the fact that this horde of men did not plunder their own people, the Russian colonists, and behaved in general respectably. The hungry Cossacks wanted above all to eat their fill. Yermak looked after them. Naturally the Stroganovs looked after them when they had made an agreement with Yermak. Then the Cossacks felt the desire for action, and Yermak allowed them to fleece the surrounding Voguls, Ostyaks and Cheremisses.

Meanwhile there had been changes in the Stroganov family. Grigory and Yakov had died and had been succeeded in the direction of the business by their sons Nikita and Maxim. These two lived on the Kama and Chusovaya, but Uncle Semyon still remained in the rear, in Solvychegodsk. Yermak entered into negotiations with Yakov's son, Maxim.

It did not take Yermak long to reorganize his band and intro-duce some discipline into it. But the negotiations with Maxim took time, and Maxim's negotiations with his cousin Nikita and his uncle Semyon took even longer. The latter was not opposed to the enterprise in itself, but he did not like dipping into his purse. Nikita had no liking for military adventures. He had all kinds of affairs on hand and could not spare any of his labour force. In addition, a fairly long period of quiet had lulled his fears.

But this feeling of security was premature. In order to attack the Stroganovs the enemy did not need to stand continually before their gates. He could appear in a flash and disappear again just as quickly. In July 1581 Prince Beguli came storming up from the River Pelym in Siberia with a force of seven hundred men. They attacked the Stroganov townships on the Chusovaya, that is to say, territories that had once been leased to Yakov Stroganov and had now been inherited by Maxim.

The attack was a violent one and a large number of people were killed or robbed of all their possessions and carried off into cap-tivity. The danger was great, and Uncle Semyon at once sent reinforcements from distant Solvychegodsk. When they arrived, Beguli had already departed again, but his tracks were still fresh.

With his own men and Semyon's, and thanks largely to Yermak's help, Maxim not only put Beguli to flight, but caught him up and took him prisoner. In the hour of crisis Nikita sent word that he relied on God's help and all his men were indispensable.

It is not difficult to imagine the fury of Maxim and Semyon. The intensity of their anger can be gauged from the fact that they did not shrink from complaining about Nikita to the Tsar himself. Moscow realized what was at stake. The prince of Pelym was a vassal of Kuchum. Only yesterday Kuchum's nephew had been outside the gates. Tomorrow he might come himself.

Maxim and Semyon emphasized in their complaint that Beguli had come 'to reconnoitre the road to Perm'. They took the view that their family quarrel was an affair of state.

The answer to their complaint was a threatening letter from Moscow to Nikita Stroganov. The letter was sealed with a black seal. In it the Tsar ordered Nikita to give Maxim and Semyon every assistance in their military activities. It was also made clear that the imperial *voivode* of Perm had orders to respond immediately to any call for help from the Stroganovs.

Before Yermak marched into Siberia he had discussed everything thoroughly with Maxim. The expedition was primarily a commercial enterprise, but both Maxim and Yermak realized that there was an important political background to it. Yermak was sent out to take *de facto* possession of the lands on the Tobol and Irtysh which the Stroganovs already owned *de jure* on the basis of the imperial charter of 1574. It was a somewhat vague task. In practice Yermak had orders to deal Kuchum such a blow that he permanently lost the desire to send his vassals into Stroganov territory. It was hoped that the consequence of this blow would be the opening-up of a southern route to Siberia for furs.

Such were the purely commercial considerations that induced Maxim and Semyon to equip Yermak. Yermak undertook in return to repay these expenses with interest. In other words, Maxim and Semyon financed the expedition and shared in the profits.

If we disregard the details, we have here a typical colonial enterprise of that period. In 1670 Prince Rupert of the Palatine founded in London the Hudson Bay Company. His cousin, Charles II, gave the company a charter to import furs from Canada, which did not belong to him at all. Close relatives of the beaver, sable, black foxes and ermine which had attracted the Russians to Siberia and kept them there incorporated the dominion of Canada in the British Commonwealth.

The Stroganovs' charter was not couched in such nice legal terms as that of the gentlemen-adventurers of London, but the Stroganovs were in the field a hundred years earlier. Tsar Ivan knew much better than Charles II what he was doing when he granted the Stroganovs their charter, and the latter knew much more about furs than the English gentlemen. But the beaver, sable and foxes were the same. They opened up for humanity the whole north of the Old and New Worlds.

Eventually Yermak and his troops were ready. He had reinforced them with a special detachment of 'Russians, Tartars, Livonians and Germans'. The last two categories consisted of prisoners from the Livonian front. All told, there were just over eight hundred men. Three hundred of these had been provided by the Stroganovs.

Maxim and his Uncle Semyon had to equip this little army. They provided three cannon, so the story goes, 'some flintlocks' and for every single participant three pounds of powder and shot, three *puds* of rye flour, a *pud* of biscuit and salt, and two *puds* of buckwheat and 'tolokno' (roasted ground oats). Furthermore – and this has a fairy-tale quality – Maxim gave each warrior two and a half pounds of butter and half a pig.

We know precisely how Russian soldiers on active service were fed at that time; they carried neither ham nor butter with them. We also know which way Yermak set out on his campaign; he went up the Chusovaya and its tributary, the Serebryanaya, to the watershed; then he had to get all his baggage over the watershed. The mountains are not high in that region, but the Cossacks had no horses and had to carry everything on their own backs.

Obviously Yermak did not in fact have any cannon. There is no mention of them anywhere later on. Nevertheless, Yermak was well equipped. The expedition is said to have cost the Stroganovs twenty thousand roubles. Even Tsar Ivan did not always have a sum like that ready to hand.

The Stroganovs even provided the army with flags, which were at the same time pictures of saints. The Stroganov seamstresses had embroidered every conceivable saint on them.

By the end of September, Yermak had crossed the Urals and reached, via eastward-flowing streams, the River Tura. At this point the realm of the great Siberian Tsar Kuchum began.

II

FROM THE URALS TO THE PACIFIC

YERMAK CONQUERS AN EMPIRE

KUCHUM'S REALM did not embrace the Siberia which we know from the map. It consisted only of the small part of it which lies on the rivers Ob and Irtysh; but it lay astride the roads from the Urals to China, Bukhara and Mangaseya. It barred these roads like a felled tree-trunk. It had to be removed, and this is just what Yermak did.

He succeeded in achieving this aim very swiftly and with very small forces. He had eight hundred men; Kuchum had far more. In arms he was somewhat superior to the Siberian Tsar, but not nearly as superior as, for example, the Spaniards in America were to their opponents, who did not even possess iron weapons. Yermak had no cannon and only a small proportion of his men were equipped with flintlock guns. The Cossacks did not have a single horse; Kuchum and his men on the contrary were mounted. His cavalry could move quickly in any direction; the Cossacks were tied to their rafts, which carried all their supplies.

Finally, there was yet another difference between the Tartars and the Aztecs: the Tartars were descendants of the Mongol conquerors; warfare was their only trade, and they knew how to practise it.

This raises the question why Yermak was so successful. His success was the result of clever strategy and a still cleverer policy. Kuchum's empire was not a unified state. It was a federation of numerous small vassal princes to whom Kuchum was a foreigner. Their peoples differed in speech and religion from the Tartars. Kuchum and many of his Tartars were Mohammedans; his vassals were pagans. They had to pay Kuchum tribute. At bottom it made no difference to them to whom they had to pay this tribute. They were therefore poor defenders of the Siberian realm.

To understand and make use of these facts, it was not enough

to be a brave *hetman* or a good general. It was necessary to possess
the capacity to subordinate both strategy and policy to a higher
aim.

The Cossacks sailed along the Tura and saw on its banks
mounted Tartars and infantry; these people were nomadic
Ostyaks and Voguls. They also saw their huts. Soon the first
skirmishes occurred. From the lofty right bank of the Tura arrows
suddenly rained down on the Cossacks. The river was fairly broad
at this spot and the arrows did not do much harm. The Cossacks
fired two or three salvoes from their flintlocks. When the enemy
heard the 'thunder of heaven' echoing out on a clear autumn day
they withdrew rapidly.

This attempt at resistance had been organized by Yepancha, a
vassal of Kuchum. As a reward for his courage his little capital was
pillaged. The same fate overtook other encampments in the surrounding district. Then the Cossacks could not travel any further
along the river; the cold had set in and the Tura began to freeze
over. Yermak wintered in the ruins of the old Tartar town of
Chinga-Tura, the modern Tyumen. He released the prisoners he
had taken in the fighting with Yepancha, telling them that he
wished them no harm since he was only interested in Kuchum
himself.

In May 1582 the Cossacks repaired their boats and rafts and
sailed down the Tura, whose waters empty into the Tobol.

Meanwhile, during the winter, Yepancha's men had gone to
Kuchum and told him about the huge Russian army which was
approaching swiftly on winged ships. Kuchum collected troops,
put Tausan, his war minister, in command of them and sent him
out against the Russian warriors. Kuchum did not let his guard
of Tartars leave his side; Tausan was to mobilize Kuchum's loyal
vassals en route.

Yermak and Tausan met on the Tobol. The Cossacks were
fresh and in good heart. It was May and every day the weather
grew warmer. The forests were yielding to steppe. For the first
time since they had left the Volga they saw a level, green expanse
again.

Tausan's battle-cry to his men 'to die for the prophet' found
little response, since they did not owe allegiance to this prophet.
At the first shot the vassals fled in all directions. Tausan himself
and a small body of Tartars were captured.

Yermak received him in a friendly fashion. After giving their involuntary guest a meal the Cossacks showed him how their flintlocks worked. At the same time they told him that an army forty times as strong was following them on foot. When Tausan was sufficiently impressed Yermak released him and his retinue: 'Go to Kuchum,' he said, 'and tell him that our forces are uncountable. Let him submit and we shall shed no blood.'

But Kuchum was not the man to submit. When he heard of Tausan's defeat he set about organizing his defences. To all his vassals he sent mobilization orders. These orders were transmitted in the form of gold-tipped arrows. Details were conveyed by word of mouth.

Kuchum was the dangerous and undefeated descendant of Jenghiz Khan and heir of the mighty Sheiban, and the spell he cast was still powerful. Vassals of the same race streamed to his standard with their men. The first to arrive were the Tartars from the Baraba steppe; they were followed by the other tribes and 'tongues': Gulei Mursa the Nogai Tartar, Yambysk, Bardak, Nemcha, Binei, Obak, Umak – they all came.

Kuchum welcomed this large army. He put his son Mahmetkul in command of it and dispatched it against Yermak. He himself began to build fortifications in front of his town of Isker. Where his nephew Mahmetkul was at this time is not known.

This time Kuchum threw in his own reliable Tartar troops. The clash took place on 21 July 1582 near the old Tartar settlement of Babassar on the Tobol. The battle lasted the whole day and finally the Cossacks succeeded in fighting their way down the Tobol, but only because the enemy had no boats. But the Tartars followed Yermak's troops undismayed along the banks, and a shower of arrows met them from behind every rock.

When Mahmetkul realized that he could not hinder the Cossack's progress he returned with his army to his father at Isker. Yermak came upon a big Tartar settlement and captured it. By now it was August, and the Cossacks were sick of travelling by water and eating nothing but fish and roasted oats when horses, meadows and occasionally cultivated fields were visible on each bank.

The settlement in question was ruled by a vassal of Kuchum's called Karacha. As usual the vassal offered only feeble resistance and was beaten. The Cossacks refreshed themselves on his property and dragged on to their boats and rafts whatever they could pick up.

Mahmetkul was waiting for Yermak with his main forces at the mouth of the Tobol. Yermak was too weak to defend himself so he went over to the attack. He disembarked his whole band and attacked Mahmetkul on the bank. The Tartars fled. This battle took place on 1 October. Yermak now had to make a decision. Winter was approaching; which way should he turn? He was at the confluence of the Tobol and the Irtysh. Down the Irtysh lay the lands for which he had undertaken the campaign, and beyond these, further north, lay the land of the Yugors, Mangaseya itself.

In the opposite direction, up the Irtysh, Kuchum sat in his fortified camp. But on the other side of him dwelt farming Tartars. These people were not nomads, and there was the possibility of wintering among them. Merchants from Bukhara visited them to buy furs, merchants who made the world go round. Yermak turned right and sailed upstream towards Kuchum.

At the beginning of October the Cossacks arrived before his fortified encampment. Nor far from it lay an abandoned settlement. The Cossacks took it over and made themselves secure. Before them lay Kuchum's fortifications and the Tartar hordes.

The Cossacks spent some weeks here. They were no longer in good spirits. The recent battles had cost them many dead. Many others had been wounded and had to be nursed back to health. The Tartars' resistance was growing stronger and stronger. Until now the Russians had not succeeded in inflicting a decisive defeat on them. To winter without winning a victory first meant slowly freezing to death. A council of war was held and it was decided to provoke a decisive battle with Kuchum.

Meanwhile Kuchum was drawing up his own plan of battle with his commanders, dividing up his troops among his sons and asking mullahs and shamans for the auspices.

On the morning of 25 October the Cossacks stormed the Tartar camp. First they had to capture a wall of earth and a palisade. The Tartars defended themselves bravely. Their leading troops were commanded by the crown prince, Mahmetkul, who left the wall and went over to the attack. The struggle developed into hand-to-hand fighting. There is no knowing what the end would have been if Mahmetkul had not been wounded at the critical moment. His bodyguard just managed to get him into a boat and across to the opposite bank of the Irtysh.

When the vassal princes saw this they hurried to leave the battle-field. They did not even try to withdraw behind the earthworks; they simply made straight for home. The Cossacks broke into the camp and Kuchum bolted with his retinue and the remains of his army.

It is noticeable that Kuchum always left the leading rôle on the field of battle to his son or his vassals. He was forced to hang back like this because of a disease of the eyes, which later made him completely blind. He himself organized the resistance and made the plans, but he was no longer capable of leading his troops into battle. At Isker he gathered together all the women (he had very sensibly ordered that they should all be taken there) and took them off with him further south.

The Cossacks lost one hundred and seven men in this battle. Yermak's band had shrunk perceptibly; he now had no more than five hundred men. On the other hand, he was now master of the abandoned town of Isker and Kuchum had no forces left. Yermak had conquered Siberia.

This 'capital' of Isker was hardly more than a big village. The houses were made of wood and mud, and contained plenty of furs and carpets. The Ostyak tribal chieftains surrendered to Yermak and undertook to pay him the same tribute as they had paid before to Kuchum. Supplies for his troops were delivered by the Ostyaks and the neighbouring agricultural Tartars.

Kuchum had fled; Yermak was Tsar of Siberia. There was nothing to prevent him acting as others had done and returning with his booty to Russia, announcing in Moscow the incorporation of another territory in the Russian empire and leaving the rest to the Tsar. No one would have demanded more of him.

However, Yermak wanted a lasting union with the new territory. For this he needed his position in Siberia to be legalized. He also needed help in the way of men and arms. His powder was nearly exhausted and his fishing nets were badly eaten away by a local water-beetle.

Yermak was very soon reminded by the Tartars that his position in Isker was not very secure. A band of twenty Cossacks sailed up the Irtysh to catch fish. They put out their nets and lay down to sleep. Mahmetkul, now recovered from his wounds, was in the neighbourhood. He crept up on the sleeping Cossacks by night and they did not wake up again. When Yermak heard of this incident he set out immediately in pursuit of the Tartars. He caught them up and some of the Tartars, too, fell into a permanent sleep. Mahmetkul himself and the rest escaped.

Yermak sent out a band which succeeded in surprising Mahmetkul as he had surprised the Cossacks. Most of the Tartars were killed, but Mahmetkul himself was bound and taken back as a prisoner to Yermak at Isker.

Yermak now had a good opportunity of taking revenge for the murdered fishermen. Instead, he received Mahmetkul with a guard of honour, greeted him as a prince and promised him 'great favours' in the name of the Tsar of Russia. Yermak had no authority at all to make promises of this sort, but he did right, as the future was to show.

Kuchum was very upset at the capture of his son, and had no doubt that he would suffer an unpleasant fate. But after a few days a message arrived from his son to say that he was alive and well, but he begged his father not to attack Yermak's foraging parties or else his own rations would deteriorate severely.

After he had secured his position on this side, Yermak sent a deputation to Moscow. He needed a reliable messenger. Ivan Kolzo decided to accept the task, although he was condemned to death in Moscow. The risk was great – but so was the possible profit. In late autumn he set out for Moscow with a small troop of Cossacks.

His route passed through the Stroganov territories. Maxim did not hold him up – for a very good reason.

On the very day in September 1581 on which Yermak set out for Siberia, an army of the usual Ural mixture of races, once again led by a Pelym princeling, appeared before the gates of Cherdyn, the capital of Perm. Yermak and his Cossacks took the southern road; the attack came from the north. This time it was the Stroganovs' turn to hurry to the help of the *voivode* of Perm, but how could they with the Cossacks away and their own possessions threatened?

The *voivode* was naturally very angry and reported the incident to Moscow. The Stroganovs, he wrote, were stirring up the natives and upsetting his own policy; they were always asking for help, but sending their own men off heaven knew where. The consequences were apparent: one attack after another from Siberia, revolts with which even the *voivode* himself could not deal.

Reports of this sort provoked a swift reaction from Tsar Ivan. In addition, Moscow was in a bad mood. The rebellion in Perm was indeed flaring up violently and the war with Sweden was not going at all well; there was nothing to rejoice about in any direction.

The Tsar sent a letter to the Stroganovs sealed with a black seal and black in purport, too. It was dated the 16 November 1582 and addressed the Stroganovs in not very polite terms; in three separate places there is talk of 'theft and treason'. 'You provoke your neighbours,' wrote the Tsar, 'put me on bad terms with the Tsar of Siberia and welcome the very thieves who have alienated the Nogai Tartar and closed the Volga to navigation.' The Tsar mentions Yermak by name for the first time and calls him the chief 'thief' and 'traitor'. He accuses the Stroganovs of sending Yermak off on an adventurous expedition instead of to the defence of Perm.

The letter ends by announcing the dispatch of a *voivode* to force Yermak to return and to enrol him and his band in the regular service of the Tsar. If this object was not attained, the Stroganovs would incur extreme disfavour and Yermak and his thievish comrades would find themselves on the gallows.

When Maxim Stroganov read the Tsar's letter he sent for his cousin Nikita and his uncle Semyon. The situation was serious; it was difficult to justify oneself to the Tsar with mere words. But the Stroganovs' old luck held. Just at this moment Ivan Kolzo arrived with greetings from Yermak and the news of the conquest of Siberia. The Stroganovs realized at once what this meant for themselves. They entertained the Cossacks, equipped them, gave them plenty of money for their journey and sent them on to Moscow. They themselves followed the Cossacks.

The atmosphere in Moscow was gloomy. The Tsar looked as black as a thunder-cloud. But when Kolzo fell on his knee before him and laid Kuchum's empire at his feet – with two thousand four hundred sables, fifty beavers and twenty black foxes into the bargain – Ivan's expression brightened. Everyone else sighed with relief: the *boyars*, the court, the people of Moscow and last but not least the Stroganovs, who received fresh favours in the form of new leases of land and trading privileges.

Only Yermak's mood remained gloomy, for he was still in Isker, preserving his friendship with the tribal chieftains, hunting, counting his powder supplies and thinking that he could not go on like this much longer. Meanwhile he had pushed his advanced posts farther to the north, down the Ob. This was all freshly conquered territory; to hold it he had to show energy, and display power which he did not possess.

Kolzo's return was both a joy and a disappointment to Yermak. Kolzo brought a full pardon for all past errors. He handed over to Yermak a fur from the Tsar's own shoulder, a silver drinking-cup and two valuable suits of armour. Furthermore he brought the news that the *voivode* Prince Bolkhovsky with three hundred men was being sent to Yermak's assistance. He was bringing powder, shot and all other supplies with him. But Prince Mahmetkul was to be sent to Moscow immediately. This command did not give Yermak much pleasure. He sent Mahmetkul to Moscow with a heavy heart, for with him went Kuchum's only reason for keeping quiet.

In fact he began to stir again at once. Yermak's supply parties were once again liable to be attacked. The tributes of fur, which Yermak had imposed on Kuchum's former vassals, sometimes failed to arrive. Yermak demanded an explanation from Karacha, who replied that he could not collect the furs himself because Kuchum's men were attacking him. He asked for a small body of men to assist him.

Yermak sent him Ivan Kolzo with forty Cossacks. They were lured into an ambush. Kolzo fell with a dagger through his body and only one of his Cossacks escaped.

Yermak had never before suffered such a serious blow in Siberia. Now for the first time he felt how isolated he was in this vast and mysterious land. His reputation among the surrounding princes fell. His band was growing smaller and smaller. He now had only just over three hundred men. Karacha was regarded by the Tartars as a hero. He collected a force of Tartars, Voguls and Ostyaks, surrounded Yermak and tried to starve him out. The siege lasted almost three months. The Cossacks were on the brink of exhaustion; every shot had to be counted.

When Karacha was just getting ready for a triumphal entry into Isker Yermak led all his Cossacks out one night, attacked Karacha's forces and destroyed them. Karacha was punished for his disloyalty; two of his sons were killed.

Perhaps the loss of his sons stimulated Karacha to one last burst of energy; he collected his scattered forces and himself attacked the Cossacks the next day. The second battle ended in a second defeat for him. 'Numerous corpses were left on the field of battle,' write the chroniclers of Siberia. In fact in this second fight about a hundred Tartars fell; Yermak lost about two dozen men.

The tribal chiefs paid homage to Yermak again. They saw that he was invincible. They did not know that in this last battle the Cossacks had used literally their last shot. The ground burnt beneath Yermak's feet. Where was the promised *voivode* from Moscow? Yermak had been in Siberia nearly three whole years. The country was conquered, but at the same time still had to be properly subdued. It had surrendered, but remained hostile and unreliable.

Yermak went to meet the *voivode*. On the way he collected tributes of fur from his Vogul 'subjects'. Finally he halted. To go any farther meant going away, and that in turn meant admitting defeat. Yermak returned to Isker.

In fact, the *voivode* Bolkhovsky did not cross the Urals until spring 1584. He arrived in Isker without horses or supplies, having lost many men and himself seriously ill. He brought gunpowder with him, but scurvy as well. Bolkhovsky died from it soon after his arrival. Command of the soldiers passed to the *voivode* Glukhov.

Yermak had done his work well. The tree-trunk had been removed and the road to Siberia opened for the *voivodes*. After his historic task had been accomplished he soon met his end.

Up till now he had been prudent and calculating. He had not made one single strategic or political error. Unhesitatingly he had always chosen the right direction, defeated the most important opponent and refused to allow himself to be diverted by subsidiary considerations. One day towards the end of summer Yermak went up the Irtysh looking for some rich Bukhara merchants. His purpose was not to rob them but on the contrary to rescue them from the hands of Kuchum, who had barred their route to Moscow. This route along the Irtysh led from Chinese Turkestan (Sinkiang), known by the Russians as 'little Bukhara', to Moscow. The link with 'great Bukhara' (West Turkestan) was provided by the water-route via the Volga and the Caspian. Yermak must have learnt of the importance of the road to little Bukhara from the

Siberian princelings, whose first request to Moscow after their subjection had been for the right to continue trading with Bukhara. So when Yermak hastened to the aid of the merchants from Bukhara he was acting as the representative of Moscow and the protector of its commercial interests.

As he did not meet anyone on the Irtysh he turned back after a few days. Tired from rowing upstream, the Cossacks asked for a rest. They put in to a little island, to camp there for the night. The island was divided from the bank of the river by only a narrow strip of water. The night was stormy and the rain came down in torrents. The Cossacks hastily put up their tents, crept into them and fell into a sound sleep. Yermak went to sleep as well. That night Kuchum attacked the camp and only one Cossack returned to Isker.

This night of 4/5 August 1584 was Yermak's last. The precise circumstances of his death are unknown to us. According to tradition he tried to swim to the bank but his heavy armour – the gift of the Tsar – pulled him under.

THE END OF KUCHUM

Yermak was dead, but his Cossacks were still at Isker, and so were the soldiers from Moscow. Altogether there were four hundred men there. They formed quite a good-sized little army; the only thing lacking was a second Yermak.

When the sole surviving Cossack reached Isker and disclosed what had happened on that sinister night of 4 August, the whole garrison of Isker embarked on their boats and rafts and started out for home with Glukhov at their head. The little army was now transformed into an undisciplined rabble. The only thought in the heads of both the Cossacks and the soldiers was not to arrive home with empty hands. They sent parties into the neighbouring villages and demanded furs, although the tribute had already been handed over to Yermak and the Tartars were on their heels. Soon the Tartars attacked, but they were repulsed and suffered heavy losses. In one of these skirmishes the last of Yermak's *hetmeni*, Matvei Meshcheryak, lost his life.

By autumn 1584 Siberia had been abandoned by the Russians.

Where was Kuchum all this time? Isker had been evacuated by

the Russians and Siberia was his again. But Kuchum had lost any desire to return from the steppes into the forest. His enemy had perished and Mahmetkul was avenged. Kuchum remained on the steppes and his son Alei settled down in Isker.

It seemed as if Russia had shot her bolt in Siberia. But the barrier had been removed once for all by Yermak and it was considerably easier to conquer Siberia a second time. The Tartars themselves helped the Russians by continually quarrelling among themselves. Scarcely had Alei settled in Isker when he was attacked by Seidak, a nephew of Etiger, who had been deposed and murdered by Kuchum. Seidak had long been collecting forces in Bukhara in order to enforce his legitimate claim to the throne of Siberia. Alei was driven out of Isker and fled to his father on the steppes, where both set about gathering fresh strength and courage for the struggle.

Meanwhile, in Moscow, the people had buried and mourned their 'terrible' Tsar. The throne was now occupied by the weak-willed Fyodor Ivanovich, but the real ruler was Boris Godunov. The enterprise begun by Yermak and the Stroganovs passed into his hands, and he clung fast to Siberia.

Even before it was known what had happened to Bolkhovsky and Yermak he decided to send them reinforcements. In 1585 the *voivode* Mansurov crossed the Urals with a hundred men. Mansurov acted more sensibly than Bolkhovsky. Instead of horses he took snow-shoes, axes and ropes, and also – at the express command of Godunov – a cannon. It was the first cannon ever seen in Siberia and did a great deal to raise Russia's prestige, which had sunk fairly low after Yermak's death.

When he reached the confluence of the Tobol and the Irtysh, Mansurov found that he was not entering a conquered Siberia with reinforcements for Yermak but instead was confronted with the task of conquering Siberia afresh. He decided to turn downstream – not upstream, as Yermak had done – towards the weak Ostyaks and Mangaseya with its furs. He did not get very far, for the frost set in, and he settled into winter quarters.

But the Ostyaks attacked Mansurov and fought with him for two days. It was not until the cannon thundered and shattered their idol that they fled. Their chieftain then appeared and offered his submission.

Meanwhile news of the happenings in Siberia had finally reached

Moscow as well. The good-natured Tsar Fyodor did not let Glukhov fall into disgrace when he told the story of his hardships. In spite of everything Glukhov had succeeded in bringing back from Siberia a considerable number of furs and even a minor chieftain, who prostrated himself before the Tsar and promised loyalty and tribute in the name of all the peoples and tribes of Siberia. Glukhov was told to return to Siberia without delay, and all Yermak's Cossacks were ordered to go with him. A fresh detachment of three hundred soldiers was sent to the assistance of Mansurov under the command of the *voivode* Sukin.

Sukin knew that between the Tobol and the Irtysh Kuchum and his son Alei were on the prowl, and that Seidak was in possession of Isker. Not far away a Kirghiz sultan was on the move and finally the treacherous Karacha had not forgotten the death of his two sons. There were thus plenty of enemies about, and each had his horde of followers. Therefore Sukin did not advance to the Irtysh; instead he built the fortified camp of Tyumen on the Tura, on the site of the old Tartar town where Yermak had spent his first winter in Siberia.

This camp was the first of a long series of fortified settlements in Siberia, little fortresses called *ostrogs* which gradually attached Siberia firmly to the Muscovite realm.

In the following year, 1587, a new *voivode* appeared in Siberia: Danila Chulkov. He brought five hundred men with him, well provided with cannon, horses and all necessary supplies. Boris Godunov's interest in Siberia was growing stronger and stronger. The healing herbs that 'Doctor' Yakov Stroganov had put on his wounds were blossoming in the form of *ostrogs* in Siberia.

Chulkov penetrated farther than Sukin. He built the new *ostrog* of Tobolsk at the confluence of the Tobol and the Irtysh, not far from Isker. He took up his position here and attempted no hostile operations against the Tartars. Instead, he made an effort to deal honestly with them. Only sixteen *versts* away, in Isker, sat Seidak. He for his part had now entered into friendly relations with the wandering Kirghiz sultan and Karacha.

This situation suited Chulkov very well, and he soon dealt with his adversaries. We do not know precisely how he managed it. According to one version, Seidak fell into the hands of the Russians after being seriously wounded in an attack on Tobolsk; according to another, Chulkov lured his opponent into an ambush

73

and then overpowered him. Whatever the truth of the matter was, the hostile hordes were scattered. Isker was free; Kuchum's throne and capital were at the victor's disposal. Three years after Yermak's death his work had been built up again.

The period of heroic deeds was over. From now onwards the Russian empire exerted continuous pressure on Siberia, and the frontier was pushed ever farther north and east. No one now was interested in Isker. Even Chulkov did not bother about it. Instead, he fortified Tobolsk and built granaries and barracks there. Prisoners he sent straight back to Moscow.

This was a clever piece of psychology. One after the other the rulers of Siberia were sent off to distant, mysterious Moscow, to the great white Tsar. They did not die from a dagger-thrust – the simple and more comprehensible custom of Siberia – but lived on, beyond the Urals, an unreal white life in the white Tsar's white city. In Moscow, no one did them any harm. They were flattered, and given a pension and land of their own; many of them even became Christians, although they were by no means compelled to do so.

With the prisoners, Chulkov sent a report to Moscow that Siberia as far as the Ob and Irtysh, with all its princes, sultans and chieftains, was in his power. Moscow thanked him for the pleasant news and gave him the task of delivering two hundred thousand sables, ten thousand black foxes and five hundred thousand squirrels every year.

That was the start of the economic exploitation of Siberia.

Expansion towards the north and east was swift; towards the south it was somewhat slower, for the way was still barred by Kuchum.

He had lost Isker, and he had lost his son, who had been taken off to Moscow. He was pursued by the Russian *voivodes*, by Seidak, and by the perfidious Kirghiz, but he would not surrender although he was steadily going blind. The Russians alternately fought him and made overtures to him, but he never submitted to them. He made his way farther and farther south, and was eventually surprised and killed by Nogai Tartars in the winter of 1598 somewhere on the other side of the Ishim.

THE NEXT QUARTER OF A CENTURY

Kuchum's death freed Moscow from legal scruples and the fur-traders from needless anxiety. At Moscow every effort was made to cut the ground from under the feet of any Siberian legitimists. Life in Russia was made pleasant for Kuchum's children. The daughters were married to young *boyars* and the sons received titles and offices. Alei's son was given the whole town of Kasimov on the Oka and the title of 'Tsar of Kasimov'. He married a highly-placed *boyar's* daughter and his children were put on the same footing as those of the most respected *boyar* families. His line came to an end in the time of Peter the Great.

Altanai, another son of Kuchum, founded the house of Sibirsky, a rich and aristocratic family. In the seventies of the last century the last descendant of Kuchum by this line was working as an official in one of the ministries at St Petersburg.

Nevertheless, the magic of Kuchum's name lived on for a long time in Siberia. In the course of the seventeenth century several rebellions made it their rallying-cry. Even as a dead man, Kuchum robbed Moscow's *voivodes* of their sleep for a whole century.

But however many Tartars, Voguls and Ostyaks rose up, Siberia belonged to the Russians. That was the view of the government in Moscow, of the *voivodes*, the merchants, the Cossacks and the vagabonds.

That must have been the opinion of Anika Stroganov's descendants in particular. At any rate, they had as much right as the Tsar to regard Mangaseya, if not the whole of Siberia, as their property.

For some time it seemed as if the Stroganovs had become the masters of Siberia. The region beyond the Urals conquered by Yermak was first of all their property. But they soon had to withdraw. When the *voivodes* entered Mangaseya no Stroganov could continue to claim special rights there. Such a stream of adventurers and merchants poured into Mangaseya with the first detachments of troops that the Stroganovs were not in a position to assert any kind of monopolistic rights against them.

However, what the Stroganovs could not do, no one else could do either. The only power capable of claiming a monopoly was

75

the state, for which at this time the valuable furs of Mangaseya answered the same purpose as the gold of the Urals and the silver of the Altai did later. They formed an internationally accepted currency. With these furs Moscow paid for its foreign purchases and obtained the gold which it did not possess.

The government was aware of the significance of Mangaseya and as soon as the Russian troops had fortified Tobolsk securely they set out down the Ob towards the north. In 1592 an *ostrog*, which later became the town of Pelym, was built on the ruins of the old residence of the princes of Pelym. Lugui, the prince of Pelym, a former vassal of Kuchum's, recognized the Tsar of Moscow as his overlord. He was rewarded with a letter granting him exemption from the visits of the officials who collected the *yassak* (tribute of furs). Henceforth he was to hand over his tribute himself, and it was fixed at the modest figure of seven bundles of furs, each containing forty of the best sables, every year.

In the following year some more Ostyak chieftains made their submission and were all given exemption. In the same year, 1594, the town of Beryesov was founded, which in days to come was to harbour many famous exiles. A year later the Ostyaks rebelled, besieged Beryesov and would have captured it had the *voivode* at Tobolsk not hastened to the town's assistance.

The detachment which defeated the disobedient Ostyaks marched farther north and in 1595 founded the town of Obdorsk right at the mouth of the Ob. The whole course of the Ob, that is, the land of the Yugors, was now subject to Moscow. But the *voivodes* serving in these parts knew that the real Mangaseya lay farther to the east on the River Taz, and an expedition was quickly sent there from Tobolsk. It was attacked in the tundra by the Samoyeds and almost destroyed. Only a small number of survivors reached the Taz; there, in 1600, the town of Mangaseya was founded.

All this took place without any co-operation from the Stroganovs. They had neither a legal excuse nor the practical means to lay hands on this eldorado of furs. It may be that they would have tried to do so all the same had not a period of chaos begun in Russia – a century of wars, social upheavals and attacks from abroad. The Stroganovs took an active part in these struggles. From their northern properties they sent gold and men to Moscow, and when peace was finally restored all their rights and privileges were confirmed by Moscow. The Stroganovs decided to be content with their vast lands on this side of the Urals.

Forty years after Yermak's campaign a good third of modern Siberia was firmly clamped to the Muscovite empire by the *ostrogs*. In this enormous area the Muscovite *voivodes*, Cossacks and merchants were at work. They all addressed themselves to the task of subjecting the native population and collecting tribute. Their methods were simple. An armed detachment would arrive at a village, elders would be summoned, and the commander of the detachment would inform them through an interpreter what tribute they had to pay in future. Collection of the tribute took place on the spot. If the natives refused to hand over the furs or gave short weight, various kinds of encouragement were applied. Their huts were set on fire and their reindeer driven away; anyone who resisted was killed and the women and children were led off into captivity.

As in all colonial territories, the question of women was always a burning one in Siberia. The clergy often raised objections to the Russians' robbing the natives of their wives and daughters and 'living with the unbaptized and unbetrothed as they would with wives'. Nevertheless, the custom persisted until towards the end of the eighteenth century; old Siberian history is full of stories about it.

It was difficult for the unfortunate nomads to protect themselves. All they could do was go off farther into the tundra or the forests. Whenever they heard of the approach of troops, they fled. For good or evil the conquerors had to introduce a form of trade and offer some equivalent for the furs. At the beginning of the seventeenth century it was the custom in Siberia to pay for an iron kettle with as many sable skins as would go into the kettle. This was considered quite equitable; every Tunguse and Ostyak was firmly convinced that an iron kettle was something far more valuable than a dozen sable or ermine pelts.

But even the Russians did not possess many kettles and carrying them with you into the tundra was a pretty cumbersome business. It was far easier to take vodka and tobacco. Some time passed before the state monopolized this trade and more or less regulated it. It was impossible to introduce even a semblance of order into these things so long as the administration itself was in a state of complete anarchy. How the Siberian administration functioned at the beginning of the seventeenth century, and what protection and order it could give the native population, can be deduced from the story of a Pole called Pavel Khmielevsky, who arrived in Moscow with the Polish army which accompanied the pretender Demetrius. Having betrayed the Poles, and been rewarded by the Russians, he started a correspondence with the Poles, who were now in Smolensk. He was caught, tried and sent to Tobolsk, where he was imprisoned. But there were few people in Siberia who could read and write, and three years later Khmielevsky found himself not only free again but in command of the *ostrog* of Yeniseisk. After another two years he was sent as auditor to the richest and most important province in Siberia, Mangaseya, Moscow's chief source of income. On the return journey he was caught smuggling a large number of furs, and was promptly thrown into gaol again at Tobolsk. Three months later he was appointed head of a corn convoy to Mangaseya!

There were two *voivodes* in Mangaseya at that time: G. I. Kokorev and A. F. Palizyn. They were very different in character and neither of them was by any means a fool. Although there was a ban on the sea-route to Mangaseya (to prevent smuggling), Kokorev was interested in it and, as can be seen from a denunciation of his activities, which has been preserved, tried to use it himself in 1630. Palizyn's eyes, on the other hand, were on the east. In 1632 he sent off to Moscow a memorandum which outlined a plan for the conquest of the 'great Zera River'.

Unfortunately Mangaseya was too small to hold both of these men. There was friction, then an open quarrel and finally a regular war. Kokorev barricaded himself in the town; Palizyn sought protection in the neighbouring Ostyak encampments.

It seemed to him that the old warrior Khmielevsky would make a very useful ally, and so the latter became involved in this feud in Mangaseya. He carried on with his own private business, too, soon established himself in the little town of Turukhansk on the Yenisei, appointed himself *voivode* and raised the tribute of furs (*yassak*).

When the defeated Palizyn went off to Moscow, Khmielevsky's halcyon period came to an end as well. Soon he was in Tobolsk prison again, but only for a few weeks; afterwards he was taken back into government service. When he was transferred to Tomsk in 1638 he set out for his new post, but died on the way and was buried at government expense.

A RICH AND BEAUTIFUL LAND

The planned conquest of Siberia by Muscovite troops did not go on for long. A special ministry for Siberia (*Sibirsky Prikas*) was set up at Moscow in 1637, but from that very moment onwards the initiative passed to the *voivodes* in Siberia itself, and the *voivodes* did not even succeed in noting all the things found and taken by free enterprise.

Cossacks sailed in their boats along the northern rivers, sent out bands in all directions, forced the natives to submit and built *ostrogs*. After them came the fur-traders. Hunters and trappers spread out in the forests far beyond the limits of the conquered territory, building themselves wooden huts and blockhouses. They formed *artels* (associations or societies) for hunting and fishing; they searched for metals, mica and mammoth-bones; there were even *artels* for the excavation of Mongolian burial-mounds.

The southward advance was hindered for a century by struggles with the Kirghiz and, in the south-east, with the Kalmucks, the remains of Jenghiz Khan's once powerful hordes. These people were warlike nomads; the struggle against them was not easy. But the new *ostrogs* and towns could only be provided with wheat from the fertile southern steppes. It was not only the settlements in the far north, such as Mangaseya, that were supplied with grain and flour from Russia; until 1684 even towns like Tobolsk obtained their bread exclusively from the Kama region, whose towns were obliged to provide contributions for Siberia. In that year the bread came for the first time from the farming settlements on the Isset, a tributary of the Tobol. These deliveries of bread ruined the north Russian towns without satisfying Siberia; they arrived at irregular intervals and if the harvest was bad in Russia there was famine in Siberia. Plagued by eternal worries about the bread-supply, Russian Siberia had to push out towards the south. Gradually the belts of Russian forts hemmed in the Kirghiz, Nogai and Kalmucks more and more tightly, like the hoops of a barrel. Behind these belts farmers and Cossacks established themselves firmly.

Siberia attracted enterprising, free and easy, energetic men. To find out why, one has only to talk to a real Siberian; there is no region in Russia in which local patriotism is stronger. As early as the seventeenth century, people used to say 'the soil of Siberia is made of gold.' Foreigners have been just as impressed by it as Russians. It should be noted that the saying just quoted was current at a time when the mineral wealth of Siberia was more or less unknown. Siberia possessed riches in plenty quite apart from gold.

The conqueror's path was provided by the rivers. Yuri Krishanich said of Siberia, 'Whoever controls the rivers controls the whole land.' The rivers of Siberia are quite extraordinary. They flow like ocean currents; in spring they overflow their banks and form whole seas, in winter they freeze into glaciers. Siberia has four river-systems, which are navigable for thousands of miles. Each of these systems embraces an area bigger than western Europe. Tributaries lie so close to each other that it would not be very difficult to create a continuous waterway from the Urals almost to the Pacific. As early as Catherine II's time P. S. Pallas suggested linking Siberia to Russia by water.

Not that the Cossacks thought of things like these on their river-trips. What struck them particularly was the incredible abundance of fish. The fish swam in such close-packed shoals that they were sometimes lifted out of the water: when a boat floated into a shoal like this the fish were forced up out of the water and jumped into the boat. There were salmon-trout, sterlets, enormous sturgeon. Until the twentieth century the pike was regarded in Siberia as a cheap fish for poor people.

The first Cossacks thus had no difficulty in finding something to eat. After people had taken all the fish they wanted out of these rivers for nearly three centuries, it was still possible in 1887 to pull about seventeen tons of fish out of one deep spot on the Ob near the village of Kuninskaya. Nearby a layer of dead fish was discovered under the ice. They lay pressed together under the ice right to the bed of the river over an area of more than two hundred square yards.

By the village of Belogorye, likewise on the Ob, a huge shoal of pike and a shoal of carp-like fish had halted under a cliff. The local people were unaware of their presence. The cold set in, the stream stopped flowing, the water-level dropped underneath the ice, and the fish lay, covered in a layer of ice, on dry land. In the spring they thawed out before the ice started moving on the river. They

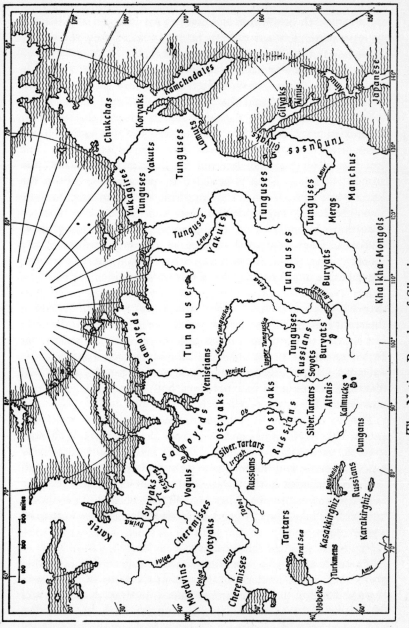

The Native Peoples of Siberia

covered the bank for a distance of three miles; the line of fish was eight to twelve yards wide and over a yard high. It is impossible to estimate how many fish there were there; they must have amounted to ten or twenty thousand tons.

The Cossacks also had the forests to see. They first arrived in the northern forests which stretch right across Siberia south of the tundra. 'Taiga,' said the Tartars and pointed to the snow-covered mountains; the Cossacks therefore used this term for mountains covered with forest. Later the word was applied to the great primitive forests of Siberia. The *taiga* is no pleasant little wood; it is vast and sinister, and the weak and imprudent often perish in it. It is often punctuated by pathless bogs. Even the bravest lose courage when they suddenly see round them nothing but dead forest, *taiga* that has destroyed itself: a bog in which everything below is decayed and rotten, and everything above withered, where only the corpses of the huge trunks slowly moulder away in the brackish water. Even when the road is open, the Siberian mosquito makes it a torture in summer for man and beast. The cedars, larches, pines and firs are so huge that they aroused wonder even in those who came from the northern forests of Russia. The Siberians' favourite tree, the cedar, is really not entitled to this name; it has little in common with the cedar of Lebanon. Its proper name is stone-pine (*pinus cembra*). Its splendid fruit, the cedar-nut, provides food for the sables and squirrels, and even for human beings, both in its natural condition and in the form of the excellent cedar oil.

Farther to the south the *taiga* changes into mixed forest. Here, by the side of the pines and firs, grow glorious birches, slender poplars, trembling aspens and fragrant lime-trees. Innumerable kinds of berries and bushes grow in the shelter of their foliage, all of them enveloped in the lush tendrils of the wild hop.

As for the mushrooms, Siberia would have been worth conquering for their sake alone. A good deal of fasting was done in Russia, and whole fortunes were later built up on mushrooms, which were the favourite food for religious fasts.

There are about nineteen hundred million acres of forest within the boundaries of modern Siberia, about six times as much as in the whole of Europe, not counting Russia. In those days the whole of western and northern Siberia was full of sables. They used to come right up to the houses and women fetching water would kill them with their yokes. When the first hunting associations were formed, a shareholder would get two to three hundred skins in a season. And what skins they were! The best individual pelt, the so-called *odinetz* (unique one), would fetch sixty or seventy roubles, a fortune at that time. There was nothing more beautiful in the world than an *odinetz* of this sort, and the diplomat, Spathari had good reason for suggesting that it was the Golden Fleece: 'The little animal is truly wonderful, it multiplies rapidly, and it occurs nowhere else on earth but in the northern land of Siberia. . . . It is a gay little animal and fair to behold; its beauty appears with the first snow, and disappears again with the thaw; it is the same animal that was known by the old Greeks and Romans as the golden fleece; for such a fleece the Greek Argonauts sailed across the Black Sea, then up a river, and found the fleece. So prolific is the animal that it is regarded as inexhaustible.'

A detail that supports Spathari's hypothesis is the fact that descendants of the old Argonauts, the Levantine Greeks, of whom Spathari himself was one, were the first foreign merchants to appear in Siberia; they came to take sable-skins from there to Turkey.

Over the centuries the habits of the sables have changed correspondingly. They no longer come into the neighbourhood of human beings and prefer to hunt for food only at night.

The Siberian red deer moved out through the forests from the banks of the Tara and populated the Altai; and there were deer everywhere. There was no need even to hunt them; they were simply driven into special enclosures. In 1754, twenty-five *versts* from Nerchinsk, over four thousand deer were corralled in this way in one single day. Wild boars lived on the Baraba steppe on perfectly good terms with the little ermines; and squirrels, bears and hares cropped up at every turn. There were beavers, wolverines and foxes of all colours: blue, red, black and even white. The foxes were particularly attractive because they did not have the cunning, spiteful nature of the western European fox. When the tribute was already being reckoned in terms of money, such a splendid black fox was delivered one day in Tobolsk that even the experts were unable to estimate its value. 'The skin must be filled with silver coins,' they said, 'and the price will be the number that go in.' In 1654, when the news of the birth of a son to Tsar Alexei Mikhailovich reached Ilimsk, a man brought in, as a gift for the

Tsarina, a snow-white fox of such beauty that the *voivode* refrained from attempting to value it. He sent the gift and its donor to Moscow, where the fur was graciously accepted and the man generously rewarded.

The conquerors made their first acquaintance with the Siberian steppe during their pursuit of Kuchum. It stretches for almost five thousand miles from the Caspian Sea to the River Amur, the largest expanse of pastureland in the world. Camels, herds of horses, innumerable sheep, cows and yaks graze there. On the stretch by the Altai it is as hot in summer as on the pampas of South America. As the traveller approaches the Altai and enters the fertile valley of Bukhtarma, he is fanned by cool breezes and surrounded by a beauty unparalleled in the rest of the world, as all who have seen it agree.

The climate is another matter; it is grim. Siberia is a 'continental' land. In latitude, the town of Omsk lies a little farther north than Berlin; Irkutsk a little farther south, but fifty and sixty degrees of frost are recorded in both places and snow lies on the ground for six months of the year. Many an army has been buried in the dreadful snow-storms of the Siberian winter and even in summer icy winter does not release its grip on the earth. The ground is continually frozen; in summer it thaws out to a depth of three feet at the most; farther down it remains frozen as hard as ice. Anyone who wishes to build a house on this ground must make laborious preparations; otherwise the earth under the house warms up, rises and slides away, so that the walls fall in. F. Shergin, a Yakutsk merchant, once began to dig a well on his property. When the pit was already some dozens of yards deep there was still no sign of warm earth or water. Shergin wished to abandon the project, but Lieutenant F. P. Wrangel, who had come to Yakutsk in 1823, persuaded him to go on digging and to send a report on the work to the St Petersburg Academy. The Academy sent Shergin instructions, together with thermometers and measuring apparatus, and the merchant went on excavating at his own expense, for which he was rewarded by Tsar Alexander I with a diamond ring. After Shergin's death his son continued the work, which was followed with interest by the Prussian Academy of Sciences as well as by the Russian one. When Professor A. von Middendorff arrived in Yakutsk in 1844 to study the problem of frozen ground, he was full of respect for Shergin's work and the respect turned into amazement when he had seen the means by which it had been carried out. At this time the pit was three hundred and eighty feet deep, and the ground at the bottom was still frozen. More recently, Soviet scientists found that the frozen ground on the Taimyr peninsula went down more than sixteen hundred feet. If European Russia is included, the total area of frozen ground amounts, according to the latest calculations, to about four million square miles.

In this ground the roots of the trees grow out instead of down, so that the forests are thin. Everything spreads outward, and there are no sharp boundaries. The tundra spreads out through the ice into the sea. Farther south there is endless forest.

But in general the climate is healthy. Russians became acclimatized very quickly, and so did the Yakuts, a Turkish race that came from the south. Animals, too, soon began to thrive in Siberia: Caucasian sheep, Don horses, Dutch cows. Wherever the local population had more or less enough food, it was extremely healthy.

The most rugged and inhospitable region is Polar Siberia. Verkhoyansk on the River Yana is the coldest spot on earth; in the winter the temperature falls to seventy degrees below freezing point. But it is possible to live even there. Polar Siberia has a flora and an abundant fauna; men grow accustomed to it and come to love it. When there was a rumour that the government was going to abandon the town of Turukhansk and move the inhabitants farther south, the latter sent a deputation to object. They refused to migrate to the fertile Minusinsk steppe and requested permission to move farther north, to the mouth of the Yenisei.

Siberian frosts are terrible. In winter the mercury in the thermometer usually freezes for several weeks, a sign that the temperature is below minus 38·4 degrees centigrade. 'In Yeniseisk in January,' writes J. G. Gmelin, 'the sparrows and jays fell from the air as if they were dead and froze immediately if they were not taken into a warm room. . . . By day there were always rings and secondary suns round the sun, and by night the same phenomena were observable round the moon.' On the other hand there is no wind in Siberia in winter, except on the east coast, and dry cold without a wind is a splendid thing. In forty degrees of frost all living things creep into their holes and nests; only man remains active as usual, building up and tearing down.

The Cossacks saw that you could live in this land. There was plenty of freedom, plenty of natural resources and little authority. They decided to settle down there.

MAP P. 146

DESHNEV, A SIMPLE COSSACK

In 1620, Cossacks from Mangaseya appeared on the Vilyui, a left-bank tributary of the Lena, and brought back the first news of the 'great River Lena, famous throughout the world'. A few years later two groups reached the Lena almost simultaneously. The Cossack Vasily Bugor, who led one of these expeditions and is regarded as the discoverer of the Lena, explored its upper reaches between 1628 and 1630, and set up two winter camps in the region. In 1632, that is, exactly fifty years after the capture of Isker by Yermak, the Cossack captain Peter Beketov built the *ostrog* of Yakutsk. Ten years later it had become an important administrative centre of eastern Siberia, like Tobolsk in the west. From here the conquest proceeded in three directions – north-east to the Bering Strait and Kamchatka, due east to the Sea of Okhotsk and south to the Amur.

Detachments of Cossacks sailed down the Lena, up its tributary, the Aldan, and, travelling from river to river by water and by land, reached the Kolyma. Others went straight down the Lena to its mouth and from there along the shore of the Arctic Ocean. They travelled in their *kochas*, flat-bottomed wooden boats with a deck and primitive sails, with which, as J. E. Fischer writes in his *History of Siberia* (1768), 'one could only sail before the wind and make little use of a cross-wind.' Fischer continues: 'A European would scarcely have dared to entrust his life to such flimsy craft on a sea that is never free from ice. But in earlier times the inhabitants of Archangel knew of no other sea-going craft and ventured on them to Mesen, Pustosersk and even as far as Novaya Zemlya.' There people at any rate lived on the coast and were seafarers. The Cossacks were familiar only with rivers; they were freshwater vikings, and now they were trying to conquer the salt sea too.

They ventured on the stormy sea for the same reason as usual: the quest for furs. The north had its own special treasures: whale-bone, walrus teeth and mammoth tusks. In the tundra they found frozen mammoths. In the course of two centuries twenty-two thousand of them were discovered in polar Siberia.

A year after the foundation of the *ostrog* of Yakutsk two

Cossacks called Rebrov and Perfilyev sailed down the Lena and eastward to the Yana. From there Perfilyev returned with a report and the usual tribute of furs to Yeniseisk, but Rebrov sailed on farther and in 1636 discovered the River Indigirka. Unfortunately he did not leave a written record of his trip.

We are better informed about the expedition of Yelissey Busa. He was sent out from Yeniseisk to the Lena in 1636 with a detachment of ten men, 'to visit the rivers that flow into the Arctic Ocean and to levy tribute on any inhabitants whom he met.' On the way Busa picked up another forty Russian freebooters, built two *kochas*, sailed the following spring down the Lena, then westward to the Olenek and finally up this river. From the Tunguses (Evenki) who lived there he collected a modest tribute: only five bundles, that is, two hundred sable skins; but they were probably pelts that paid for the whole enterprise, for the shores of the Olenek were the home of the finest black sables in Siberia.

The next year Busa went back to the Lena by land, built two new *kochas*, sailed down the river and then eastward. Not far from the mouth of the Yana ice-floes forced him in to the land. He abandoned his *kochas* and after marching for three weeks reached the upper Yana. The Yakuts who lived there were not so affable as the Tunguses on the Olenek; there were sharp skirmishes, but as a result the *yassak* (tribute of furs) was much richer. But Busa was not satisfied. He went down the Yana again and then to the east. At the mouth of the Chendon he made the acquaintance of a new people, the Yukagires, who handed over the 'proper' tribute without further ado. ... Only then did Busa turn back; he arrived home in 1642, six years after his departure, laden with furs.

Another Cossack from Yeniseisk, Posnik Ivanov, was on the Yana in 1639 at the same time as Busa, with a troop of thirty-five men. His trip is of particular interest because, contrary to the normal custom in Siberia, but in accordance with old Cossack tradition, he explored the land-route to the north-east on horseback instead of by water. He levied tribute from the Yakuts, fought with the Yukagires, who had never seen horses before, and returned with a good pile of furs and mammoth teeth, for which he paid with the loss of half his men.

Cossacks perished at sea, of hunger, of scurvy, from the poisoned arrows of the Yukagires and sometimes even from the blows of each other's sabres. This happened because the different bands competed with each other for the best districts and the 'best' natives. Amid the ice and fog of the north the vision of sudden wealth hovered before their eyes. Whether this dream came true for any of them is another matter; but those Cossacks were tough characters.

In 1644, one of them, Mikhail Stadukhin, set up his winter camp on the River Kolyma. This was the origin of the town of Nishne-Kolymsk. Later on a fur-market was held there, and the Tunguses, Yukagires and Yakuts would bring in sables, beavers and walrus-teeth, and exchange them for knives, vodka and tobacco. Stadukhin stayed there for two years and collected information about the way to the land of the Chukchas on the River Pogicha. He was told that it was only three days' journey and that there were plenty of walrus-teeth and sables there, and even gold.

This River Pogicha crops up in all the contemporary stories of eastern Siberia. Everyone looked for it, but no one found it. Most modern authorities think that it is probably to be identified with the River Anadyr, which flows into the Bering Sea.

In the next year Stadukhin repeated his attempt to reach the Pogicha. He reached the Kolyma, built two boats on it and sailed eastward through the Arctic Ocean. After he had sailed for seven days and nights, lost one boat and found no estuary, he made for the legendary river by land. What it was called made no difference to him; the main thing was the walrus-teeth and the sables.

At the same moment another expedition was making for the Pogicha. It was headed by Fedot Alexeyev, a daring merchant and adventurer who had come to these remote regions from the White Sea. He was in the service of a Moscow merchant called A. Ussov; another Moscow business may also have had a share in the enterprise. It was thus Muscovite capital that was at work beyond the Kolyma in the middle of the seventeenth century. However, a tenth of the furs obtained had to be handed over to the state, which also took an interest in the *yassak*, so the expedition was joined by a government representative, an experienced traveller and *yassak*-collector called Semyon Ivanovitch Deshnev.

Alexeyev built four boats on the Kolyma and sailed out in search of the Pogicha. A thick barrier of ice forced him to turn back. But he was by no means discouraged by this failure and decided with Deshnev to repeat the attempt the next year. This time he had a fleet of six *kochas*, each with a crew of fifteen men.

The boats reached the sea and set course for the east. Not far from the Bering Strait one of the boats was wrecked and its crew was taken on board the others. An attempt to land on 1 October 1648 was foiled by the Chukchas. As they sailed round the eastern tip of Asia, now called Cape Deshnev, a storm overtook them and carried the boats out to sea. Deshnev's boat was blown far to the south, past the mouth of the Anadyr, and then driven ashore.

This took place in 1648. It means that the Cossack Deshnev was the first man to sail from the Arctic into the Pacific and that he discovered the Bering Strait eighty years before Bering.

In 1655 he sent in his report to the *voivode* of Yakutsk, who was to forward it to Moscow. Deshnev had two reasons for making this report. First of all, Deshnev, in his own view, was in the service of the Tsar and, although he also tried to make as big a private income as he could, he wanted to receive a regular salary. Second, he wished to record his discoveries, not for scientific reasons, but so as to be able to exploit the walrus-teeth alone and undisturbed.

His report is simple and clear. He says that his vessel was driven ashore by the storm and that he then turned northward with twenty-four companions and after ten weeks of difficult going reached the Anadyr not far from its mouth. On the way he lost thirteen men. At the Anadyr he found neither forest nor Chukchas. Deshnev wintered at this inhospitable spot and the following spring travelled up the Anadyr. Higher up it he met people called 'Anaules'. They looked very martial, but this did not prevent Deshnev immediately collecting tribute from them. Here he laid the foundation stone of the *ostrog* of Anadyrsk. At that time it marked the eastern limit of the Russian advance in Siberia.

In April 1650 Deshnev had the pleasure of welcoming at his *ostrog* a new expedition which had come from the Kolyma by land. The arrival of the Cossack Motora, who led this expedition, gave Deshnev fresh courage. But his spirits sank when Mikhail Stadukhin appeared on Motora's heels. Stadukhin began collecting from the Chukchas tribute which they had already paid to Deshnev. There were quarrels, and even fighting, between the Cossacks. Eventually Deshnev and Motora succeeded in getting rid of their unwelcome comrade. He went off to the south, taking with him most of the *yassak* collected by Deshnev. Deshnev and Motora heaved sighs of relief. They built boats and in summer 1652 sailed down the Anadyr to its mouth. They were the first Russians to reach the Bering Sea via this river. In the estuary they hit a sandbank which rewarded them richly for all their hardships, for on it they found mountains of walrus-teeth. Motora was unable to make use of the discovery, for he was murdered by the Chukchas in the same year.

Deshnev had to return to the Anadyr *ostrog*, where he began to fell wood with which to build boats. He wanted to reach the mouth of the Kolyma by sea. A year passed in preparations for the return journey and then a fresh troop of Cossacks arrived, led by Yuri Seliverstov. The land-route to the Kolyma was also open.

Not far from the mouth of the Anadyr, in a Koryak camp, Deshnev met a Yakut woman whom Alexeyev had taken with him on his journey. Deshnev asked her about the fate of her master. 'The master and his companions lost their teeth,' she said, 'and all died down to the chief *hetman*; others were slain by the Koryaks and the rest floated away in small boats.'

Deshnev realized that Alexeyev had died from scurvy. He heard no more of his companion, but an echo of Alexeyev's further travels has reached us through S. P. Krasheninikov, the explorer of Kamchatka, who visited the peninsula in 1737. The natives told Krasheninikov about the Russian fur-hunter Fedot Alexeyev, who had sailed into the Kamchatka River with two vessels. He had gone up the Kamchatka, they said, and pitched camp for the winter on the Nikul, one of its tributaries, which since then has been called the River Fedot. He and his companions had later been killed by the Kamchadales.

Krasheninikov found no traces of this first Russian colony on Kamchatka, but everything, including other traditions of the natives reported by G. F. Müller, points to the conclusion that the man in question was Fedot Alexeyev's son, who had accompanied his father on the trip with Deshnev in 1648 and bore the same Christian name as his father.

Deshnev's story has been subjected to the most searching investigations, but in spite of all kinds of objections it seems likely that it is true. His geographical, meteorological, ethnographic and other observations have all proved faultless. At the end of a thorough survey of the evidence, the Russian scholar L. S. Berg wrote: 'What Deshnev describes, he did!'

It may be asked why the Russian government, after being informed of Deshnev's sea-trip, still did not know whether

Siberia was joined to America, and why Peter the Great later posed this question to Bering. The answer is typical of the history of geographical discoveries, not only in Siberia. Deshnev sent his report to the *voivode* of Yakutsk in 1655; it only became known in St Petersburg eighty-seven years later, when it was published by G. F. Müller, the famous historian of Siberia. Müller himself discovered it in the archives of Yakutsk in 1736, eight years after Bering's first expedition.

None the less Deshnev's discovery had become known in Siberia. All the Russian maps made between his and Bering's journey show north-eastern Siberia as washed by the sea. These maps exclude the possibility of a land bridge between Siberia and North America. In his *History of America* (1777) the Scotsman, W. Robertson speaks of 'a mysterious Siberian tradition of a successful sea-voyage round the east cape in 1648'. Vague rumours about Deshnev's voyage had reached Europe by the middle of the seventeenth century. In 1652 the Swedish 'commercial factor' in Moscow reported to Queen Christina's government that the Russians were on the point of sending a group of officers to America. The report gave the impression that the Russians had discovered a way to America; it must have been an echo of Deshnev's enterprise. In the 'Notice about the River Amur' drawn up by N. Gavrilovich Spathari, the Russian ambassador to China, in 1678, we find this passage: 'It is impossible to reach the mouth of the Amur from the mouth of the Lena by sea, because great blocks of ice float on the sea . . . and crush the ships.' The existence of a sea passage between Siberia and America is thus taken for granted by Spathari. Finally, on the map of Siberia by Philip von Strahlenberg, which was published at Stockholm in 1730 but had been drawn in Siberia about 1715 on the basis of older Russian maps, we find the statement that the Russians reached Kamchatka by sea from the River Indigirka *'magno labore et vitae discrimine'* (with great difficulty and danger).

Deshnev made one of the greatest geographical discoveries without realizing its scientific importance; on the other hand, he understood very well what its practical value was. In that he resembles many great discoverers whose names are immortalized on our maps. Eighty years before Bering and a hundred and thirty years before Cook he sailed between Asia and America, and like these two men he will not be forgotten.

III

THE STRUGGLE
AGAINST THE BLACK DRAGON

———⟐———

COSSACKS DISCOVER DAURIEN

WHATEVER ONE'S view of the value of Deshnev's seafaring exploits, the fact remains that, thanks to him, sixty-seven years after Yermak had set out with his little army from the Stroganovs, Russia had advanced to the eastern tip of Siberia. In the space of a lifetime a whole continent had been crossed and incorporated by Russia.

About the middle of the seventeenth century a real rush to eastern Siberia started. Rumours of its fantastic riches made both great and small lose their heads. Every *voivode* equipped his own expedition. People came from Yakutsk, from Yeniseisk, even from Tobolsk and Tomsk. Merchants in Kazan, Kholmogory and Moscow sent their representatives.

The *voivodes* competed with each other. Dimitri Kopylov's detachment of Cossacks, whose second-in-command, Ivan Moscovitin, set up the first winter camp on the Sea of Okhotsk in 1639 and brought back the first information about the Amur and the agricultural possibilities of its basin, had been sent from Tomsk, in spite of the objections of the *voivode* of Yeniseisk. Nine years later the *voivode* of Yakutsk sent his troop out. This band found a better route and in 1649 built an *ostrog* at the mouth of the Okhota which later became the town of Okhotsk.

At the same time the Cossacks were moving south. They travelled along the Yenisei and its tributaries to Lake Baikal, the 'Holy Sea' of the Buryats and Tunguses. It was sighted in 1643 by Kurbat Ivanov, the 'leader of fifty men'. Three years later the *hetman* Kolesnikov travelled round Baikal from the north-west and built an *ostrog* on the upper Angara. In the next year the *boyar's* son Pokhabov reached Lake Baikal from Yeniseisk and crossed it on the ice from north to south. Another year later the Cossack Galkin went round it from the north, reached the River Bargusin and built an *ostrog* there.

Galkin was a man of exceptional daring and energy. On the other side of Lake Baikal he arrived in a region swarming with sable, ermine and Tunguses. He dealt successfully with all these, but before the lake he stood speechless.

It is certainly a great lake: with a length of four hundred and twenty miles and a breadth of fifty, it is longer than the Adriatic and not much narrower. Galkin tried, without success, to determine its depth. We know it now: nine hundred and twenty fathoms. Its autumnal storms are as dangerous as those at sea, and it harbours the same animals as the Arctic Ocean, such as seals. It is the Arctic Ocean in miniature, situated fifteen hundred feet up in the middle of a continent!

On the far side of the lake Galkin saw valleys with the remains of irrigation canals and learnt that corn had once been sown there. He returned to Yeniseisk and reported his impressions. The reference to crops fell here on deaf ears, but in Yakutsk a different view was taken. There the *voivode* collected plenty of furs and they had an abundance of fish, walrus-teeth and even mammoth-teeth, but no corn. The Tunguses and Yakuts asserted unanimously that somewhere in the south, in a region known as Daurien that could be reached along the rivers, fields of golden wheat waved in the summer sunshine. There flowed the 'black river', said the Tunguses, and by this river corn grew. The first Cossacks who sailed up the Vitim, crossed the mountains and gazed down into the valleys of the tributaries of the Amur confirmed these stories; for example, Maxim Perfilyev in 1640 and Bakhtiarov in 1641.

In Yakutsk this news was received with the greatest excitement. A year before, people there had seen no corn for ten months. The *voivode*, Peter Golovin, decided to send a fresh expedition to the land of Daurien. He collected a detachment of one hundred and twelve Cossacks and fifteen soldiers, to which he added two clerks, two interpreters, a guide and a smith. Vasily Poyarkov was appointed commander. Little is known of this man. He was no ordinary Cossack, but a chancellery official, well versed in trade and the collection of *yassak*, who could handle a quill, and a sabre still better. His most striking characteristic was an inflexible will unhampered by scruples or nerves.

Poyarkov set out from Yakutsk in July 1643. This time the route chosen was the Aldan instead of the Vitim. In November, Poyarkov had to desert the upper reaches of the Aldan for its banks, because the river began to freeze over. He set up a winter camp and left his heavy baggage there with an armed guard; with the rest of his men he crossed the mountains and in December reached the Seya. Here he halted for the winter and started questioning the local inhabitants about the land of Daurien. They told him that on the Shilka oats, barley, buckwheat and peas grew. Poyarkov had already heard about all this, but he had not seen it himself.

He would have been only too glad to find something of the sort, for his men had nothing to eat. In the winter their hunger reached such a pitch that the Cossacks started hunting the Dauriens and feeding on this 'game'. Poyarkov lost half his party through starvation and scurvy, and discipline began to break down. Only Poyarkov's unfeeling cruelty enabled him to preserve his authority and to stifle all attempts at mutiny. Every day, indeed every minute, he had to be prepared for a dagger-thrust in the back; thus he could have no mercy for the backs of others.

In the spring the Cossacks who had been left behind at the winter base caught up with Poyarkov. Together they sailed down the Amur in home-made boats. Every time they put into the bank they were met unfailingly by a hail of arrows, for the news of their arrival preceded them. On one occasion, of the twenty-six men he sent out to look for food, only two returned.

Poyarkov spent the next winter at the mouth of the Amur. This time things were easier, for he had a few captured Gilyaks whom he held as hostages in order to force their fellow-tribesmen to provide him with supplies. When the ice melted in the spring he sailed out of the Amur and turned north through the Sea of Okhotsk. He was just two years too late, otherwise he would have gone down in history as the first seafarer on the Sea of Okhotsk; as it was, the Dutch captain de Vries had entered this sea from the east.

Poyarkov spent his third winter at the mouth of the River Ulya. In the spring he rowed up the river, crossed the most inaccessible mountains in eastern Siberia and arrived back in Yakutsk on 12 June 1646, after an absence of two years and eleven months. He had lost three-quarters of his men, suffered unparalleled hardships and made a journey that only one man – Ivan Nagiba in 1652 – was able to repeat during the course of the next two centuries. In addition, he succeeded in arriving hale and hearty with four hundred and eighty sable skins, six sable cloaks and some captured Gilyaks. But like many others, he was unable to enjoy the fruits of his labours. The Cossacks who came back with him raised complaints against him. They accused Poyarkov of behaving cruelly towards the natives and themselves.

Poyarkov did not deny the charges; he simply pointed to the special circumstances of the expedition. The *voivode* of Yakutsk sent him to Moscow. What happened to him there is not known.

KHABAROV'S CONQUESTS

While Poyarkov was travelling down the Amur, the search for an access to the Shilka and the Amur was being continued from Yakutsk. Two fresh reconnaissance parties reached the Shilka and although they returned without fame or booty they confirmed the stories of abundance and wealth, of the crops and numerous population of the land of Daurien.

About this time Yerofei Pavlovich Khabarov turned up in Yakutsk with a plan for an expedition to the Amur.

Khabarov had seen a good deal in his time. He came from north Russia, from Deshnev's native town, Ustyug. He had gone on trading journeys to Mangaseya and been as far as the Taimyr peninsula. Obviously his travels had not been completely fruitless; he brought a small fortune with him to eastern Siberia and set up a salt works not far from the town of Kirensk on the Lena. He was thus not just a commercial adventurer but a solid business man. Salt was a safe proposition in eastern Siberia. Soon ploughed fields were to be seen round the salt works, and then a mill. Khabarov became a wholesale corn-dealer – again a solid and vital line of business. In 1641, after eleven years of constructive work the *voivode* of Yakutsk requisitioned the whole concern for the state. The reason why this step was taken is not known. It may be that Khabarov's arbitrary behaviour on his own property was at the bottom of it, for he was hot-tempered by nature and wielded a heavy hand.

Just when Khabarov's fortunes were at their lowest ebb he met the newly-appointed *voivode* of Yakutsk, who late in 1648 was on the way to his post and had to winter at the *ostrog* of Ilimsk, not far from Kirensk. The *voivode* had, for a Russian, the strange-sounding name of Franzbekov. He had originally been called

Fahrnsbach and was a German from Livonia. As he belonged to the Greek Orthodox Church nothing prevented his being employed in the government service. Clever, experienced and a linguist, he had spent some time as Russian agent in Stockholm and had then decided to make a career and a fortune in Siberia. He had a receptive ear for grand ideas and Khabarov suggested an expedition to Daurien at his own expense and risk; all he asked of Franzbekov was to provide him with arms and government support.

This suggestion appealed at once to Franzbekov. The attractive thing about it was that Khabarov wanted to try a new, better and shorter route to the Amur, not via the Vitim, like Poyarkov, but up another tributary of the Lena, the Olekma. This was certainly a fresh and promising idea. No less seductive was the fact that Khabarov, although according to his own assertions he had been unjustly ruined by the previous *voivode*, was offering to finance the expedition from private means and was only asking for moral support.

But how could he undertake an enterprise like this without money? It was precisely in this point that his business sense showed itself. Khabarov simply pointed out to the *voivode* that he, the *voivode*, could have a private share in the expedition, that is, contribute the necessary money.

This bold proposal was adopted. Franzbekov provided Khabarov, out of government supplies, with arms and ammunition for seventy hired freebooters. He also gave him written orders. But that did not affect the essential nature of this expedition, which was fundamentally a private venture by Franzbekov and Khabarov. Just as in the case of Yermak, Moscow was only subsequently informed of the affair.

But the Stroganovs were private persons, while Franzbekov was a representative of the government. His enterprise was therefore not a completely straightforward matter, as had been the case with the Stroganovs and Yermak. From the start it had a tinge of the illegal and piratical. This is clearly shown by Franzbekov's deceitfulness. After he had dispatched the party he informed Moscow that he had commissioned Khabarov to bring the rulers of Daurien 'under the Tsar's exalted hand . . . not by force, but by friendliness.' But what the *voivode* said to Khabarov was rather different; there is no mention of friendliness in his instructions. On the contrary, Khabarov is told not to shrink from any measures:

'If these people should show themselves disobedient . . . it is permissible with God's gracious help to use force . . . to subdue them by the customary means of waging war, to attack them unexpectedly . . . and to seize tribute for the Tsar.'

In March 1649 Khabarov sailed down the Lena and then up the Olekma. He tried to find out more about the route, but this was difficult, for since Poyarkov's expedition people fled in all directions at the sight of a Cossack. Finally he reached the Amur. In a deserted village he found an old woman who was probably a magician and soothsayer, or else simply clever enough to act as if she was. At any rate, she told Khabarov during the night of the treasures of the land of Daurien. She confided to him that in the nearby mountains lay gold, silver and precious stones. In addition, there was corn in Daurien; but what was corn compared to gold?

The old woman also told Khabarov about the political situation on the Amur. That part of Daurien where the Cossacks were was ruled, she said, by Prince Lavkai, her brother. The farther bank of the river was under the sway of a still more powerful prince, who possessed an army armed with bows and fire-arms and ate and drank from gold and silver vessels; his capital lay on the River Non (the Nonni, a tributary of the Sungari) and was very big and wealthy. And this powerful prince was subject to a still more powerful one, the omnipotent ruler.

This was a fairly clear picture. The left bank of the Amur, Daurien proper, was ruled by the minor Tunguse prince Lavkai; the right bank, Manchuria, was a province or vassal-state of the Great Khan of China.

The old woman was wrong in only one detail. Twenty-five years earlier the capital of Manchuria had been moved to Mukden. This move was carried out by Khan Nurhachi, who founded by conquest a Manchurian empire that stretched from the Amur and the Yellow Sea to the Great Wall of China. The old woman could hardly know that Nurhachi's son, Abakai, who had meddled skilfully in the Chinese civil war, had made his Manchus masters of Peking and been declared in 1636 the founder of the new Tai-Tsing or Manchu dynasty; and that in 1644 – when Poyarkov was on the Amur – his grandson had been proclaimed emperor of China under the name of Shun-chih and thus inaugurated the Manchu period of Chinese history, which did not end until 1912.

So these Cossacks had stumbled not just on a frontier territory of the Chinese Empire, but on the nucleus of the new Chinese power, the homeland of a young, vital, ambitious dynasty. If the Siberian *voivodes* had considered all this a little more carefully, they would probably have been more cautious.

In May 1650 Khabarov returned to Yakutsk, leaving some of his men to wait for him on the Amur. He brought little booty back with him, but he did not have to render an account to his partner, for Franzbekov had already been removed from his post and was now far away. Khabarov confirmed the story of corn in Daurien. He brought samples with him and also a map of Daurien, which unfortunately has not been preserved. In Khabarov's opinion, grain could be transported from there to Yakutsk, but only if the country was conquered first; for that about six thousand men would be needed.

Immediately after his return he began to make preparations for a second expedition. He equipped it carefully, obtaining horses and three cannon. His band consisted of one hundred and seventeen volunteers and twenty-one government Cossacks. In the same year he appeared on the Amur again, advanced to Prince Lavkai's residence, the village of Albasin, and captured it. He fortified this spot, left a small garrison behind and himself went on farther down the Amur. He attacked the Daurians wherever he met them and returned to Albasin with prisoners and a rich haul of booty. He sent a report back to Yakutsk that he had found plenty of food on the Amur.

After wintering unmolested in Albasin, in the early summer he led his Cossacks down the Black River again. His account of this trip is sober and factual:

'After making ready big and small boats, and asking God for his grace, we set out from Albasin on 2 June. After two days we came upon tents abandoned by the Daurians and seized one woman only for questioning. . . . After bitter fighting we took three forts belonging to the princes Olgemoa, Gugudar and Latodi. 661 Daurians were killed; 243 women and girls were taken prisoner, and also 118 children, 237 horses and 113 head of cattle. Our losses were 4 dead and 45 wounded, all of whom soon recovered.'

Peking soon heard what was happening on the Amur. Orders were sent from the capital and the Manchus were soon on the march. The clash occurred below the modern Khabarovsk. When the battle was over, the Manchus had left behind many dead, seventeen muskets, two cannon, eight silk flags, eight hundred and thirty horses and large stocks of supplies. Khabarov's losses were ten dead and seventy-eight wounded.

The captured supplies enabled Khabarov to winter at the scene of his victory. The rumour that the road to the Amur was open began to exert its effect. Troops of bold fellows joined Khabarov from the north. It was the beginning of the rush to Daurien, which was to last, in spite of setbacks, for several decades. The word went round that Daurien was not only warm but also free from government officials. Exiles, prisoners, deported peasants and independent hunters all streamed into the land of freedom during the next few years. After the mutinies at Verkholensk in 1653 and at Ilimsk in 1655 they were joined by deserters from the army.

In Moscow, Khabarov's adventures were compared with the heroic deeds of Yermak. Khabarov had removed the barrier to the Amur, just as Yermak had opened up the path to Siberia. Now it was a matter of consolidating these conquests and bringing them under government control. In 1653 the Muscovite nobleman Sinovyev arrived on the Amur with reinforcements and munitions. He gave the Cossacks gold medals and pay for the time they had served, but at the same time he deprived Khabarov of his command, which he gave to one Onufry Stepanov. The transfer of command took place at the mouth of the Seya. Rather strangely, Khabarov made no objection. Sinovyev behaved in a rude and overbearing way. One can imagine how often Khabarov's 'fingers twitched', as the Russians say. But the 'nobleman' came direct from Moscow, and a whole army of three thousand men was supposed to be following him, under the command of an important man from the court, Prince Lobanov-Rostovsky. Khabarov accepted the situation in silence and went off with Sinovyev to Moscow, where a mass of complaints awaited him.

At Moscow things went badly for him at first. All his property was confiscated, and he was threatened with an even worse fate. But the force of his personality and his powers of persuasion saved him again. He explained to the Muscovite officials all about the Black Dragon and how he had driven a few nails into its back in the way of *ostrogs*. He told them about the grain that could be shipped to Yakutsk and about the silver and silk that streamed from China to Daurien. He also mentioned gold, sable and ermine.

The resemblance to Yermak became obvious. People understood. His fortune was returned to him, he was raised to the status of *boyar's* son and he received some villages near Ilimsk to administer.

There he spent the rest of his life and there he died. But the things that he had created lived on. Even the salt-works which he had founded before the expedition to the Amur proved to be a sound enterprise. That, too, lived on. It passed out of the hands of the government into the possession of a merchant called Voroshilov from Irkutsk and was taken over again by the state at the beginning of the nineteenth century. Even his mill remained in service, and the farm near Kirensk flourished.

STEPANOV'S MISERABLE END

Khabarov was cruel and covetous, but he was also clever and daring; he procured much useful information about Daurien and the Amur and opened a new road to this region. The next step was to make use of these achievements, and for this men with a better knowledge of the political aspects of the situation were needed; hence the plan to send Prince Lobanov-Rostovsky to Daurien with three thousand men. But this plan was never put into effect; it was impossible to collect such an army and to supply it from Siberia.

As we said above, Onufry Stepanov took over command of Khabarov's brigade. He wintered in the land of the Gilyaks and then in spring 1654, when his supplies were exhausted, went on to the River Sungari. There was nothing more to be won on the Amur; the local inhabitants had been transferred to Manchuria by the Chinese authorities and the fields lay fallow. Stepanov had just received a fresh reinforcement of fifty men; perhaps it was this that encouraged him to take the bold side-step to the Sungari. After travelling for three days up the Sungari, Stepanov met a body of Chinese and Manchurian troops and after bitter fighting was forced to retreat. He was already short of gunpowder.

He had lost time and men, and discipline was beginning to break up. On the return journey he kept collecting little groups who had set out to make their fortune in this strange land. These adventurers did nothing to improve discipline, and Stepanov hastily built an *ostrog* in which to winter peacefully. In spring 1655 the Chinese attacked him again; this time they had an army of 'ten thousand men, with fifteen cannon, and fire-arms with and without locks'. For three weeks the Chinese and Manchus besieged the *ostrog*, which was defended by about five hundred Cossacks, but they were unable to capture it.

Stepanov was stuck there with his hungry and now undisciplined band. The worst of it was that he was now receiving no munitions or provisions from Yakutsk. This was due to Sinovyev, who at his departure had told Stepanov to send the *yassak* straight to Moscow instead of to Yakutsk. He was following the new Moscow policy; Daurien was already regarded as imperial territory. In 1655 Pashkov, *voivode* of Yeniseisk, was appointed first *voivode* of Daurien. In 1656 he started out for his new post with five hundred and sixty-six men. The hardships he suffered on the way are known to us from the autobiography of the exiled archpriest Avakum, who travelled to Daurien with Pashkov, as well as from Pashkov's own reports. In 1656 Pashkov built an *ostrog* on the River Nercha, four miles from its confluence with the Shilka. This *ostrog* was at first called Nelyudskoi (human-less, inhuman), but two years later it was rechristened Nerchinsk, the town on the Nercha.

It is clear that Sinovyev's arrangement was sensible: the *yassak* was bound to take the new route via the Shilka and Lake Baikal; the enormous detour through Yakutsk was unnecessary. But the *voivode* of Yakutsk felt neglected and left the support of Stepanov's band on the Amur to Pashkov, who at first had nothing himself and was waiting for supplies from Yeniseisk. Stepanov was thus left to his own resources. He did the worst thing he could have done. Instead of building permanent fortifications, provoking a decisive battle with the Chinese or returning home, he wandered about on the Amur for another two years, looking for a district that would provide food.

When Chinese regular troops finally brought him to battle at the confluence of the Amur and the Sungari in June 1658, he was no longer capable of offering serious resistance. Two hundred and twenty-seven of his men succeeded in breaking through and escaping up the Amur; the other two hundred and seventy disappeared.

Stepanov himself was in all probability killed, like most of those who disappeared. However, a number of them were taken prisoner and were well treated by the Chinese, who settled them near Peking and gave them Chinese wives. This was a deliberate policy, which aimed at breaking down the morale of the starving Cossacks by making captivity attractive.

THE COSSACKS START AFRESH

The Black Dragon was in the power of the Chinese. The *ostrog* of Albasin was burnt to the ground. But the Cossacks did not retreat far; they left the Amur, but dug themselves in on the Shilka.

However, the pressure from inner Siberia continued. Six years after the Chinese victory a successor to Khabarov appeared in the heart of Daurien.

He was a Polish prisoner-of-war called Nikifor Chernigovsky, who had been foreman of the salt-works at the *ostrog* of Ustkut. In 1665 something rather unusual even for Siberia had occurred. Obukhov, the *voivode* of Ilimsk, was attacked and murdered while on a journey by a gang led by Chernigovsky. 'It is not known precisely what caused this bitterness against Obukov,' writes G. F. Müller. According to Siberian tradition, the reason was the *voivode*'s passion for Chernigovsky's pretty wife.

Chernigovsky went off with his men to the Amur and came to the very spot where the ruins of Albasin lay. He set to work without delay and built new fortifications. Then he began to hunt the famous 'Albasinian' sables. And as the memory of the fate of the *voivode* of Ilimsk upset his peace of mind, of his own accord he sent a delegation to Moscow with a large parcel of the very best sable skins.

There his case was investigated. On 15 March 1672, Chernigovsky and six others were condemned to death in their absence, and forty-six accomplices to severe whippings. But these sentences were only passed in order to preserve appearances. Chernigovsky had killed an inefficient *voivode*, but not without a reason; on the other hand, he had led the Cossacks back to the Amur. In addition, the sables which he sent were absolutely first-class skins. So the delegation returned with a full pardon from the Tsar and a reward of two thousand roubles as well.

Meanwhile the fields round Albasin had been tilled, gardens

laid out and a big village built. A monk called Germoger had already settled there and founded a monastery nearby. In this monastery there was a much-revered icon of the Virgin Mary. Even genuine farmers began to settle there.

In 1674, Chernigovsky was replaced as commandant of Albasin by a *boyar's* son. In another ten years a regular *voivode* appeared, Alexei Tolbusin. He received a seal of office with the arms of Albasin on it: an eagle with a bow in one claw and an arrow in the other. These were almost the only Siberian city arms without a furry animal in them; apparently furs were no longer the important thing about Daurien.

But this peaceful life did not last long. The Chinese were still there. The replacement of the old, tired Ming dynasty by the energetic Manchu emperors had already made itself felt in the resistance to Stepanov. Now the vigorous and warlike K'ang-hsi was on the throne. In 1684 he was thirty years old, and he began to give clear indications of his claims to all the lands round China proper. He built fortresses in Manchuria at Mergen, Tsitsihar and Aigun; the last was in fact on the left or 'Russian' bank of the Amur.

In June 1685 Albasin was besieged by Chinese regular troops. The Chinese brought a large number of guns with them and on the very first day of the siege the garrison lost a hundred men. Tolbusin had no stock of supplies. Food and munitions which had been on the way from Yeniseisk for months were halted on the frozen rivers and snowed-up roads. After a few days Tolbusin capitulated on honourable conditions. The Chinese allowed the garrison to keep their weapons and provided them with food and horses. Tolbusin took the holy icon and went off to Nerchinsk.

Albasin was burnt down for the second time and the Chinese returned in triumph to Aigun. They took about thirty prisoners with them, who were lodged at Peking. As there was a priest among them, they were allowed to hold religious services.

However, Tolbusin and the *voivode* of Nerchinsk did not feel entitled simply to abandon the 'district of Daurien' to the Chinese. Moreover, they found out that the cultivated fields of Albasin had been neither harvested nor burnt down by the Chinese. Meanwhile, too, the reinforcements from Yeniseisk arrived; they consisted of a regiment of Cossacks, which had shrunk on the way and had no horses. The Cossacks were led by an experienced warrior, a Prussian officer who had been taken prisoner when he was serving as a lieutenant in the Polish army. The Russians called him Afanasy Ivanovich Beiton; it is difficult to decipher his proper name from the Russian transliteration. He had been promoted to captain and sent to Daurien. He made a map of the country, the first that is known, for Khabarov's map has not been preserved.

At the end of August 1685, Tolbusin appeared with his troops before Albasin again and immediately started to bring in the harvest. All the settlers returned with him and proceeded without delay to rebuild the *ostrog*. Under the leadership of Beiton they made it stronger than before, for it was realized that the Chinese would return. About this time they transferred Aigun to the right or Manchurian bank of the Amur and fortified it strongly. From there they continually sent out small reconnaissance patrols.

The Amur was considerably nearer to Peking than to Moscow. At Moscow, the throne was occupied by two minors, Ivan and Peter; at Peking ruled the one, determined K'ang-hsi. On 7 July 1686 Albasin was besieged again. Tolbusin had seven hundred and thirty-six men under his command, and in Albasin there were eight cannon, one hundred and thirty *puds* of powder and sixty *puds* of lead. The Chinese army consisted of about seven or eight thousand men, with forty cannon.

Tolbusin made amends for his earlier surrender. He led the defence energetically and was killed in September, personally leading a sally. The command passed to Beiton.

The Chinese did not succeed in taking Albasin. After besieging it for ten months, in May 1687 they withdrew. Negotiations between the Russian and Chinese governments had already begun. A peace had to be signed.

MOSCOW APPROACHES PEKING

At this time all Moscow's energy and attention were concentrated on Poland, the Ukraine and the Baltic. The only thought in the Kremlin was how to finance the struggle in the west, for the treasury was empty and gold was badly needed. Trade with China offered the possibility of obtaining some. China was the best market for Siberian furs. Moscow was therefore ready to give up a good deal in exchange for the opportunity to trade with China.

In any case, without an understanding with China, Daurien was more or less worthless.

Moscow had long been interested in Siberia's eastern neighbours. The advance into the south-eastern steppes was always meeting resistance. Who was behind all these Marzas and Tarichas who pretended to submit one day and burnt down Russian settlements the next? Somewhere beyond the Kirghiz horde lay the encampments of the Mongolian 'golden Tsar', Altyn Khan, who possibly embodied the old tradition of Jenghiz Khan. Kuchum had been a descendant of Jenghiz Khan and those of his sons who had stayed in Siberia gave the Russian authorities trouble for a long time. Moscow was therefore quite right to establish relations with Mongolia where, as it proved later, the enterprising attitude of Jenghiz Khan's successors was still very much alive.

Nor was this Moscow's only interest in Mongolia. The route to China led through Altyn Khan's settlements. The first Russian ambassador to Altyn Khan was therefore commissioned to investigate ways and means and, if possible, to reach China.

In 1608 the Cossacks Belogolov and Litvin were sent to Altyn Khan 'to offer him greetings from the Tsar'. The Cossacks brought back the first authentic information about Altyn Khan. His nomad kingdom, they said, embraced all the Kalmucks, who lived beyond the Kirghiz; their horsemen were equipped with bows and arrows, but had no fire-arms. Three months' journey beyond lay the Chinese Empire, in which settled people lived, with big commercial cities and an army equipped with fire-arms.

The Cossacks had made many other observations touching geography, economics, manners and customs. Their report served as a rough guide; in the years that followed Moscow continued its investigations. The most interesting of these was the embassy of the Cossacks Tyumeretz and Petrov.

These two rode out of Tobolsk in 1616 towards the upper Yenisei. Then they crossed the Tannu Ola mountains and met Altyn Khan in person on the shores of Lake Ubra Nor. The Cossacks were hospitably received and given mutton and mare's milk. When it came to the audience in the felt tent of the Khan himself, 'the latter, who sat in the Turkish fashion, pulled off his cap when the name of our Tsar Mikhail Fyodorovich was mentioned, while his *boyars* rose and bared their heads; and the Khan interrupted the conversation and asked how His Majesty was . . .'

The kernel of the ambassadors' speech was the suggestion that the Khan should put himself under the protection of the Tsar and pay him tribute in return for his help and support. It was clearly due to the political situation – the Khan was fighting the East Mongols and Kirghiz – that he accepted the offer and even swore an oath of loyalty to the White Tsar, 'holding his golden idol in his raised hand'. He sent two of his ambassadors to Moscow with the Cossacks.

In Moscow, Altyn Khan's emissaries confirmed his readiness to recognize the Tsar as his overlord. They went home with gifts and a letter, accompanied by a small Russian delegation led by the Cossacks Petlin and Mundov. They left Tomsk in May 1618 and at the beginning of September arrived in Peking. 'The Mongolian land,' the Russians reported, 'is big and wide; it stretches from Bukhara to the sea.' It is not clear which sea they meant; probably they counted Manchuria as part of Mongolia.

'The Mongol men are not clean,' the Russians continued, 'but the women on the other hand are very clean. The horses are good, and there are many camels; there is plenty of silk, as a result of the horse-trade with China. The Mongols plough with a hooked share, like the Tartars round Tobolsk, and make wine from every kind of corn without hops; they have no jewels and their pearls are poor.'

The Cossacks go on to describe the Chinese city of Kalgan, which lay just inside the Great Wall, and then the capital itself, where the Tsar Taibun (probably a distortion of the Chinese word 'Taming', ruler, emperor) 'dwelt in person'. The Russians called Peking 'Kambalyk', which means 'city of the khan' in Turkish, the 'Cambaluc' of Marco Polo. Kambalyk, they said, was on the River Yuko, which flowed into the Red (Yellow?) Sea; sea-going ships could not reach it, so smaller ones were used. A detailed account of China's foreign trade follows. The city itself was very large and as white as snow; it was square in shape; at the corners stood towers with big cannon pointing through the loopholes; there were guards at the gates; the streets were paved with grey stones; shops built of stone were to be seen everywhere; and inside the city lay yet another containing the imperial palace, which was beautifully decorated, with gilded roofs.

The Cossacks did not see the 'Taibun'; it was explained to them that they could not appear before him without gifts.

It should be remembered that gifts not only formed part of the normal diplomatic ceremonial but also – and this was their main significance – symbolized the submission of foreign rulers to the only sovereign of the world, the Chinese emperor. For the 'Middle Kingdom' was not a geographical but a cosmological concept. Between the one heaven and the one earth lay a kingdom, *the* kingdom, and everything else was border and subsidiary territory, inhabited by barbarians who naturally owed the emperor sub-mission and tribute. The meaning of all these 'Chinese ceremonies' was not clear to the Kremlin, which was badly informed and did not even possess a Chinese interpreter. The letter in Chinese which Petlin and Mundov brought back with them remained unread for fifty-four years for lack of an expert translator! It is true that the filing of such a document among the archives is to be partly explained by transitory disappointment in Moscow about the prospects of Russo-Chinese trade. It seemed that China was too far away and the roads to it far too insecure.

Nevertheless, even if the Muscovites had had a translator at their disposal, it is doubtful whether they would have grasped the import of the letter. In it the Chinese emperor Shen-Tsung declared himself ready to receive the Tsar's ambassadors in a fitting manner if they came with gifts and a letter from the Tsar, and to answer the letter politely; but he would not send his own ambassadors or merchants to Russia 'because this was not the custom of the Chinese'. In other words, the Chinese wanted peace, but only peace; neither war nor trade. For the Russians, on the other hand, a peace without trade was useless.

These exchanges provoked great interest in Europe at that time. The Belogolov–Litvin mission of 1608 became known in England immediately. London was informed about it by Sir John Merick, the British ambassador and governor of the Muscovy Company in Moscow, who knew Russia better than anyone else at this period. Merick also knew all about Petlin's mission; that is why *A Relation of Two Russe Cossacks travailes out of Siberia to Cathay* appeared in England as early as 1625. Three years later a Latin translation was published in Germany, and it was followed by French, Swedish and Dutch translations. The main details of the story were also recounted by John Milton in his *Brief History of Moskovia* (1682).

While Petlin and Mundov's journal was going the rounds in

western Europe, it was completely forgotten in Russia. It was only rediscovered a hundred and fifty years later by J. E. Fischer, who discussed it in his *History of Siberia*.

Many other ambassadors visited Altyn Khan. Threatened by enemies, in 1634 he accepted full Russian suzerainty. The final home of his horde became a part of the Russian realm; it corresponds roughly to the present Soviet Altai territory.

The Russian envoys to Altyn Khan brought back much interesting information. Among other things, the ambassador Starkov described a warm drink called 'chai', which he had drunk with Altyn Khan in 1638. At the time, Starkov could not be sure whether it was an infusion made from the leaves of a tree or from herbs. As a present for the Tsar he received, beside sable furs, ten *puds* of this dried 'chai', which was worth a hundred sables, so the Mongols said, whereupon Starkov asked them to give him a hundred sables instead. But the donors would not do this. This first package of 'chai' gave rise in time to the enormous Russo-Chinese tea trade.

Altyn Khan had suggested that he should act as go-between in the trade between Russia and China, but nothing much resulted from this proposal. Attempts were made, when occasion offered, to make trading agreements with the Chinese frontier authorities, and now and again these attempts were successful. It was decided to make greater efforts to come to a working arrangement and in 1654 a proper, if not very aristocratic, ambassador went to Peking with a letter from the Tsar. This ambassador, the *boyar's* son Fyodor Isakovich Baikov, was to open up diplomatic relations between the two countries and to collect as much information of a political and economic nature as possible.

Baikov did everything that was asked of him. He went up the Irtysh, then past Lake Saissan and on the far side of the Mongolian Altai he probably reached the old caravan route which led straight across the Gobi Desert to Kalgan and Peking. Baikov's route was new to the Russians and although his journey there and back lasted four years he brought home all his men and baggage safe and sound. However, his mission could hardly be regarded as a resounding success. In Peking he was received coolly from the start; his hosts behaved in a rude and provocative way. That he was asked to perform the 'kotow', an action which hardly accords with modern conceptions of the dignity of an ambassador, goes

without saying; all foreigners, including the English, submitted
to this demand until late in the nineteenth century. But when it
was suggested to Baikov that he should hand the Tsar's letter to
the court chamberlain and not to the Bogdo Khan (the emperor)
himself, he was furious; he would rather have his hands and feet
cut off, he declared, than sacrifice the dignity of his master in this
way. He also refused, when he was eventually received by the
emperor, to kneel down.

He finally went off home with the Tsar's letter and spurned gifts
still in his possession. It was suggested that his 'tactless behaviour'
had been the cause of his failure, but this was not true, for he had
been expressly instructed not to 'kotow'. The real cause of the
failure was the fact that just at the time when Baikov was in Peking,
Khabarov's successor, Onufry Stepanov, was on the Amur, and
the Chinese in Daurien had already gone over from the defence
to the attack.

In spite of this Baikov's mission was of great importance. He
had discovered a new road to China, one that was better than any
previously known. Russian caravans subsequently used this way
regularly. His achievements also formed a contribution to geographical knowledge. His detailed description of his journey was
utilized extensively in the compilation of the so-called 'Godunov
map' of Siberia, which was commissioned in 1667 on the orders
of Tsar Alexei Mikhailovich by the *voivode* of Tobolsk, Peter
Godunov, a distant relative of Tsar Boris Godunov. The author of
this map was the official Ulyan Remesov.

A second, improved edition appeared at Tobolsk in 1672. Together with other maps, most of which have not been preserved,
it served as the basis of the first geographical atlas of Siberia, which
was completed at Tobolsk on 1 January 1701 after three years'
work. The author of this atlas was the Tobolsk *boyar's* son Semyon
Remesov, son of the above-named Ulyan Remesov and author of
a history of Siberia. It contains the first ethnographical map of
Siberia, which gives its ethnographical make-up with remarkable
accuracy.

This makes it comprehensible why Moscow was always asking
for accounts of journeys and for maps. Maps of Siberia and geographical information about the country were required, and every
ambassador to China became *ex officio* a geographer.

Baikov was followed in 1659 by the *boyar's* son Perfilyev with a fresh letter for the Bogdo Khan, but in spite of careful preparation he was unable to achieve anything. The emperor did not receive him, and Perfilyev sold a package of tea and other presents given to him for the Tsar in Peking so as to be able to buy precious stones with the proceeds. He was probably afraid of losing his baggage on the return journey, and this did in fact happen: he was attacked and robbed by Kalmucks.

In 1670 the ambitious *voivode* of Nerchinsk, Danilo Arshinsky, received an interesting letter from the Chinese government. The Chinese complained about the activities of the Cossacks in Daurien and at the same time requested the Russians to hand over the Kalmuck prince Gantimur, who had gone over to the Russian side and taken his whole clan with him. The note was handed over by a mandarin, who was accompanied by a small retinue. This was the first Chinese embassy to cross the Russo-Chinese border. It almost certainly had the task of finding out what kind of forces the Russians had in Nerchinsk as well as that of getting hold of Gantimur.

Arshinsky obviously regarded the appearance of the Chinese as his great chance. Without much reflection he sent his own mission to Peking; it consisted of the Cossack Ignaty Milovanov 'with four comrades'.

The Bogdo Khan himself received the Cossacks. This fact deserves attention; Milovanov was the first Russian thought worthy of this honour. He later gave an account of the audience. 'The Bogdo Khan,' he said, 'is a young man of average height with reddish hair and no beard. He wore golden clothes and on his head a sable cap with a tassel and a red stone which was a good *vershock* (one and a half centimetres) in diameter.' The Cossacks bowed low before him, but did not bare their heads, 'since the Chinese *boyars* had caps on as well'. The Bogdo Khan and the Cossacks were then given tea, which was served not in the Chinese but in the Mongolian style, with butter and salt. The court had thus retained its Mongolian–Manchurian customs.

The 'ambassadors' of the *voivode* of Nerchinsk were thus graciously received by the great K'ang-hsi, the ruler who was officially entitled 'Lord of the universe', and who called the gifts of foreign rulers 'tribute' and his own gifts to them 'loans'.

Although Gantimur was not handed over, the Bogdo Khan wrote a very friendly letter to the Tsar in which he requested that

Chernigovsky's activities in Albasin should be halted and raised the question of Gantimur again.

Milovanov was an ordinary Cossack; he could not even read or write, and his report is simply a transcript of what he said on his return. Nevertheless the information he provided was precise and abundant. He had gone straight to Peking from the Amur via Hailar and the Nonni valley; the earlier Mongolian routes which Petlin and Baikov had taken lay far to the west. Milovanov's geographical information was used to correct and complete the Godunov map, a new edition of which appeared in 1672. His success in Peking was particularly remarkable since by any normal calculation it could have only ended in disaster. Arshinsky's orders to Milovanov instructed him to request the Chinese emperor by word of mouth to recognize the Russian protectorate and henceforth to pay tribute to the Tragan Khan, the 'white khan'! Fortunately the Chinese could not read the Russian characters of the written instruction, which Milovanov handed over to the court chamberlain, and when he was asked for an oral translation he had the sense to suppress anything insulting to the emperor. Milovanov thus put the *voivode* right and turned his tactless gesture into a piece of real diplomacy. He later had a successful career in the diplomatic service, was given the rank of *boyar's* son and took part in further Russian missions to Peking.

SPATHARI'S EXERTIONS AND HIS FAILURE

The efforts that had been made by the Russians for sixty years were beginning to bear fruit and it looked as if proper relations could now be organized. It was time for real diplomats to take the matter in hand. Gavrilovich Spathari, a Greek born in Moldavia, was indubitably a proper diplomat. His career was a stormy one and he never achieved a success commensurate with his talents. Perhaps certain defects of character were to blame. In Transylvania he was convicted of treason by his *gospoda* and sentenced to have his nose cut off; he escaped with a scar. He had studied at Constantinople and Padua, been through the mill of the diplomatic intrigues between the Porte and her Danubian satellites, and travelled in Germany, Italy and Sweden on diplomatic business. He could speak Greek, Latin, Turkish, Arabic, Russian and

Italian, and spent some time at the court of Frederick William, Elector of Brandenburg, where he met other European diplomats. 'Herr Spatharus . . . is a clever man,' wrote Nikholaus Witsen to the philosopher Leibniz. He compiled a number of theological and historical works, in which he defended various aspects of Greek Orthodox doctrine; hence his interest in Russia. In 1671 he went to Moscow and became a close friend of the *boyar* Matveyev, who was the director of Russian foreign policy at that time. He was entrusted with the responsible post of interpreter in the *Posolsky Prikars* (Foreign Ministry) and in 1675 he was sent as a special ambassador to China.

Careful preparations for the expedition were made. All the documents in the archives were put at his disposal, and it was at this time that the message in Chinese brought back by Petlin and Mundóv in 1619 was finally translated.

Including the guard, the embassy consisted of one hundred and fifty men. It left Moscow on 3 March 1675 and arrived in Tobolsk on 30 March. Spathari stayed at Tobolsk for a month while preparations were made for the journey across Siberia. He did not waste his time but made a thorough study of all the material available about China. He was given considerable help in this by one of the most famous Siberian exiles, the Croat Catholic priest Yuri Krishanich. Krishanich had come to Moscow as an advocate of a pan-Slav political and ecclesiastical union, but found no response. The author of many learned works, he was working at the time on a book about Siberia. He showed Spathari his account of trade with China and advised him to travel through Manchuria rather than through Mongolia. He also translated a number of foreign books on China for him.

Spathari left Tobolsk on 2 May 1675 and arrived in Peking on 15 May 1676. He stayed there for three and a half months. He started negotiations with the Jesuit Verbiest as intermediary, was received in audience three times by the Bogdo Khan, drank tea with him and had some meals from the imperial table sent to his lodging, which was reckoned a mark of great favour. Then suddenly everything changed. People began to cheat him; his letters were no longer answered; and his refusal to accept the Chinese gifts on his knees in the courtyard of the palace was treated as unparalleled impudence. He was required to depart and not even provided with sufficient provisions for the journey.

Tobolsk, at the confluence of the Irtysh and the Tobol and for a long time the chief city of Siberia

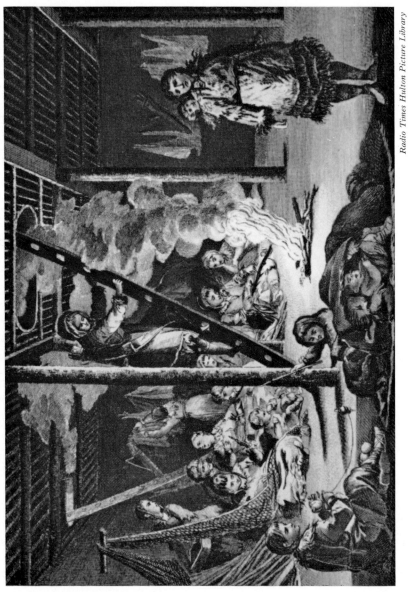

Kamchatka: Peasants in winter quarters. An engraving from Bankes's *New System of Geography.*

It is interesting to speculate on the reasons for this sudden change of attitude. It is not impossible that with the help of Russian prisoners living in Peking the Chinese had finally succeeded in translating Milovanov's written instructions. But in any case the Chinese had other reasons to be dissatisfied. The Russians had not handed over Gantimur, and for the Chinese this was a matter of honour and an important political precedent. Peking feared an alliance between the Russians and the Kalmucks. There was a rumour that Spathari was conducting secret negotiations with the latter. At the same time Albasin had been occupied again by the Russians, and the Chinese had no intention of retreating from the Amur. Spathari was told by word of mouth that Peking would only negotiate with Moscow when Gantimur was handed over and an ambassador was sent 'who was a sensible man and did everything required of him by Chinese usage.' The further condition was laid down that the Russians must 'keep quiet' in the frontier regions.

Spathari's return to Moscow was thus not exactly a triumphal one. Unluckily for him, his patron, the *boyar* Matveyev, had in the meantime fallen into disgrace and been banished. Spathari himself only just managed to escape a similar or even worse fate. In the end he succeeded in rehabilitating himself and even in retaining his post. He subsequently took part as an interpreter in many important negotiations, but he never played an independent rôle again.

From a political point of view Spathari's mission did more harm than good, but its cultural significance was enormous. The literary spoils of his trip to China were considerable, and of lasting value, although they are marred by one defect. As J. F. Baddeley has shown, in Spathari's book on China only the three chapters dealing with north China are original; the rest is a translation of the Jesuit Martini's *China Atlas* (Amsterdam 1655), which Spathari probably got from Verbiest in Peking. Spathari does not mention Martini's name anywhere in his book, although he added Martini's *De bello tartarieo* to it as a supplement and expressly said that this was a translation.

On the other hand, the chapters written by Spathari himself are full of the most valuable observations and descriptions, and his *Report on the Great River Amur* is nothing less than the first geographical account of this river in the literature of the world. The diary of his journey also forms the first geographical description of Siberia. The breadth of his interests is amazing. Spathari was geographer, historian, naturalist, ethnographer and economist, and in all these fields he was equally observant, accurate and un-prejudiced. In addition, there is the charm of an unusual historical situation in which a Byzantine Greek representing Eastern Orthodoxy and the most characteristic representative of Roman Catholicism arrive at the foot of the Dragon Throne, on which sits a sinocized Tunguse. Byzantium and Rome act as the first mediators between Moscow and Peking! Can this interpretation stand up to sober criticism? Yes, it can, for even if Rome was not directly involved, her representatives in China did really do everything they could to establish a link between the two empires. Verbiest was Spathari's only friend in Peking and the letter to the Tsar which he gave to Spathari with his astronomical work con-tains nothing that would justify us in accusing him of Jesuitism or double-dealing. It is quite understandable that Verbiest should seek the favour of the Moscow court. What he dreamed of was a land link between Europe and China by way of Russia and Siberia. That was the old ideal of missionaries in China; Leibniz later took it over from the Jesuit Grimaldi. There was more to it than a mere attempt to gain advantages for the Jesuit order.

Spathari may have had the same idea in mind. We cannot say for certain, because in any case it was impossible for him to speak or even write about it. Neither he nor Yuri Krishanich ever dis-closed the subject of their private conversations. But we know that they were both capable of taking the long view of things. Spathari nourished the hope that in time the Chinese would join the Greek Orthodox rather than the Roman Catholic Church. After Spathari's departure from Tobolsk in May 1675 Krishanich wrote: 'I pray to God that He may bring him safely home after he has advanced the good cause for the salvation of the Russian people.'

BOYARS, MANDARINS AND JESUITS

The situation on the Amur continued to remain uncertain and dangerous. Since Daurien was always in a state of war and there was no hope of trade with China, the region held no interest for Moscow. In the end the two sides would have to define the fron-

tier between them and find a *modus vivendi*. This was also the
wish of the Chinese, as they made clear in a letter which they gave
to the ambassadors Venyukov and Favorov, who spent some time
in Peking in 1687, that is, after Spathari's visit. By this time the
Chinese had sent a whole army up to the Amur. So the Kremlin
decided to bring the matter to a conclusion, cost what it might.

In 1685 an embassy left Moscow under the leadership of Fyodor
Alexeivich Golovin. His instructions were to conclude a lasting
peace with China and to establish the right to trade. He was under
orders to demand that the River Amur should form the boundary
between the two empires.

However, while Golovin was travelling through Siberia, which
took two years, the Chinese had already captured Albasin once
and besieged it a second time, so further instructions were hastily
sent on to Golovin. He was left free to give up the Amur as far as
the mouth of the Seya and, if need be, even to give up Albasin,
which was equivalent to abandoning the Amur as a frontier, for
Albasin was the only Russian base there. Moscow stood firm on
one point only: Gantimur and his followers could not be handed
over because in the meantime they had been converted to the
Orthodox faith and become subjects of the Tsar.

Golovin was a statesman of some standing. The dying Tsar
Alexei Mikhailovich had entrusted his son Peter to him. From
that time onwards Golovin's fate was bound up with that of the
young Tsar. He remained loyal to Peter during the struggle for
power, and the main reason why he was sent to Daurien was that
his opponent, Prince Vasily Golitzyn, who at that time was all-
powerful, wanted to have him as far as possible from Moscow. A
good deal of testimony, both Russian and foreign, to his political
and personal qualities has been preserved. Leibniz met him in
Germany eight years later and considered that 'the fat war minister
was the cleverest and most intelligent' of the Tsar's companions.
Golovin was quite at home in Siberia; he had grown up in Tobolsk,
where his father had been *voivode*. He was accompanied on his
mission by a seasoned diplomat called Kornitzky and the shrewd
voivode of Nerchinsk, Vlassov. His escort consisted of five hundred
regular *streltzy* (guards), who were joined in Siberia by about
fourteen hundred Cossacks.

K'ang-hsi, too, was represented by his best men. His embassy
was headed by Prince Songgotu, commander of the emperor's

bodyguard and 'dignitary of the first rank'. He was an uncle of the empress, great-uncle of the heir to the throne and his 'chief tutor', just as Golovin had been to the Tsar's son, Peter. One of the richest men in China, he was not only an experienced statesman but also an art connoisseur and a patron of literature; his liking for the Jesuits was well known. He was accompanied by the mandarin Sabsu, twice victorious at Albasin and governor of northern Manchuria, and a number of other mandarins, all from the ranks of the imperial guard and all Manchus. Thus in the 'Chinese' delegation there was not a single Chinese.

Men of this eminence were entitled to large retinues. Songgotu's personal household consisted of a hundred servants, three hundred camels and five hundred horses; it was the same with the other mandarins, and in addition there was a military escort. Altogether the Chinese delegation comprised about ten thousand men, three or four thousand camels and fifteen thousand horses. Infantry and artillery sailed up the Amur and the Shilka; the delegation itself and the cavalry came by land. During the negotiations reinforcements were continually sent up from Manchuria and Mongolia. At the decisive moment Songgotu must have had about fifteen thousand men under his command.

Amid the shimmering gold of the dignitaries two modest interpreters, Father Gerbillon and Father Péreyra, remained almost unnoticed. The former was a French mathematician and historian, the latter a Spanish philosopher and musician. Both were excellent geographers and astronomers; Gerbillon, who had come to China only two years before, could already speak Manchu perfectly. Both interpreters were members of the Society of Jesus.

The Society was a power which it is unwise to underestimate. Since 1294, when the first papal delegation arrived in Peking under the leadership of the Franciscan Giovanni de Montecorvino, who became the first Bishop of Kambalyk (Peking) and died there in 1328, Rome had never ceased to hope for the conversion of China. The achievements of the missionaries under the tolerant Mongolian Yuan dynasty were destroyed by the nationalistic Ming dynasty. However, in the fifteenth century the missionaries started again. The Chinese did not make things easy for them. At one moment they would reluctantly leave the missionaries in peace, at the next they would put them in cages and kill them. However, towards the end of the sixteenth century the Jesuit Matteo Ricci established a firm foothold in Peking. The German Jesuit Adam Schall, who had experienced the last twitches of the dying Ming dynasty, won the trust and sincere respect of the first Manchu emperor, Shun-Chih, who called his Catholic friend *mafa*, which means 'grandpa'. He put him in charge of the college of astronomy and entrusted him with the task of reforming the Chinese calendar. This post was one of the most important in an empire which stood in a direct relationship to heaven; the foretelling of eclipses of the sun and moon was an affair of state. Adam Schall played an important rôle at court and Baikov, who calls him 'Adamscha', speaks of him in his report. According to Spathari, who also frequently mentions the then dead Jesuit, Schall had been a 'mandarin of the first rank'.

After Shun-chih's death Schall fell into disgrace as a result of the intrigues of Chinese astronomers. He was cast into prison and condemned to be cut up into ten thousand pieces. However, after the announcement of the sentence, 'the earth trembled under the feet of the judges and the walls of the palaces collapsed;' on the orders of the empress the gaolers hastened to release their powerful prisoner.

At this time the eleven-year-old K'ang-hsi was on the throne and the country was ruled by a regency council, which in 1665 banned the Christian religion in China. The venerable priest died in deep sorrow the next year. Before he died he appointed Father Verbiest as head of the Jesuit mission, and after seven years Verbiest had succeeded in restoring the former reputation of the missionaries so well that he himself was appointed president of the college of mathematics and astronomy. He was on intimate terms with the Emperor K'ang-hsi and gave him instruction in astronomy, mathematics, military science and geography. The Jesuits put together the first maps of China and K'ang-hsi was the first emperor to have an approximately correct notion of the limits of his realm.

The Jesuits had long been interested in Siberia, and indeed in Russia as a whole. There were already some of them in Moscow. Father Avril tried to travel through Siberia to China, and although from Astrakhan, where he had arrived via Turkey and Transcaucasia, he was taken to Moscow and not allowed to go any farther, Prince Golitzyn and other notabilities had frank conversations with him in Latin. They even lent their learned guest

Spathari's account of his journey to China, of which Avril made good use. For a long time it was only from his somewhat distorted reproduction that Spathari's map was known. The original eventually turned up in Germany.

Such 'interpreters' were worth a good deal, and Golovin was well aware of this. He tried to make sure of their co-operation; he sent presents to Gerbillon and Péreyra and promised them 'the favour of the Tsar'. The Jesuits let him know secretly that they were interested in 'good wine'.

The mandarins were also eager to ensure the success of their mission. We must not forget that regular Chinese troops were already on the Amur. That is how it came about that an army of fifteen thousand men, with fifty cannon cast in accordance with Father Verbiest's instructions, was at the disposal of the 'prefect, paladin and consilarius' at the decisive moment. It was a nasty pill for Golovin to swallow; the Jesuits were the only two specks of sugar on it.

It seemed unlikely that any other unpleasant surprises could await the Russian delegation since Moscow had already renounced its claim to the Amur. But after Golovin's arrival other events had occurred in Selenginsk which once again altered the whole situation. After a long period of civil war the Kalmuck tribes had finally united under the rule of the mighty conqueror Galdan. The latter had invaded the frontier territory of Sinkiang, defeated the Mongolian princes – K'ang-hsi's vassals – and chased them farther east, that is, in the direction of China. This suited the Russians quite well; for the Chinese, Galdan was an enemy who weakened them, for the Russians he was a possible ally.

At this point Golovin was in great difficulties. In January 1688 a Mongolian band of four thousand men, armed with Chinese muskets and even cannon, attacked Selenginsk and Udinsk. The situation was extremely critical. When the attack was beaten off, the enemy fled, pursued by the Cossacks.

That the attackers, who were far superior to the Russians in numbers, should have taken to flight so swiftly was rather curious. It was only discovered later that at that moment the Mongolians were threatened by Galdan, who was on the point of cutting their communications. He was already far to the east. Even the Chinese delegation, which was on the way to meet Golovin, had to turn back precipitately.

Under these circumstances it would have been very natural for Galdan to seek an alliance with the Russians. But he did not do so; he felt strong enough alone.

For Golovin the game was up. He realized how weak he was. In front of him on the Amur were K'ang-hsi's troops and behind him the wandering Mongolian hordes. One after the other the Buryat tribes deserted the Russians and went over to the Chinese. Golovin wasted his time fighting them, and instead of going to Albasin, as he had been expressly ordered to, he remained in Selenginsk so long that one day he received the news that the Chinese delegation, accompanied by a large army, was at the gates of Nerchinsk. To let the Chinese come so far was, of course, a bad mistake, for it was a practical demonstration that the Amur was not a frontier.

NEGOTIATIONS ON THE NERCHA

The ambassadors of the two empires finally met on 12 August 1689 between the Shilka and Nerchinsk. In front of Golovin rode five trumpeters and a drummer, and he was followed by a body of two hundred and sixty guards on foot. The Chinese ambassadors had a similar escort. The Russians wore brocaded caftans lined with black sable; the Chinese were dressed in golden garments trimmed with sea-otter and beaver. Golovin was 'somewhat under-sized and corpulent, but otherwise he looked well and understood how to preserve his dignity without affectation', wrote Gerbillon. Presumably the 'Paladin' was not inferior in appearance to the Russian ambassador. The difference between the two was that Golovin had a detachment of under two thousand behind him in Nerchinsk, while the Chinese had an army fifteen thousand strong on the opposite bank of the Shilka.

The ambassadors sat down opposite each other in a big tent. Between them was a table covered with a silk Persian carpet embroidered in gold. On it stood silver writing materials and a valuable striking clock.

After the preliminary greetings Golovin made a short speech. He spoke of the reciprocal friendship which rightly bound the two sides together. It would be a good thing, he said, to put an end to misunderstandings. Permanent trading relations should be established. The most important thing was to come to some agreement about the frontier. The simplest course would be to make the Amur the boundary, since the population on the left bank had already recognized the authority of the Russian Tsar by paying him regular tribute.

Prince Songgotu endorsed Golovin's words about the traditional friendship between China and Russia, agreed fully with the desire for peace and trade relations and suggested, for his part, making Lake Baikal the frontier line.

The Jesuits said later that even they had been amazed at this Chinese demand. The Chinese were suggesting nothing less than the surrender of the whole of Eastern Siberia. There was no possibility of achieving a peaceful settlement on these conditions, and the Jesuit fathers immediately offered to use all their influence to curb the appetite of the Chinese.

The next day the Chinese said no more about Lake Baikal, but they demanded the whole of the Amur for themselves and the Shilka up to Nerchinsk. In accordance with his instructions Golovin agreed to cede the Amur as far as Albasin.

After two further sessions the negotiations came to a halt; the two sides could get no farther. Golovin demanded from the Chinese ambassadors an official communication about the reason for the breakdown. At this point Gerbillon and Péreyra suggested a compromise, namely, that the border should be the Gorbiza, a tributary of the Shilka. Golovin was unwilling to agree to this. He returned to Nerchinsk and made preparations to depart. But he could no longer do so. The Chinese troops crossed the Shilka by night and surrounded Nerchinsk. They explained that they had been compelled to do this because their camp was threatened by floods. It was in fact raining the whole time. Nerchinsk was now completely cut off from Albasin, whence Beiton was sending despairing calls for help. The town had no food left and the harvest was not yet ripe; the Chinese blockade was having its effect.

Golovin was not easily dismayed; he had demonstrated this when confronted by the Mongols and on other occasions, too. But he was no longer of an age when one makes admirable but pointless gestures. He knew that the unfortified town of Nerchinsk would be captured and his detachment annihilated. There were no other troops in the neighbourhood. When the Chinese had destroyed him they could in fact take the land to the east of Lake Baikal and march unopposed to the shores of the lake itself.

The negotiations and disputes lasted another twelve days. Time, too, was against the Russians. When two thousand Buryats joined the Chinese army, Golovin signified his agreement.

The treaty was signed on 27 August 1689 by the Russian (Julian) calendar. It was drawn up in Russian, Latin and Manchu. The Latin text, the work of the learned Jesuit fathers, is regarded as the most reliable.

In the west, the border between Russia and China now ran up the Gorbiza and then along the Argun into the mysterious distance of Mongolia. In the east, it was to lie along the crest of the Stanovoi mountains. In the very far east, a region of which the Russians had only a vague notion and the Chinese none at all, it was left to be settled in future negotiations.

One thing at least became quite clear as soon as the Nerchinsk treaty had been concluded: the whole course of the Amur – both banks – came under Chinese rule. Albasin had to be torn down. Golovin had insisted on this condition so as not to leave the Chinese with a ready-made fortress on the Amur. He himself now supervised the work of destruction; at the same time he fortified Nerchinsk and had its garrison reinforced.

He had already reached Irkutsk on his return journey when ambassadors from Galdan arrived offering an alliance against the common enemy. Golovin heaved a sigh of relief and sent the surprised ambassador on to Moscow to negotiate the alliance there.

In the Kremlin no tears were shed for the loss of the Amur. At that time Siberia was not yet ripe for the Amur; it was not seen in Moscow as the 'natural boundary'. In the treaty of Nerchinsk Golovin had won for Russian merchants the right to travel unhindered to China and to trade there. Even before his departure he himself dispatched a big trade caravan to China. There was more joy in the Kremlin at this gain than sorrow at the loss of Albasin.

All the same, Golovin did not escape the reproach that he had surrendered Albasin too easily. But the Tsar was pleased to be free of the worry of Daurien and he did not wish to lose a loyal and clever friend. He made Golovin a *boyar* and appointed him governor of Siberia with his residence in Moscow, in other words, minister for Siberian affairs. Later he became a field-marshal, admiral of the fleet, 'president of diplomatic affairs' and the first Russian Count of the Holy Roman Empire as well. But he realized himself at the time that the Nerchinsk affair had not been conducted too brilliantly. He complained about the Chinese breach of faith and the 'double rôle' played by the Jesuits. After this the Society of Jesus had to abandon all hope of winning over the Russian 'heretics' to the true faith.

On the other hand, after the signing of the treaty the reputation of the Jesuits at K'ang-hsi's court rose still higher. That is hardly surprising, for they were the godfathers of the first treaty that the Chinese had signed with a Christian state, the only one until modern times resting on the principle of equality, a treaty which relieved China of any worry about a powerful neighbour for a hundred and fifty years. Three years after the treaty of Nerchinsk K'ang-hsi issued a decree permitting Chinese to become Christians. The emperor did not cancel this decree until 1717, when Pope Clement XI published a Bull condemning the Confucian rite as superstition. At that point there were some hundreds of thousands of Catholics in China.

But K'ang-hsi retained his personal liking for the Jesuits until the day of his death, and the Christian God rewarded him for this. After the Russian danger had been removed the emperor turned his attention to the Kalmucks and conquered them. Defeated and homeless, Galdan put an end to his own life.

After him, the great emperor's other enemies fell like broken ears of corn. When heaven finally called its beloved son to it, in the 8th moon of the 60th year of K'ang-hsi (1722), he left behind on earth seventy sons and an empire that in the north embraced Daurien, Manchuria and Mongolia.

MOSCOW DISCOVERS PEKING

Even after Nerchinsk Moscow did not relax its efforts to create settled conditions for trade with China. Fresh embassies were sent to China by Peter the Great; the most important were the missions of Irbrandt Ides (1692–5) and the 'guards captain' Lev Ismaylov (1719–22). None of them achieved anything, because the Russians and Chinese were talking at cross-purposes. For the Russians, the chief question was trade; for the Chinese, it was the border between Siberia and Mongolia. It was true that Galdan had long been dead, but the struggle with his successors was not yet over; East Turkestan was finally conquered only in 1757, by the Emperor Ch'ien-lung. The Kalmucks fought bravely, and to counter the Jesuit cannon of the Chinese they brought their own into the field, cast for them by the Swedish 'bombardier' J. G. Renat. The Chinese troop movements aroused strong disapproval in Mongolia because cavalry fought on both sides and as a result the reserves of horses in Mongolia were dropping steadily. A tendency to look towards Russia arose in Mongolia and more and more tribes went over to the Russians. They could do this quite easily as there was no definite border and, since Altyn Khan had accepted the protection of Russia, the 'white Khan' could be regarded with some justification as the protector of the Mongols.

The first man to succeed in creating a firmer foundation for Russo-Chinese relations was the ambassador Sava Vladislavich-Ragusinsky, Count of Illyria. A Serb from Bosnia, he began his career as a Russian secret agent in Constantinople. About 1700 he went to Russia and in 1716 he was made a count by his birthplace, the Republic of Ragusa. He enjoyed the good will of Peter the Great and executed many public and private commissions for him; among other things, he bought *objets d'art* for him abroad, but at the same time he also played an important part in the diplomatic service. Among the curiosities which he sent to the Tsar from Constantinople was a little Negro from Abyssinia, who was brought up by the Tsar and sent to France to complete his education. This Negro, who was called A. P. Hannibal, was the grandfather of the great Russian poet Pushkin.

After about eight months in Peking and fifty-eight conferences on the border, on 20 August 1727 Sava concluded an agreement recorded in the history books as the 'Treaty of Kyakhta', from the exchange of documents at Kyakhta on 14 June 1728. The treaty laid down two places, both on Russian soil, as permanent centres for the exchange of goods. These two places were Kyakhta and Nerchinsk. A trade caravan 'of two hundred merchants at the most' was allowed to travel from Siberia to Peking once every three years. A church was built on to the 'Russian House' in Peking, and a priest and some boys were allowed to reside there, the latter in order to learn Chinese. A precise frontier was drawn only between Siberia and Mongolia; from the Yablonoi mountains to the Sea of Okhotsk the border was left undefined, as before. Boundary posts were erected by the two countries only in Transbaikalia and Mongolia.

This last decision was nevertheless an important one, because the boundary marks halted the Russian advance towards Mongolia. From this point of view the treaty of Kyakhta once again represented a victory for the Chinese and a renunciation on the part of the Russians. It could scarcely be otherwise, for at that time relations with China were reaching the point where only compliance or war was possible, and for Russia there was no question of fighting China either then or later. Even two hundred years later Russia was not equal to a test of strength in the Far East, as the war with Japan showed. Spathari had delivered a warning against conflicts with China so long as Siberia was not in a position to defend Daurien. Sava Vladislavich expressed the same view with much greater force in his secret memorandum of 1731. A war with China, he wrote, would demand such sacrifices in men, time and money that even in the case of final victory the damage would take a hundred years to repair. Worst of all, the mighty Chinese empire would be Russia's enemy for ever after. On the other hand, from good-neighbourly relations with China immense advantages could be expected. The first of these was security, the second 'trade', and hence the prosperity of Siberia.

These were not casual arguments. As we have seen, from the start trade was one of the most important aims behind Muscovite probes in the east. The treasury needed gold and silver, and it was fancied that both were to be found in China. The whole business was quite simple. The instructions to Golovin and Spathari, who were asked, amid the lofty political negotiations, to purchase certain 'quantities of gold and silver, reflect fairly petty fiscal considerations rather than large-scale political thinking. A fresh tone is apparent in official papers after Nerchinsk and Kyakhta. The potential economic resources were now clearly assessed for the first time and placed in a broader geo-political context. This corresponded to the new spirit abroad in the reign of Peter the Great; when Sava Vladislavich was negotiating with the Chinese, Bering was making his first voyage of discovery and St Petersburg had already caught a glimpse of the Pacific. From all he saw and heard in Siberia, wrote Sava, the land was not a province but a whole empire, containing over forty rivers bigger than the Danube and another hundred bigger than the Neva. . . . There was no other land so richly blessed by God in the whole world. The possibilities of development were enormous, he said, if the roads to China and Japan were opened. But at the moment Siberia was weak, thinly populated and held back by the enormous distances between each place. What was needed was organized government, and roads, river-traffic and trade.

This programme, which had in fact been already sketched by Yuri Krishanich, makes clear the relationship between the economic potentials of Siberia and China. This relationship is a primary fact which lies at the bottom of all Russia's attempts in those days to open up China. In the seventeenth and eighteenth centuries, not only Siberia but also many European countries seemed backward and poor in comparison with China. Like all the earlier Russian ambassadors, Spathari was amazed when he saw the highly-developed state of Chinese road construction, river traffic and architecture. The same was true of agriculture. In China this was based mainly on artificial irrigation and manuring; in Siberia between 1733–43, according to J. G. Gmelin, 'it was not the custom to try to improve poor land by manuring it or by fetching good earth to put on it.'

The relationship becomes still clearer if we compare the articles exported by each country. Siberia exported to China almost nothing but raw furs; in return it obtained from China only industrial products or valuable consumer goods. According to the testimony of A. N. Radishchev, a writer who was exiled to Siberia towards the end of the eighteenth century, two-thirds of the imports into Siberia from China were textiles and a quarter of them tea. P. A. Slovtzov tells us that all the Siberian women, even farmers' wives, wore underwear and clothes made out of Chinese materials. Chinese ink was used in Siberian government offices and cheap Chinese porcelain and wooden crockery was to be seen everywhere. Everyone drank Chinese tea and smoked Chinese tobacco. All these goods travelled right to the tundra and as far afield as Mangaseya and Kamchatka.

In general, the Siberian 'empire' obtained far too little from the mother-country and had to turn to China. There is no doubt that Siberia needed China more than China needed Siberia.

This is the key to the 'China doctrine' propounded by Sava

Vladislavich. Here we find formulated for the first time the political principles which made it possible for undefended and thinly populated Siberia to develop peacefully for almost two centuries. Russia left the neutralization of the Mongolian powder-magazine to the Chinese. China performed this task and in doing so was working for Russia. The Chinese government encouraged and supported Buddhism in Mongolia in every possible way, with the result that almost half these erstwhile conquerors of the world were to become mendicant monks or hermits. It hindered the colonization of Mongolia and Manchuria and left them depopulated. For a long time they were more or less dead. So far as the Russians were concerned, this policy made the treaties of Nerchinsk and Kyakhta into the finishing touches to their five-hundred-year struggle against the steppes. These two diplomatic defeats became the foundation of the Russian empire's stability in the eighteenth and nineteenth centuries.

Vladislavich himself regarded the two treaties as the beginning not the end of Russia's policy towards China. History proved that he was right about this, too. At the end of the forty-year fight for Daurien Russia was left with an advanced post on the Shilka, which was in fact the upper Amur. If Daurien had been lost, Transbaikalia had been finally won, and the latter was not only richer in minerals than any other part of Siberia, it was also the last stage on the road to China. Today we can see clearly what Moscow could then see only hazily; the real historical significance of the struggle on the Amur and in Mongolia in the seventeenth century was that Russia made the first direct contact with China and restored the old land-link between East and West. Only from this point of view can the achievements of the Cossacks on the Amur and those of the innumerable embassies to the Altyn Khan and the 'Chinese Tsar Taibun' be properly assessed. If the Russian adventurers in Daurien did not behave too politely, they did discover and explore the Amur and the names of men like Poyarkov and Khabarov are to be found today in every history of geographical discoveries. But what the ambassadors to China had accomplished in the course of a century was understood even then by the best contemporary experts on Asia, the Jesuits. Father Avril wrote as follows about the Russian envoys to China: 'I know very well that they did not get there at the first attempt and that it cost some trouble before the route was as well known as it is now

. . . but of all the routes to this flourishing and glorious realm (China), the one which the Muscovites take today is the sure stand above all the shortest.'

It was that great European cosmopolitan, Leibniz, who took up the idea of a land-route to China and transformed it into the vision of a spiritual community embracing both Europe and 'another civilized world and anti-Europe' (that is, China). Part of this vision was the 'great Siberian post-road' and the north-east passage. He was only formulating and providing an intellectual basis for aims which Russia had long pursued.

From a historical and geographical point of view, the treaties of Nerchinsk and Kyakhta were only stages on that 'surest and shortest' route to China of which Father Avril had written. This route spans the whole north of Asia. Two and a half centuries of unexampled sacrifice were required to open it up properly. Only at the end of this development did it become clear that this route means much more than trade and commerce. A transcontinental route carries not only goods; it also carries ideas, and he who controls it dominates the continent.

IV

THE LEAP ACROSS TO AMERICA

————◆◆◆◆————

ATLASOV'S WORK

AFTER DESHNEV'S adventures on land and sea the Cossacks realized that they could not go any farther east; the ocean barred the way. The region that led up to the ocean was still unexplored.

The route to the ocean had already been found by Deshnev's rival, Mikhail Stadukhin. In 1651 he had travelled from the Anadyr to the River Penshina, that is, the immediate neighbourhood of Kamchatka, and he returned to Yakutsk with news of a new land unusually rich in furs.

At that time the *prikastshik*, that is, the government fur supervisor, at the trading post of Anadyr was Vladimir Atlasov. He was a Russian merchant who had come to Siberia because to him even the vast expanses of the Muscovite empire seemed too narrow. He had devoted himself entirely to the fur trade and in 1672 had already been commissioned to accompany a government convoy of furs from Yakutsk to Moscow.

After he had heard enough reports about Kamchatka – which most of those who told these stories did not know at all themselves – Atlasov sent one of his own men, Luka Morosko, there. He gave him sixteen Cossacks and the task of finding out everything worth knowing about the new land and of collecting furs from the inhabitants.

Morosko returned not only with furs but also with three Koryaks and a mysterious roll of writing which no one could understand. It was a Japanese letter which had fallen into the hands of the Chukchas from a stranded Japanese vessel.

Atlasov now gathered a detachment of sixty Russian Cossacks and as many Yukagires and set off on his campaign. From the mouth of the Penshina he crossed the mountains to the mouth of the Olyutora. Here he divided his expedition into two; he himself sailed on the Sea of Okhotsk along the west coast of Kamchatka,

A trapper returning to base with a collection of valuable furs.

The River Yenisei, which rises near the Mongolian frontier and flows into the Arctic Ocean.

while the loyal Morosko advanced southwards along the east coast to the Pacific. However, one dark night the faithless Yukagires attacked the Cossacks while they were asleep, killing three and wounding fifteen. Atlasov himself received three wounds. He saw that it was unwise to split his forces and recalled Morosko. Together they advanced to the River Kamchatka.

There he built an *ostrog*, and to mark the conquest of a new country he erected nearby a cross with the inscription: 'This cross was erected on 18 July in the year 7205 by the *pyatideryatnik* (leader of fifty men) Vladimir Atlasov and his companions.' Atlasov's date is based on the creation of the world. According to Greek Orthodox tradition the birth of Christ occurred in the year 5508 after the creation of the world, so Atlasov conquered Kamchatka in 1697.

Atlasov travelled down the River Kamchatka, collecting the usual tribute of furs from the local people as he went. He himself admitted later that it was not always a peaceful journey. Nevertheless he already regarded the Kamchadales as his own people, and when he heard that one of their reindeer herds had been attacked by the Koryaks on the upper Kamchatka he turned round, chased the thieves for a few days and recovered the reindeer. 'About a hundred and fifty Koryaks' were slain.

Atlasov was now made a prince of Kamchatka. He marched through the whole country with his men and stopped only five days' march short of the southern tip, Cape Lopatka, in the 'land of the Kuriles'. These 'Kuriles' were Ainus who had mingled with the Kamchadales. We do not know what made Atlasov turn back. Probably it was the disinclination of his companions to go any farther. At any rate, the story is that after wintering on the little River Ucha he 'yielded to the pleas of the Cossacks' and went back to the Anadyr. On the way he founded the *ostrog* of Vershne-Kamchatsk on the upper reaches of the Kamchatka and left there his retainer Seryukov with fifteen Cossacks and four Yukagires.

In February 1700 Atlasov reached Yakutsk and exactly twelve months later he was in Moscow, where he announced the annexation of Kamchatka; as proof, he delivered to the ministry for Siberian affairs 3,200 sables, 190 red foxes, 10 silver foxes and 4 beavers. In addition he brought with him the first Japanese to tread on Russian soil.

When Atlasov arrived in Kamchatka the natives told him that

there was a Russian living among them. On closer inspection this 'Russian' turned out to be a Japanese, who probably came from the same ship as the mysterious writing which Morosko had brought back. The Japanese was called Denbe and came from Nagasaki. Atlasov liked him very much. According to the Cossack, the Japanese was 'clean, polite and clever', and at the sight of an icon 'he wept a great deal and said that they had similar ones at home'. Peter the Great grew interested in the prisoner. Denbe, who in the meantime had learnt a little Russian, was presented to the Tsar on 8 January 1702 and was questioned by Peter for a long time about Japan. Denbe's statements were recorded in writing. They certainly aroused the Tsar's curiosity about Japan. That the Japanese had much gold and silver, wore all kinds of cloth and traded with the Dutch all seemed very important to the Tsar. After the interview he gave orders that Denbe should be supported at government expense and given further instruction in Russian; in return Denbe was to 'teach four or five young Russians his language and script'. Eight years later Denbe joined the Orthodox Church and was christened Gabriel. He asked to be allowed to go home. But it was difficult to grant this wish as no Russian had ever set eyes on Japan and poor Denbe remained in Russia to the end of his life.

Atlasov's report was received very favourably. He was appointed 'chief', with a salary of ten roubles a year, and he also received one hundred silver roubles and a piece of German cloth to the same value with which to clothe himself. The Siberian Ministry was well disposed towards him and wrote down his report word for word. This was a sensible thing to do, for his report contains the best and most abundant information about Kamchatka to be found in eighteenth-century sources. The Cossack had an unusually sharp eye for both men and nature. He gives concise and accurate details of the geography and climate of the peninsula, its mineral resources, plants, animals, fish and export and import possibilities. His estimate of the population was used as a starting point by all later students of Kamchatka. His statements were utilized by that tireless cartographer, Semyon Remesov, in the production of maps of Kamchatka which are not to be found in the Remesov atlas. Unlike the atlas, these maps already show Kamchatka as a peninsula; the map of 1700 gives all the mountains and rivers, even the *ostrog* at Vershne-Kamchatsk founded by

Atlasov, and other details, too. On it we see for the first time, opposite the Chukcha peninsula, a tongue of some land or other (Alaska!) with the inscription: 'The land that has recently become known.'

It is quite understandable that Atlasov impressed the Muscovite officials. He was fêted, especially as he had brought back, besides the *yassak* for the Tsar, four hundred and forty of the best sable skins for himself, and doubtless knew how to distribute them to the best advantage. He set off on the return journey with orders to the *voivode* of Yakutsk to give him every assistance in the assembly of a troop of one hundred Cossacks. He was to have guns, powder, shot and a flag from government stocks, and also one trumpet and one drum. For bartering with the natives he was to be provided with a *pud* of blue glass pearls and a hundred knives.

On the journey Atlasov began to pick the 'right types' for his troop. But the 'spirit of his own boldness', as he expressed it later at his trial, carried him away. On the upper Tunguska he met a Russian merchant travelling west with a load of Chinese goods. All these goods – silk, tea and spices to a total value of sixteen thousand roubles – found their way into the hands of Atlasov and his companions.

Probably Atlasov did not hurry back to the east, but had a good time on the way. At any rate, the merchant reached Yakutsk before him. As soon as Atlasov arrived he and ten companions were arrested, tried and thrown into prison. The stolen goods were returned to the merchant and the 'chief' had to stay behind in Yakutsk.

A TROUBLED TIME

Meanwhile Atlasov's work on Kamchatka was carried further; but it was a difficult and bloody business.

Seryukov lived at Vershne-Kamchatsk on friendly terms with the Kamchadales. As his detachment was only a small one he made no attempt to collect tribute. After three years he started off back to Anadyrsk. His route led through the territory of the Koryaks. They remembered Atlasov very well and took their revenge by killing Seryukov and all his companions.

Meanwhile fresh troops were on the way to Kamchatka. In place of Atlasov, who was still in prison, came the *prikaschik* (supervisor) Zinoviev, who set to work energetically. In 1704 he built an *ostrog* on the west coast, by the River Bolshaya. This *ostrog* later became the town of Bolsheretsk, the administrative centre for the whole of Kamchatka. Zinoviev imposed regular tribute on the Koryaks and Kamchadales, and in order to deprive them of any possibility of resistance, he introduced '*yassak* books', in which he recorded the names of those liable to pay. Whoever had his name inscribed in this book knew that it was all up with him; he had either to deliver the skins or be thrown into the water. The book had a magical effect.

At the end of 1704 Zinoviev was succeeded by Vasily Kolesov, who had to stay longer than intended in Kamchatka because two men sent to relieve him were both murdered by the Koryaks. And when Kolesov himself set off for Yakutsk the Kamchadales burnt down the *ostrog* of Bolsheretsk and killed the garrison to the last man.

About this time Atlasov was released before he had served all his sentence. He had sent a message from prison asking the *voivode* of Yakutsk for an interview and had discussed the situation with him. Almost no furs were arriving from Kamchatka. The governors were sending nothing and usually themselves failing to return. Atlasov had served four years; the *voivode* cancelled the rest of the sentence and freed him. He appointed him commander of all armed forces in Kamchatka, but ordered him not to offend the natives and expressly deprived him of the right to sentence Cossacks to death.

Atlasov collected a detachment of Cossacks and armed them well; he even obtained two small copper cannon. But on the way to the scene of action he apparently tried to recompense himself for the hardships of prison life and by the time he arrived in Kamchatka he had made enemies not only of the Kamchadales but also of the Cossacks. He took up the reins of government and first of all punished the Kamchadales cruelly for their attack on Bolsheretsk. When he entered the territory of the Koryaks, they attacked him. He defeated them and returned to Vershne-Kamchatsk.

Now he felt himself master of Kamchatka again. Furs began rolling in; but the Cossacks also began to disappear. Atlasov had become drunk with power and the Cossacks' resentment grew steadily stronger. In December 1707, five months after Atlasov's arrival, a revolt broke out. The Cossacks arrested Atlasov, took over the private property of their former leader – 1,234 sables, 400 red foxes and 75 sea-otters, all 'won' in only five months! – and chose a new 'chief'. Since in the Cossack's view Atlasov's fortune had been acquired illegally, they divided it up among themselves.

However, Atlasov soon succeeded in escaping to another *ostrog*, Nishne-Kamchatsk. His attempt to take charge of it failed; he could only stay there as a private citizen.

In 1709 a new chief appeared, Peter Chirikov. He took up office without learning about the rising against Atlasov. On the way he was attacked by the Koryaks, who killed eleven of his fifty-five men. He just managed to fight his way through to Vershne-Kamchatsk, where he was shut up as though in a beleaguered fortress.

A year later another new chief arrived, by name Lipin, alias Mironov. Chirikov handed over his office to him. At this point there were more officials than were necessary in Kamchatka, and they were of every kind: the new chief, Lipin; the old one, Chirikov; Atlasov, who considered himself the rightful chief; and finally the future chiefs Anzyferov and Kosyrevsky.

The two last started a conspiracy. When Chirikov and Lipin went off together to Nishne-Kamchatsk, the rebels killed Lipin without any ado. They wanted to do the same to Chirikov, but left him alive to start with, 'from religious considerations', so the story goes. When they found Atlasov at Nishne-Kamchatsk they killed him, too, without ceremony.

The usurpers Kosyrevsky and Anzyferov now enjoyed their period of power. The Kamchadales could detect no difference; the methods of the government remained the same. The Cossacks kept Chirikov in chains for three months and then drowned him in the River Kamchatka.

Anzyferov and Kosyrevsky were now masters of the situation, but they knew that a reckoning with the rightful government was unavoidable sooner or later. They therefore hastened to forestall the official report to St Petersburg. In April 1711 the seventy-five rebels sent two humble petitions to the Tsar. In one they presented the murder of Atlasov as self-defence against his violence. In the other they enumerated all the illegal actions of Chirikov and Lipin, emphasizing particularly that these two had hindered the exploration of Japan, an opportunity for which had arisen when another Japanese vessel was stranded on the coast of Kamchatka. The Cossacks, on the other hand, were ready to proceed, on behalf of the Tsar and their country, to the investigation of the unknown islands.

And in fact the little band did travel at once to the River Bolshaya, pacify the Kamchadales there and go on to Cape Lopatka. There the Cossacks embarked in little boats and at last sailed over the sea to the first of the Kurile Islands. So the Kurile Islands were discovered in August 1711 by the rebellious Cossacks Kosyrevsky and Anzyferov from Kamchatka.

Just at this moment the new chief, Savostyanov, arrived. Anzyferov did not want to come to blows with him; he preferred to legalize his own position. He turned up before Savostyanov and introduced his doughty men. When he saw the latter, Savostyanov hastened to confirm Anzyferov in his position of fur-collector. It was a legalization from necessity, and it remained open to question whether it would be recognized in higher quarters. His men also knew that they still had to deal with the *voivode* of Yakutsk. So the rebels seized their last chance of a pardon. They sent a third petition straight to the Tsar, in which they gave a detailed description of their expedition to the Kurile Islands, emphasized its geographical results and promised further achievements of the same sort.

All these petitions, drawn up no doubt by Kosyrevsky, are very significant. These military mutineers adduce their geographical accomplishments as a sufficient reason for pardoning them. Such a course could only be pursued by men who had clearly grasped the value of such accomplishments and assumed a corresponding attitude in the Tsar. They knew that the chief Lipin had already been urged to collect information about Japan and that Savostyanov's instructions were even more precise on this point; all this was a consequence of the Tsar's conversation with Denbe. It was the beginning of the reconnoitring of Japan from Kamchatka, like the probing of China through Mongolia which had begun a century before. Savostyanov had been ordered to start trade with Japan 'like the trade already carried on between the Russians and the Chinese.' This probing of Japan reached its climax a hundred and fifty years later with the 'opening up' of Japan by Admiral Putyatin.

Anzyferov now set about collecting *yassak* with redoubled energy. The results were soon apparent. On one of his trips Anzyferov and his twenty-five Cossacks were besieged by the Koryaks in a blockhouse and burnt to death.

Anzyferov's death made things easier for Savostyanov. The Cossacks felt that they had gone too far. Savostyanov imposed some prison sentences and had a number of men flogged. Then, for the first time in seven years, he personally took the skins intended for the government to Yakutsk, where they had not been expecting a delivery like this: 13,218 sables, 3,282 red foxes, 48 other foxes and 259 sea-otters. It is true that the sables from Kamchatka did not enjoy a particularly high reputation, but such a large number nevertheless formed a valuable consignment. The sea-otters, on the other hand, called by the Russians 'sea-beavers' or 'Kamchatka beavers', were highly regarded.

During Savostyanov's absence rebellions flared up again everywhere. Kamchadales, Koryaks and Cossacks all revolted. In 1712 power passed into the hands of the former chief Vasily Kolesov. In the meantime he had been in Moscow and had become an enthusiastic disciple of Peter the Great's new ideas. He was burning with eagerness to restore peace and order to Kamchatka and to provide the Tsar with fresh information about Japan. He held an inquiry into the murders of Atlasov, Lipin and Chirikov, had a number of Cossacks hanged and many others flogged. He even succeeded in putting Kosyrevsky in prison, but not for long. He released him on condition that he set out to explore the Kurile and Japanese islands. Kosyrevsky accepted the task without hesitation. He had already visited the Kurile Islands a second time; he now set out for the third time. He took possession of the first two islands, robbed the inhabitants of all their furs and decided to sail on farther. However, he was forced to turn back by a typhoon.

This Ignaty Kosyrevsky was a remarkable man; even in Siberia there were not many like him. He was of Polish origin, but a zealous member of the Greek Orthodox Church. The archimandrite Martian, who had come to Kamchatka in 1705 as the first Russian missionary, several times took him under his protection, and that is why Kosyrevsky did not end on the gallows. A swindler and murderer with a mystical temperament, he was not only the first Russian to visit the Kurile Islands but also put together four maps, which served as a basis for the work of Semyon Remesov and the other Russian cartographers and thus also influenced contemporary European cartography.

The various governors of Kamchatka never stayed there very long at that time. In 1713 a fresh 'chief' again appeared to relieve Kolesov. The new man was an aristocrat called Yeniseisky. He and Kolesov set out together for Yakutsk with a rich tribute of furs. But the fateful Koryak barrier came down in front of them too; they and their escort were all murdered on the way and the skins never reached Yakutsk.

But the *voivode* of Yakutsk was not prepared to accept the loss. He sent his men with a consignment of tobacco and the Koryaks were quite happy to hand over all the furs in return for the tobacco.

Things went on like this for quite a time. After the death of Kolesov and Yeniseisky the route from the Kolyma to Kamchatka, through the territory of the Koryaks and Chukchas, was in fact regarded as impassable. The barrier raised by Atlasov had fallen again. Just at that moment the Tsar sent a personal command to explore the sea route to Kamchatka from the mouth of the Okhota. In 1714 a Cossack officer called Kusma Sokolov was sent to Okhotsk to carry out the command. As assistants, he was given the 'sailor and pilot' Yakob Neveizyn and two more sailors, a Russian and a Swedish prisoner-of-war. In addition, Sokolov had two carpenters and thirteen Cossacks with him. The Swedish prisoner was in fact a Dutch sailor in the service of Sweden, Heinrich Busch by name. As Busch later told G. F. Müller, 'The carpenters built a vessel like the Russian *lodshas* in which they used to sail from Archangel to Mesen, Pustosersk and Novaya Zemlya.' Busch said the ship had proved good and strong, and in fact several trips were later made in it to Kamchatka and even the Kurile Islands. In 1716 Sokolov sailed across the Sea of Okhotsk to Kamchatka, visited the *ostrog* of Nishne-Kamchatsk in the winter and returned to Okhotsk the next summer.

This was not the first Russian voyage in the Sea of Okhotsk, for as early as 1646 Poyarkov had sailed from the mouth of the Amur to somewhere near the mouth of the Ulya and in 1651 Stadukhin had made much the same voyage from the River Penshina to the Okhota. But these were coastal voyages, while Sokolov, with Neveizyn and Busch, sailed right across the Sea of Okhotsk from west to east and thus opened up the sea route to Kamchatka, which now for the first time really became part of the Russian empire.

THE TRAGEDY OF THE KAMCHADALES

But whether you travelled to it by land or water, Kamchatka remained what it was. Governors, chiefs and *hetmeni* collected furs, and the natives killed them whenever they could. It was simply a question of who could last longest; the result showed that it was the administration.

In this paradise of lawlessness only the Church had retained a semblance of moral authority, and this circumstance was sometimes exploited by clever adventurers. For instance, in 1716 Kosyrevsky donned a cowl and founded a monastery near Nishne-Kamchatsk. Three years later, the monk Ignaty Kosyrevsky was sent under guard from Kamchatka to Yakutsk for making seditious speeches. There he prospered at first; he was taken into a proper monastery and made the abbot's deputy. But the authorities soon recalled this monk's earlier activities; Kosyrevsky was arrested and things looked black for him. But he escaped again and once more tried his luck with geography. He told the *voivode* of Yakutsk that he knew all about the sea-route to Japan and conditions in the eastern ocean. He played his hand so well that when Bering stopped at Yakutsk in 1726, Kosyrevsky managed to see him, showed him his sketch-maps and asked to be included in the expedition. Bering prudently declined the offer; but soon afterwards the situation changed again.

The Cossack chief Afanasy Shestakov offered to put an end to the thievish activities of the Koryaks and Chukchas and the islanders beyond Kamchatka. He travelled to St Petersburg and laid before the senate not only a plan of campaign but also a new map of eastern Siberia, Kamchatka and all the surrounding islands. In 1727 his plan was approved and means were put at his disposal. The next year Shestakov was in Yakutsk again. There he heard that Kosyrevsky had spoken in prison of gold-bearing islands which he claimed to have discovered at the mouth of the Lena.

Shestakov put the monk aboard a boat, which Kosyrevsky seems to have built at his own expense, and sent him off down the Lena. Before the boat reached the mouth of the river it broke up in the ice and Kosyrevsky hurried straight off to Moscow. There he was well received, and in the imperial capital on the Neva the *St Petersburg Advertiser* praised his administrative and geographical achievements. But the dead of Kamchatka did not leave him alone even in Moscow. He was charged with murder and condemned to death; then the Senate interfered, a new inquiry was ordered. . . . We do not know what the end of it all was.

Meanwhile Shestakov had arrived in Okhotsk. From there he went to the River Penshina, to conquer the Koryaks. The Koryaks welcomed him as they had welcomed many others before him. On 14 March 1730 his neck was pierced by an arrow in a bloody battle. He collapsed on to a sleigh and the reindeer harnessed to it pulled him straight into the Koryak camp.

Kamchatka was still seething with revolt. The Kamchadales were declining in numbers but they still retained their capacity for rebellion. In 1731 there was a general rising. Several *ostrogs* were burnt down and all the small Cossack detachments which had ventured deeper into the country were destroyed. The hero of this rebellion was the Nana-Sahib of Kamchatka, the baptized Kamchadale Kharchin. According to legend he could run fast enough to overtake a wild reindeer. This detail particularly struck Pushkin's poetic fancy when he was studying the history of Kamchatka a hundred years later.

The rebellion was savagely crushed and by June 1732 'peace and order' prevailed again. We do not know precisely how many people lost their lives in these eleven months. They were counted in dozens on the Russian side but in hundreds on the side of the Kamchadales.

Like many other fighters for freedom, Kharchin ended on the gallows. News of the rebellion reached St Petersburg, and in a remarkable contemporary document, the 'Supreme Personal Order' of 9 May 1733, the commission of inquiry was instructed to punish only the guiltiest of the instigators with death and to let the others go free, because, in the words of the order, 'they are a wild people and had good grounds for rebelling against the wickedness of their governors. They could not make a complaint because of the great distance and perhaps did not understand how to.' On the other hand, the utmost severity was to be employed against the governors and their subordinates because it was their evil and destructive deeds which were mainly responsible for the revolt.

In accordance with these instructions nine Kamchadales, including Kharchin, and four Russians were condemned to death by the commission. Forty-four Kamchadales and sixty-one Russians were flogged. Considering the time and the place, the impartiality of this verdict is amazing.

Another 'personal order' considerably eased the situation of the Kamchadales. It reduced the rate of tribute and introduced some order into the collection of the furs. Bering's second expedition also provoked a rebellion, but it was an insignificant one. After that peace reigned in Kamchatka and we hear of no more revolts until 1756, when eight Russian soldiers were killed in a local uprising. The Kamchadales no longer had the strength for anything bigger. Their numbers were continually dropping, while those of the Russians in Kamchatka rose. The native population of the peninsula was finally decimated by smallpox brought in from Siberia.

Five years after the rebellion of 1731–2 a student from the Russian Academy of Sciences, Stepan Petrovich Krasheninikov, arrived in Kamchatka. He compiled a book about the peninsula that is still the best ever written on Kamchatka. Krasheninikov paints a vivid picture of the Kamchadales, who were still living in the Stone Age, were slaves to the most primitive shamanism and were often repulsive in their naïve and bestial sensuality. An upright and pious man, Krasheninikov sometimes puts his excellent observations in the form of a moralization. Thus he writes in one place: 'The Kamchadales have a completely distorted idea of virtue and vice; in their view the greatest happiness consists of gluttony, idleness and copulation; physical desire is aroused by singing, dancing and the telling of love stories. To them, the greatest sin is boredom which they try to avoid by every possible means.'

Other statements of Krasheninikov lift the two-hundred-year-old curtain hiding the tragedy of that forgotten land: 'In moments of unhappiness the Kamchadales had always resorted to suicide, which was common among them even before they were conquered. After the conquest this fondness for self-destruction increased so much that special orders were issued from Moscow that the Russians were to prevent the Kamchadales from taking their own lives.'

THE LEGACY OF PETER THE GREAT

Kamchatka was in Russian hands. But what lay beyond it? That was what Peter the Great wanted to know more than anything else. He had already discussed the subject with scholars on his first trip abroad in 1697–8. In Holland he spent much time with his friend Nikolaus Witsen, the burgomaster of Amsterdam, whose book and map provided the eighteenth century with its first source of information about Siberia. The problem of Gama land and the Terra de Jeso – those mysterious islands which were supposed to lie to the south-east of Kamchatka between Japan and America – was naturally among the matters discussed. The Tsar's interest continued to grow. In Moscow little Denbe had told him about Japanese ores and silks. From Vasily Kolesov he learnt of Kosyrevsky's claim that there was gold on the Kurile Islands. On some maps published in Europe which the Tsar possessed, a narrow strip of water, called the Anian Straits, was shown between Asia and America – a centuries-old creation of the cartographical imagination, evoked by an obscure passage in Marco Polo's book, which corresponded in a remarkable fashion to a geographical reality but was continually doubted.

This doubt was confirmed by the views of Guillaume de Lisle, the famous French geographer, who in 1706 published a map of 'Tartary' on which, at the extreme north-eastern edge of Siberia, a long tongue of land with a chain of mountains on it can be seen. Beside it is written: '*On ne sait pas où se termine cette chaîne de montagnes, et si elle ne va pas joindre quelque autre Continent.*' De Lisle was still doubtful; shortly afterwards a new map appeared at Amsterdam, and at the same spot it was stated that this mountain-chain ran on into America.

Peter had every reason to be interested in the Anian Straits. The question of the north-east sea-passage to China had been raised by Gerasimov in the sixteenth century. English and Dutch activity had made it acute, and at the end of the seventeenth century the presence of the Jesuits in China gave it a fresh topicality. The Jesuits dreamed of a land-route to China through Russia and Siberia, but the Russians knew from experience how difficult this land-route was, and naturally returned to the idea of a sea-route to

China, which would also be under Russian control but considerably easier and cheaper than the land-route. The question was thus occupying people's minds both in Russia and in Europe. The most enthusiastic protagonist of the idea in Europe was Leibniz. As early as 1697 he suggested in a memorandum which he wrote for Lefort, the Tsar's most trusted adviser, that the question whether Asia and America were joined together should be settled by an expedition to those parts. It is not known whether the Tsar saw this memorandum, but in any case Leibniz clung to his idea. He met the Tsar twice in October 1711 at Torgau, several times in November 1712 at Karlsbad, Teplitz and Dresden, and again in June 1716 at Bad Pyrmont. On these occasions the Asiatic–American riddle was among the many matters discussed. Leibniz returned to the same theme later on in several memoranda to the Tsar and his advisers.

It was also discussed when the Tsar visited Paris in 1717. There Peter met Guillaume de Lisle, the *'premier géographe de sa majesté'*, and showed him two new Russian maps. One embodied the results of the latest explorations in the neighbourhood of the Caspian Sea, the other did the same for Siberia. The unsolved problems of the geography of Siberia were also raised. The story was even current afterwards that the Academy had asked the Tsar for permission to send a French expedition to north-eastern Siberia. In reality such a suggestion was never made officially, but private conversations with the Tsar always centred round the same theme. A concrete proposal for an expedition from the mouth of the Dvina or Yenisei to China was also made about the same time by the Russian naval architect F. S. Saltykov, and some of his ideas were later included in the instructions given to Bering.

Peter's interest in geography is well known. In it political and economic considerations were combined with real scientific curiosity. It was only natural that a Tsar who had personally supervised the surveying of the whole course of the Don and had written in his own hand the sailing instructions for his captains should attempt to solve the Anian riddle.

The whole Pacific complex – Japan, Kamchatka, America – seemed to be extremely important. Hence the orders to the governors of Kamchatka to collect information about Japan and the Pacific islands, and the opening of the sea-route to Kamchatka at the Tsar's personal behest. In 1719 Peter sent two geodesists,

Yevreinov and Lushin, to the Pacific. Their orders were 'to establish whether Asia and America are joined or not . . . and to carry out any other tasks enjoined on them.' The two geodesists also had other secret instructions which no doubt referred to Japan and the Kurile Islands.

At the 'fifth or sixth Kurile Island' the geodesists turned back because they had lost their anchor. Yevreinov made his report in person to the Tsar at Kazan in May 1722. 'The emperor showed great pleasure at Yevreinov's work,' wrote Müller, but the contents of the report were never known. The map brought back by the geodesists was not found until 1945.

Three weeks before his death, at the beginning of January 1725, Peter summoned Admiral Apraxin. 'His Majesty already felt the onset of illness,' wrote Peter's favourite, his 'mechanic and master of the lathe', Nartov. Nevertheless the Tsar had drawn up a few days earlier the instructions for a maritime expedition 'that should decide by sea the question whether Asia and America are joined together.' 'Since at that time I was with the Tsar the whole time, I saw with my own eyes how anxious His Majesty was to complete the instructions for this important undertaking, as though he felt that his end was near, and how peaceful and happy he seemed when he had finished them. The emperor immediately summoned his admiral-in-chief and gave him the document with the words: "My poor health has confined me to my room; and so in the last few days I have been thinking of something which I have long had in mind and which other matters have prevented me from investigating, namely, the route through the Arctic Ocean to China and India. The way shown on this chart, known as Anian, is not drawn without good reason. During my last journey abroad I learnt in conversation with learned men that such a discovery is quite possible. If our country is safely protected against the foe, let its fame be furthered through the arts and sciences. Should we not have more good fortune in the exploration of this route than the Dutch and the English, who repeatedly tried to use it for the investigation of the coast of America? For these reasons I drew up these instructions; I leave it to you, Fyodor Matveerich, because of my illness, to see that they are carried out in every detail by the proper authorities." '

The sheet of paper which Peter handed to the admiral contained the following instructions, written in the Tsar's own hand.

1. Construct in Kamchatka or elsewhere two ships with decks.

2. In these vessels, sail along the coast which runs towards the north and, because its end is not known, seems to form a piece of America.

3. See where this coast joins America and whether a town belonging to Europe is not to be found; if a European ship is encountered, inquire from it what this coast is called and make a note of it; land, describe everything in detail, draw a map and then return.

PETER

BERING'S FIRST VOYAGE

Peter himself chose the men who were to sail to the Anian Straits. As their leader he appointed Vitus Bering.

Bering was a Dane. He was born in 1680 in the Danish town of Horsens, where his forefathers had long been established. He had begun his career as a sailor on the ships of the Dutch East India Company and after sailing on many seas and oceans had entered the Russian Navy as a lieutenant in 1704. In 1710 he was promoted to commander and in 1724 to captain, first class. According to G. F. Müller he took part in the hostilities against Sweden and this seems more than likely, for during the great Northern War he was serving in the Baltic fleet. When Peter wrote down his three points Bering was forty-four years old, and twenty of these years he had spent on board Russian ships. He was regarded as a brave officer and an excellent seaman, and was popular with everyone because of his open and good-natured character. No one could suspect at this time that he had something of his countryman, Hamlet, in him.

Two officers were assigned to Bering as lieutenants. One of them was likewise a Dane, Martin Spangberg, a good seaman but a boorish and unattractive man. He soon succeeded in falling out with everyone, beginning with the good-natured Bering.

Lieutenant Alexei Chirikov was one of the young men called by Pushkin 'Peter's nestlings'. He was full of enthusiasm for the idea of Russia as a sea-power. Even as a cadet he was marked out by his exceptional gifts, was promoted before his time to officer and appointed an instructor at the Naval Academy. As one of his superiors put it, 'he had a pure heart and a great love of the sea'.

Special mention should be made of the young midshipman Peter Chaplin, whose diary is an important source of information about the expedition. He drew the map of Bering's voyage.

The first party left St Petersburg on 24 January 1725, twenty-four hours before the Tsar's death. Bering had to wait behind for his instructions, which were given to him on 5 February. He set out the same day. But all the members of the expedition did not meet until two years later, in Okhotsk. Their journeys through western Siberia had been difficult enough, for they had an enormous amount of baggage with them, but the last stage, from Yakutsk to Okhotsk, was frightful. The ship for the expedition was to be built at Okhotsk, and all the instruments, ropes, anchors, chains, tar and sails had to be taken there. Spangberg's party almost perished from hunger and cold; many members of it did in fact die, among them the talented explorer of the Kurile Islands, the geodesist Lushin.

At Okhotsk a small ship called the *Fortuna* had already been built before Bering's arrival. In two trips it carried the expedition to Bolsheretsk on the west coast of Kamchatka. From there, men and baggage had to be conveyed about 550 miles over the mountains to Nishne-Kamchatsk. For this purpose Bering mobilized almost all the dogs in Kamchatka. Most of them died on the way. The services of the Kamchadales were also called upon in large measure. All this provoked the last great rebellion of the Kamchadales in 1730–1, which has already been described.

There is one point about these activities which even the old historians of Bering's first expedition found difficult to understand: why did Bering not sail direct from Okhotsk to the mouth of the River Kamchatka? In other words, why did he not circumnavigate Kamchatka? By doing so he could have saved two years and avoided large losses of baggage, the physical exhaustion of his men and the enormous burden placed on the Kamchadales. The answer is provided by a description of the *Fortuna*, which ferried him to Kamchatka. This 'ship' was a so-called *shitik*; the name was derived from the verb meaning 'to sew'. Its keel consisted of a tree-trunk, to which planks were 'sewn' with osier switches! It is perfectly comprehensible that Bering should have considered such a boat unsuitable for the circumnavigation of Kamchatka. This in turn throws an interesting light on Bering's psychological attitude to the whole enterprise. He did not trust his first vessel and one can imagine that he did not feel any more comfortable on the second one, which was built in Kamchatka. He lacked that organic 'Siberian' sympathy with nature, that capacity for adapting oneself to one's surroundings, which the Russians possessed in such large measure. Very significant in this connection is a remark in the diary of his companion, Steller. Steller says that Bering wished that the whole affair could be entrusted to 'a young and impetuous man from the country', that is, a Russian, instead of to himself. These words refer to the second expedition, but they illuminate many points in the history of the first.

On 8 June 1728 (this date, and those that follow, are calculated according to the old Russian or Julian calendar) the new ship, the *Saint Gabriel*, was launched at Nishne-Kamchatsk, and on the 13 July it put to sea with Bering, his two officers and a crew of forty-one on board. The *Gabriel* sailed along the coast towards the north. The weather was good, land was in sight the whole time and everyone was in a cheerful mood.

They sailed steadily on until August arrived, and with it fog and rain. On 6 August they took fresh water on board, conversing with some Chukchas, who had rowed up to them in a boat made of skins. The Chukchas reported that there was sea all round the land in these parts; but there was an island in the sea inhabited by people of 'their own blood'. On 9 August, Bering sailed round Cape Chukotski and on the 11th did in fact sight an island, which he christened 'Saint Lawrence Island'.

On 13 August, Bering discussed the situation with his officers. He thought that they had already passed round the north-eastern tip of Asia; he raised the question whether they should sail on farther and, if so, for how long.

Spangberg suggested that they should go on for three days and then turn back. In contrast to the two Danes, Chirikov maintained that the expedition's task had not yet been completed. In his view, to provide a real answer to the question whether Asia and America were divided by water, the *Saint Gabriel* ought to sail farther west along the coast, at least as far as the mouth of the Kolyma. If this could not be done by 25 August because of ice, he was in favour of looking for a suitable spot in which to winter, either on the coast or the one opposite Cape Chukotski, where, according to the Chukchas, there was forest.

Here spoke a man of quite different character, with a different

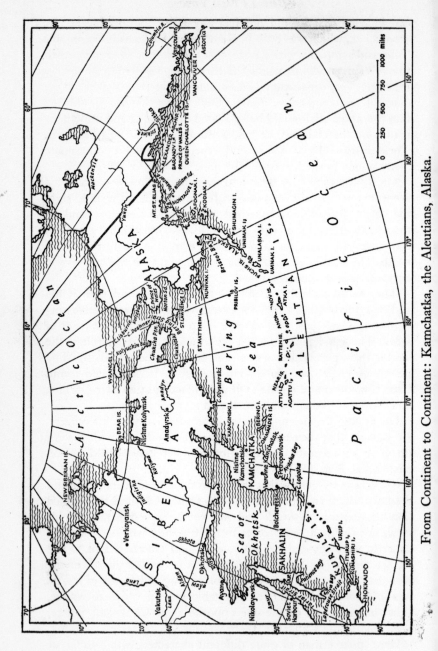

From Continent to Continent: Kamchatka, the Aleutians, Alaska.

attitude to his environment. His reference to forest is characteristic enough, for there is no forest on the Asiatic side of the Bering Straits and in contemporary reports 'forests' always meant the other side, whether this was an island or the American continent. Chirikov thus wanted to look for this *other* side; and he wanted to winter there, or even, if need be, on the Russian side. He trusted his vessel and both the unknown shores. He also took the reports of the Chukchas seriously. Only a man who felt at home in these surroundings could do this.

Bering was rather dubious about Chirikov's proposal. He considered it impossible to winter without wood and fire, and, like Spangberg, he was disinclined to rely on the words of the Chukchas. So he took Spangberg's advice, not Chirikov's, sailed north for another three days and then turned back.

This was on 16 August. The *Saint Gabriel* had reached latitude 67° 18′ north; that is, it had already sailed through the strip of water between Asia and America. The sea was free of ice. On the way back they discovered another island in the Diomedes group.

On 1 September the *Saint Gabriel* dropped anchor in the mouth of the Kamchatka. Bering repeated his attempt the next summer. This time he turned back after only three days; the weather was too unfavourable. He then sailed round Kamchatka, stopped for a while on the west coast and arrived in Okhotsk on 23 July 1729. From there he went straight to St Petersburg, which he reached on 1 March 1730.

The Senate, the Admiralty and the Academy of Sciences were all waiting impatiently for his return. But the results of the expedition disappointed them, and they said so. It was pointed out that the fundamental question about the relationship between Asia and America was still not finally answered; that the required astronomical observations had not been made; and that the detailed information about the 'peoples, customs, fruits of the earth, metals and minerals' had not been collected.

These accusations were only partly justified. Bering's first voyage was by no means fruitless. The information which he brought back made it possible to draw new maps, and his trip strengthened Russian contact with Kamchatka and the north-east of Asia. As for Bering's astronomical fixes, they were later confirmed and praised by Cook, who also christened the passage between Asia and America 'the Bering Straits'.

But it was true that Bering had not carried out his appointed task. To prove that Siberia and America were divided by water, he ought to have sailed at least to the mouth of the Kolyma, that is, to a spot which was positively known to lie on the north coast of Siberia. This was just what Chirikov had suggested. When Bering declared on his return that he was finally convinced that there was water between Siberia and America, he was not saying anything new. Almost everybody else was convinced of this too. What was needed was concrete proof, and Bering had not produced it. There is a personal tragedy here which deprives us of the right of speaking of a 'mistake' in the accepted sense of the word. It was almost a century before the required proof was produced, and even then the sailors had to be helped by the landlubbers. The last doubt was only removed in 1822, when Baron F. P. Wrangel travelled by land from the mouth of the Kolyma as far as the island of Kolyuchin, which Captain Billings had reached in 1791 from Kamchatka, also mainly by land. It was then quite clear that there was a continuous coast-line from the White Sea to the Pacific, and the fateful question put to Bering was finally resolved.

Exploration of the Pacific coast by no means came to a halt while Vitus Bering was talking with the authorities and scholars at St Petersburg. On his way back in July 1729, Bering had met the Cossack chief Afanasy Shestakov, who was riding, full of confidence, over the mountains to Okhotsk, to lead the great expedition on which he was to lose his life. At Okhotsk, Shestakov found the two ships of the Bering expedition, and he himself built two more. In 1729–30 they carried out various assignments in the Sea of Okhotsk, in the Kuriles, and along the east coast of Kamchatka.

After Shestakov's death the leadership of the expedition passed to his subordinate, Captain Pavlucky. In accordance with Shestakov's instructions he sent another ship – the tried and tested *Gabriel* – round Kamchatka to the north. The second mate, Ivan Fyodorov, was appointed captain of the ship and he was given the geodesist Michael Gvosdyov as cartographical expert. Fyodorov was ill with scurvy even before the ship sailed; he was carried on board on a stretcher.

In 1732 Fyodorov and Gvosdyov sailed through the Bering Straits and past the Diomedes Islands. Gvosdyov went ashore on the southern side of Cape Deshnev and suggested that the Chukchas there should pay him a tribute of furs. The proposal remained unanswered. The *Gabriel* then sailed eastward to the unknown 'great land' and anchored two and a half miles off the coast. From there it sailed south and next day reached King Island. With the help of a Chukcha interpreter whom he had brought with him Gvosdyov talked to an Eskimo who came rowing up to the ship. From the Eskimo he learnt that in the 'great land' there were forests, rivers, reindeer, martins, foxes and beavers.

Fyodorov and Gvosdyov were thus the first sailors to reach the coast of Alaska, the first to set eyes on both sides of the Bering Straits, and thus the real discoverers of the latter. The American historian H. H. Bancroft drew attention to this about seventy years ago. Fyodorov, the responsible leader of the expedition, ought to have gone ashore to secure the fame of this deed for himself, but he was seriously ill and his exhausted crew demanded that he should turn round.

Soon after his return Fyodorov died. The report on the voyage was made by Gvosdyov, to whom all the historians subsequently ascribed the expedition's achievements. But this is not correct. Fyodorov was the actual leader of the expedition and it was he who kept the log of the *Gabriel*. It was only in recent years that a fragment of this log-book was found, but it was used in its entirety by Martin Spangberg to draw the map on which the *Gabriel*'s voyage was marked. This map, too, has been lost, but a contemporary copy was discovered in 1943. It assures Fyodorov and Gvosdyov of a place in the history of geography.

BERING'S SECOND VOYAGE

It was becoming more and more clearly understood in St Petersburg that the exploration of Kamchatka and the surrounding area was a matter of first-rate political importance. Peter the Great was naturally fully conscious of the political significance of these activities. The renunciation of Daurien in the treaty of Nerchinsk had, as a corollary, increased Russian interest in Kamchatka and Japan. From the Russian point of view, the relations of eastern Siberia with its neighbours, its opening-up and its annexation were all parts of the same problem. As early as 1722, during the Persian campaign, it had been suggested to the Tsar by Lieutenant F. I.

Soimonov that a route to Kamchatka and thence to Japan should be sought along the Shilka and the Amur. 'I know that,' the Tsar replied, 'but it must come later.' Soimonov was thus the first to express the thought that the Amur forms a link with Kamchatka and is Siberia's outlet to the sea.

Two years after the conversation with Soimonov the Tsar had talks with the chief secretary of the Senate, I. K. Kirillov. Like Soimonov, Kirillov was one of the Tsar's 'nestlings'. He was keenly interested in geography and cartography and in 1734 published on his own account the first printed atlas of the Russian Empire. He has left us an account of his conversations with the Tsar. It concerned relations with China and the question of the Russo-Chinese border. The Tsar wanted to see a map of eastern Siberia, and Kirillov had to make a new one in one night, using available Russian maps, including Yevreinov's map of Kamchatka, and a Chinese – i.e. Jesuit – one of eastern Asia.

The conversations began in December 1724, and on 23 December the Tsar put down his three points for the Kamchatka expedition. Their connection with the Amur and Japanese problems is unmistakable. But the connection was not clearly formulated, probably on purpose, and it seems likely that Chirikov was the only member of Bering's expedition who grasped the political significance of its task. However, he played only a subordinate part in the first expedition. So far as Bering was concerned, Kirillov was convinced from the start that he would only bring back the answer to the question whether Asia and America were joined together, and that nothing concerning the 'real interest' could be expected from him.

Where the 'real interest' lay in this connection is not difficult to see: in the political at least as much as in the geographical aspects of the project. It is understandable that the 'imperial historiographer', G. F. Müller, should have supported the official 'geographical' thesis, as the geographer L. S. Berg has done in our own day. But K. E. von Baer pointed to the political side of the affair, and the famous historian S. M. Solovyev emphasized its economic aim, namely, the development of the Russian function as trade-link between East and West, a conception that is doubtless near the truth. On the other hand, the recent attempts of some Soviet writers to present Bering's two expeditions as purely political and nationalistic enterprises look like a distortion of the truth which

is contradicted both by the behaviour of the expeditions themselves and by Russia's hesitant and apathetic attitude towards
Alaska in the eighteenth century. It remains true that Kirillov
himself had a solid grasp of the general political significance of the
whole enterprise; in his 'Proposals' to the Senate even Korea was
mentioned for the first time in Russian official documents as part
of the Far Eastern political complex. But this memorandum is
undated; it was probably drawn up in 1733, but perhaps even later.
In any case, the leaders of the expedition cannot have received
corresponding instructions, otherwise their actions are difficult to
understand.

There can be no doubt that Bering's two expeditions had their
political side; they were intended above all to provide geo-political
information. But it is unlikely that Peter the Great had a clear
conception of the 'Russian position on the Pacific'. Such conceptions ripen slowly and at that time the premises were still lacking.
Bering's first trip looks more like a reconnaissance, comparable to
the first Cossack reconnaissance of the routes to China: a cautious
probing of a problem that would soon arise.

As Kirillov goes on to say, Shestakov was sent to the east immediately after Bering to consolidate as far as possible this 'real
interest'. From this point of view, the information gained by
Shestakov's successor, Pavlucky, and by Fyodorov and Gvosdyov,
were really more valuable than the results of Bering's first
expedition.

It is apparent that at the time of Bering's return interest in the
Kamchatka enterprise was by no means lacking at St Petersburg.
Moreover, Count Apraxin had been succeeded as head of the
Admiralty by Count N. F. Golovin, a well-educated naval officer
obliged by his very origins to take a special interest in everything
to do with Siberia. He was the grandson of a *voivode* of Tobolsk
and the son of the man who signed the treaty of Nerchinsk and
later became the governor of Siberia. The powerful chancellor,
Count Ostermann, was also keenly interested in the expedition,
and with him the whole court. Bering had many friends among
all these people, and this assured him of a favourable reception for
the proposals with regard to Siberia which he put to the government in 1730. Among other things, Bering suggested developing
the cattle-raising industry in Yakutia, introducing it into Kamchatka, improving the facilities for shipbuilding at Okhotsk and on

the River Kamchatka, and reorganizing the administration of the Far East. He also recommended measures to check the epidemic of suicides among the Kamchadales described by Krasheninikov in his book. Not satisfied with all this, Bering proposed that he himself should once more explore the sea-routes from Kamchatka to America, the mouth of the Amur and Japan, and that the Arctic coast of Siberia from the Ob to the Yenisei and from the Yenisei to the Lena should be investigated.

These proposals were far-reaching enough in themselves, but Kirillov built them up into the greatest piece of geographical research ever planned. More remarkable still, the plan was actually carried out. It comprised seven big undertakings; four of them were concerned with the exploration of the whole north coast of Siberia, the aim of the fifth was to find America, that of the sixth was to explore the coasts of Japan and the Kurile Islands, and that of the seventh was to explore Siberia from the points of view of natural history, ethnography, history and archaeology. The three last projects were put under the overall command of Bering; they formed what was known as the 'Second Kamchatka Expedition', while the whole enterprise was called the 'Great Northern Expedition'.

The composition of the Kamchatka expedition could not have been better. The two senior officers after Bering were Chirikov and Spangberg, and next to them, with the rank of lieutenant, came the Swede Sven Waxell as mate and Sofron Khitrovo as naval chief-of-staff. All the other officers and sailors were experienced and reliable men. Louis de Lisle de la Croyère, a stepbrother of the Guillaume de Lisle with whom Peter had talked in Paris, was taken as astronomer and geographer.

Louis de Lisle had already been in the east of Canada. He took a whole observatory with him on the expedition, including four telescopes, four theodolites, twenty thermometers and twenty-seven barometers. The transport of these instruments cost enormous trouble, which was unfortunately not repaid by the results.

The second scientific member of the expedition did not join Bering until much later. This was George Wilhelm Steller, a doctor who had studied at Wittenberg, Jena and Halle. He had entered the Russian army as a medical officer in 1734 during the Polish war of succession, and had come to St Petersburg with a column of wounded. On the recommendation of his patron, the famous archbishop Feofan Prokopovich, he was appointed to the expedition as 'natural history adviser'. This was in 1737. Steller did not arrive in Okhotsk until August 1740. Together with Waxell's report and Khitrovo's journal, his diaries form the best source of information about the second expedition.

The expedition was grandiose in conception but overloaded in practice. Bering was right to point out to the Senate that this was a mistake. It took eight years to move all the men and baggage from St Petersburg to Kamchatka; the distance to Okhotsk alone is well over six thousand miles.

The members of the expedition were divided into three groups, which left St Petersburg one after the other at the beginning of 1733. Spangberg was the first to arrive at Okhotsk, and he took a year and a half; Bering himself spent almost three whole years in Yakutsk, supervising the transport of the expedition over the roadless Stanovoi mountains to Okhotsk. The main body of the expedition reached Okhotsk in the summer of 1738, more than five years after leaving St Petersburg.

This continual travelling exhausted the members mentally and physically before they could set about their real tasks. Bering had been given special powers. He mobilized men and horses, requisitioned food from government stores and quartered his men on the Russian settlers. The appearance of his detachments always meant trouble for the local inhabitants and sometimes ended in catastrophe, which in turn led to protests and disputes. While the expedition crept at snail's pace across the Siberian mountains and swamps, criticisms and complaints streamed back swiftly to St Petersburg.

In fact, Bering's salary was cut and Soimonov suggested making Spangberg leader of the expedition in his place, a proposal which shows that Soimonov was no judge of men. Admiral Golovin, on the other hand, suggested quite sensibly that a fresh expedition should be sent straight from St Petersburg to Kamchatka and America via Cape Horn, and was ready to lead it himself. His plan was executed sixty-five years later by Krusenstern and Lisyansky.

All this was a heavy burden on Bering. There is another very important factor to be considered too: nine years passed by between the approval of the expedition and the day Bering sailed from Kamchatka. In 1732 he was fifty-one; when he set sail he was sixty. As time went by he found it more and more difficult to answer the missives from St Petersburg and to smooth over clashes with the local authorities.

SPANGBERG DISCOVERS JAPAN

To judge by what we know of Martin Spangberg, he lacked the most important quality of a real leader, the ability to manage men. As a seaman and organizer in the narrow sense, on the other hand, he was first-class. He was the first to arrive in Okhotsk and there he built magazines, barracks and, above all, ships: the hooker *Saint Michael* and the sloop *Nadeshda* ('Hope'). He also refitted the old *Saint Gabriel* and *Fortuna*, and began to build two ships for the voyage to America, the *Saint Peter* and the *Saint Paul*. He set sail with the first three of these on 18 June 1738. He himself hoisted his flag in the *Michael*, the *Nadeshda* was commanded by Lieutenant Walton and the *Gabriel* by Midshipman Shelting. They explored the Kurile Islands and in August returned to Bolsheretsk for the winter.

There Spangberg built another sloop 'from birch wood', and in May of the following year set out, with four ships, for Japan. Walton was parted from him on the way, and on 16 June Spangberg alone reached the Japanese coast. A few days later he was at anchor off the island of Hondo, in latitude 38° 25' north. The sun was shining, the sea was calm and on land they could see groves of trees in blossom, cultivated fields and numerous villages: the heavenly scene that again and again was to enchant Russians coming from Siberia or Kamchatka. Spangberg made contact with the Japanese, and various exchanges were made: linen, linen clothes and glass beads were handed over in return for fresh fish, rice, tobacco and pickled cucumbers. 'On the other hand,' says the historian Müller, 'the Japanese were not interested in cotton and silk goods, mirrors, knives, scissors, needles or things like that which were shown to them, because they have all these things in their own country.'

Four officials also came on board and talked to Spangberg. He showed his guests a chart and a globe. They immediately recognized their own country, which they called 'Nippon', and told him the names of the individual Japanese islands.

Spangberg did not succeed in entering into closer relations with
the islanders; his water and food were running out and he had
several sick men on board. He sailed back to the north, visited the
southern islands in the Kurile group on the way and arrived at
Okhotsk on 29 August. Even on this idyllic trip he had lost thirteen of his crew of sixty-three from scurvy.

At Okhotsk Walton was waiting for him. Walton had reached
the coastal waters of the island of Hondo, about five degrees
farther south. He, too, had been compelled to turn back by heat
and lack of water.

Spangberg now obtained permission from Bering to travel to
St Petersburg with his report. He started out, but on the way received orders from the capital to return to Okhotsk and sail to
Japan again. St Petersburg was not satisfied with the results of his
expedition. People there did not even believe that Spangberg and
Walton had reached the coast of Japan; it was assumed that the
land they had reached was Korea. It is true that Spangberg might
have been able to find out a little more about Japan, but the
reproaches to which he was subjected were unjustified. He and
Walton had in fact explored the way to Japan from the north, they
had fixed the position of northern Japan and the Kurile Islands,
they had refuted the old story of Gama-land and finally they had
shown that De Vries's 'Company-land' was simply one of the
Kurile Islands.

Spangberg returned to Okhotsk 'in a different mood', as Müller
puts it. There he built a sloop and tried to sail to Japan again.
His voyage did not achieve its aim, but his companion, Shelting,
touched the coast of Japan and on the return journey sailed along
the whole east coast of Sakhalin. This was the Russians' first
acquaintance with Sakhalin (1742).

BERING'S VOYAGE TO AMERICA

Spangberg's trips to Japan affected Bering's American expedition
unfavourably in so far as they claimed a considerable portion of
the stores collected at Okhotsk and caused Bering to lose further
time waiting for replacements. On the other hand, Spangberg
brought back with him an important piece of information. After
his trip to Japan it was clear that the land of Gama, if it existed

at all, was not to be found south-east of Kamchatka. In everyone's view, this was an important, indeed decisive, moment. Should they waste valuable time looking for the land of Gama to the south-east of Kamchatka, or should they steer north-east straight away? Everybody, including Bering, was in favour of the latter course. Chirikov saw the situation most clearly; already in 1733 he had proposed to the Senate that the expedition should sail straight from Kamchatka to the north-east.

Bering arrived in the bay of Avacha, on the east coast of Kamchatka, in the late autumn of 1740. The bay was calm and deep, one of the best he had ever seen, said Sven Waxell. Granaries, barracks and houses had already been built in the summer. So a new port came into being. Bering christened it Petropavlovsk (Peter and Paul's Town) in honour of his two ships, and wintered there.

On 4 May 1741 Bering held a conference with his colleagues to decide what course to steer on the approaching voyage. Louis de Lisle brought a copy of a map made by his stepbrother, Joseph Nicolas, which showed the land of Gama as lying to the south-east of Kamchatka. No one except Louis believed in this land, but according to the supplementary instructions which Bering received from the Senate in 1733 he was to keep strictly to this map. So they decided on a south-easterly course in order to look for Gama-land first.

One wonders why Bering held this conference if the question had in any case been decided in advance by the Senate. There was only one other possibility open to him: to disregard the instructions and take the responsibility for doing so on himself. Could he dare to do this? Obviously he could, for the authors of the instructions did not know the results of Spangberg's voyages and Bering could naturally have refrained from looking for a land of whose non-existence he had meanwhile been informed. A word from the commander of the expedition would have sufficed to produce a corresponding decision, but Bering did not utter that word. Why not? When one understands how Bering's position had been undermined by that time, and what his mental state was, it is difficult to reproach him for his irresolute behaviour. The fact remains that the wrong course was chosen and this meant that time was wasted.

A month later, on 4 June 1741, both ships put out to sea, with

Bering on board the *St Peter* and Chirikov in command of the *St Paul*. After sailing for sixteen days, during which no land at all was seen, the two ships lost sight of each other in storm and fog. Each sailed on independently. After five days Bering had, so to speak, sailed right through 'Gama-land' and the *St Peter* turned north-east. On 12 July there were signs that land was near: seaweed and reeds in the water. Steller examined them and said that they did not seem to come from Kamchatka. After another four days they sighted land. As they approached it the weather was very clear and they could see several bays and cliffs, and farther off a range of mountains higher than any in Siberia or Kamchatka. It was the range containing Mt Elias, the highest peak in North America.

This meant that they were saved, for their water was coming to an end and scurvy was breaking out. One of the first victims was Bering himself. Steller's account makes it clear what sort of condition he was in. The leader of the expedition listened apathetically to the congratulations of his delighted officers 'and even shrugged his shoulders for all to see as he looked towards the land.' When he was alone in his cabin with Steller and another of his companions he said: 'We think now that we have found everything and many are full of bluster, but they forget where the land is, how far from home we are, and all the things that can still happen. Trade winds may start to blow and prevent us returning. We are not familiar with the land and we have no stores to see us through the winter.'

The *St Peter* sailed cautiously towards the land and on 20 July anchored off the island now known as Kayak. The first mate, Khitrovo, was sent ashore in the big rowing-boat to fetch water. The scientist, Steller, was given a small boat and a sailor to accompany him. He reported later that Bering had been reluctant to let him go. Steller is full of cutting remarks about Bering and his officers: 'We had only come,' he writes, 'in order to take American water back to Asia.' He had lost his affability and smelt treason and treachery everywhere. 'Ten years were devoted to the preparations for this great enterprise,' he writes further on, 'and ten hours were devoted to its main purpose.' No doubt Steller's outbursts were exaggerated, but Bering's indifference to the scientific and political aspects of the expedition was rather curious. He was certainly ill and in a depressed frame of mind. But the similarity of his attitude to the one which he adopted on the first expedition is striking. He paid no more attention to Steller's representations now than he had to Chirikov's on the earlier occasion. As a commentator on Steller's diary pointed out later, it is incomprehensible that no serious effort was made to explore and take possession of the land that had been discovered. It almost seems as if Bering's instructions were inadequate. Yet the instructions spoke clearly of 'exploring the new lands' and of investigating trading possibilities 'to the advantage of the state'.

Steller used the short time at his disposal to make a truly scientific record. He explored the island; noted, described and, in many cases, sketched about 160 different kinds of plant as well as many animals, birds and molluscs; he found a store of provisions hidden by the inhabitants – probably Eskimos, who did not show themselves – and took various objects and examples of food from it. In exchange he left a piece of cloth and some kettles, knives and glass beads. On the tiny neighbouring island Khitrovo found an Eskimo hut and took various objects of daily use from it. Then they had to return to the ship, which drove Steller to despair. On board, they tried to cheer him up with a cup of chocolate which was served to mark 'the discovery of America'.

From Kayak they steered south-west. On 25 July they sighted a 'high land', probably the island of Kodiak, and on 2 August a little island which fifty-three years later Vancouver christened 'Chirikov'; today it is called Ukamok. Throughout August they drifted on without sighting land. They had had no fresh water for some time and at the beginning of August twenty-six of the crew of seventy-seven were already ill with scurvy. Bering could not leave his bunk and the command was in the hands of Sven Waxell and Khitrovo. These two were good friends and so all went smoothly.

On 30 August they anchored in the middle of a group of islands. Scurvy claimed its first victim here; the sailor Shumagin died as soon as they landed, and the islands were named after him. Here, too, Steller was the first to land, so as to be able to make a thorough exploration. They took water on board, but it was salty. For the first time they met other men, Aleutians, who only received the name later; at that time they were called 'wild Americans'.

September, the season of storms, had arrived. The cockle-shell of a ship, its crew sick and depressed, sailed on past the long, curving line of islands which blocks the entrance to the Arctic Ocean from the Pacific. The sailors had no food, almost no water, no strength and no commander. 'Our ship drifted along at the mercy of the winds and waves, with almost no guidance, like a piece of dead wood,' wrote Waxell. Only nine or ten members of the crew were still capable of working. Steller alone seems to have remained perfectly healthy.

BERING DIES ON HIS ISLAND

They drifted on, 'under two leaders, sold and betrayed', as Steller somewhat uncharitably puts it, until they sighted land on 5 November. What land was it? Only Bering, Steller and Ovzyn realized that it was not Kamchatka and that, even if it had been, they would have had to harness all the strength they had left in order to reach the bay of Avacha. But the captain was ill and apathetic, Steller, as a landlubber, was not consulted, and Ovzyn was only a seaman; in reality he was an able young naval officer, but he had been demoted for 'political unreliability' and his views were therefore not given their full weight. Waxell and Khitrovo were convinced that the *St Peter* was off Kamchatka and that they would soon be able to call on assistance from Petropavlovsk. This energetically supported view won the day at the conference which took place at Bering's bedside on 5 November 1741.

As they approached the coast the *St Peter* ran aground on a sandbank. Then two anchors were lost. The sailors took the view that the two corpses they had on board would not let them reach the shore. They tied a cannonball to each and dropped them overboard.

Meanwhile the weather had cleared up a little and a start was made with unloading. The rough sea made this very difficult and it took until 21 November. In this time they could have easily reached the bay of Avacha and many lives would have been saved.

The sick were put ashore and miserable mud huts were built for them. Now that almost everyone was ill the comical pedant Steller became the strongest personality among them. He was a doctor and was an expert on herbal remedies and many other things. Under his supervision Bering was brought carefully ashore. He could no longer move. His legs were swollen and his frozen body showed almost no sign of life. To alleviate the icy frost in his legs he had them covered with sand. But his mind was clear to the end. He did not wish to rob his comrades of hope, but he himself, as some of his remarks indicate, considered the situation hopeless.

He died on 8 December and was buried, as Steller describes, 'with Protestant rites, near our hut, where he lies between his adjutants and two grenadiers.'

Sven Waxell now took over command. Still supported by Khitrovo, he succeeded in maintaining discipline among the men. In the course of the winter the survivors gradually realized that the wind had driven them to an uninhabited island, not to the mainland. This island now bears Bering's name. The climate there is not very severe and the winter not particularly cold, but almost all the survivors were ill with scurvy and completely exhausted. Many of them were near madness and some suffered temporary blindness. Steller's 'fauna' saved them from dying of starvation.

There were many marine animals there. The whole coast was seething with sea-otters. They ate the flesh of these animals and carefully collected the skins. Altogether the crew of the *St Peter* killed nine hundred sea-otters during the winter, as well as a number of sea-lions and 'sea-bears', a species of seal called *sivuch* or *kotik* by the Russians. They also hunted that curious animal which was discovered and described by Steller, and bore his name – 'Steller's sea-cow', *rhytina Stelleri* – until it was finally exterminated. This did not take long; the last sea-cow was killed in 1768.

But the real lords of this island were the stone-foxes, which barked like dogs and were therefore christened by the Russians *pestzy* ('little dogs'). They often had valuable bluish fur. Steller has a great deal to say about the foxes: 'They penetrated into our dwellings by day as well as by night and stole everything they could carry away, even things which were of no use to them, such as knives, sticks, sacks, shoes, stockings, and so on. When we were skinning an animal, it would often happen that we killed two or three foxes with knives in the process, because they tried to tear the flesh from our hands. . . . If we kept something on a pole to preserve it, they would undermine the pole so that it fell, or else one of them would climb the pole like a monkey and throw down whatever was on top with incredible skill and cunning. At night, when we were sleeping in the open, they would pull off our night-caps, gloves and beaver rugs.'

The *St Peter* was stuck so fast on the sandbank there could be no question of refloating it. Instead, Waxell had the ship dis-mantled and built a lugger of the same name from the pieces. This was Waxell's own idea and he put it into effect with great skill and ingenuity. In general, the services he rendered in bring-ing the survivors home were extremely valuable and they have rightly been emphasized in the most recent Soviet books.

The construction of the lugger took most of the summer. They set sail towards the west on 13 August and after four days sighted the coast of Kamchatka. Before leaving they erected a wooden cross over Bering's grave. The cross was also to serve as a sign of Russian sovereignty.

Of the seventy-seven members of the crew of the *St Peter*, forty-six returned to Kamchatka, and many of these died soon after landing. Apparently only Steller and little Waxell remained hale and hearty. They had not developed scurvy. After all he had gone through Steller still had enough strength left to busy himself with the exploration of Kamchatka.

CHIRIKOV'S VOYAGE TO AMERICA

Where was the *St Paul* all this time? She was drifting along not far from the *St Peter*. When Chirikov lost sight of Bering on 20 June, he too steered south, in accordance with instructions. But the very next day he turned east and after three weeks saw the first signs of land.

On 15 July, twenty-five days after being parted from her sister-ship, the *St Paul* arrived at a little island that lies close to the present Prince of Wales Island. This was America, which Chirikov thus sighted about a day before Bering. The boat sent to survey the coast returned with the news that there was no suitable anchorage to be seen, so the *St Paul* sailed on northward for two days and finally anchored off the island now known as Khikhagov. On 17 July one of the mates, Dementyev, rowed ashore with ten armed men to explore the country. Smoke had been seen rising, which meant that the region must be inhabited. They waited a long time for Dementyev to return and when, after six days, there was still no news of him, a second boat, containing the mate Savelyev and three men, was sent to look for him. This second boat did not return either. No light was ever thrown on this catastrophe, although Russian efforts to solve the mystery went on until 1820.

Chirikov had lost not only fifteen good men but also any possibility of landing, for he had no other small boats. He cruised to and fro for a few days and made signals, but the sea was growing rougher and the wind was driving the ship against the cliffs. Eventually he had to turn back. He sailed along the coast of Alaska and then along the Aleutians, taking much the same course that Bering had followed a few days before. He approached the island of Kodiak, where Bering had also been, and received a visit from an Aleutian, with whom he exchanged gifts. But he was no longer in a position to take on water or food. When the *St Paul* entered Avacha Bay on 8 October, he had lost twenty-one out of his crew of seventy-five. De Lisle died in the harbour before he could set foot on land.

Chirikov was carried ashore seriously ill. But by the spring he had recovered sufficiently to be able to stand, and he put to sea in search of Bering. He sailed to the Aleutians and reached the island of Attu, that is to say, he went much farther out from Kamchatka than Bering Island, to which he passed quite close. Bad weather forced him to turn back.

From Petropavlovsk he sailed to Okhotsk, and from there he went to Yeniseisk. He was seriously ill, probably with tuberculosis. Only a milder climate could have saved him, but he was not summoned to St Petersburg until four years later. There he was received in audience by the Tsarina Elisaveta Petrovna, who informed him that he had been promoted to captain-commander. He died two years later in Moscow.

Since Lomonosov's time, Chirikov's voyage has been regarded by Russian nautical experts as a masterpiece of navigation. It was certainly a more difficult undertaking than Bering's return trip, since the loss of the two boats had deprived Chirikov of the chance of renewing his water supplies and he had to make do with what he had taken on board in Kamchatka. In spite of this he lost only six men from scurvy. He succeeded in bringing his ship straight into the bay of Avacha, and the course steered by the *St Paul* shows considerably fewer zig-zags than the course of the *St Peter*.

THE CONQUEST OF THE ARCTIC COAST

We have not yet told the full story of the Great Expedition. As we know, it was also entrusted with the task of exploring the whole Arctic coast from the White Sea to Kamchatka and solving the problem of the north-east passage.

Several expeditions were equipped for this purpose. They were given specified periods in which to carry out their tasks, and these periods were lengthened if they were not long enough. Money was never refused, and there was no lack of men either, for young officers were glad to volunteer for the work.

In 1734 Lieutenant Dimitri Ovzyn sailed from the mouth of the Ob to that of the Yenisei, and in 1738 he and the boat-builder Koshelev succeeded in sailing up the Yenisei as far as Yeniseisk in a boat built by Koshelev at Tobolsk.

Because of his friendship with the son of the 'political criminal' Prince Dvolgorukov, Ovzyn was demoted to seaman and banished to Kamchatka. There he joined Bering. This young officer showed himself remarkably cool in the most difficult situation and he was the only one, except for Bering and Steller, who opposed the fateful decision to winter on Bering Island. On his return to Petropavlovsk he found a decree of the Senate reinstating him as an officer.

After the Yenisei it was the turn of the Taimyr peninsula. The coxswain Minin made three attempts in 1738–40 to sail round it from the west, but all three failed. In 1740 Minin did manage to reach latitude 75° 17′ north, and until recently this was regarded as the northern limit of old Russian voyages in the eastern Kara Sea. Minin probably shared this view, for he recorded the latitude on a memorial plaque which was found in 1932 by Soviet Arctic explorers.

Nordenskiöld, too, thought that his ship, the *Vega*, was the first to anchor off 'the northern tip of the old world' (on 19 August 1878). However, a discovery made by a Russian Arctic expedition on the eastern side of the Taimyr peninsula in 1940 proves that Russians sailed round Cape Chelyuskin at the beginning of the seventeenth century. Besides many articles of everyday use and coins, fishing and hunting equipment, glass beads and mirrors were found – typical adjuncts of a trading and hunting expedition.

In 1735, before Minin, Captain Vasily Pronchishchev had begun the assault on the Taimyr peninsula from the east, from the mouth of the Lena. He was accompanied on this trip by his wife, Natalia, the first woman in the history of polar exploration. The couple tried twice to circumnavigate the Taimyr peninsula and reached 77° 29' north, so that they were only a few minutes of latitude short of their goal, but the ice prevented them going any farther. Both husband and wife died from scurvy on the return voyage. Pronchishchev's companion, the coxwain Chelyuskin, returned to Yakutsk with the remainder of the crew.

In 1739, Chelyuskin and Captain Khariton Laptev repeated the attempt. When their ship was crushed in the ice they went on through the tundra with dog-sledges. They explored the peninsula separately, and after spending two winters there Chelyuskin reached the northernmost point of continental land on the globe in 1742.

In the first half of the nineteenth century Russian writers cast doubt on the truth of Chelyuskin's assertions; people were unwilling to believe that he had really conquered the Taimyr peninsula. These doubts were removed in 1851 by the publication of Chelyuskin's journal. Nordenskiöld later confirmed Chelyuskin's statements in every point. It was only then that Cape Chelyuskin .received its present name.

The other points in the programme of the Great Expedition concerned the strip of coast from the Lena to the Anadyr, that is, the extreme north-eastern tongue of Asia. In 1735 Lieutenant Lasinius sailed eastward from the Lena with a crew of forty-four; thirty-six of the party, including Lasinius himself, died from scurvy during the winter.

The project was taken over the next year by Dimitri Laptev, Khariton's cousin. Three years later he left the Lena for the second time, wintered twice in the ice, but could not reach the Bering Straits. As Deshnev's sea-route was a failure, he decided to try Stadukhin's land-route. This decision cost him another winter, but he finally reached the Anadyr, built two boats and sailed down the river to its mouth. He returned to Yakutsk by land.

When he arrived in St Petersburg in 1743, the 'Second Kamchatka Expedition' was already being wound up, since in the view of the Senate 'it had borne no fruit'. This was a superficial judgement by the men who now sat in the Senate in the place of Bering's old patrons and friends. However, the immense consequences of the expedition for Siberia, its economic development and Russian political expansion in the North Pacific could not be immediately apparent to everyone. Moreover, it is not difficult to understand the disappointment of uninstructed people when they suddenly heard that the question of the north-east sea passage still remained unanswered. Even Müller considered that one of the undisputed results of the Great Expedition was confirmation of the fact that navigation along the northern shores of Siberia was impossible because of the ice.

M. W. Lomonosov alone did not share this view. He believed in the possibility of finding a north-eastern sea-route to China and America 'to the greater glory of Russia, together with unparalleled gains', as he wrote in his memorandum.

Today, it looks as if both Müller and Lomonosov were right. No doubt the north-east passage could not be opened up with the ships and equipment available at that time. To that extent, Müller was perfectly right. But this did not mean that the problem would always be insoluble. Lomonosov represented the old Russian tradition which was embodied earlier in Gerasimov, Saltykov, Peter the Great and Kirillov, and which was fed by the imagination. Müller on the other hand remained true to the facts. But even he suspected what Lomonosov already knew: that the 'Second Kamchatka Expedition' was a beginning, not an end.

SCIENCE OPENS UP SIBERIA

A great deal of pioneering work in the exploration of Siberia was also done by that part of the Great Expedition which was commissioned 'to compile an account of the past and present and also of the natural resources'. We possess much valuable information about Siberia from earlier times – accounts of official journeys, reports from Cossacks about annexations and discoveries, and many maps – but the first explorer who went to Siberia for the express purpose of studying the country was a doctor of medicine called D. G. Messerschmidt, one of the most tragic figures in the history of the exploration of Siberia. After obtaining his doctor's degree at Halle in 1716, he went to Siberia at the request of Peter the Great. He travelled for many years in western Siberia, Daurien and parts of Mongolia. Among other things he discovered deposits of graphite, coal and rock-salt on the lower Tunguska. His special interest was ornithology.

In 1721–2 he was accompanied by a Swedish prisoner-of-war, an officer called Strahlenberg. This meeting not only provided Strahlenberg with intellectual stimulation; it also enabled him to become acquainted, through Messerschmidt, with earlier Russian maps of Siberia. A close friendship developed between the two Germans exiled in Siberia, for Strahlenberg was also a German: he had taken this name when he was elevated to the ranks of the Swedish nobility, but he had been born with the homely name of Tabbert during the Swedish occupation of Stralsund. An entry in Messerschmidt's diary gives us a clue to the intellectual climate in Siberia at that time. 'I parted,' wrote Messerschmidt in May 1722, 'from the pious, honest, industrious, loyal Tabbert, my only friend and support, with many tears. . . . I shall never forget dear Tabbert. . . .'

These words alone hint at an over-sensitive nature and a fear of loneliness. Three years later Messerschmidt returned to St Petersburg in a state of complete physical depression. He died there in 1735, poverty-stricken and forgotten by everyone. His manuscript notes, which filled thousands of sheets, remained unpublished.

Strahlenberg parted from Messerschmidt because his freedom had been restored by the Peace of Nystad. In 1723 he was received by the Tsar at Moscow and discussed his map with him. This conversation was not without influence on Peter's decision to have the Anian problem investigated by an expedition, for, as we know, Strahlenberg's map provided indirect evidence for Deshnev's voyage round the eastern tip of Siberia. Seven years later he published his map at Stockholm, together with a book on Russia in German, which was soon translated into various European languages.

This work contains many inaccuracies and a number of sheer errors, but all the same it possesses great value. Although he had never seen Deshnev's report, Strahlenberg presented the question whether there was a strip of water between Asia and America as answered in the affirmative. He had seen the importance of Atlasov's report and was the first to publish it. It was Strahlenberg who suggested that the Urals should be regarded as the boundary between Europe and Asia, basing his proposal on the differences '*in regno animali, vegetabili et minerali*' to be observed on each side of these mountains. Previously the Don had been regarded as the dividing line.

The scientific study of Siberia began with the academic group consisting of G. F. Müller, J. G. Gmelin, and de Lisle de la Croyère, who were later joined by G. W. Steller, S. P. Krasheninikov and J. E. Fischer. They were all very young when they first went to Siberia. Müller was twenty-eight, Gmelin was twenty-four and Krasheninikov was not quite twenty-two – a mere student.

They could not complain about lack of support from the government. Their journey has only to be compared with that of Messerschmidt, who received a yearly salary of 500 roubles and could not afford to employ a servant. These academics, on the other hand, each received a salary of 1,260 roubles and 40 *puds* (about 1,400 lb.) of flour a year as well, which was quite a fortune in Siberia. They were abundantly provided with everything they needed, including some cases of Hock. They were accompanied by a whole staff of students, who were to act as secretaries, clerks, artists, collectors and translators. Moreover, they were equipped with all kinds of letters of recommendation, and all the local authorities were warned of their coming and instructed to provide all possible assistance. It is easy to imagine what poor Messerschmidt would have accomplished with help like this.

Müller, Gmelin and Krasheninikov left St Petersburg with their followers on 8 August 1733. As a botanist, Gmelin was to deal with the natural history of Siberia, while Müller looked after the 'past and present'. They arrived in the following January at Tobolsk, where they found Bering. They went on to Irkutsk via Yeniseisk, and in August 1736 reached Yakutsk. In between they visited Daurien, returning by way of Lake Baikal.

Their toils and troubles were great, but so were their interest, enthusiasm and optimism. The mere fact that they had gone to Siberia of their own free will showed that they were optimists. Rich, wonderful, mysterious Siberia gripped them and cast its spell on them as it had on everyone else before them. The Siberia they saw was, of course, more or less untouched; valuable beavers wandered about Cossacks' kitchen-gardens and food was so cheap that, in Gmelin's words, 'everyone could lie down on a bed of ease'. At least, those were the impressions they received of western Siberia. The farther east they advanced, the more serious their mood became. They travelled across the prairie against the dark background of forest fires, they were devoured by mosquitoes in the daytime and by bugs at night, and at Yakutsk they found out what frost means in Siberia: 'a *voivode* there got frostbite in his hands, feet and nose on the way from his house to the chancellery.'

At Yakutsk, too, they had a piece of very bad luck; they lost everything they had collected and most of their manuscripts in a fire during the night of 8 November 1736. Things were not going too well in other ways either. Gmelin, a good-natured, somewhat corpulent Swabian, could think of nothing but returning to 'civilized lands', Müller, a morose Westphalian, still possessed his tremendous capacity for work but was already suffering the first depressing attacks of the hypochondria which was later to torment him for years. Both of them already shivered at the mere idea of Kamchatka. When the commandant of Okhotsk informed them that no ship was available to take them there, they decided to return to Irkutsk. They sent the 'student' Krasheninikov to Kamchatka, on the assumption that some sort of ship would soon be found for him.

The two scholars spent the next four years at Yeniseisk, whence they surveyed the region between the Ob and the Yenisei.

The arrival of Steller in January 1739 was a great joy to them. In the six weeks which they spent with him they recognized his exceptional talent. 'He will do the job better than I could myself,' wrote Gmelin to St Petersburg, delighted at being finally rid of the nightmare of Kamchatka. Steller set off for the east in March 1739, equipped with detailed instructions; for Müller and Gmelin, their hard Siberian life, in spiritual exile and physical discomfort, went on as before.

They were both dead tired, and gradually grew more and more irritable and difficult. There was constant friction with local authorities, and people were beginning to notice Müller's hypochondria. He started to suffer from insomnia and groundless worries. What had he been doing all these years? He had, in fact, been working harder than most convicts in Siberia. Nor had Gmelin been idle. His botanical work is still regarded as exemplary by experts today, and his *Journey Through Siberia* contains a host of valuable observations on natural history and geography.

But Müller's accomplishment was stupendous measured by ordinary standards. Surrounded by a crowd of secretaries and translators, for ten years he ploughed through the archives of Siberian chancelleries and monasteries, organized excavations, had drawings of the local costumes made, crept round old mines and caves, wrote memoranda for the local authorities on the natural resources and trading possibilities, and drew up for his colleagues instructions so detailed that in many cases they form complete scientific treatises. Müller's so-called 'portfolios' in the Russian archives have not been fully utilized even today.

The innumerable 'observations' which Müller sent to the Academy were themselves almost ready-made sections of the future *History*. He devoted the rest of his life to putting them together, and if he did not succeed in leaving behind him a rounded literary work, the part of the *History* which he published does embrace the whole course of events in Siberia from Yermak's expedition up to Müller's own time.

That is the Cyclopian background against which this athlete of historical scholarship stands before us. For Müller may certainly be described as a real scholar even though some later writers have tried to dismiss him as a mere compiler. This view is lacking in historical perspective. Those who hold it forget that Müller was the first man in Russia who tried to write history based on the facts, not on a preconceived scheme. To this extent he was certainly a 'compiler of facts'. But he was not an uncritical compiler; he always tried to get back to the original sources, and to distinguish the truth from legend or deliberate fiction. It is not surprising that he did not always succeed; sifting of this kind takes generations. Moreover, he could not be too objective, for at that time in Russia all history was official history and Müller himself was an 'imperial historiographer', a position which involved certain obligations. It goes without saying that, as a foreigner, he had to be particularly careful.

Müller was the first to investigate chancellery archives. He discovered the Remesov *History* at Tobolsk and made considerable use of it. He also utilized the authentic original reports of Deshnev, Khabarov and many others. In addition, he consulted private archives and in those of the Stroganovs at Solikamsk he found a mass of documents dealing with the preparations for Yermak's expedition. To illuminate the course of events he used oral tradition as well as the geographical, ethnographical and archaeological evidence which he had collected himself. The general picture of the Russian advance into Siberia which he drew still serves as a guide today. It says a good deal that Soviet editions of the works describe Müller as 'the father of Siberian history'.

We can hardly reproach Müller for seeing the history of Siberia as, in the first place, a political expansion and for being guided in his account of it by the idea of 'the advantage of the state'. This was not toadying to the Tsar; it simply reflects the intellectual climate of the age, the age of enlightened absolutism with its elevated conceptions of the interest of the state and reasons of state. It was not until fifty years after Müller's death that an attempt was made by the most important nineteenth-century historian of Siberia, P. A. Slovtzov, professor of philosophy at Tobolsk, to present the history of Siberia from the point of view of sociology and economic geography as an example of colonization by a whole people, and even Slovtzov dedicated his history of Siberia to the memory of Müller.

Müller and Gmelin returned to St Petersburg in February 1743, after living in Siberia for ten years; during this period they had travelled about 23,000 miles. In 1747 Gmelin went to Germany on leave and never returned. Müller stayed in Russia. He spent the evening of his life in charge of the Foreign Office archives. He became a privy councillor, was knighted, and for some time was rector of Moscow University. Catherine II knew him and valued him highly. She always summoned him when she went to Moscow; this happened seven times, as Müller himself proudly tells us. The English clergyman William Coxe, who later wrote a very well-known book about Russian discoveries in the Pacific, visited Müller at Moscow in 1778. 'His memory is still amazing,' wrote Coxe, 'and his precise knowledge of the smallest details in the Russian chronicles is simply incredible. ... His collection of documents and manuscripts is priceless; they are all kept in the most careful order, arranged in several volumes according to their titles. ...'

Shortly before his death Müller expressed the wish to be appointed governor of a remote Russian province. He died in 1783 at the age of seventy-eight.

KRASHENINIKOV AND STELLER

The exploration of Kamchatka forms a separate chapter in the history of the 'Great Expedition'. Müller and Gmelin had entrusted it to the young 'student' S. P. Krasheninikov. Their assumption that he would find ways and means of getting to Kamchatka turned out to be justified. Krasheninikov arrived in Kamchatka all right, but only just. On the way the old *Fortuna* started to leak. The cargo and the passengers' personal baggage had to be thrown overboard and Krasheninikov stepped ashore on 28 October 1737 'with nothing but the shirt he wore'.

The two academicians were right. Kamchatka would not have suited them at all. Not only had Krasheninikov lost his clothes, books and instruments; for two years he did not even receive his salary – a hundred roubles a year! – because communications with St Petersburg were cut. In spite of this he did not waste a single day. He toured the peninsula in every direction, mainly on foot, and carried out systematic investigations, assisted no doubt by Müller's 'observations' as well as by his instructions.

Like other explorers of Siberia at that time, he was interested in more or less everything. The result of his labours was thus a real encyclopedia of Kamchatka, whose historical parts are as impressive as the sections dealing with geography. His own special interest was ethnography, and in this field he excelled all his colleagues.

Krasheninikov's interest in ethnography had only been awoken in Siberia; by training he was a classical scholar. He also filled the many gaps in his scientific knowledge in Siberia, where the academicians' library was at his disposal and Gmelin gave him lessons.

To arrive at a just estimate of Krasheninikov's character and his somewhat pathetic position in the world of scholarship we must take into account his lowly origin, which put obstacles in the way of his advancement. He came from a social environment devoid of any intellectual tradition; his father was a farmer and soldier. At his entry into the Academy he had to conceal his origin because as 'a common person' he would not have been admitted. It is noteworthy that even the Germans did not treat him as a colleague. For example, Müller protested strongly at Gmelin's wasting his time giving geography lessons to the 'student'. Müller tried to hinder Krasheninikov's later rise to assistant and professor with every means at his disposal, and the words which he wrote as an epitaph to the dead author in the preface to Krasheninikov's book on Kamchatka were probably the tribute he had to pay his own conscience. 'He was one of those,' writes Müller, 'who are distinguished by neither their origin nor fortune's favours, and who rise by their own qualities and achievements, who receive nothing from their forbears and may be described as the authors of their own success.'

Like most of his colleagues, Krasheninikov had seriously damaged his health in Siberia. His *Description of the Land of Kamchatka* was published at St Petersburg in 1755, some months after his death. This modest man thus did not live to see the world-wide success of his book; in 1764 the English edition appeared, in 1766 the German edition, in 1767 the French translation, in 1770 the Dutch translation, and in 1786 the second Russian edition. The third Russian edition followed in 1818 and the fourth appeared in 1949.

Steller arrived at Bolsheretsk in 1740, having come by the usual route through Yeniseisk, Irkutsk, Yakutsk and Okhotsk. From Irkutsk, where he was stationed for a whole year, he crossed Lake Baikal to the Bargusin mountains and brought back a large collection of botanical and mineralogical specimens. He sent them all straight back to the Academy at St Petersburg with his reports. This led to a breach with his superior, Gmelin, which could only be healed later. However, the first thing that Steller did in Kamchatka was to demand that Krasheninikov should hand over everything – his manuscripts, collections of specimens and notes – to him, Steller, the assistant. It did not occur to Steller that by doing this he was robbing a scholar of his intellectual property.

After returning from the fateful voyage on board the *St Peter*, Steller set about exploring Kamchatka with undiminished energy. In May–June 1742 he travelled to the south of the peninsula and visited the first three Kurile Islands. This journey produced some interesting geological finds, and, spurred on by success, he planned an expedition to the north, to the valley of the Kolyma, where he hoped to find a mammoth in the permanently frozen ground. At the end of August he went from Bolsheretsk to Nishne-Kamchatsk, on foot, because there was no snow on the ground and dog-sledges could therefore not be used. On the way he lived on fish, herbs and berries, like the Kamchadales. From Nishne-Kamchatsk he went on farther north to the River Olyutora with dog-sledges.

Altogether Steller spent two years and eight months in Kamchatka. His travels in Kamchatka would alone be sufficient to assure him of an honourable place in the history of the exploration of Siberia, but they are put in the shade by his work in Alaska and on Bering Island. His heroic enthusiasm for scientific research was boundless. Gmelin did not exaggerate when he wrote in the preface to his *Flora Siberica*: 'Steller was a born naturalist. . . . He was a man who never avoided difficulties and dangers; on the contrary he sought out work, toil and danger and actually despised the pleasures and enjoyments of this life. . . .'

Like Krasheninikov, he was very interested in the natives. As the officers of Bering's expedition had been given special powers *vis-à-vis* the Russian authorities in Kamchatka, Steller too was regarded to some extent as a government official. This opened up various possibilities for him. For example, he set up a school in Bolsheretsk, baptized some of the Kamchadales, and on one occasion he even freed a group of natives who had been arrested on suspicion of being involved in a conspiracy. Naturally he soon quarrelled with all the local authorities. He sent complaints to St Petersburg and his opponents did the same. On his way home Steller was stopped in western Siberia and sent back to Irkutsk. Meanwhile, however, the affair had been cleared up at St Petersburg and all charges against him were dropped. News of this reached him at the town of Tara.

He immediately turned round and hastened to Tobolsk. There he received a warm welcome from Archbishop Antonius, a pupil of his old patron, Feofan Prokopovich. But Steller was already ill with the 'evil fever' which had already carried off so many in Siberia. His condition grew worse from hour to hour, but he travelled on. He died on 12 November 1746 in the town of Tyumen, at the age of thirty-seven. The stories which circulated for some time in Germany about his miserable death, without attention or medical help, do not correspond with the facts: he was treated by two doctors, who did all they could for him with the facilities available in a small Siberian town.

Steller left behind a series of specialist works, mostly on zoological subjects, which were all published after his death. His particular speciality was marine animals. Since Gmelin's *Flora* and *Journey Through Siberia*, enthusiastic acclaim for Steller's character and work has never ceased. His gifts as an analyst and systematizer, combined with a capacity for making big syntheses, certainly border on genius. But his character was not so unequivocal as many of his admirers imagine. As a man he was unhappy, unbalanced and problematical; his judgements were egocentric and unjust. He did not shrink from political denunciations, probably under the influence of alcohol. The only man in the Far East with whom he was really friendly was Skornyakov-Pisarev, the commandant of Okhotsk, an informer of the worst sort, who bombarded the government with complaints about Bering and his colleagues.

But the most curious characteristic of this problematical personality was his cruelty to animals. It was a complete riddle to all his companions. Krasheninikov relates how Steller experimented with sea-bears, putting their eyes out and then provoking the others to attack the blind one. A senseless fight then started in which the blinded animal was naturally at a disadvantage. Steller watched the spectacle from a small hill 'for some hours'. Steller himself tells of his war with the foxes in his *Description of Bering Island*: 'The more we killed and cruelly martyred for revenge before the eyes of the rest, letting them go half-skinned, without eyes, ears or tail and half-roasted, the more spiteful and bold the rest became.' This all sounds extremely odd. A man like that could not be happy.

A good deal was said in Europe at the time with the aim of putting the rôle of the Russian government in a bad light. The government had provoked this by making the expedition a state secret. It could naturally not remain a secret, but news about it was distorted and criticism became malicious. In reality the government may have made mistakes but it was not lacking in good will. In such enterprises the best measure of good will is always money and from this point of view the government's attitude was irreproachable. 'Money was never refused,' wrote Sven Waxell, and this was the truth. Quite apart from the assistance rendered by the population by way of goods and manpower, the expenditure in cash, up to and including 1742, came to 361,000 roubles; expressed in terms of modern purchasing power, this sum is equivalent to over three and a half million gold roubles. In addition, there were the expenses involved in winding up the expeditions. In general, the participants were treated generously. For example, Bering's wife received her husband's whole salary, a gratuity of five thousand roubles and a pension of two thousand roubles for the rest of her life. Bering's personal belongings were sold by the government in Petropavlovsk and the proceeds, which amounted to a thousand roubles, were sent to his widow. All in all, these payments assured the family of a life free from financial worries.

As for the treatment they received as individuals, Bering's three sons were privileged to enter the cadet academy and the family was obviously in a good social position, for Bering's only daughter married a member of the aristocracy, Baron von Korff, chief of the St Petersburg police. All the other members of the expedition were promoted after their return and they or their dependents received pensions and cash gratuities. Waxell was promoted to captain-commander and given a quiet and well-paid post at Kronstadt. After his death, his three sons, all naval officers, were elevated to the ranks of the hereditary nobility. Khitrovo died in St Petersburg with the rank of admiral, and the academic members of the expeditions ended their days as professors, privy councillors and the holders of important decorations.

V

RUSSIAN AMERICA

————◆◆◆◆————

THE OPENING UP
OF THE ALEUTIAN ISLANDS

THE MEMBERS of Bering's expedition had brought back with them not only scurvy and depressing memories but also sea-otter skins. The value of these skins was appreciated at once by the fur-dealers. Even before Chirikov had arrived in St Petersburg new ships were being built at Okhotsk and in Kamchatka. Men and capital streamed to Kamchatka. Those in a position to do so equipped their own ships; those who were not rich enough set up companies with others. Five years after Bering's death fifteen such companies were active, and after another five years there were twenty-five of them. By the end of the eighteenth century eighty-five expeditions had already been sent out to America by forty-two companies.

One did not have to go to a nautical college before sailing the ocean in those days. Anyone who dared to be a captain could be one. In 1743 Sergeant Yemelian Basov appointed himself captain. He took with him one of the members of the crew of the *St Peter* as pilot, on the assumption that he must know the way. Basov first sailed to Bering Island, where he spent the winter; the next year he visited Copper Island, then sailed on farther. He saw many of the Aleutian Islands, but could not land because of bad weather. He returned to Petropavlovsk in 1746 with a good haul of furs.

The very next year, Basov equipped a fresh expedition, this time in conjunction with a merchant called Trapesnikov. Another merchant, Chuprov, acted as leader of this expedition, and an experienced sailor called Nevodchikov, who had been to America with Bering, was appointed captain. Chuprov and Nevodchikov reached the first group of islands in the Aleutians, which Chirikov had also seen but taken for the American continent. Nevodchikov made a map of the islands of Attu, Agattu and Semikhi; so he and Chuprov may be regarded as their discoverers.

Chuprov's party had behaved badly on the islands and their cruelty to the natives led soon after their return to legal proceedings and the punishment of the guilty. But their haul of furs was worth 112,000 roubles and this spurred on enterprising business men in Kamchatka. In the next few years one expedition after the other was dispatched to the Aleutians, with the result that the individual groups of islands were explored and mapped. Many of these trips were extremely successful from a business point of view; one merchant returned with over two thousand sea-otter skins.

Orders were issued at this time that the natives were to be treated with care and no acts of cruelty committed. In point of fact, the hunters tried unfailingly to win over the natives by kindness. Andreyan Tolstykh, for example, used these sensible methods and they brought him more furs than his competitors obtained by brutality. But to achieve their full effect humane methods demand time – Tolstykh's expedition had lasted four years – and most of the fur-trappers had no time to be humane. Nor is there usually much charity in evidence when men are half-crazed from hunger. But the basic cause of the brutality was the difficulty which the private merchants found in controlling the sailors and hunters whom they had engaged. On foreign soil, with the sea between themselves and the authorities, they tried to make sure of their share of the spoils as quickly as they could. The government was a long way off and its orders were usually not obeyed. Three years after the appearance of the first hunter on the islands of Umnak and Unalaska, open warfare broke out between the Russians and the Aleutian islanders.

In the summer of 1763 three ships, all belonging to the same company, arrived at Umnak together. The head of the company was Nikifor Trapesnikov, a pioneer of the Aleutian fur trade who had helped to finance the expeditions of Basov and Tolstykh. His ships were commanded by Captains Drushinin, Korovin and Medvednikov. Off Umnak they met another Russian ship commanded by Stepan Glotov, who was returning to 'his' island for the second time.

The three captains went on to Unalaska and each set to work on his own. The islanders gave them a friendly welcome. Drushinin, who was pleasantly surprised by the nature of this reception, divided his men into three groups, sending two of them into the interior of the island to hunt and trade and himself remaining behind with the third near the coast. Drushinin's group was attacked by the islanders and only four men escaped with their lives. When these four had fought their way to the shore they found that their ship had been burnt and the watch on board killed. There was no trace of the other two parties and neither of them ever returned.

Captain Korovin made the same mistake as Drushinin. He trusted the islanders and was cut off and besieged. When he had held out for more than three months the four survivors of Drushinin's group managed to join him. Korovin finally succeeded in reaching his ship, but he had to fight a night battle with several dozen Aleutian boats before he could manage to weigh anchor. His ship was wrecked on the rocks off Umnak; he and sixteen of his crew were saved. After searching for a month he found the remains of a camp on the shore and the third captain, Medvednikov, dead in the midst of the corpses of his nineteen companions. There was no sign of his ship.

Korovin set about building a winter camp, expecting a fresh attack at any moment. Fortunately for him Glotov returned again to Unalaska at this time. Meanwhile he had sailed on much farther and reached Kodiak. He was the first seafarer to set foot on this island.

Autumn had now arrived and they decided to winter on Unalaska. One can imagine how Korovin longed for revenge, but Glotov was against it. At this point a new ship, *The Holy Apostles Peter and Paul*, sailed up, manned by a fresh party of hunters and commanded by the doughty Captain Ivan Solovyev. It is only fair to emphasize that at first Solovyev was not out for revenge; he repeatedly tried to come to an agreement with the islanders, on condition that they returned their booty. But his proposal was answered with another attack and a new fight broke out which ended in the complete defeat of the islanders.

James Cook, who visited Unalaska fourteen years later, found peace and order there and a fairly numerous native population. 'If there was cruelty there to start with,' he wrote in 1778, 'its beneficent results are its best excuse; at present the two races live in perfect harmony with each other.' The two opposing sides had paid dearly for this harmony.

Thus in the thirty years after Bering's second expedition the Aleutians were taken over by Russian merchants. The maps they made complemented the provisional information supplied by Bering and Khirikov (or rather, Waxell-Khitrovo and Chirikov) and provided the basis for the Russian claim to have been first in the field in the exploration of the northern Pacific and the north-west coast of America. The Russians' work was later to some extent corrected and completed by Cook.

A striking characteristic of Russian enterprise in these regions at that period was their purely private nature. The usual arrangement was that the merchants would promise to levy a tribute of furs from the islanders; the government contented itself with occasionally sending along a minor official as a supervisor. It did not itself even raise the question of tribute from the Aleutians, but the merchants sent in the tithe usual in Siberia and also sent the best furs as presents to St Petersburg. It is not difficult to understand why they did this. To send out a ship a licence had to be obtained; and to build and equip it, and usually to man it as well, every enterprise needed assistance from the government. Competition among the merchants, of whom there were dozens, was inevitable, and every one of them did all he could to make himself useful and pleasant to the government and to present his own private business as a matter of concern to the state. Hence the levying of tribute and the reports and maps which they laid before the commandants of Kamchatka and Okhotsk on their return, and which the latter were pleased to forward to St Petersburg with their own comments and suggestions. It was also quite a good thing if a governor of Siberia could present the empress on her birthday with half a dozen newly discovered islands, as D. I. Chicherin did after Tolstykh's expedition.

What happened in Kamchatka was the normal process of accumulation of capital and natural selection among the entrepreneurs. The fur trade was eventually dominated by a few groups with plenty of capital, each group consisting usually of two or three merchants. In the list of businessmen active in Kamchatka in the seventies of the eighteenth century, certain names keep recurring: those of Grigory Shelikhov and Ivan Golikov from Rylsk, three Panovs, probably brothers from Totyma, Kholodilov from the same town, Lebedev-Lastochkin from Yakutsk and a few others. It may well be that one or two of them were already toying with the idea of a fur monopoly in the Aleutians. Monopolies had long been known in Russia; some were held by the state, others were farmed out to individuals. Even in the reign of Catherine, who was opposed to monopolies, the state leased a monopoly in the production and sale of vodka to private persons; the best known of these in Siberia, Ivan Golikov, was eagerly engaged in the Kamchatka–America business. The idea of a monopoly was at the back of men's minds. Everyone knew that in 1749 the Empress Elizabeth's favourite, General-Field Marshal Count P. I. Shuvalov, had been granted, in addition to the privilege of exporting wood, a monopoly in the catching of marine animals in the Arctic Ocean. Many of the younger and more astute merchants realized that they were wasting their resources by competing against each other.

HESITATION AND FUMBLING

The question naturally arises, what was the government doing at this time? It was usually quick to seize the initiative and take control itself. The answer is that it was continuing Peter's struggle for the two seas in the west and its resources did not extend to activity in the Pacific as well. During the thirty years in question there was a war with Sweden, the Seven Years War, four years of fighting against Bar's Polish confederation and the start of a war with Turkey. Only at the beginning of this period was the memory of Peter's testament still alive. In 1753 it was even decided to resuscitate to some extent Bering's second expedition and to send some ships down the Amur to Japan and America. This project was never carried out, but its author, F. I. Soimonov, was appointed governor of Siberia and during the seven years of his tenure of office a number of new enterprises were undertaken in the Far East. The results were not very striking, however, and in fact during this period the merchants accomplished far more on their own account. The government showed no intention of taking official possession of the American islands; it confined itself to encouraging private enterprise. For example, Glotov and Bechevin were presented with gold and exempted from handing over 10 per cent of their furs to the state. On the whole, St Petersburg had a very vague idea of the situation in the new Pacific 'possessions', and so eventually the government decided to clarify the whole question of its new subjects and their obligations in the way of tribute. This was among the tasks given to the expedition of Captains Krenitzyn and Levashov.

This expedition is of particular interest because it was based on a grandiose plan drawn up by M. W. Lomonosov, who had once again raised the question of the north-east passage. Lomonosov proceeded on the assumption that the ocean was free of ice in the high latitudes. He now suggested two simultaneous expeditions: one was to sail north-west from Spitzbergen and steer across the North Pole to the Bering Straits, while the other was to steer from the Bering Straits towards the North Pole. The two expeditions were supposed to meet half-way.

In pursuance of this plan Captain W. I. Chichagov's expedition was sent out to explore the north-west passage. Chichagov made two attempts, in 1765 and 1766, to circumnavigate Greenland, but on each occasion he was forced to turn back by the ice. He lost eight men on these two voyages. The other expedition had a far worse time. The original plan was abandoned and the aim restricted to exploring the Aleutians and regularizing the payment of tribute. Captain Krenitzyn's first attempt in 1766 came to a most unfortunate end; of the four ships with which he put to sea from Okhotsk, he lost three.

Two years later Krenitzyn and Levashov made another attempt. They were separated by a storm; Levashov wintered on the island of Unalaska and Krenitzyn on Umnak, whence he also explored the coast of Alaska. During this winter the two captains lost thirty-six men from scurvy, among them the brave Stepan Glotov, the discoverer of Umnak, Unalaska and Kodiak. The two parties joined up again in the spring of 1769, but on the return journey Captain Krenitzyn was drowned in the River Kamchatka. Altogether the expedition lost seventy of its original one hundred and eighty-eight members.

Krenitzyn and Levashov brought back with them fresh geographical information, but so far as the natives were concerned the expedition was a failure. Complete anarchy continued to reign in the collection of the tribute of furs. There were many voluntary collectors, but the treasury did not always receive what it should have. The methods and times of collection were subject to no control. The tribute also lacked any legal basis, for the annexation had never been officially announced in Russia or communicated to other countries. Not until 1770 was a decree passed forbidding the collection of tribute without the express authority of the government, and then the intended proclamation of the incorporation of the American islands into the empire was postponed again and again. The government continued to hesitate and to remain content with a cautious probing of America.

There were reasons for this hesitant attitude. First of all, in the government's view, the islands were of no economic importance. The original interest in trade with the supposed neighbour 'on the other side' soon declined. America had been found all right, but not the neighbours. There remained the Aleutian tribute, with which the merchants of Kamchatka continued to try to tempt the government. But in the second half of the eighteenth century furs had long ceased to play the rôle in the Russian official economy which they had played a hundred years before, when they had been almost the only source of currency. Russia now exported many other things, including ore and even the finished product, iron. She was also mining gold and silver in her own territory. The tribute which came from and by way of Kamchatka did not even cover the cost of administering the region.

Finally, St. Petersburg had no clear idea of the strategic significance of Kamchatka and the America coast opposite. It was realized, of course, that the Aleutians formed a bridge between Asia and America. But their strategic position in the North Pacific was not grasped, because the Russians had no foothold on the American continent and no contact with any neighbour there. Even Kamchatka, which had long been an integral part of the empire, had not yet attained the political significance which only danger from outside can confer by giving strategic importance to a half-forgotten frontier region. This transformation was brought about in Kamchatka by a highly dramatic event, which marked the beginning of a new epoch in the northern Pacific.

KAMCHATKA BECOMES WORLD-FAMOUS

In 1768 some of the Polish nobility, united in the so-called Confederation of Bar, rebelled against their king, Stanislaus Poniatovsky, who was no more than a tool in the hands of the Russians. The consequent Russian intervention ended in the first partition of Poland. Most of the captured confederates were sent to Siberia and those of them who committed any further offence, such as attempting to escape, were dispatched to Kamchatka. Two officers who arrived there in this fashion were the half Polish, half Hungarian Count Benyowszky and the Swedish Major Wijnbladh. The place of residence assigned to them was the 'fortress' of Bolsheretsk, and here Benyowszky saw an opportunity to escape which he proceeded to utilize with tremendous energy and audacity. The circumstances of this escape throws a great deal of light on the situation in Kamchatka in those days.

The 'fortress and port' of Bolsheretsk was a small settlement with a simple church, a house for the commandant, his office with four storehouses alongside it, twenty-three 'merchants' shops', that is, wooden sheds for the storage of furs, and forty-one scattered farmhouses. The fortifications consisted of an old moat, into which the inhabitants threw all their rubbish. Seventy Cossacks and their families formed the garrison. Three-quarters of this garrison were away most of the time; the Cossacks went off to hunt and to collect the tribute of furs from the Kamchadales. The commandant of Bolsheretsk was Captain Grigory Nilov, a good-natured old Army officer 'with a weakness for drinking'. This masterly strategist was in charge not only of Bolsheretsk but also of the whole peninsula.

Benyowszky soon won Nilov's complete confidence; he even went off on official trips on Nilov's behalf. This enabled him to become familiar with the general situation and to meet a number of different people. There were Russian political exiles in Kamchatka at this period, most of them intelligent nobles and bureaucrats, personal opponents of the 'usurper' Catherine. However, Benyowszky succeeded in creating a broader social basis for his conspiracy. At Bolsheretsk there was the crew of an old schooner, which had been sent out from Okhotsk by the merchant Kholodilov to America, but had only just managed to reach Bolsheretsk. The crew refused to sail on to the Aleutians in this old tub. Nilov locked up some of the mutineers and threatened the rest with various punishments; in short, he sided with the 'capitalists'. Benyowszky, on the other hand, scented an opportunity to escape and tested the men's feelings. They declared themselves ready to help and to man a suitable ship.

A ship soon turned up, the galliot *St Peter*, which belonged to the government and plied between Okhotsk and Bolsheretsk. Her captain, an experienced seaman, had long been a malcontent and put his ship at Benyowszky's disposal. Two more young seamen, the boatswains Bocharov and Ismaylov, joined the conspiracy, but when Ismaylov saw which way the wind was blowing he tried to warn Nilov at the last moment.

Nilov was also tipped off by someone else as well and although he was unwilling to listen to 'old women's gossip' he decided to question his favourite. This was the signal for the revolt. In the night of 26 April 1771 the conspirators broke into Nilov's house, murdered Nilov and elected Benyowszky commandant. The very next day they began to load the *St Peter* with food and furs, and on 12 May they set sail for Japan. On board the ship were seven women and sixty-three men, including one Aleutian, a Koryak and three Kamchadales.

The *St Peter* sailed south past the Kurile Islands, touched the coasts of Japan and Formosa, and on 12 September 1771 dropped anchor in the port of Macao. There Benyowszky sold the ship and its cargo of furs. With part of the proceeds he paid for passages on a French ship, which took him and his companions on to Mauritius and finally to Lorient in France.

The appearance of a group of Russian political *émigrés* in France – the first political refugees from Russia ever to reach the west – aroused a great deal of attention. Relations between France and Russia were poor at the time. Benyowszky was welcomed and fêted everywhere. He gave long talks in the political salons to specially selected audiences, which included members of the government and ambassadors of foreign powers, about the ease with which Formosa and Kamchatka could be conquered. The Russian envoy reported all this at once to St Petersburg, adding that a rumour was current that the French government was going to put a frigate at Benyowszky's disposal for the voyage to Kamchatka.

St Petersburg had already had news of the events in Kamchatka. According to the inhabitants of Bolsheretsk, Benyowszky had promised to return soon and take them all over to California. It was particularly noted in St Petersburg that some natives had left their country with Benyowszky. All this put Kamchatka in a new light.

In the summer of 1773 some of the refugees from Kamchatka called on the Russian ambassador in Paris, asking for pardon and permission to return to Russia. Catherine agreed at once, and seventeen men returned. They were allowed to reside wherever they liked in Russia and only a few went back to Kamchatka, among them the boatswain Bocharov, who later made his name as a seaman, like his friend Ismaylov. Ismaylov became known internationally through Captain Cook, who held a long conversation with him on Unalaska in 1778. The two men exchanged geographical information to their mutual satisfaction.

Benyowszky had made Kamchatka famous and exposed its weakness to the whole world. It was suddenly realized at St Petersburg that Kamchatka was completely unprotected and that anyone who obtained possession of it could deny Siberia access to the sea and perhaps even march into Siberia. It was decided to strengthen Kamchatka's defences. After Cook's visit the seat of the commander-in-chief was moved from Bolscheretsk to Petropavlovsk and poor Nilov's residence lost its former rank of 'capital'.

In the effort to make Kamchatka capable of resistance, Nilov's successor, Boehm, even formed the plan of fortifying the island of Urup – one of Kuriles, well on the way to Japan – and founding a Russian colony there which could supply Petropavlovsk with corn. Whether this was Boehm's own idea or not is a question that must remain unanswered; at any rate, an expedition was equipped and, led by Antipin and Shebalin, it levied tribute from some of the Kurile Islands. In the same year the natives of the Kuriles, the Ainus, known by the Russians at that time as *mokhnatye kuriltzy* ('hairy Kurilers'), were released from paying tribute by a decree of Catherine's; but Antipin and Shebalin did not know that.

Just at this time the Spaniards began to move northwards from southern California. In 1769 the *visitador* José de Galvez came to Mexico from Madrid. When he had assessed the situation for himself on the spot, he decided to take counter-measures against the Russian advance and to move the Spanish missions and garrisons as far north as possible. People in California already felt threatened by Russia, although the Russians had so far gone no farther than Unalaska. The *visitador* sent two ships to the north from Mexico, and two land expeditions as well. As many Franciscan missionaries accompanied these expeditions the whole enterprise was known as the 'Expedición Sacra'. A mission was set up in Monterey and in 1771 a ship commanded by Captain Juan Pérez visited San Francisco bay.

The expedition found no traces of the Russians, but this only made them seem more dangerous. If only the Spaniards could have seen the ships which the Russians used for their ocean voyages at this time, and what their 'bastion' in Kamchatka was really like! 'Monterey will soon be a flourishing Spanish colony,' wrote a contemporary, 'but even this will not protect the Californian coast against an attack by the Muscovites, for there are plenty of harbours besides Monterey where they could gain a foothold.' Hence other expeditions soon followed.

All these undertakings were backed by the power of Spain. Operations like this were watched attentively in England, and the Russians now began to hear of them too. However, what gave St Petersburg a good deal more to think about was the appearance of Captain Cook in Alaskan waters. Cook's official task was to discover the north-west passage and eventually the north-east passage as well. This alone meant that England was in the process of moving a good deal closer to Kamchatka and the American islands. In fact, Captain King did land on the southern shore of the present Cook Inlet in Alaska, and at one spot, which he named Point Possession, he declared the surrounding area to be a possession of the British crown.

Nothing was known of this in Kamchatka. When Cook's *Resolution*, under the command of Clerke, appeared off Petropavlovsk on 29 April 1779, ten weeks after the great explorer's tragic death – the *Discovery* under King arrived two days later – the Russians' surprise was so great that it turned into panic. The garrison was alerted, two old cannon were wheeled into position and the inhabitants began to flee. They thought that Benyowszky had come with the French.

When the truth was learned, the English were given a hearty welcome which King could not praise highly enough in his report. Nevertheless, just when the expedition was dropping anchor in the bay of Avacha again after another trip to the Bering Straits, with the corpse of its second leader, Clerke, on board, a detachment of infantry with two small cannon came sailing up from Okhotsk. It was not difficult to guess the meaning of this. 'It seemed,' wrote King, 'that our visit had drawn the attention of the Russian authorities in Siberia to the unprotected situation of this spot; the good commandant told me, with a shrug of his shoulders, that other nations which were not at all welcome could find their way there as easily as we had done.' It was now realized in Russia that two good well-armed ships were sufficient to shake Russian power in Kamchatka and America. No one realized it more clearly than Grigory Ivanovich Shelikhov.

SHELIKHOV'S 'FATHERLY KINDNESS'

Shelikhov was born in 1747 at Rylsk in the district of Kursk, a region that is famous for its nightingales and race-horses and has little to do with oceans. But Shelikhov, who seems to have come from a line of small traders, had an urge to see the world. It is not known precisely how he reached Siberia, but at any rate he turned up in Nishne-Kamchatsk in 1775, that is, after Benyowzsky and before Cook. A little while before he had married the young widow of a Siberian merchant, who brought a small dowry with her. It may be assumed that this formed the capital with which he started. But the unanimous verdict of all who knew his wife, Natalia Alexeyevna, is that she was exceptionally brave and clever, and that is the best dowry any man can receive.

Shelikhov built his first ship, the *St Paul*, in co-operation with the Kamchatka merchant Alin; it was sent out to the Aleutians in 1776. Without waiting for the *St Paul* to return, Shelikhov equipped another ship, the *St Nicholas*, this time with a new partner, the Yakutsk merchant Lebedev-Lastochkin, and sent it off in 1777 under the command of the 'Siberian nobleman' Antipin to the Kurile Islands, whence Antipin was to start trade with Japan. No trading with Japan took place, but the Ainus were forced to hand over plenty of furs. In the following year the partners sent out their representative, Shebalin, in the brigantine *Natalia* to assist Antipin, whose ship had run aground on the island of Urup. Antipin and Shebalin visited Hokkaido, exacted tribute from the Ainus there and returned in 1782.

These were Shelikhov's first attempts. At first he was over-shadowed by his more powerful partner, but he was there all the same and numerous documents now make it clear that the 'Kurile idea' was his very own. He clung to it throughout his life. It deserves to be emphasized that he was the first to think in modern terms and to propose the annexation and fortification of the Kuriles. He is always returning to the theme in his later letters and memoranda, and the empress's Commission for Commerce reported in 1788 as follows: 'He has already taken steps to build a fort and harbour on one of the Kurile Islands in order to begin trading with Japan and China when a favourable opportunity arises.' It subsequently emerged that it was Shelikhov's particular method to build small private 'fortresses'.

Shelikhov hardly needed any encouragement from outside at this time. He worked like a maniac and sent out one ship after another without waiting for the results of previous voyages. On the River Urak near Okhotsk he built a proper shipyard; what this meant only becomes apparent when one thinks of the enormous transport difficulties between Yakutsk and Okhotsk, not to mention the fact that at that time every bit of iron had to be carried right across Siberia from the Urals. It is remarkable how gaily this calculating merchant, who was greedy for profits, risked his own and Natalia's money, and that of his partners as well. Even before he had got his first big haul of furs safely home from the Aleutians in the *St Paul* in 1780 he had sent out another five, if not six, ships. All these ships returned with rich cargoes, but Shelikhov's luck as a businessman is reflected in the fact that two of them were wrecked on the Russian coast on the way back, yet their whole cargoes were saved and brought in undamaged!

These ships did not arrive back until 1784 and at first all Shelikhov had at his disposal was his share in the seventy-five thousand roubles brought in by the cargo of the *St Paul* in 1780. Nevertheless, in 1781, he equipped a fresh and extremely risky expedition. His first partner, Alin, had no share in this project; probably it seemed too uncertain and pioneering, for Shelikhov wanted to send the ship not to the Aleutians but to the north, in the direction of the Bering Straits, to find the places where the Aleutian sea-otters probably bred. So Shelikhov looked round for a new partner and found him in Lebedev-Lastochkin, who had plenty of capital. With Lastochkin's assistance he dispatched the *St George* to the north. He had even been lucky enough to find a really good captain, the 'mate' Gavrila Pribylov, who discovered on his voyage a whole group of islands which is famous even today for its marine animals and bears its discoverer's name.

Pribylov's voyage of discovery became one of the most successful enterprises of its kind every undertaken in the North Pacific. He was away for eight years and the haul he brought back with him broke all records: two thousand beavers, forty thousand sea-otters, six thousand blue foxes, seventeen tons of walrus-teeth and eight-and-a-half tons of fishbone. Altogether the value of this cargo amounted to 258,018 roubles. It is interesting to recall at this point that the whole tribute from Kamchatka and the Koryak territory amounted at this time to about eight thousand roubles a year.

This expedition made Shelikhov a real millionaire and the leading merchant, not only in Okhotsk or Petropavlovsk, but in Irkutsk as well. But this was only apparent in 1789, when Pribylov returned from his islands; no one could know it at the beginning of the 'eighties. For none of his most successful ships was back when Shelikhov himself went off to America.

He did this as founder, part-owner and representative of the 'North-Eastern American Company', which was created in 1781 in St Petersburg, where Shelikhov entered into partnership with a merchant called Golikov and his nephew, Captain M. Golikov. The senior partner was the uncle, Ivan Larionovich Golikov. He, too, came from Kursk, and Shelikhov had long been associated with him in business.

The company's original capital was seventy thousand roubles, just enough to equip the first expedition. In order to be able to afford a share in it at all, Shelikhov had to borrow money from the wealthy Ural and Altai mine-owner, Demidov. We do not possess the original text of the agreement with Golikov, but according to Shelikhov it contained the following aims: 'Voyages in the Northern Ocean to discover unknown islands'; exploration of the 'American mainland'; transference of the peoples there to the sovereignty of the Russian empress and the conduct of 'voluntary trade' with them. The 'imperialist' character of this private agreement is obvious; the members of the company wanted to gain a firm foothold on the American continent and to make the people there Russian subjects.

Shelikhov left St Petersburg as soon as the agreement had been signed. In his yard near Okhotsk he built three galliots: *The Three Patriarchs*, *Simeon and the Prophetess Anna* and *St Michael*. All these set sail on 16 August 1783, with 192 men on board. Shelikhov himself was on board the first, 'together with his wife', who, in his own words, 'followed him everywhere and was prepared to endure every hardship.'

In the late autumn Shelikhov arrived at Bering Island with two of the ships; the third had disappeared on the way in storm and fog, and only caught up with the expedition two years later at the island of Kodiak.

After wintering successfully on Bering Island Shelikhov sailed first to Unalaska, then to Kodiak. At Unalaska they took on board two interpreters and ten friendly Aleutian Islanders.

Shelikhov knew very well that he would not have an easy time with the natives on Kodiak. According to Russian descriptions they were 'Konyages', a warlike Eskimo tribe which up to then had defied all Russian attempts to gain a foothold on the island. Shelikhov behaved very diplomatically; he avoided quarrelling with them and kept his men under tight control. This was all the more necessary because the Konyages were numerous and without the crew of the *Michael* Shelikhov had only 132 men at his disposal. But the Konyages, like all islanders, were determined to safeguard their independence; moreover, their experiences with previous visitors had not been happy. Shelikhov sought in vain to remain on peaceful terms with them. One night they attacked him and only withdrew with their dead and wounded after a hot fight.

The state of war lasted for a little while longer but ended in victory for Shelikhov. He took many prisoners, whom he quartered away from his harbour, which he had christened 'Three Saints'. He took hostages and formed the prisoners into a 'volunteer working party'. How voluntary the work was we cannot tell; but the emphasis which Shelikhov puts on 'free will' in all his reports and memoranda looks today not so much like hypocrisy and clever self-advertisement, of which many people accused him, as the expression of a far-sighted policy. Moreover, as we know today, 'free will' is a relative concept. Perhaps the Konyages really did seek work of their own free will; the Russians were certainly too weak to compel them to work. But the size and nature of the reward was determined by Shelikhov, and that was the important thing. The American fur trade involved a considerable financial risk. Ships were often lost and men died in large numbers. In the long run there could be no profit in the business unless labour costs were brought down. In all probability Shelikhov simply wanted to create a sound and lasting basis for his colonial enterprises by balancing the high costs of transport with a reduction in the price of the raw material and labour. There was no room in these careful calculations for sentimentality or personal cruelty.

In fact Shelikhov does not seem to have been a cruel man, although our only evidence for his 'mildness' and 'fatherly kindness' comes from his own reports. On the other hand, we know of cases in which he dealt very severely with the 'rebellious savages'. This is hardly surprising in an age when the rack was still in use in France and in every country corporal punishment was employed to maintain military discipline. It should be remembered, too, that the days of *Uncle Tom's Cabin* were far from over. The hostility of the Konyages sprang from the mere fact that the Russians had come to their island and were lording it there. Even if the Russians had been mild and kind they would still have been 'colonial exploiters', like anyone else in the same situation. Consequently, there were revolts, and Shelikhov had either to suppress them energetically or to leave the island, which was the last thing he wanted to do. He fortified his harbour and organized beaver and sea-otter hunts. He sent out large groups of native hunters in their light boats, under the supervision of one or two of his Russian hunters. This method would have been impossible if the Konyages had not been treated with a minimum of humanity. 'I have never thought of making them pay tribute,' he wrote, 'in case their mistrust was aroused and they took offence; I only tried to give them a good opinion of the Russians and to introduce them gradually to our customs. . . . I can certainly say, and I pride myself on the fact, that when they heard of my approaching departure they were as upset as if they had lost everything.'

This sounds by no means unlikely, for one can imagine that the natives were only expressing in this way their fear that after the departure of the great chief they would have a still worse time with the minor chiefs. All the same, Shelikhov's utterances were received with scepticism by many of his Russian contemporaries. In general, a large number of people felt that he was not so concerned with the spiritual enlightenment and Christianization of the American savages as he pretended; they took the view that his real interest lay elsewhere, and they were right. Nevertheless, Shelikhov's motives were not determined by his purse-strings alone. For him, as for all his contemporaries, conversion to the Orthodox Church was synonymous with the recognition of everything Russian, including the majesty of the Russian state. As his widow

wrote soon after his death, he considered that his noblest task in
America was 'to lead the natives to the true Christian faith and to
make them subjects of Your Imperial Majesty.' One part of this
conception could not be separated from the other. Shelikhov was
neither a pirate nor a missionary; he was a merchant, out for
profit, and at the same time an empire-builder, an eighteenth-
century Russian Cecil Rhodes.

After Shelikhov had consolidated his position on Kodiak he
sent out several parties of hunters to the American coast and the
surrounding islands. His men explored Cook Inlet and the strait
between Kodiak and the mainland, which has since borne Shelikhov's name. On the little island of Afognak and at Cook Inlet
small forts were built.

The first part of the work was now complete. Kodiak was Russian. It was a base or pivot, but the lever had to be worked, as
Shelikhov knew, from St Petersburg. The length of this lever or
arm was one hundred and eighty out of the three hundred and
sixty degrees of longitude, and this distance had now to be travelled by sea and land, over the ocean and across Siberia.

In May 1786 Shelikhov loaded *The Three Patriarchs* with furs,
and after a parade and salute of guns he weighed anchor for the
journey home. Unfortunately we do not know how big the cargo
of furs was, but he seems to have been pleased with it. Just as he
was putting to sea the *St Michael* turned up. Shelikhov turned
back and made the final arrangements. He left the *Simeon and
Anna* and the *Michael* in American waters and appointed his
representative, Samoilov, governor of the new colony.

The voyage to Bolsheretsk took eleven weeks and almost the
whole crew went sick with scurvy. Goodness knows what would
have happened to *The Three Patriarchs* if Shelikhov had not, with
his usual foresight, taken with him a number of native 'Americans',
who were supposed to be following him to Okhotsk 'by their own
wish, from curiosity'. They did all the sailors' work during the
voyage. It is clear how methodically and logically the man worked.
The colonies could certainly not get on without 'voluntary work by
the natives'.

He arrived safely at Bolsheretsk and intended to sail straight on
to Okhotsk, but while he was ashore with Natalia a sudden squall
caused the galliot to drag her anchor and blew her out to sea.
Shelikhov would have liked to wait until the ship was driven in-

shore again, but he received news that an English merchantman was at anchor in the bay of Avacha. Although they had been struggling for three years with the Eskimos, and were in the middle of a journey from Kodiak to St Petersburg, Shelikhov and Natalia leaped into the saddle and rode off to Petropavlovsk without even waiting for news of their ship with its valuable cargo.

The English ship was really there; it was an East Indiaman from Calcutta with a cargo of colonial produce. The deal was done in three days. Shelikhov bought goods to the value of 6,611 roubles. He paid one thousand roubles in cash; the rest was payable in bills two months later in Moscow. Shelikhov took delivery of the last bales and sacks on 1 September; a few weeks later they were all sold in Bolsheretsk to Okhotsk merchants at a profit of 50 per cent!

He did not wait for *The Three Patriarchs* this time either, rightly foreseeing that it would sail straight to Okhotsk to save time. So Grigory and Natalia went to Okhotsk by land, across the ice of the gulf of Penshina and past the Koryak 'barrier'. They travelled first in dog-sledges, then in reindeer-sleighs, and on the way were subjected, as Shelikhov wrote later, 'to unspeakable difficulties and dangers'. They arrived in Okhotsk on 27 January 1787, three and a half months after leaving Bolsheretsk; on 11 March they were in Yakutsk and on 6 April in Irkutsk.

THE 'RUSSIAN COLUMBUS'

Only a month later Shelikhov handed over to the governor-general of Siberia, I. W. Jakobi, two memoranda. In one he described his 'Wanderings in the Eastern Sea'; the other dealt with the question of privileges for his company. Naturally Shelikhov was not sparing with the colours in his picture of his 'Wanderings'. He estimated the native population of Kodiak at some fifty thousand and the savages who had attacked him at not less than four thousand. He said that he had converted a large number of natives to Christianity and that he thought they loved him 'like their own father'.

All this was advertisement, of course, and it has to be separated from the many objective facts in the first memorandum. But it is only in the second memorandum that Shelikhov comes to the real point. There he says in plain, unadorned language what he expects from the government. He needs a military guard of at least a hundred men, this number to include miners, surveyors, iron-founders, carpenters and sailors. He also requests permission to employ men with 'lapsed passes', undischarged bankrupts and people of that sort, who stood outside the law in Russia. He further seeks approval to make slaves out of captured members of the American tribes. On the other hand, he promises to enrol Aleutian and Kurile islanders only as volunteers. He asks for permission to trade with Japan, China, Korea, India and the Philippines, and requests a twenty-year loan of half a million roubles to make up for the losses the company has suffered. He ends with a plea for crown protection.

Shelikhov's mental processes are as clear and consistent as his deeds. He had completed the first part of his programme: he had founded permanent settlements in American waters, pushed out from the islands to the mainland, and begun the organization of a labour force. Now he was ready for the second part of the programme, trade with the outside world. Here national interests were involved, and he needed the protection of the state. If the programme was to be successful Shelikhov now needed a monopoly.

However, he did not dare to use this word. Like Jakobi, he knew that Catherine was opposed to monopolies and he could see that a governor-general could ask for one as an exception, but not he himself, a trader, whose edifying patriotic speeches were not believed by anyone as it was.

Although I. W. Jakobi was a German by birth, he was never-theless a genuine Siberian. His father, W. Jakobi, was the com-mandant of Selenginsk who thirty years before had suggested occupying and fortifying Daurien. The younger Jakobi was in close contact with Siberian business circles and it was even whis-pered that he had an interest in some of their activities. We do not know if this was really so; at any rate, Shelikhov did not share his profits with him and Jakobi acted quite loyally in supporting him. All the expeditions to America were financed by Irkutsk capital, which had been built up by the Russo-Chinese trade. Between 1764 and 1792, however, as a result of friction with Peking, turnover in the China trade had dropped to nothing, and this forced the merchants of Irkutsk to put their capital into the Kam-chatka–America trade. 'Irkutsk is populous and wealthy,' wrote

I. G. Georgi in 1772 in his *Travels in Russia*, 'but development is halted by Chinese chicanery; if the Kamchatka trade gets going, it will be more profitable.' That was just what Shelikhov thought, too.

Jakobi explained all these problems in his report to the empress. He backed up Shelikhov's requests in the interest of the state, and he hinted in prudent circumlocutions that by 'crown protection' Shelikhov meant the exclusive right to hunt marine animals on the coast of America.

Jakobi's report was handed over to the 'Commerce Commission' in St Petersburg, a high authority consisting of three persons close to the empress, who reported their findings direct to the monarch. Catherine's answer was found only recently in the form of notes in her own hand in the margin of the memorandum. The combination of political considerations with the sound common sense of a German housewife give them a charm of their own. The proposal of an interest-free loan for twenty years reminds Catherine of 'the man who was going to teach an elephant to talk in thirty years. When he was asked why he needed so much time, he replied: "either the elephant or I will die, or else the man who gave me the money for the elephant's education will." ' Catherine refused to grant the loan or the military guard, and displayed a reserved attitude to the whole enterprise. She mistrusted colonial conquests, for she had just observed for herself the successful revolt of the American colonies against the British Crown and the complete failure of the French East India Company, which in her opinion would be followed by the collapse of the French company's English equivalent. 'The discovery of new regions brings all kinds of difficulties with it; in particular, every discovery leads to a monopoly.' Catherine wanted no monopolies, for the grant of a monopoly in the Pacific would be followed by an attempt to gain one in the Caspian, and so on in other regions; it was the path to the 'hundred-headed monster'. Shelikhov's and Golikov's plan aimed, in her opinion, at a real monopoly, and monopolies were against her principles. The notes end with a proposition that sums up Russian policy in the Pacific: 'Wide expansion in the Pacific Ocean will bring no lasting gain. It is one thing to trade and another to seize possession (of places).'

Catherine wanted to trade and she also wanted to collect information about America. In both these directions she was ready to encourage private initiative. She found that the information provided by Shelikhov was inadequate; nevertheless she rewarded both Shelikhov and Golikov with swords, decorations and written testimonials, as she had rewarded others earlier on. She did not object when, on his own initiative, Jakobi provided, for transport to America, thirty iron coats-of-arms of the Russian Empire and the same number of copper plaques bearing the inscription: 'Land belonging to Russia.' She had even less objection to Jakobi's prudent instructions that the coats-of-arms should be erected 'in suitable spots', but the plaques 'stuck secretly in the ground', so that proof should be at hand in the case of future disputes. There seemed to be no danger in this.

The answer to Shelikhov did not mean that Catherine had no interest in Siberia and the Far East. During her reign the Academy of Sciences organized expeditions which made enormous contributions to contemporary knowledge of the eastern and southern parts of Russia and Siberia. A man who made his mark was P. S. Pallas, who travelled all over European Russia and Siberia between 1768 and 1774 and later became one of the Russian government's chief advisers in matters of geography. Among the plans he put forward was one for the 'physical exploration' of eastern Siberia and the Pacific Islands. This plan was not realized in the form which Pallas wished, but it was not entirely fruitless, for it led to the dispatch of an expedition under Billings and Sarychev with the task of exploring the north-east passage and acquiring fresh information about the northern Pacific.

One of the points in favour of Billings was that he had accompanied Cook on his last voyage. However the choice did not turn out to be an entirely happy one; the results of Billings' expedition, which lasted from 1785 to 1793, did not correspond to its long duration and enormous cost. It had sailed along the coast of America as far as the island of Kayak.

Shelikhov returned before Billings and in his memoranda he put questions of a political nature in the foreground. The Aleutian Islands had been gradually made into Russian islands. Both Jakobi and the Commerce Commission in St Petersburg had proposed officially securing the Pacific territories for Russia. The question was becoming more and more urgent, for just as a hundred years before the Jesuits had followed attentively the Russian move towards China, so now Europeans, especially the English, were watching the Russian advance across the Pacific to the American continent.

Interest in the Russian colossus was in general considerable. While the French encyclopedist Diderot was conversing in St Petersburg with the empress, the Englishman Jeremy Bentham, later famous as a philosopher, was visiting his brother Samuel, who was building ships on the Dnieper for Potemkin's Black Sea fleet. In 1781–2 Samuel Bentham travelled to Siberia, and there was a story that he built a ship for Shelikhov at Okhotsk. This cannot be correct, for Bentham only went as far as Nerchinsk and Kyakhta, but mistakes of this sort were bound to occur, for at that time there were many foreigners in Siberia.

It will be recalled how pleased the English had been at Cook's reception in Kamchatka. Many of Cook's companions declared themselves ready, like Billings, to enter Russian service. One of them, an American called John Ledyard, visited Pallas in St Petersburg and went on to Yakutsk with a letter of recommendation from him. He showed such a lively interest in Russian plans with regard to America that he was suspected of being a French spy and deported from Russia. In reality he was not a spy, but he did constitute a danger in another sense: he was the first American to realize the commercial possibilities of the marine animals of Alaska.

Just at the time when Catherine was busy with Shelikhov's memorandum, there appeared at the Russian court a Spaniard from Venezuela called Francisco Miranda, a champion of independence for the Latin-American colonies. He was received in audience by Catherine and probably talked to her about Mexico and California. It had then been finally decided to clarify the situation in the northern Pacific, and to send an expedition consisting of four warships and a transport round Cape Horn to Alaska. All the preparations were made, Captain G. I. Mulovsky was appointed leader of the expedition and in 1787 the flotilla was ready to sail when the outbreak of war first with Turkey and then with Sweden made it necessary to abandon the plan. The brave Captain Mulovsky was killed in a sea battle with the Swedes.

Catherine did not revive this plan. Shelikhov was granted neither political nor financial support and received no monopoly. However, he did not allow himself to be discouraged. On the contrary, he managed to form connections in St Petersburg which themselves amounted to something like a monopoly. He even found his way to Catherine's last favourite, the omnipotent Subov.

Shelikhov also had a good friend in Irkutsk, the impoverished nobleman Resanov. Resanov had a son, an extremely well-educated young man who wanted to make a career in the imperial entourage. This was difficult to arrange without money and influential connections. In 1790 the young man came to Irkutsk, became acquainted with Anna, Mrs Shelikhov's daughter by her first marriage, and realized that she could give him what he lacked, for Anna was Shelikhov's favourite. In deference to the truth it must be emphasized that the marriage which soon took place was one of love as well as of convenience.

Resanov soon returned with his young wife to St Petersburg, and after a short period of service in the empress's private chancellery obtained the influential post of a secretary in the Senate. He soon moved into his own new house to which all the fashionable people of St Petersburg came as guests. Here at the supper-table the senator and later minister of justice Dershavin, who was also a famous poet and Pushkin's teacher, celebrated in verse Grigory Shelikhov, 'the Russian Columbus'. The highest officials of the empire were frequent guests in the house, and Nikolai Petrovich Resanov thus became Shelikhov's permanent ambassador at the imperial court.

Even this was not all. Shelikhov's missionary activity, or rather his accounts of it, had not been in vain. He secured a patron in the person of Gavriil, metropolitan of Novgorod. This did not mean a great deal at Catherine's sceptical court, but the support of the official church probably raised the prestige of Shelikhov's colonial enterprises in the eyes of Siberian officials and possibly in those of the empress as well. In any case it gave Shelikhov himself, who in this respect had followed the old Stroganov mercantile tradition, a certain satisfaction. Thanks to the metropolitan's initiative, the first mission was sent to Kodiak in 1794: ten monks from the island monastery of Velamo in Lake Ladoga, led by the archimandrite Joseph Bolotov. In 1796, a year after Shelikhov's death, the diocese of Kodiak was set up and the archimandrite Joseph was consecrated bishop. The expenses of developing and maintaining the new bishopric were taken over by the government. Traces of the missionary activity of these Russian monks in Alaska were preserved until our own day.

At the end of 1788 Shelikhov returned to Irkutsk and continued to direct his American enterprises from there. Although he had not attained all his objects in St Petersburg, the distinctions he had received spoke for themselves. The new governor of Siberia, I. A. Piel, a man of great integrity, became Shelikhov's friend, an even closer friend than Jakobi had been.

Shelikhov did not rest on his laurels for a single day. Immediately after his return he began to make preparations for a fresh expedition to America. He went off to Okhotsk and supervised the building of a new ship, the *North-eastern Eagle*, which set sail for Kodiak in 1791. He used to spend the winter in Irkutsk and the summer in Okhotsk. There was much to do, and he had still more plans in his head. At that time he was a little over forty; full of physical and mental energy, he felt capable of anything and shrank from nothing.

We know about his plans, thanks to Piel's detailed reports to St Petersburg. These reports were necessary, for Shelikhov's plans always exceeded the governor-general's authority; they were the plans of an empire-builder, which brought the Russian government face to face with problems of international politics. Shelikhov no longer asks for money, but only for men: craftsmen and ship's carpenters. He requests farmers for the agricultural colonies to be founded in America and the Kurile Islands. He points to the complete inadequacy of Okhotsk as a harbour and suggests a better one at the mouth of the River Ulya. His attention is always focused mainly on the development of sea trade, as important for Siberia as for Russian America. The Kuriles, too, have their place in this conception, for they open up the possibility of trade with Japan. He repeats his first suggestion: trade relations must be sought with the Dutch East Indies and the Philippines; he urges negotiations with China for the opening of Canton to Russian ships, and demands Russian consulates in all the centres of trade on the Pacific.

Shelikhov recommends the construction of a new harbour on the Sea of Okhotsk, but he knows that this will not solve the problem. Siberia needs an ice-free and easily accessible port on the Pacific. Is there not such an access, asks Shelikhov, 'along the ridge of the mountain-chain' which stretches eastward from Lake Baikal and ends on the shore of the Sea of Okhotsk? There may be a suitable harbour near the mouth of the Amur. 'And if we do not find a harbour there,' Shelikhov continues, 'at any rate we shall get to know the region between the Amur and the sources of the Rivers Vitim, Olekma, Aldan and Maya, for up to now these places have remained unexplored and undescribed.' He is even ready to finance an expedition to these regions, and would be glad to take part in it himself.

In the memorandum of Shelikhov's from which we have quoted the question of a Russian base on the Pacific was clearly posed for the first time. Such a base was found sixty-five years later in Port Arthur. A straight line of historical development leads from Shelikhov to Muravyev-Amursky and Witte. The suggested exploration of the watershed between the Amur and the right-bank tributaries of the Lena was carried out fifty years later, by A. T. von Middendorff.

Interested as Shelikhov was in China, he did not forget that all the problems of the northern Pacific meet in the Bering Strait and its two shores. He suggested sending several expeditions in that direction 'to measure latitudes and explore the routes', and also when possible, 'to start trade and establish friendly relations with the native peoples'. He wrote about these projects to Piel in 1790; four years later he informed him that he also meant to discover the north-west passage!

Shelikhov died quite suddenly on 20 July 1795 at Irkutsk, 'in the midst of his heroic deeds', as contemporaries wrote, 'leaving his mourning widow and his children to look after his American enterprises.' He was only forty-eight. He was buried in the cemetery of the monastery at Irkutsk. An obelisk made of marble from the Urals still stands on his grave today, adorned with a copper compass, anchor, chart and sword, symbols of the imperial and maritime conceptions of the merchant from Rylsk. The poets of the Russian Rococo, Dershavin and Dmitriev, added florid epitaphs to the tomb. In 1895, on the centenary of his death, a monument to the 'Russian Columbus' was erected in his native town of Rylsk.

GOVERNOR BARANOV

For all the breadth of Shelikhov's plans his eyes were always on 'Russian America'. He had a grip on the Siberian authorities through his friend Piel, and in St Petersburg he had many other patrons in high places besides Resanov. In America, however, it was not patrons he needed but governors, not bureaucrats but pioneers. A real man was wanted there. In 1786 he had left behind the old fur-hunter Samoilov as governor of Kodiak, and commissioned him to explore the waters to the south. But Samoilov did not carry out these orders; he did not even stop the rival firm of Lebedev-Lastochkin from establishing itself near Alexandrovsk on Cook Inlet. So Shelikhov replaced Samoilov with a Greek called Delarov, who turned out to be an intelligent but rather too talkative governor. Above all, he lacked audacity and initiative. Someone else had to be found.

Shelikhov discovered him in the person of Baranov, a small merchant who turned up in Irkutsk in 1780. Alexander Andreyevich Baranov came from the north Russian town of Kargopol, a staging-post on the road from Moscow to the White Sea. The local inhabitants had long been concerned with hunting and the fur-trade, so Baranov was at home in Siberia from the start. He had set up as a trader in Irkutsk, but as he possessed no capital he had soon entered the service of Golikov, a vodka-manufacturer and a partner of Shelikhov in the American trade. That was how Baranov came to know the 'Russian Columbus'.

After four years Baranov gave up his position with Golikov to devote himself to a project which made his name known even in St Petersburg: in 1784, with a new partner, he founded the first glass-works in Siberia on the River Talza, about twenty-five miles from Irkutsk. The originator and technical director of this enterprise was Baranov's partner, Erik Laxman, a Finn by birth, who was a noted scientist, a member of the Academy of Sciences in St Petersburg, and at the time the greatest expert in Siberia on all questions of political and economic geography. Baranov became the sales director and factory manager. The two partners worked together for four years without any friction. The friendship between them lasted even after Baranov had left Irkutsk, and the contact with Laxman certainly influenced his intellectual development.

We do not know precisely what induced Baranov to leave the enterprise in Irkutsk suddenly in 1788 and to throw himself into the fur trade. Probably it was the desire that every businessman feels one day to be his own master. Perhaps he was helped in this new start by his brother Peter, who bought furs on the River Anadyr. Just at that moment Shelikhov, who had recently returned from St Petersburg, suggested to Baranov for the first time that he should go to America. But Baranov rejected the proposal and went off to his brother on the Anadyr instead of to America.

A year later, as he was returning to Irkutsk with a large load of furs, he was attacked by the Koryaks, who robbed him of every single fur. This meant complete bankruptcy after years of successful work. At Okhotsk he met Shelikhov again, who repeated his offer. This time Baranov did not refuse it, and on 30 August 1790 he left Okhotsk on board the *Three Patriarchs*. He took with him stores for the colony on Kodiak and fifty-two men as well: hunters, craftsmen and workers. The ship was commanded by the experienced seaman Bocharov, a former companion of Benyowszky's on the trip from Bolsheretsk to Paris and the man with whom Shelikhov had sailed to America in the *Simeon*.

On the 9 October they dropped anchor off the cliffs of Unalaska. These cliffs were to prove fatal to the ship. While the crew were still busy unloading the cargo a storm tore the ship from her moorings and smashed it against the rocks. Baranov now showed his mettle. He saved as much as he could of the cargo and settled in for the winter. He managed to establish tolerable relations with the Aleutians, and in the eight months of his stay learnt their language and methods of hunting. In the following April he constructed three big *baidarkas* (Aleutian boats); two of them he sent off under the command of Bocharov on a reconnaissance trip to Bristol Bay, and in the third he set off himself with fifteen men for Kodiak. His boat entered 'Three Saints' harbour at the beginning of July 1791 after covering a distance of over six hundred miles.

Baranov had been favoured with good weather during the voyage and bright sunshine greeted him as he landed on Kodiak. The sun does not often shine in those regions, but when it does Kodiak is a sight that has delighted every visitor. John Burroughs, a member of the Harriman expedition to Alaska in 1899, describes with great enthusiasm its emerald hills, flowery valleys, blue waters and 'vast green wilderness stretching north, south and west. . . . Enchanting Kodiak!'

But it was nature that was enchanting; the work of human hands was not so captivating. Captain Sarychev, who had been on Kodiak a year before, had found that 'Shelikhov's township' consisted only of 'a few mud huts, a granary and two farmhouses inhabited by Russian hunters'. Sarychev also mentions some native children who lived in a separate hut and were well treated by the Russians. The last detail is also mentioned by all later observers. It is to be explained partly by the Russians' love for children in general, but more particularly by the fact that a large number of children on Kodiak were only half-Aleutian, since their fathers were Russians. By the time Baranov arrived the settlement had grown a little bigger; storehouses, new huts, a forge and many other buildings had been put up. Nearby there was a camp of Aleutian workmen. Nevertheless, the reality was less dazzling than it appeared in Shelikhov's reports. The saddest thing of all was that the bulk of the cargo of the *Three Patriarchs* had been lost, while Baranov's arrival meant that there were another fifty mouths to be fed in the colony.

Baranov did not have much time to look round at his new surroundings. 'Three Saints' harbour was open to every wind and quite unusable, as the first storm showed. Baranov found a sheltered bay surrounded by forest on the north-eastern coast of Kodiak; he christened it St Paul and transferred his residence to this spot. Then he went off with a fleet of 450 Aleutian *baidarkas* eastward to Prince William Sound (Chugatskaya Guba) and the little bay of Nutkhek, where it was thought that the sea-otters had their breeding-grounds.

Here Baranov made his first acquaintance with the Tlingite tribe – the Russians called them Koloshes – and he was to remember the meeting for a long time. At first the Indians were not particularly hostile; Baranov brought presents for their chieftains and established good relations with them. But the Indians had met white men before. Since Cook's time a whole string of English and Spanish captains had visited them and they knew that these visits always began with presents and ended with extortions. Baranov sent the Aleutians away and set about building a blockhouse with a palisade and ramparts. This was 'Fort Constantinovsky', which, as Baranov knew, would be transformed by Shelikhov's pen into 'the fortress of Constantinovsky'.

But the Indians did not like the look of the 'fortress'. They kept quiet at first because a new ship appeared in the bay, the schooner *Phoenix* from Calcutta. It had been driven off its course and needed assistance. The captain was an Irishman called Hugh Moor.

Baranov gave him everything he needed, and with the help of some German words which he had learnt from Laxman he was able to converse with both the captain and his mate, O'Cain, who was also an Irishman. He questioned his guests eagerly and learnt much from them about the situation in the Pacific and the interest of the Americans, Dutch and British in Russian America and its furs. But to assume, as some American authors do, that it was only through Moor that Baranov learnt of the existence of California and the Dutch East Indies is naïve; Shelikhov's letters and memoranda prove that the economics and political problems of the Pacific were understood in Irkutsk and Okhotsk at that time just as clearly as in Boston and Calcutta. Baranov's friend at Irkutsk, Erik Laxman, could probably have taught Moor quite a lot about them.

They parted good friends. Baranov gave Moor some valuable furs and the Irishman left behind as a souvenir his boy, the young Bengalese Richard, who became Baranov's loyal servant and his interpreter as well.

After the departure of the *Phoenix*, Baranov went to the island of Nutkhek (Montague). Here his party was attacked by the Koloshes while it was asleep. There was a hot fight, which lasted until dawn. It might have ended unfavourably for Baranov if a big boat full of Russian hunters had not appeared at dawn in the entrance to Nutkhek Bay. The Indians withdrew with their dead and wounded. Baranov lost two Russians and ten Aleutians, and all the rest of his party, including himself, were wounded.

The first three years were full of difficulties and worries of this sort. Baranov expanded his headquarters, explored Bristol Bay and the coast of Alaska, and established posts on Cook Inlet and Prince William Sound. But the lack of food and good ships and the numerical weakness of the colony hindered its development. In addition, Russian competitors were not letting the grass grow under their feet. In Cook Inlet, by the side of Baranov's post, 'Fort Alexandrovsk', there were already two other forts, built by the Lebedev-Lastochkins, who made friends with the Indians and egged them on to attack Baranov's men.

Meanwhile Shelikhov was not asleep in Okhotsk, as was soon apparent. In the summer of 1793 a new ship belonging to the company arrived at Kodiak, the *North-eastern Eagle*. It had been built by an Englishman called James Shields who had drifted somehow or other to Siberia and immediately been snapped up by Shelikhov. Shields brought the *Eagle* to Kodiak himself.

His arrival marks the beginning of a new era in Russian America. Originally Shields wanted to return to Okhotsk, but Baranov succeeded with great difficulty in persuading him to stay. Now Shelikhov's old idea could be put into effect and ships built on the spot. Baranov and Shields looked round for a suitable site and found it in Resurrection Bay (Voskresenski Bay) on the mainland. Soon the crash of axes was to be heard. On 15 September 1794 the first Russian ship built in America, the three-masted schooner *Phoenix*, glided down the slipway, to be followed the next year by the *Olga*.

At the end of 1794 Ismaylov arrived at Kodiak from Okhotsk with a new ship, *The Three High Priests*, and a large number of men: hunters, farmers and the archimandrite Joseph Bolotov with ten monks. *The Three High Priests* was soon followed by a second ship, the *Katherina*, commanded by the famous Captain Pribylov. These two vessels brought mail, cargo and 123 new colonists. Baranov now had 272 subjects on Kodiak and a flotilla of seven ships.

In 1795 the governor sent the *Phoenix* off to Okhotsk with a cargo of furs worth three hundred thousand roubles. His victory was now assured; he no longer needed to fear Russian competitors. Those in Cook Inlet were having a bad time. Their friendship with the Indians had turned into a bitter feud which cost thirteen men their lives. When Baranov sailed there in 1796 his former enemies welcomed him as a liberator and recognized his authority without any limitations.

However, Baranov had his own difficulties; he was tired and ill. No ship had arrived at Kodiak for three years. He had succeeded in pacifying the Russians, but it was difficult to come to terms with the Indians. They would not let the Russian hunters advance any farther south, and every year more of them were armed with American guns. Old guns from the War of Independence could be bought cheaply in America and American captains regarded them as excellent objects for bartering. They also supplied the Indians with other things – knives, axes, blankets – more cheaply and better than Baranov, who received almost nothing from Russia. Baranov estimated that, on an average, ten English and American ships appeared every season in 'his' waters and carried away with them no fewer than twenty thousand skins. They went straight to

Canton, quickly and punctually; the Russian furs went first to Okhotsk and then had to be sent to China by land via Kyakhta and Mongolia. One wonders in what conditions the goods reached the customers.

At last, in 1797, the old schooner *Alexander* arrived from Okhotsk, and with it a letter from Natalia Shelikhov to Baranov informing him of the death of her husband two years earlier. She wrote that the financial position of the company was not brilliant; Baranov knew this better than anyone else, for since his arrival he had sent back only one consignment of furs of any size to Okhotsk. But the company would not for that reason cease its activities, Natalia continued, and as Baranov was irreplaceable she and Golikov begged him not to resign but to carry on in accordance with her late husband's instructions and his own good sense. Baranov decided to 'wait', and waited twenty-one years.

In April 1799 he set out on board his flagship, the schooner *Olga*, with some Russian hunters and a flotilla of about 500 small boats, each manned by two Aleutians, towards the south-east. The sea was rough and it was impossible to land. On 2 May thirty of the small boats were swallowed up by the waves off the rocky island of Nutkhek. After an exhausting day the boats finally managed to reach the shore. Even before night fell the Koloshes attacked the hurriedly built camp. The Aleutians either fled, as they usually did, to the woods and were scalped by the Indians, or else hid in the cliffs on the shore. Baranov and his Russians, although outnumbered, fought their assailants. In this battle he lost another twenty-six men, including two Russians. Altogether the trip had cost him eighty-six men.

Fighting, hunting and collecting furs, he reached in July the island then called Sitka and now known as Baranov Island. He landed in one of its bays and announced to the chief of the tribe which lived there that the island had been annexed by the Russian empire. He handed over presents and objects of daily use as a price for the island and explained that he wished to live in peace with the natives and to trade with them. The very next day he began to build Fort Mikhailovsky.[1] By the spring of 1800 it was

1. In Russian sources it appears on one occasion as 'Arkhangelsk' (Archangel) and in another as 'Mikhailovsk' (Michael). There is no contradiction here; in both cases the full name 'Mikhail Arkhangel' (Archangel Michael) is meant.

finished, and in the course of the next two years Baranov moved about two hundred Russian hunters and workmen there. He had recognized the strategic and economic importance of the island. From it he could bar access to Alaska and put an end to visits from Boston and Calcutta. For this he needed a legal title and an internationally recognized frontier. The relationship of Russian-America to the Russian empire had at last to be legally defined.

THE RUSSIAN-AMERICAN COMPANY

Baranov knew that after the death of Catherine II in 1796 her son Paul had ascended the throne. What he did not know was that with this change of monarch the attitude to monopolies in the highest circles had also changed. In the last analysis Catherine had previously been the only person who was opposed to monopolies on principle. The formation of a monopoly company in Russian America had been favoured not only by the Commerce Commission but also by many people in government and even academic circles as well. It is hardly likely that Paul had a well-based opinion of his own about this question, but, like most St Petersburg politicians, he did not share Catherine's conviction that the British East India Company was going to collapse. On the contrary, he regarded it as a very effective instrument of British policy. He was no economist; the forefront of his mind was occupied by political questions, and it is not difficult to imagine how he must have been attracted by the possibility of replying to the intrigues of the English in the Mediterranean with their own weapon, a privileged company, in the Pacific.

As Paul himself desired a merger of Russian enterprises in America, Shelikhov's heirs only had to ensure that they and not their competitors obtained control of it. When a strong, competitive group, headed by the merchant Mylnikov, was formed in Irkutsk, Paul decided that it could not be allowed to damage 'the already existing company of the first man in the field, Shelikhov'. This was a clear warning, and after a few weeks, in June 1797, the two groups merged together into the 'United American Company'. Mylnikov thought that the union would be only a formal one, and that he could continue to work independently, but pressure from St Petersburg increased and in August of the same year there was a directive from the Tsar referring to the disadvantages involved in the existence of several companies in America and emphasizing the need for their fusion into one single one.

It was now clear which way developments were tending and the struggle for control of the coming company grew tense. The Mylnikov group were prepared to use any methods they could find. They accused Shelikhov of overstepping the law and even of committing crimes in America; two Aleutian chiefs were brought before the Tsar to make complaints in person. They were given an audience, treated kindly, presented with gifts and sent home again with good wishes but with no consequences for Shelikhov. The Mylnikov group also tried to use the Tsar's favourite, Lopukhina, as a pawn in their manoeuvres, but they were unlucky, for the lady very soon fell out of favour. Naturally, Shelikhov's successors were not slow to counter their competitors' intrigues. After all, at their head stood the cultured lawyer and diplomat Resanov, an important figure in government circles and a friend of the military governor of St Petersburg, Count P. A. Pahlen, the man who three years later organized the murder of Paul but at that time enjoyed his full confidence.

The outcome of the struggle was a foregone conclusion. Since Shelikhov's competitors were opposing the will of the monarch they could not achieve victory. On 8 July 1799 the 'Crown-protected Russian-American Company' was established.

The documents make it clear that it differed substantially from the earlier companies. The imperial decree assured the company of 'the support of our land and sea forces'. Its management had the right to put requests 'direct to His Imperial Majesty'. Its seal was adorned with the imperial eagle.

The company received for a period of twenty years the right to hunt land and sea animals and to exploit the other natural resources on the American coast from 55 degrees North to the Bering Strait 'and beyond', likewise in the Aleutians and Kuriles and 'the whole area of the north-eastern sea, which belongs to Russia by the right of first discovery'. It was also given the right 'to make further discoveries south of 55 degrees North and to take possesson of territories discovered . . . so far as they had not been occupied already by other peoples.' The company was allowed to found settlements, build fortifications, deal with neighbouring powers, employ people, and to make unfettered use of the forests in the

whole region of Okhotsk. No other company or person was
allowed to do any of these things in the company's territory without
its agreement.

The new company was also given another important com-
mission, 'to look after the spiritual mission whose task it is in
America to pass on the knowledge of the true God to the heathen
American population.'

So Grigory Shelikhov's dream was realized; the company which
he had founded received the monopoly. The question arises
whether it could still be called 'his' company. The answer, at the
time of the company's foundation, was on the whole 'yes'. Of
724 thousand-rouble shares, his heirs owned 239½, or about a
third. Such a block, even if it does not mean an absolute majority,
does give a group control unless the other shareholders form one
unit, and in this case they did not. Of the four directors of the
company, one was Shelikhov's son-in-law, M. M. Buldakov, and
another was his son, Ivan. In addition, by command of the Tsar,
Buldakov had been appointed managing director. Still more
important, the post of 'Correspondent', who was supposed to
supervise the company on behalf of the government, was entrusted
to N. P. Resanov. The opposition group, which was able to appoint
Mylnikov and one of his adherents to the board, had every reason
to regard itself as blocked.

Right from the start the government took steps to ensure that
other people could acquire shares. Ten shares were enough to
confer voting rights, and at general meetings those actually present,
not shares, were counted. This made possible the acquisition of
more and more influence by people acceptable to the government
from the ranks of the higher civil servants and court officials.
Further development was in fact in the direction of bureaucratiza-
tion, and in practice the company was gradually nationalized. In
1801 Tsar Alexander bought twenty shares in the company; the
grand dukes followed his example, and this was the signal for the
court and administrative aristocracy to enter the company. As
the author of the most recent book on the Russian-American
Company, S. B. Okuny, shows, at the general meeting of the
company in 1819, of the eighteen shareholders present, ten were
representatives of the higher civil service and only eight were
merchants. After the new statute had been drawn up in 1844, of the
five new directors (instead of the previous four), only one was a

businessman; the rest were admirals and generals. After 1857 there was no merchant at all on the board.

But all this was only apparent later. At the time of the company's foundation Baranov was busy building his Gibraltar. During the next few years he divided his time between the mainland, Kodiak and Sitka. He worked tirelessly and damaged his health as a result. His support was Anna Grigorievna, a beautiful Indian girl, daughter of a Tlingite chief, who was first his friend and then his wife. His great joys were his son Antipatr and his daughter Irina, who were both born out of wedlock but later legitimized. A man like Baranov could not exist without friends and colleagues, and he had them. But he worried a great deal and was plagued by doubts because he did not receive any news from Russia. Four years had passed since 1798, and during this period he had received neither mail nor supplies. The *Phoenix*, which had been sent from Okhotsk, never reached him; it was wrecked on the cliffs of Unalaska.

It was not until 1802 that he finally received news of the great changes in Russia. He learnt that the new Russian-American monopoly company had already been in existence for three years; that the Emperor Paul, by whose wish it had been founded, was no longer alive; that he, Baranov, was one of the shareholders of the new company, which had allotted him ten shares; and that, as a reward for his services, he was entitled to wear the order of St Vladimir (it was enclosed in the letter). He also learnt now for the first time that the rights of the Russian-American Company extended to all the Russian possessions in America, the Aleutians, the Kuriles and all the regions between them, and finally that the man appointed as 'chief administrator', that is, governor and ruler, of this empire was himself, Alexander Andreyevich, the erstwhile small trader from Kargopol.

Baranov assembled the whole colony and had a Mass said for his namesake, the new Tsar Alexander I. This was followed by a Requiem Mass for the dead Tsar Paul. Then Baranov read out the decree appointing him governor, put on his decoration, and announced that he was putting down one thousand roubles for the construction of a new school for Russian, Aleutian and Russo-Aleutian children. The school was built that same year.

THE STRUGGLE FOR SITKA

Fort Mikhailovsk or Arkhangelsk on Sitka now appeared as fully justified. Baranov built a real castle there; it was a triangle, with a base line of seventy yards on the side facing the sea. The fort was protected by a palisade of spruce-trunks, covered outside by three and inside by two layers of the same wood. This wooden wall was proof against the cannon-balls of contemporary naval artillery. Captain Lisyansky, an experienced naval officer, speaks in his journal without any irony of 'the fortress of Mikhailovsk'. Inside this palisade there were houses, granaries and offices – fourteen buildings in all. The Russian population of the fortress amounted to about two hundred persons.

However, as so often is the case, a fortress can be impregnable against an enemy who knows the rules of the game but an easy prey for 'idiots with no idea of strategy'. That is just what the Tlingites were. They did not find it difficult to get through the impenetrable fortifications when all the inmates of the fortress, including the guards, were peacefully sleeping. The Indians always knew exactly what went on in the fortress because the Indian girls used to visit their unmarried Russian friends there. The attack was carried out late one Sunday evening in 1802. Baranov was on Kodiak at the time. A large number of the hunters were away in Yakutat Bay catching marine animals with the commandant, Baranov's accountant, Kuskov. Twenty-six Russians had stayed behind at Mikhailovsk, together with a number of Aleutians and all the women and children. Most of these people were killed immediately; those who stayed in the houses were burnt to death inside them. A few were carried off as prisoners and slaughtered later.

The Indians pulled bales of furs out of the burning houses and dragged them off into the forest. They were helped to do this by some white men; who they were is not clear. According to Russian sources they were deserters from an American ship who had been held under arrest at Mikhailovsk and were freed by the Indians. This seems credible, since an American sailor was later found among some dead Indians. But in general the Indians had no more cause to love the Americans than the Russians. One of the reasons for the revolt was in fact the violent deeds of English and American captains cruising in these waters. One of them, Captain Barber of the *Unicorn*, had a reputation that extended along the whole north-western coast of America. Obviously the Indians were not enchanted by the Russians either, but as permanent residents of these regions the Russians naturally had to take more account of the manners and customs of the natives than these captains who just came and then disappeared again. The Indians had attacked American and English ships more than once, but without much result. The Russians now had to foot the bill for everyone.

As always in the hunting season, there were some foreign ships cruising off Sitka. Three of them arrived at Mikhailovsk immediately after the drama; two were English, the *Unicorn* commanded by Captain Barber and the *Alert* under Captain Ebbets, and the third was the American *Carolina*, under the command of Captain Sturgis. They took on board those who had escaped the massacre. The Russian refugees were worried about the fate of Kuskov. When he returned with the Aleutians from Yakutat he might fall into the hands of the Indians. Curiously enough, none of the three captains felt inclined to warn Kuskov of the danger. Apparently none of them wished to leave the scene of the disaster since they reckoned there must still be a lot of furs there. Fortunately Kuskov was informed about the events on Sitka by an old Indian friend.

Barber assumed the leadership against the Indians. He collected on board his own ship all those who had been saved and called on the Indians to hand over their prisoners and the furs. A chieftain of the Tlingites and his nephew, who came to see Barber, were arrested. When the nephew tried to escape Barber hanged him. After that the prisoners and a considerable number of furs were handed over.

Barber sailed to Kodiak with the twenty-three rescued Russians and Aleutians. When he arrived at St Paul's Harbour he told Baranov that he would only hand over the Russians in return for a ransom of fifty thousand roubles in cash or furs. Baronov retorted that the rescue had already been paid for by the furs which Barber had received from the Indians. 'I shall shoot,' said the captain. 'So shall I,' replied Baranov. Both men knew that they were only bluffing. In the end they agreed on ten thousand roubles, for which the unselfish saviour gave a receipt.

The loss of Mikhailovsk was a blow which Baranov could not

take lying down. With his fortress he had also lost Sitka, that is, he had had to abandon the best hunting-grounds to the English and American captains and above all he had lost the possibility of barring access to Alaska from the south. And all this had happened just when the Russian-American Company had been recognized as an instrument of Russian policy and he himself appointed to carry out this policy. Mikhailovsk had to be recaptured; but how was this to be done now that the Indians, who in any case were already supplied with American arms, also had Russian guns and the cannon at Mikhailovsk into the bargain? Baranov waited for the arrival of at least one decently equipped vessel from Okhotsk, but again he was disappointed. In 1803 Lieutenants Khvostov and Davidov brought him a valuable cargo from Okhotsk in the *Zacharias and Elizabeth*. Their schooner was armed and they themselves were proper naval officers, but they had no time for an expedition to Sitka, for they were under orders to load up with furs and return before winter. Moreover, Baranov himself could not concentrate exclusively on mounting the operation against Sitka for the company wanted furs from him. Between 1802 and 1804 he delivered cargoes of them worth two and a half million roubles.

Just at this time a new commercial possibility presented itself to Baranov. An old acquaintance, the mate O'Cain, now himself a Boston captain, who had been Baranov's guest ten years before with Captain Moor, arrived at Kodiak with a cargo of provisions and general stores for him. The Irishman wanted to barter these for furs, but just at that moment Baranov had none. He conceived the idea of a new kind of deal, which he subsequently made with several other captains as well. He lent O'Cain a party of Aleutians with some Russian hunters and they all went with O'Cain to the coast of California. The spoils were divided. Baranov's share enabled him to pay a handsome price for the goods he had received from O'Cain.

While O'Cain went hunting, Baranov prepared for warlike operations. In 1803 he built two schooners at Yakutat, added a couple of old ships and 450 *baidarkas*, and with this armada sailed on Sitka. On the way he ran into a storm, and lost about fifty *baidarkas* and as many Aleutians.

Baranov first tried negotiating. He renounced the idea of reprisals and simply asked for the fortress and the stolen property to be returned. But the Indians dragged out the negotiations and were in fact not ready to accept the proposal. What was to be done? At this very moment, on 20 August 1804, the frigate *Neva*, under the command of Captain Yuri Lisyansky, sailed into the little harbour near Mikhailovsk where Baranov's fleet lay at anchor.

The *Neva* was one of the two ships of the Russian expedition round the world led by Krusenstern. Lisyansky had heard of Baranov's misfortunes from American captains at Hawaii and had hurried to join him. He had unloaded his cargo at Kodiak and sailed on to Sitka.

Lisyansky's arrival altered the balance of power and Baranov decided to storm the fortress. A bombardment by the *Neva* did not damage the fort; the cannon-balls, fired at fairly long range, could not penetrate the palisade. Baranov marched to the attack at the head of his detachment. The Aleutians dragged the cannon with which Baranov intended to shatter the gates of the fort. When the defenders opened fire the Aleutians left the cannon where they were and fled. Baranov was wounded in the hand. He started to retire, the Indians pursued him, and if the guns of the *Neva* had not opened fire the battle might have ended disastrously for the Russians.

The next day the Indians sent representatives to parley, but they still could not make up their minds to surrender Mikhailovsk. Their boats, drawn up on the shore, were seized and destroyed by Baranov's men, and their stocks of fish were discovered and distributed among the Aleutians. It had already been decided to make a second attack on the fort when the negotiators promised to hand it over the next night. As a sign of surrender, the garrison would shout 'u-u-u' three times. This sinister cry did, in fact, echo out that evening and was answered by a triple cheer from the Russians.

The next day, 8 October 1804, Baranov and Lisyansky entered the fortress. It was empty. In the central square they found what Lisyansky describes as 'a most barbaric sight such as to make even the hardest heart tremble. On the assumption that we might be able to track them down in the forest from the cries of the children and the barking of the dogs, the Sitkans had killed all the children and dogs.' Alongside lay the bodies of thirty men who had fallen in the fighting.

Baranov did not rebuild Mikhailovsk. He moved the fortress farther south to a more strategic site with a better harbour. There a new fort and settlement soon arose, which were christened Novo-Arkhangelsk.

Neither before nor after his victory did Baranov raise the questions of punishment for the perfidious attack or of the surrender of those responsible. In Lisyansky's view he even showed 'far too much moderation'. In the spring of 1805 he invited the chieftains to meet him, gave them presents, smoked the pipe of peace with them and declared the incident closed.

THE FIRST RUSSIAN CIRCUMNAVIGATION OF THE GLOBE

Lisyansky's voyage forms part of the history not only of Russian America, but also of Russian seafaring in general, for it took place within the framework of the first Russian circumnavigation of the globe under the leadership of Captain, later Admiral, I. F. von Krusenstern. This was the old plan of N. F. Golovin, president of the Admiralty in Bering's time. The aim was quite simple and must have been clear to everyone after Bering's expedition, namely, to find a sea route to Kamchatka and Alaska, for otherwise those territories could not be developed or defended. At the end of the eighteenth century this idea became part of a still broader conception: the necessity of enabling the Russian territories on the Pacific to establish a sea-trade with the outside world, particularly with China. The dream of Shelikhov and all the merchants of Irkutsk, direct trade by sea with China, was now taken over by the Russian Navy in the person of the young Lieutenant I. F. von Krusenstern.

Krusenstern was a talented and ambitious officer. He had distinguished himself in the war against Sweden, like his comrade Yuri Lisyansky, who was three years younger. Krusenstern's superior officer in this war had been Captain Mulovsky, the man who in 1787 was to have taken the Russian ships from Kronstadt to Alaska. In 1793 Krusenstern, Lisyansky and fourteen other young officers were seconded to the British Navy for training. They all fought on the English side against the French revolutionary fleets, including Lieutenant Jakob Bering, a grandson of the famous Vitus. Under the English flag they visited every part of the world. Krusenstern went to India and from there made a trip to China on his own account. At Macao he witnessed the return of an English ship from a five-month voyage to the west coast of America. The vessel brought back a cargo of sea-otter skins worth sixty thousand piastres.

This incident formed the final stimulus to the plan which was to carry the young naval officer into the ranks of the world's great sailors. During his journey home Krusenstern compiled a memorandum which he handed over to the Navy Ministry at St Petersburg in 1799. In it he suggested organizing sea-trade with China direct from Russia, 'in order to stimulate our foreign trade' and to prepare the way for the export of furs straight from Alaska to Chinese ports instead of by the senseless route through Okhotsk and Kyakhta. He considered it possible to supply Russian America by sea from Kronstadt, and recommended the dispatch of a trial expedition which at the same time could carry out the first Russian circumnavigation of the world.

It was due to the Minister for Trade, Count N. P. Rumyantzev, that Krusenstern's plan was put into effect. Two ships were acquired in England for the expedition, the *Nadeshda* (Hope), of 430 tons, and the *Neva*, of 370 tons. One of the ships was paid for by the government, the other by the Russian-American Company and Count Rumyantzev personally.

During the preparations the original plan was widened in scope, apparently thanks to Resanov. It was decided that a Russian mission to Japan should sail with the expedition to conclude a trade agreement with the country and thus open it up for trade with Russia. It is understandable that it should have been Resanov, Shelikhov's son-in-law, who championed this idea, for ever since the Kuriles had come under the jurisdiction of the Russian-American Company Japan had entered the sphere of its commercial interests. It thus seemed natural to entrust Resanov himself with the negotiations. He was granted the rank of royal chamberlain and decorated with one of the highest distinctions in the empire, the order of St Anne, first class. He was to sail to Japan as envoy extraordinary and minister plenipotentiary, and to Alaska as 'correspondent' of the Russian-American Company.

The importance of the expedition was underlined by the fact that Tsar Alexander made a visit to Kronstadt a few days before it was due to leave. The ambassador Resanov, with a suite of seven, was escorted aboard the *Nadeshda* by the Minister for Trade and the Deputy Minister of the Navy, Admiral Chichagov. The two ships left Kronstadt harbour on 8 August 1803. They sailed in company through the Kattegat, and then via Falmouth, Teneriffe, Cape Horn and Easter Island to Hawaii. From there Lisyansky in the *Neva* sailed to Kodiak, and Krusenstern and Resanov in the *Nadeshda* to Kamchatka.

After a seven-week stay in Petropavlovsk, Krusenstern put Resanov ashore at Nagasaki in September 1804. We shall discuss Resanov's mission, which ended in complete failure, later on (p. 292 *et seq*). He left Japan on 6 April 1805. The *Nadeshda* sailed through the Straits of Tsushima into the sea of Japan; she was the first Russian vessel to enter these waters, which were to be so fateful for Russia.

On 23 May Krusenstern entered Avacha Bay and Resanov landed at Petropavlovsk. A month later Krusenstern set off for Sakhalin again, sailed round it from the north-east and steered south in the direction of the Tartar Strait. Shallow water prevented him going very far and on 19 August he returned to Petropavlovsk. There he had some repairs carried out and loaded freight, and on 23 September 1805 set sail for Macao, where he had arranged to meet Lisyansky and sell the furs which the latter was to bring from Alaska.

The *Neva* and *Nadeshda* then set out for home together. They parted company again at the Cape of Good Hope; Lisyansky sailed straight to England and from there to Kronstadt, while Krusenstern went round the north of the British Isles and arrived home a fortnight later. The whole expedition formed a chapter of its own in the history of Russian activity in the Pacific, and one that was to have a great many consequences.

Resanov had decided to inspect his Company's possessions. He sailed from Petropavlovsk to Novo-Arkhangelsk in the brig *Juno*.

He was welcomed by Baranov with a salute of guns and a full-dress parade. The diplomat from St Petersburg was captivated by the governor. 'A rough diamond, but a diamond all right,' Resanov wrote of him. He was immediately struck by the difficulties with which Baranov had to cope, especially by the colony's lack of provisions. 'There is no flour here,' he reported to St Petersburg, 'because there is no labour force on Kodiak, and in Sitka the colonists are perishing from hunger because they are continually at war with the Koloshes, who are armed with the finest guns and falconets, and fishing takes place in pouring rain.' The Russian colonists' supply difficulties were also noted by Krusenstern: 'They lack even salt, that indispensable seasoning of our food,' he wrote, pointing out that the permanent state of hunger in the colonies should be taken into account when people felt inclined to criticize the Russian-American Company's 'unrestrained drive' towards the south.

In the long winter evenings Resanov found plenty of time to discuss all these questions with Baranov. Kuskov also took part in these conversations. In the meantime he had been promoted to commercial adviser and Baranov's official deputy; he was a quiet and clever man whom Resanov liked as much as he did Baranov. Resanov himself turned out to be a mild, simple and good-natured man. With Baranov he worked out a comprehensive programme which provided for improvements in the living conditions of the company's employees and the natives, the recruitment of doctors, the construction of hospitals and schools, and the extension of missionary activity. It was decided to purchase new ships. While he was still at Sitka Resanov asked the government in St Petersburg to allow the emigration of Russian peasants to the colonies as independent farmers. However, this suggestion was turned down; the government was afraid that in these circumstances all the Siberians would move over to America.

No doubt the two men also discussed political and strategic problems. Now that Resanov had visited Hawaii, Japan and Kamchatka and seen Sakhalin and the Kuriles, he could be regarded as the best-informed diplomat of his time on questions connected with the North Pacific. Baranov, too, had given him important information. Perhaps it is not a great exaggeration when Baranov's most recent biographer, Hector Chevigny, makes this assertion: 'Resanov was the first man in the world to understand that he who controls Alaska can also control the Pacific.' The documents available make it clear that Resanov and Baranov understood the significance of Alaska at that time far more clearly than their foreign counterparts.

The most urgent of all the problems discussed seemed to be the question of trade with California, known more often in those days as New Albion. A diplomat was needed for this task, and Resanov undertook it himself. After spending the winter at Novo-Arkhangelsk he sailed in March 1806 on board the *Juno* to San Francisco.

The *Juno* anchored in San Francisco harbour on 4 April. The Russians were given a friendly welcome and Resanov succeeded in establishing excellent relations not only with the Spanish officials but also with the superiors of the Catholic Mission.

He was perfectly frank about his aims with the governor of California, Don Arillaga. 'We need corn,' he said. 'We could get it from Canton, but California is nearer.' Resanov suggested drawing up a trade agreement and leaving the rest to their respective governments in St Petersburg and Madrid. To start with, he asked only for permission to sell the goods he had brought in the *Juno* and to buy corn with the proceeds.

But with the best will in the world Arillaga could not agree to these proposals. The Spanish colonies could only trade with foreign countries through the mother-country. This was the notorious 'colonial system' which had cost England her American colonies and was soon to bring about the breakaway of the Spanish colonies in America. It should be noted that from the beginning the Russian government strove for the opposite of this system, namely, direct trade by Alaska with foreign countries. This had been particularly emphasized in the statute of the Russian-American Company in 1799.

So the negotiations with the Spaniards produced no result. Arillaga would not even allow the goods on board the *Juno* to be sold. The only thing he could permit – no doubt to some extent on grounds of common humanity – was the purchase on this one occasion of corn and provisions for cash.

THE RUSSIANS IN CALIFORNIA

During his stay in California, Resanov became convinced that the colonial system was provoking considerable discontent there and that the example of the American states' successful revolt had not been lost on the Spanish colonists. Baranov, too, was well informed on this subject, for his friends, the Boston and East Indian captains, all carried on a contraband trade with California. The fact was that California simply could not exist without smuggling.

Nothing was more natural from the Russian point of view than to exploit the situation in order to acquire their own source of supplies for Alaska in California. Resanov wrote to St Petersburg pointing out that the section of coast between the Russian and Spanish colonies had so far not been occupied by anyone and that it was particularly important to gain a foothold on the Columbia River.

These ideas were not new to Baranov; in fact, he may have been their author. After Resanov's departure he gave serious thought to the question of the Columbia River and in 1808, when his first party of hunters went off to the coast of California, he gave them some of the old plaques inscribed 'Land belonging to Russia'. One of these plaques was buried on the shore of Bodega Bay. The expedition to the Columbia River had to be cancelled. Baranov had been told by St Petersburg that he could plant the flag of the Russian-American Company wherever he liked so long as such action involved no political complications. He was now warned to be particularly careful in his relations with the United States. In 1808 the first American consul arrived in St Petersburg and Tsar Alexander appointed his first *chargé d'affaires* in Washington; in 1809 Russia became the first of the great powers to grant *de jure* recognition to the United States.

Friendly relations began with a protest by the Russian government against the activities of American captains who were supplying the Indians in the territory of the Russian-American Company with weapons. Washington replied with the rather curious suggestion that if the Indians were to be regarded as Russian subjects it was up to the Russian government itself to prevent them buying weapons from foreigners, but if the Indians were not Russian subjects they could buy their weapons where they pleased. Two years later both sides appointed permanent ambassadors and Rumyantzev raised the question of the arms trade again, only this time he put it differently: he suggested that the Americans should take over the sale of Russian furs in China and in return stop selling guns to the Indians.

It is interesting to note that this plan was in fundamental agreement with the project already suggested to the American government by a private individual, John Jacob Astor, president of the American Fur Company. Shortly before, Astor had founded the Pacific Fur Company, whose object was the fur trade in the north-western territories on the far side of the Rocky Mountains.

In 1810 Astor sent two expeditions to the Columbia River, one up the Missouri and over the Rockies, the other by sea from New York. After incredible adventures and losses Astor's men succeeded in establishing a fortified post at the mouth of the Columbia. This post was christened 'Astoria'. Then war broke out between the U.S.A. and England, Astoria passed into the hands of a Canadian company and the British flag was hoisted there. It made no difference to Baranov whether it was British or American; in either case the Columbia River was barred to him. Only California was left.

In 1808 Baranov sent two vessels into Bodega Bay under the command of the faithful Kuskov. One of them ran aground under the cliffs; some of the crew were drowned and others fell into the hands of the Indians. The next year Kuskov tried to gain a firm foothold on Charlotte Island, but was prevented from doing so by the Indians. In March 1811 he appeared again off the Californian coast with hunters, tradesmen and all the necessary stores, and founded the Russian colony of 'Ross' on a little bay which he called Rumyantzev Bay, not far from Bodega Bay. The construction of a fort began at once. On 30 September (12 October) 1812 – it was St Alexander's Day, when Russian troops at the other end of the world were retreating from Smolensk, just occupied by Napoleon – the ten cannon of Fort Ross fired a salute for the Tsar. Three years later the fort was surrounded by the houses of Russian settlers and the huts of Aleutians brought from Alaska. There was also a flour-mill, a big farmyard, a tannery, barns, forges, workshops and baths. Wheat and hemp were grown and purchases gladly made from English and American captains. We are told about all this in the memoirs of Adalbert von Chamisso, the German writer and botanist who visited Fort Ross in 1817 when he was taking part in the Russian voyage round the world with Otto von Kotzebue.

By this time Baranov was seventy. He had several times requested permission to retire, but had not yet been relieved. His successor was to have been General Koch, the former commandant of Okhotsk, but Koch died before he could set out for Kodiak. In 1812 a second replacement was on the way, but went down with his ship and its crew of thirty-three in a storm. Shelikhov had long been dead and Resanov, too, had sunk into the grave. He had been on the way to St Petersburg through Siberia, but the hardships of the journey were too much for him; somewhere near Krasnoyarsk he fell off his horse with a heart attack.

The old governor had become lonely; really he should have retired long before. He suffered from gout and sometimes drank more than was good for him.

With Resanov's death the last living link between himself and the management of the company in St Petersburg had been snapped. Golikov was dead, and Natalia Shelikhov, if she was still alive, had certainly ceased to play an active part in the business. The Company had become a joint stock company, whose only real shareholder was the government; everything was depersonalized and bureaucratized. But Baranov still ruled his huge oceanic empire, which stretched from the Bering Strait to Bodega Bay, and before he resigned he even tried to extend this empire towards the south. This time the goal was Hawaii.

HAWAIIAN INTERLUDE

The Hawaiian Islands are the same as the Sandwich Islands, so named by their discoverer, Captain Cook, in honour of the First Lord of the Admiralty. Baranov knew all about the Hawaiian Islands, for they were a port of call on the way to Canton both from Alaska and California. The ruler of the islands, Kamehameha, called Tomi-Omi by the Russians, was also well informed about the 'Russian lord of Alaska'. Tired of his English and American friends, Kamehameha had perhaps thought at times of an alliance with Baranov, whom he probably imagined as an emperor like himself. At any rate, after the first greeting, which he sent in 1803 through O'Cain, he always sent his best wishes to Baranov and even expressed the wish to visit him. Fuller information was brought to Baranov by Lisyansky, who visited Hawaii in 1804 and gave a detailed description of the islands in his journal. From him Baranov learnt that coconuts, bananas, yams or sweet potatoes, onions, cabbage, melons and pumpkins grew in Hawaii, and that there were pigs, cattle, sheep and goats there, which had multiplied so fast that preventive measures had become necessary. It is not difficult to imagine the effect of this story on the ruler of a permanently hungry colony. In addition, the sandalwood tree also grew there, the article most in demand in the Chinese market.

Lisyansky also threw light on the political situation. Kame-hameha was striving to unite all the islands under his own rule; he had no particular love for the English, but they had helped him to build up an army and a fleet. Kamehameha needed both because the two northernmost islands, Kauai and Niihau, were under the sway of King Tamori, who did not recognize the authority of the emperor and was supported by the Americans; the two sovereigns were thus in a permanent state of war, a situation which opened up all kinds of possibilities for a third power.

The success of the Krusenstern-Lisyansky expedition had filled the Russian-American Company with enthusiasm for fresh enterprises. As soon as it had returned to Kronstadt the *Neva* took on board a fresh cargo and sailed under the command of Lieuten-ant L. A. von Hagemeister on a second trip round the world. The next year it was already at Novo-Arkhangelsk. Baranov sent Hagemeister to Hawaii to negotiate with Kamehameha, but he turned out to be a poor diplomat for he held conversations not only with Kamehameha but also with his enemy, Tamori. As a result the emperor's Russian sympathies cooled off noticeably. Tamori had asked for help and offered desirable concessions in return. But Baranov remained loyal to Kamehameha and wanted to work only through him.

When war broke out between England and the U.S.A. in 1812, several American captains suggested to Baranov that he should buy their ships, either in fact or only on paper, so that they could fly the Russian flag. Baranov acquired in this way one of the best American vessels, the *Atahualpa*. He re-christened it the *Bering* and sent it in 1813 under the command of Captain Bennet with a cargo and presents to his friend Kamehameha. The *Bering* met a storm and was driven off its course to the island of Kauai, where King Tamori seized the cargo as a prize. Bennet returned to Sitka and told Baranov what had happened.

The captured goods had to be recovered from Tamori by force and an opportunity to do this soon occurred. In 1814 a warship arrived from Kronstadt, the frigate *Suvorov* under the command of Lieutenant M. P. Lazarev. No one was better equipped than he to carry out the task. But Lazarev had no intention of taking orders from a 'trader'. He stayed at Sitka as long as he deemed necessary and then sailed home. However, before he departed he put ashore his medical officer, Dr Scheffer.

Georg Anton Scheffer was a German from Würzburg who had come to Russia in 1808 and became a police surgeon. He could speak Russian and English besides his native German. This man seemed to have arrived just at the right moment for Baranov. When Lazarev had begun to quarrel with the governor, Scheffer took the latter's part, and the old man would not pay attention to Lazarev's repeated assertions that Scheffer was an unreliable adventurer. This turned out to be a fateful mistake on Baranov's part: for the young Lazarev already showed that knowledge of men which later made him the educator of the best men in the Russian Navy, the heroes of the Crimean War.

Baranov sent Scheffer to Hawaii with the task of making Tamori return the *Bering* and its cargo, but he explained to him at the same time that this was really only a secondary aim. The most important thing was to find a good harbour and to conclude a trade agreement with Kamehameha. Force was not to be thought of; on the contrary, it was a question of obliterating the unpleasant impression which Hagemeister's haughty manner and intrigue with Tamori had made on the 'Imperator'.

All this was very well planned, but Baranov's mistake consisted in trusting Scheffer too far and setting no bounds to his enterprise. He put considerable power in his hands and had to cash the cheques which Scheffer issued in Hawaii. Scheffer did not deceive or rob Baranov; the affair simply went to his head and on his journey to Hawaii he thought rather too often of those of his countrymen who had been made generals, counts and chancellors by Tsars in return for their services.

In October 1815, Captain Bennet of the *Peddler*, which was sailing under the Russian flag, landed Scheffer on the enchanting island of Oahu, where the emperor and his court were at the time. Kamehameha received him coolly and would not even read the message from Baranov. However, Scheffer showed that he was a learned man and a doctor, and gradually won the ruler's confidence. In return for his services he was given a large piece of land, on which he immediately began to grow tobacco and yams. He put up some houses and set about buying up pieces of land from the natives. All this went on in the strategic centre of the Pacific, between Honolulu and the modern Pearl Harbour.

Scheffer's spirit of enterprise was highly displeasing to the Americans, who already owned plantations on Oahu. They were still more seriously displeased by Scheffer's frantic buying up of sandalwood and his attempt to persuade Kamehameha to give him a monopoly in the export of this valuable natural product. They pointed out to the 'Imperator' what dangers this involved to the independence of his kingdom.

In these circumstances Scheffer soon began to feel uncomfortable and when in spring 1816 two armed vessels of the Russian-American Company arrived, the *Kodiak* and the *Ilmen*, both of them acquired by Baranov from the Americans and under the command of American captains, he went off to King Tamori on the island of Kauai, leaving some of his men behind to guard the plantations. Tamori was in need of help and therefore quickly agreed to an alliance with the Russian Empire in the person of Herr Scheffer. The king not only granted Scheffer the exclusive right to export sandalwood but also conceded half the island of Oahu to the Russian-American Company 'in permanent usufruct'. There was only one snag: this blessed isle still contained the Emperor Kamehameha, who had therefore first to be chased off it. For this purpose Scheffer promised to write to Russia for no more and no less than five hundred soldiers; as a beginning, he bought an armed schooner from an American and handed it over to Tamori.

In order to waste no time, Scheffer began to lay out plantations and to build forts on Kauai. He constructed three of the latter, equipped them with cannon and hoisted the Russian flag over them. He possessed great initiative but only small forces: a few Russians and about fifty Aleutians.

In everything he undertook Scheffer acted on his own responsibility. Baranov was worried and had him warned, but the doctor already felt like the Baranov of Hawaii. His alliance with Tamori had naturally become known at once to the latter's opponent, Kamehameha, and all relations between the doctor and the emperor were broken off at once. When the Russian ship *Rurik*, commanded by Lieutenant Otto von Kotzebue, arrived at Hawaii in November 1816, panic broke out, for Kamehameha thought that the five hundred soldiers who were to conquer his realm had now arrived. But, instead of soldiers, the only person Kotzebue had on board was Kamehameha's old friend and personal physician Don Eliot y Castro, a Brazilian who had entered the service of the Russian-American Company. Eliot pacified the emperor, who received Kotzebue and informed him that 'as a hero himself, he respected the other hero, Emperor Alexander'. But the emperor made some extremely sharp complaints about Scheffer; they culminated in the accusation that Scheffer had encouraged Tamori to defy the emperor. In answer, Kotzebue swore to Kamehameha that, as he wrote later, 'Scheffer's bad behaviour could in no way be attributed to the wish of the Russian emperor.' Kotzebue convinced Kamehameha that the Tsar had no desire to seize possession of his islands.

It is clear from this episode that Kotzebue, who had left Russia in 1815, had no idea of the plans of the Russian-American Company with regard to the Hawaiian Islands. This effectively disposes of the story that the Russian government had long-matured plans for the conquest of the most important strategic point in the Pacific. There was no word of any such plan in Kotzebue's instructions, which had been drawn up by Krusenstern. Kotzebue's arrival, which showed that neither the Russian government nor Russian military power was behind Scheffer, put paid to all his plans.

In actual fact Tamori had been influenced to such an extent by Scheffer that in May 1816 the doctor had enrolled him as a Russian citizen 'with the hoisting of the Russian flag in front of his palace'. The Tsar was informed of this event the following year, and at the suggestion of the Russian-American Company it was decided to send to Tamori 'a gold medal on the ribbon of the order of St Anne, together with a suitably mounted sword and a crimson cloak adorned with gold lace.' In spite of this the Russian-American Company was officially informed by the Foreign Ministry that 'the acquisition of these islands would bring no gain to Russia and might well involve her in considerable difficulties. For this reason His Imperial Majesty was not inclined to confirm Tamori's acquisition of Russian nationality.'

This decision was conveyed to the management of the Company on 24 February 1818, that is, five months before the arrival of Scheffer's report describing the collapse of his enterprises. What had happened meanwhile in Hawaii? Just what the Foreign Ministry in St Petersburg and Baranov in Novo-Arkhangelsk had probably feared. While Scheffer and Tamori were planning the seizure of the island of Oahu, Kamehameha's 'imperial guard', under the command of an English seaman called Young, had destroyed Scheffer's post there. His representative, Tarakanov, had to flee with all his men to the island of Kauai in the very schooner which Scheffer had bought for the conquest of the Hawaiian empire. In Hawaii, to use Scheffer's own words, 'a revolution began'. The people behind it were the Americans. The American captain of the *Ilmen* betrayed Scheffer and joined his own countrymen. Scheffer, together with the Russian employees and the Aleutians, was put on board the *Kodiak* and requested, in Tamori's name, to leave the island. But the *Kodiak* had no water on board and was leaking into the bargain. The ship was disarmed and only then allowed to enter harbour, when the captain ran it aground on a sandbank.

That is where Kotzebue found the ship when he arrived at Hawaii for the second time in October 1817. By then Scheffer had already sailed off to Canton in a foreign ship. The crew of the *Kodiak* were starving, and Kotzebue provided them with food. Tarakanov then 'lent' the Aleutians to an American for hunting on the Californian coast, in return for which the American delivered them at Sitka at the end of the expedition. Tarakanov himself and his Russian companions went back to Baranov.

In September 1817 Scheffer sent a report from Canton to St Petersburg describing what had happened; he himself arrived in the capital twenty-one months later, long after it had been decided to give up the idea of making Tamori's kingdom a Russian protectorate. When he appeared in St Petersburg in person he produced a long memorandum on the economic and political importance of the Sandwich Islands and recommended their immediate occupation.

However, his reflections provoked nothing but ironic remarks, whereupon the energetic doctor went off to Brazil, which had been recommended to him, probably by Eliot, as another land of 'unlimited possibilities'. There he was made a count by the Emperor Don Pedro I as a reward for special services and was given the task of recruiting soldiers for the Brazilian Army in Germany. The 'Count' then went to Germany; whether or not he ever returned to Brazil is not known.

BARANOV RETIRES

Baranov had asked several times to be relieved. But, as usually happens, he had probably been quite pleased at heart each time he had learnt that his successor had not reached Alaska. He had lived too long in his oceanic empire and grown too accustomed to power; moreover, he was an emotional person, who could not tear himself away from the people whom he had tyrannized and loved for almost three decades. In St Petersburg he had always been regarded almost as part of Russian America, and so long as Shelikhov's and Resanov's old friends were alive and influential Baranov was looked upon as irreplaceable. The first naval officers who had worked with him in America – Davidov, Khvostov, Lisyansky – were still under the spell of the 'governor's' powerful personality. But later on sharp criticism was heard. During their stay in American waters the smart commanders of the corvettes and frigates were officially 'at the governor's disposal', for the Company financed their trips and it was always their task to carry freight to and from Alaska. This led continually to friction and clashes; the naval officers often refused to follow the directions of the 'shopkeeper' Baranov. When they returned home they were at pains to emphasize the governor's authoritarian ways and the lack of order in the colony. When Lazarev reported how Baranov had shown favour to Dr Scheffer, whom Lazarev had dismissed, the naval ministry was furious. Worst of all for Baranov was the fact that Scheffer's conduct in Hawaii very soon showed how right his young critic had been. Baranov had involved the Company in an affair which brought it a loss of several hundred thousand roubles and caused serious displeasure in higher quarters. It was the first time that anything like this had happened, and when account was taken of the fact that Baranov was over seventy there could be no doubt that he had overstepped the age limit. His personal fate was now decided.

In 1816 a new expedition of two ships under the command of Captain von Hagemeister, who was already known at Sitka as well as in Hawaii, was dispatched to Alaska. The frigate *Kutuzov* arrived at Sitka in July 1817, the frigate *Suvorov*, with Hagemeister himself on board, in November. Hagemeister had been commissioned to inspect Baranov's activities and to appoint a successor.

This meant that a naval officer without any commercial experience was taking on the job of inspecting the greatest trading enterprise in the Russian Empire and of finding a man who could manage it. His assistant in the task was to be Lieutenant S. Yanovsky, who had already been on Sitka with Lazarev and was naturally prejudiced against Baranov.

It turned out that the business was in perfect order, so far as one can speak of 'perfect order' when the book-keeping was so primitive, for the supporting documents often consisted only of a note or a scrap of paper. At any rate, the two officers convinced themselves of one thing: beyond the thirty shares in the Company which belonged to him officially, Baranov did not possess any private capital of his own at all. The directors in St Petersburg, whose jobs cost the Company a third of its total income, bought houses and jewels; Baranov possessed neither.

Even the dry Hagemeister had to recognize this. The young Yanovsky was already under the spell of the mighty old man. A contributory factor in this was Baranov's daughter, the beautiful Irina, a proud and religious girl. Her romance with Yanovsky, worthy of the pen of a Chateaubriand or Turgenev, was pure and charming. When the lieutenant asked Baranov for her hand, he knew that he was wooing a maiden who was penniless. There is a small detail which is worth mentioning in this connection. In the document legitimizing *post factum* Baranov's marriage with the Indian Anna Grigorievna, the latter is described as 'Princess of Kenai' (her Indian tribe) and, as Baranov at that time had already been ennobled himself, their children were recognized as hereditary Russian nobles. This enabled the aristocratic officer Yanovsky to conclude a legitimate marriage with the half-Indian Irina in the church of St Michael in the town of Novo-Arkhangelsk.

Hagemeister soon saw that it was not so easy to replace Baranov. The Indians as well as the Russian employees and foreign captains continued to recognize only him as governor. Finally Hagemeister found a solution: he appointed Baranov's new son-in-law, Yanovsky, as his successor!

This eased the pain of parting for the old man. He was also cheered by the arrival at Sitka of the ex-naval captain W. M. Golovnin in the gunboat *Kamchatka*. Golovnin suggested to Baranov that he should come to St Petersburg and take over the post of adviser to the Russian-American Company. Golovnin also promised to take young Antipatr Baranov to St Petersburg and to have him enrolled in the cadet corps. The old man, who had previously made up his mind to spend his last days with old Kamehameha in Hawaii, agreed to 'go home' to the icy tundra of St Petersburg where so many hot-blooded men had already frozen to death.

On 27 November 1818 Baranov went aboard the frigate *Kutuzov* and looked back at his island for the last time. As usual the ship was laden with furs. A crowd of people – Russians, Aleutians and Indians – had gathered on the shore. They all found it hard to take their leave of this man: a rough diamond, at once harsh and kind, who feared nothing, took all responsibility on himself, was capable of admitting his own mistakes and also ready to forgive those of others. The *Kutuzov* headed for Batavia. There Baranov went ashore to see the sights. He returned on board with a high fever. He died on 16 April 1819 and his body was consigned, after a few short prayers, to the waters of the Indian Ocean.

Almost all colonial pioneers have enjoyed a bad name in their own countries and Baranov was no exception. Naval officers had undermined his reputation and Speransky set the seal on their views. The famous statesman's description of Baranov as 'resolute and daring, but drunken and cruel' was repeated by later historians of Siberia. But Speransky never went farther east than Irkutsk and he never saw Baranov. He founded his opinion on the stories told by others. How little he understood conditions in the American colonies is clear from his accusation that Baranov let his employees starve for seven years. Baranov himself was starving during these seven years, for not an ounce of flour was sent to him from Okhotsk. Naturally he was rough, but no rougher than his surroundings. Most of the men with whom he had to deal were ecsaped convicts and deported criminals. If he had not treated them roughly he could not have maintained discipline amid the continual struggle against the Indians and the ocean, and the permanent hunger and undernourishment. It was the hard colonial life to be found in all colonies in those days. Baranov served the system of cruel exploitation and slave-labour; but no other was at his disposal or even in existence.

In the early years he ruled his America without vodka, and almost without rations either. How was he to keep his men under control? When vodka arrived as well as food, it eased the situation. The Company began to sell vodka as well as bread and clothes on credit, and thus finally enslaved everyone. Baranov could see how hateful this system was, but without vodka, as he wrote to St Petersburg, he could not rule. This statement is understandable seeing that it came from a man who drank himself and considered it impossible to live in the conditions of the 'accursed American life' without drinking. All Russian finance ministers considered it impossible to govern without vodka, at any rate up to the October Revolution – and even after it. We cannot judge a man too severely because he expressed this opinion a hundred and fifty years ago.

The Russian-American Company simply reflected conditions as a whole in the Russia of those days, with its serfs, small-scale economic organization and lack of personal freedom. And all this was accentuated by the monopolistic character of the Company. Yet the Russian-American Company would have had the chance to develop into a normal and sound colony, if it had been regarded as a colony by the Russian government. But in fact this was not the case. There were never any colonists in Russian America, only employees and workmen. Shelikhov, and after him Resanov, had dreamed of founding an agricultural colony, and to this end had requested the dispatch of peasant colonists from Russia. They succeeded once in obtaining a few dozen families of colonists, but that was the end of it. Afterwards the government rejected all requests that farmers should be settled in Alaska.

So there grew up a colony without colonists, an enterprise which was administered by the St Petersburg civil service but at the same time had at any cost to provide a profit for the shareholders. Baranov could not alter this situation. He was coarse, often even brutal, but personally honourable and upright. These qualities were not denied even by the monk-missionaries who in general were hostile to him and criticized him sharply, on much the same grounds as Catholic missionaries criticized the activities of the French and Spanish colonial rulers in the eighteenth century. The main charge of both the Orthodox and Catholic missionaries was that of disorderly or immoral behaviour, especially 'illegitimate unions' with native women. The monk Yuvenaly was tortured to death by the Indians because of his opposition to polygamy. The other monks could hardly be pleased when the governor himself set an example of immorality by living with an Indian woman and having two illegitimate children by her. Baranov's union with Anna Grigorievna was only legalized several years later. Nor could the monks applaud Baranov's readiness to protect Russians who acquired illegitimate wives and children in America. That he built the schools and churches in which the monks taught and preached moderated only a little the righteous anger of these stern preachers of Christian morality.

Amid hardships and dangers that would have been unimaginable to a Hastings or a Bourdonnais, Baranov had built up in the course of twenty-eight years by remarkable strength of will and foresight one of the biggest commercial enterprises in the world. He was a first-class business organizer and it was only during his tenure of office that the Russian-American Company made a real profit. In the last few years before his retirement the shareholders were receiving a dividend of 15 per cent, in spite of the fact that most of the Company's income was swallowed up by the management in St Petersburg.

Baranov was a merchant and had no exclusively political aims. Both in California and Hawaii he was acting only in the interests of his great enterprise. But the limits he set to these interests were wide and his plans thus overstepped purely commercial calculations and automatically became political. Baranov brought to life the old Siberian ideas of a warm water outlet and trade with economically more powerful neighbours. Like all Siberian governors and diplomats, Baranov did not want to wage war but to trade. He was a living embodiment of the old Siberian dynamic. The old Siberia, which had leaped across to the other side of the Pacific, gazed from there, through Baranov, at China. Therein lay Baranov's significance and strength.

THE LEGACY LEFT BY BARANOV

If Baranov had not succeeded in gaining a base in Hawaii, the base in California was still there after his death. The management of the Russian-American Company understood very well that the actual occupation of Ross had to be confirmed legally. It had therefore approached the Tsar with the request that the situation should be clarified by means of negotiations with Spain. But Alexander I did not wish to take active steps in the Pacific; he had no intention of thereby uniting two competitors, England and the U.S.A. When in 1817 the Spanish government handed over a protest, St Petersburg made no reply and confined itself to sending Hagemeister to legalize the position of Ross on the spot. Hagemeister executed this commission with his usual diplomatic talent: he sailed from Sitka to California and concluded with some Indian chief a treaty ceding the territory round Ross to the Russian-American Company.

At this time the Company was very worried about the barter trade with the Indians. It was not in a position to give the Indians so much in the way of blankets, powder, guns and gin for its furs as foreign captains did. The clever Golovnin told the government bluntly that there was no point in extending the Company's monopoly without giving it effective protection against foreign captains. His words made an impression and in September 1821, simultaneously with the renewal of the Company's privileges, a decree was issued forbidding all foreign ships 'not only to put in to coasts and islands under Russian protection but even to approach any nearer to them that one hundred nautical miles'.

This brought protests from both the American and British governments. It also happened that the Holy Alliance, in which Russia was the senior partner, did not recognize the independence of Mexico but continued to regard it as a Spanish colony. The American answer to both these acts was President Monroe's message to Congress of 2 December 1823, which was directed primarily against Russia. This statement proclaimed that from then onwards the American continent could not be regarded as a possible site for future colonization by a European power. This is the famous 'Monroe Doctrine', which gained more and more importance as time went by and was theoretically the basis of American foreign policy right up to our own day.

The negotiations on Alaska at St Petersburg in 1824 were thus conducted after the proclamation of the Monroe Doctrine. They ended in the signing of treaties with the U.S.A. in April 1824 and with England in February 1825. The contents of the treaties were the same in each case and although Russia abandoned any attempt to stop foreign ships sailing into Alaskan waters the treaties cannot be regarded as a defeat for Russian diplomacy. On the contrary, the Russians were skilful enough to exploit the rivalry between England and the U.S.A. and to prevent them establishing a common front by dealing with each partner separately. Originally the British were unwilling to put the Russian frontier in Alaska farther south than 60 or 59 degrees North. However, as the Americans recognized 54° 40′ North as the border, the British were compelled to do the same.

The eastern boundary of Alaska fixed by the Russo-English conference, 141 degrees West, was also very advantageous to Russia. It is sufficient to point out that the huge basin of the Yukon River was left to the Russian-American Company, a fact whose importance, in the prevailing ignorance about the American north-west, was naturally not fully grasped by any of the diplomats assembled in St Petersburg. But others grasped the essence of the problem. Count N. S. Mordvinov pointed out to the foreign minister, Nesselrode, that 'the uselessness of possessing large tracts of wilderness' may be more apparent than real, for their 'use' only became evident later. It should be added that this delimitation of frontiers was equivalent to international recognition of the Russian-American Company's territorial rights.

The Monroe Doctrine had no direct influence on the St Petersburg negotiations but it was taken into account by the Russians in their consideration of the Californian question. It had now become clear that the opponent to reckon with in California was no longer Spain but the United States. Monroe's message was a warning backed by real power.

However, the political situation in California automatically demanded negotiations. Mexico had already broken away from Spain and California lived its own life. There were no armed forces there at all, and when the guns of the Russian frigate *Kreuzer* fired a salute on entering San Francisco harbour in 1824 the coastal batteries did not reply because they had no powder. That made a deep impression on a young lieutenant on board called D. I. Savalishin. The *Kreuzer* was commanded by Captain M. P. Lazarev, Baranov's old opponent, who had meanwhile made his name through his voyages to the Antarctic with Billingshausen. Lazarev himself did not dabble in politics, and this made Savalishin do so all the more enthusiastically. It is a dangerous game for young lieutenants; a year later Savalishin joined the Decembrist conspiracy and ended his political career in Siberia.

His plan was to encourage the Californian separatists to proclaim their independence and then to demand the right to colonize

California freely as the price for recognition by Russia. Savalishin had thought it all out and already made contact with the head of the Catholic party in California, Joseph Altimira, prior of the mission at San Francisco. The youthful lieutenant described himself to this worthy Catholic as 'Grand Master of the Order of Restitution', whose aims were, so he said, 'the protection of religion and the throne and the struggle against freemasonry'. The head of the order, according to Savalishin, was Tsar Alexander I. We do not know whether Altimira believed all this; he must have seen what kind of a man Savalishin was, but at any rate he conducted conversations with him.

Savalishin also disclosed his plans to his comrade, Lieutenant E. W. Putyatin, who was obviously the better politician of the two, for he declared the project to be utopian. Thirty years later he was able to give further proof of his political judgement.

Soon afterwards Alexander I died and the Decembrist revolt broke out. When the new Tsar, Nicholas I, finally gave his opinion on Savalishin's Californian plan, the latter was already shut up in a lonely fort. The imperial government flatly declined to have anything to do with the fantastic plan which was directed, into the bargain, against the lawful King of Spain and might have caused serious political complications.

By this time the Russian-American Company's interest in California was already on the wane. The gains brought in by Ross were far smaller than the costs of its upkeep. It had no land for agricultural purposes, and it was impossible to acquire any because in the meantime Spanish and American ranches had been established all round the colony. Corn had therefore still to be purchased in San Francisco or Santiago.

When in 1836 California declared itself independent of Mexico, there could be no further doubt that the 'protector' of the country in the sense intended by Savalishin could only be the great American republic. So in 1841 Ross was sold. The buyer was a private individual, the German Swiss Johann August Sutter, the 'emperor of California', on whose land, bought from the Russian-American Company, the first gold in western America was found. The 'emperor' had made a pretty good deal; the purchase price of the colony was only thirty thousand dollars. Through some swindle on the part of the middlemen, even this sum never reached the till of the Russian-American Company.

VI

MURAVYEV TAKES THE AMUR

———◆•◆◆•◆———

ON THE THRESHOLD
OF THE NINETEENTH CENTURY

THE ATTEMPT to create an outlet for Siberia to the world market through Russian America had failed. Baranov's realm finally became a proper overseas colony, and the shortest way to it was across the sea. Siberia remained off the beaten track and continued to form a world of its own.

For a long time Moscow, and later St Petersburg, regarded Siberia simply as a source of income. One of the first decrees dealing with Siberia had been the introduction of the *yassak*, the tribute in fur, in 1586. Some years later the original collective payments were replaced by individual taxation: five sable skins a year from every adult man and woman, and in addition every tenth skin from any further animals killed. Russian hunters thus had to hand over a tenth of their spoils.

Interest in other natural resources was also considerable right from the start. Even before Yermak's expedition, Ivan the Terrible had commissioned the Stroganovs to look for iron, copper, lead and sulphur in Siberia. All through the seventeenth century the government required the *voivodes* to prospect for ores, mica, sulphur and precious stones. People were firmly convinced that sooner or later ores would be found; both in the Altai and in Transbaikalia the natives showed the Russians disused pits overgrown by trees a hundred years old, in which they found primitive tools and the skeletons of ore-miners.

However, it was not until the time of Peter the Great that the search for useful minerals was crowned with success. In 1704 the Nerchinsk works was founded to process the lead and silver deposits of Daurien and four years later Henning, the 'chief miner' of Siberia and the Urals, announced to the Tsar the extraction of the first pound and a half of silver. Before the end of Peter's reign Akinfy, son of the famous pioneer of the Urals, Nikita Demidov, had prospected for ore in the Altai mountains and quickly discovered rich deposits.

Demidov set to work at once on a big scale. He recruited master miners from Saxony and at the end of ten years he was the owner of seventeen copper mines and thirty gold, silver and lead mines in the Altai. In 1745 he extracted the first Siberian gold. It was only a by-product of the silver and the event was of no real significance. All the same, gold is gold, and two years later Demidov's mines were bought by the Empress Elizabeth and after that were the private property of the Tsar's family. In 1787 Catherine II bought up the Nerchinsk silver and lead mines in the same way.

Iron-works sprang up only after the death of Peter the Great. The first iron-works was founded in 1734 on the River Tuba, not far from the modern Minusinsk, the second near Kuznetsk in 1771 and the third, the Petrovski works, in Transbaikalia in 1789. Their equipment was primitive and their production insignificant.

Real gold-dust was found at the beginning of the nineteenth century, in the Nerchinsk region. Gold was immediately declared a government monopoly. To start with, private individuals were forbidden even to look for it. Not until 1826 was this veto lifted; ten years later private exploitation was also allowed, on condition that all gold produced was handed over to the treasury.

The question arises, what profit did the state gain from its huge colony? Originally, the tribute of furs paid by the natives formed the main source of income. According to Dr Giles Fletcher, who went to Moscow in 1588 as English ambassador, the export of furs brought in at that time four or five hundred thousand roubles every year. According to G. K. Kotoshikhin, a Russian living in Sweden who wrote a great work on the Russian Empire in 1666–7, round the middle of the seventeenth century Russia obtained furs worth more than six hundred thousand roubles every year from Siberia. At that time, this sum was about a third of the state's total income. From the time of Peter the Great onwards there was the silver and copper as well, and the relative importance of the furs gradually declined. Soon customs dues from trade with China and licences for the production and sale of vodka came to the fore. To collect all these taxes the state had to pay a host of officials, who received twice the salary of those in Russia; it had to maintain frontier guards, keep such roads as there were in good repair, often feed the starving population, and finally make good the deficit on the state mines, which, as time went on, grew less and less productive. What had once been the main source of income, the famous *yassak*, sank almost to nothing as the animals were gradually exterminated and in 1769 it was brought to an end.

If the state itself got relatively little out of Siberia, there were a large number of people for whom it was paved with gold. As in all colonies, this was particularly true of the officials and merchants. In the seventeenth century Siberia was divided into districts governed by *voivodes*. At first there was only one, that of Tobolsk; as more land was occupied others were added (Tomsk in 1629, Yakutsk in 1638, Yeniseisk in 1676), and in 1678 the district of Verkhoturye was separated from that of Tobolsk.

Peter the Great ended the division of Siberia into districts and formed instead a unified 'Siberian government' consisting of five provinces, with Tobolsk as the capital. The *Sibirsky Prikas* became the 'government chancellery' in Moscow. The governor appointed by Peter was the former *voivode* of Nerchinsk, Prince Gagarin. With his appointment, his fortune began to grow like a snowball. He built himself a palace in Tobolsk, where he held 'court' and had his own theatre and orchestra. He had another palace built in Moscow. 'The finest of all the houses is the house of Prince Gagarin in Tverskaya Street,' says an old guide to Moscow. The Tsar gradually began to grow suspicious of the prince's luxurious living. After a long and wearisome investigation Gagarin was tried, condemned to death and cruelly executed in the square outside the senate-house in St Petersburg.

According to the official explanation the reason for the governor's execution was his readiness to accept bribes, but this seems hardly credible. The 'fattening' of the *voivodes* on perquisites was common knowledge; it was a tradition that had come down from the seventeenth century. Peter was certainly concerned to put an end to this practice, but the discovery of an offender is not sufficient to explain his furious anger, frantic behaviour and undeniable cruelty in the case of Gagarin. The truth was that the governor's position had been undermined by the catastrophic failure of the two expeditions he had dispatched to the gold-fields in Chinese Turkestan, those of Colonel Buchholtz in 1715 and Prince Beckovich-Cherkasky in 1716. The two detachments together numbered several thousand men, and only a few hundred returned. The Tsar did not soon forget mistakes of that sort. Moreover, there was another point as well. Gagarin was known as a friend of the Swedish prisoners-of-war. Strahlenberg mentions his benevolence, and so does F. W. von Bergholz, a young court chamberlain from Holstein, who lived in St Petersburg from 1721 to 1725. The latter also indicates the real reason for Peter's anger: Gagarin was suspected of wanting to detach Siberia from the Russian empire with the help of the Swedish prisoners-of-war.

This accusation is interesting inasmuch as a hundred years later, in a somewhat milder form, it brought about the fall of another governor of Siberia, Nikolai N. Muravyev-Amursky, who will be discussed later on. As for the 'fattening', it went on as before.

After Gagarin's execution Peter offered the post of governor to his friend Grigory Stroganov, but Stroganov declined it. He could 'fatten himself' at home, for his wealth was enormous. Of Anika's three sons, only Semyon, the youngest, had descendants still alive. Grigory's and Yakov's lines had become extinct in the second and third generations. In the hands of Grigory, Anika's great-great-grandson, lay all that the descendants of the colonizer of Perm had collected in the course of a hundred and fifty years.

The post of governor was taken instead by Prince Cherkasky. His father had been a *voivode* in Siberia and had returned fabulously wealthy. His son did not waste his time either; as his biographer remarks tersely, 'no one came back from Siberia empty-handed'. The prince's only daughter married Count Sheremetev, who owned seventy thousand serfs and a corresponding acreage of land. His wife brought him as a dowry another eighty thousand serfs and estates amounting to almost half the land in the province of Moscow. The lucky pair owned the biggest fortune in all Russia.

It was already the ostentatious age of Catherine, and Peter's modest 'Siberian government' was now called the 'Tsardom of Siberia'. It received its own coat-of-arms, with the two inevitable sables, and from 1763 to 1781 special Siberian coins were minted. From 1764 onwards the tsardom consisted of two governments, those of Tobolsk and Irkutsk.

The period of the 'Siberian Tsardom' included the 'reign' of Denis Ivanovich Chicherin, 'father Denis', who really did rule like a Tsar and nearly drove the Siberians crazy with his pretentious ways. Not a wicked man in himself, he was nevertheless a typical Siberian despot, accustomed to make his plans without consulting any experts and to carry them through regardless of the human sacrifices involved. His particular concern was the construction of the great road from Tobolsk to Irkutsk. For this project the marshy Baraba steppe had to be conquered and colonized. 'Father Denis' used exiles and recruits, with whose bones, so they used to say in Siberia, the road was paved.

In 1803, under Alexander I, there was a fresh administrative reform. After an inspection, which, as usual, brought all kinds of abuses to light, Siberia was again united in one government. The inspector, Senator Selifontov, was appointed governor-general and at once began to act in an even more arbitrary way than his predecessors. As a result of reports by Count Golovkin, who in 1805 travelled through Siberia to China, Selifontov was dismissed and 'forbidden to set foot in Moscow or St Petersburg'.

Now began the era of Governor-General Pestel, who held office from 1805 to 1819 but spent only three of these years in Siberia. As a senator and member of various important committees and commissions, he compiled memoranda and drew up new laws. Most of his time, however, was devoted to protecting his Siberian deputy, Treskin, against the 'malicious slanders of grumblers', who, in Pestel's view, formed most of the population of Siberia. As a good Saxon and former post-office official, Pestel distinguished himself by his industry and integrity; after ruling Siberia on paper for fourteen years he had collected nothing for himself except debts. The Siberians would not have grudged him a few perquisites if only he had shown the slightest interest in their real needs. While Pestel sat in St Petersburg the corruption of the officials in Siberia grew absolutely intolerable. Treskin took no bribes personally; it was all done by his wife, who was imitated by all her husband's colleagues.

Pestel's tenure of office ended with a fresh review in 1819. The inspector, Speransky, the famous legislator of Alexander I's reign, was appointed governor-general. He regarded the post as a kind of banishment, and felt lonely and unhappy in Irkutsk. 'For nearly three years I have not heard one single intelligent word,' he wrote to his daughter. His reform of the Siberian administration turned out to be more modest than had been expected even in St Petersburg. In 1822 Siberia was again split into two, a western half with its capital at Tobolsk and an eastern half with its capital at Irkutsk.

The two governors were given advisory councils, the judiciary was divided rather more clearly from the general administration, and the nomads of the steppes were granted a shadowy kind of self-government. At bottom, very little had changed.

There must certainly have been many governors who did not think only of their own interests, for in spite of everything Siberia made economic progress, its farmers were prosperous, the Cossacks were loyal to their Tsar, and the natives were not completely exterminated by merciless pioneers. We must not forget one thing: supported by the Russian Church, from the beginning of the eighteenth century onwards the government was carrying on a struggle for the poor 'savages' with adventurers and fortune-hunters of every kind.

Bad as the Russian administration in Siberia may have been, it was no crueller or more barbaric than the colonial governments of the other European powers in the seventeenth and eighteenth centuries. Rather the reverse; in the expansion of Russian rule the native population was nowhere completely exterminated, as was the case in Australia, Haiti, Newfoundland and a large part of North America. The worst sufferers were the Kamchadales and the Aleutians, but even these peoples were not absolutely destroyed; the Tartars of western Siberia, the Buryats and the Yakuts even began to increase again in the nineteenth century. And Russia was the only one of the old colonial powers which never tolerated slavery and slave-dealing as legal institutions in her colonies.

The only form of serfdom in Siberia was the 'enrolment' of Russian peasants for the royal mines; at the end of the eighteenth century there were about sixty thousand 'enrolled workers' of this sort. Otherwise there was no serfdom either for Russians or for native Siberians. Illegal enslavement of individual 'savages' did nevertheless take place, especially in remote border territories, as the government prohibitions of 1726, 1741 and 1748 indicate. Speransky's decree of 1826, which laid down severe penalties for depriving the natives of their freedom, put an end to this practice.

All these decrees dealt not with the legal possession of slaves but with kidnapping. There was never any mass slavery in Siberia, simply because there was no economic occasion for it as there was in the Spanish colonies with their gold-mining or the North

American colonies with their cotton plantations. In Siberia the native had to bring in sable skins from the *taiga*, and for that he had to be and remain free. The old Siberian writer Shashkov describes in picturesque language how 'the Siberians of all classes, from the *voivodes* down to the last little trader, all robbed the natives.' It is the usual story of the chase after women in the colonies. The old sources cited by Shashkov tell how 'servants and all kinds of traders took away the natives' women and girls by force and kept them', and how the Cossacks in Kamchatka 'abducted the natives' women and shared them out . . . but after the birth of children they mostly married them.' As the frontier regions were colonized cases of women being kidnapped grew rarer and rarer.

'Down to the last little trader,' says Shashkov. But even the smallest shopkeeper somewhere in Mangaseya or Yakutia was a personality, not to mention the big merchants in the towns. The latter regarded themselves as the masters of Siberia, and not without reason. They were the economic pioneers of Siberia. They financed the bands of Cossacks who in the course of a few dozen years conquered a land bigger than the Roman empire.

The only person from whom a Tunguse or a Yakut could buy powder, lead, a fishing net or a bottle of vodka was 'his' merchant. In return he had to deliver so many furs or work for so many days. In the region of Yakutsk the merchant Chartkov sold his goods on credit at prices about which the buyers did not even inquire; they took their goods in silence and went off, knowing that at a certain time Chartkov would appear and claim what was due to him. In this way, particularly by selling on credit, the firms of Kandinsky and Butin made millions in Transbaikalia. A merchant called Saltanov obtained control of the Turukhansk region. He forbade the local inhabitants to buy anything from any other merchant, he bought and sold his own customers, and when there was an outbreak of smallpox he announced that the property of those who had died had passed into his own possession; for all the local people without exception were his debtors!

There was no lack of attempts to control the traders' greed for profit, but even the most honest and human *voivode* could see that trade in Siberia was bound to be in the nature of exploitation. With the huge distances involved and the absence of roads and security, transport risks were enormous; capital took a long time to show a return; and customs dues and bribes formed another heavy expense. A businessman could not make ends meet with a normal profit; he had to demand an excessive profit.

Tender-hearted men could not have overcome these obstacles, and the merchants were therefore all more or less men like Atlasov or Khabarov. When all is said and done, they brought the most essential goods to the consumers, they organized trade with China and they opened the way to America. But for them, Siberia would never have emerged from the seventeenth century.

Towards the end of the thirties of the last century the merchants were joined by the gold-seekers. The 'fur age' in Siberian history was drawing to a close, and the 'gold age' was beginning. At first gold was found only in the neighbourhood of Nerchinsk; then came the *taiga* of the Yenisei and after that the valleys of the Lena and the Vitim. Gold enticed the prospectors in the same direction as the sables and foxes once had, farther and farther east. They perished singly and in groups without finding anything; if they made a find, the booty was divided according to the laws of the *taiga*.

The unknown soldiers of the gold dream marched out into the *taiga* and perished without trace to the last man. The 'secret' was known only to the heroes back at base. By the middle of the nineteenth century there were many of these 'heroes'. Most of them had never seen their own mines. Men who had connections in St Petersburg or with the Siberian authorities received gold-bearing pieces of land in the form of 'remnants' or 'unowned lots' and sent out their trusty representatives to feed the mosquitoes of the *taiga* with their blood and suck the life and energy out of vagabonds and farmers.

To be sure, it was not easy to deal with these peasants. Only the most luckless were ready for drudgery in the mines. In the course of two and a half centuries a string of Russian settlements had spread across Siberia from the Urals to the Amur. Many of their inhabitants were the descendants of the first colonist-exiles, deported peasants, Old Believers and all kinds of rebels; but greater still in numbers were the peasants who had gone to Siberia of their own free will, looking for space and freedom. In Siberia there were no landowners and no serfs!

Thus Siberia became the land of freedom and daring as well as the land of exile and grief. Free and energetic men went there, and the Siberian peasant was never so badly oppressed as the Russian peasant. These free men pushed the frontiers of Russian-occupied land outwards in all directions. The government not only gave them no support; it even opposed the natural urge towards the wide open spaces. None the less, wherever Russian troops went, they always found Russian villages which had sprung up on their own. Their inhabitants fought and traded with the natives, made treaties with the Chinese, Kalmuck, or Kirghiz chiefs, and then later on became Russian subjects again because the boundaries of the state had caught up with them.

The peasants were free and for the most part prosperous. Every peasant was a trader as well as a landowner. Both the peasants and the Cossacks were experts at trading with the natives and in their leisure they all looked round to see if there was gold anywhere in the neighbourhood. They would take on a bear unaided, and did not fear the cold, escaped convicts or even the authorities in the towns. They were sharp-eyed and inventive. Colonel de Belcourt, who was in Siberia at the same time as Benyowszky, remarks in his book: 'The Siberians are such rascals that they could double-cross the smoothest Italian.'

These 'rascals' understood very well how to look after their own interests. They worked and drank, earned money and waited for a man who would understand what Siberia needed and what it had to offer.

MURAVYEV, NEVELSKOI AND THE AMUR

Siberia lived its own life and also had its own time-scale. It was only just entering the nineteenth century when the first half of the century was already drawing to a close in Europe. In eastern Siberia the new age began with the appointment of Nikolai Nikolayevich Muravyev as governor-general. Muravyev's ideas and deeds not only marked a turning-point in the history of Siberia, they also determined Russian policy in the Far East for the next century and thereby influenced the whole course of Russian history.

Muravyev came from an old Russian aristocratic family whose numerous branches were active before and after him in many fields of public service. His father had begun his career as a naval officer and was later for quite a long time in charge of the Tsar's private chancellery; nevertheless he did not leave his children a fortune. Young Muravyev, who had already been at court as a page, began his military service as a guards officer, took part in the war against Turkey and then entered the Caucasian army, where he displayed exceptional talent as a military and political leader in the pacification of warlike mountain tribes and was wounded in the arm. He showed that he was both determined and flexible, firm and yet human. For all that, his character was anything but integrated and harmonious and his inner development was partly determined in advance by a number of discrepancies. He was an aristocrat, but poor; he was proud and ambitious, but small and unimpressive in appearance; reddish hair and pink cheeks were not exactly conducive to a brilliant career as a guards officer – this was probably the reason why he never wanted to stay in St Petersburg and was always trying to reach the front line. It would perhaps be too facile a piece of psychology to attribute his tremendous thirst for action and his desire for self-assertion to these outward characteristics, but they were certainly not without significance and it may be guessed that it was they which determined his democratic outlook and his opposition to the haughty military bureaucracy of St Petersburg, where the tone was set by Tsar Nicholas I, a handsome, cold giant, a sort of superman in guards uniform. Yet, in spite of differences in temperament, these two men were drawn to each other. When Muravyev left the Caucasus to become governor of Tula he became a supporter of the movement to free the serfs and induced a group of landowners to hand an address on this subject to the Tsar. This was a 'liberal' and 'democratic' action which made Muravyev permanently suspect in the eyes of many influential people, but it was welcomed by the Tsar; the 'superman' was himself a supporter of emancipation and reflected all through his reign on this act of humanity, although he eventually showed that he was not a big enough man for the task.

On the occasion of a trip through the district of Tula in 1847 the Tsar came to know Muravyev personally and informed him of his appointment as governor-general of eastern Siberia. There had just been an inspection there, and Count Tolstoi's report disclosed the usual administrative abuses, well-known old failings such as bureaucracy, bribery, lawlessness and nepotism, the last especially in connection with the distribution of gold mines. It was

an old, yet ever new story: again and again inspectors were sent to
Siberia, but it never occurred to the demi-gods in St Petersburg
that it was the system, not the men, which needed replacement.
People in St Petersburg held the good old belief that all Russia
needed was the 'right' men, and so Nicholas, too, was looking for
'men'. He had found one in Muravyev, and he sent him to eastern
Siberia to establish law and order.

There could naturally be no question of any fundamental alteration of the system. The old bureaucracy immediately scented
danger even in this promotion of a young man of liberal views
(Muravyev was only thirty-eight). It subsequently did all in its
power to wreck the measures suggested by Muravyev.

Before his departure for Siberia Muravyev went to St Petersburg to receive his last instructions. In the discussion of Siberian
problems the conversation kept returning to the Amur. In the
years just before Muravyev's appointment the Amur question had
again become topical. To be more precise, what had really become
topical was the problem of China, but the route from Russia to
China led down the Amur; for Russia, China began on the Amur.
After the British had opened China to sea-trade through the
Opium War, and thus started the partition of the Yellow Empire –
for the cession of Hongkong in 1842 obviously formed a precedent
– the old question of Russo-Chinese trade was bound to enter a
new phase. Russia could hardly remain content for ever with the
old caravan trade via Kyakhta while the ships of the other powers
sailed straight to China.

Another factor which helped to bring the Amur question to
life again was a purely scientific enterprise, A. von Middendorff's
Siberian expedition of 1843–5. In itself this expedition had nothing
to do with politics, for its promoter, the famous naturalist K. E.
von Baer, had given it the task of exploring the Taimyr peninsula
and Yakutia. It was also left to Middendorff to investigate afterwards the flora and fauna of the coast of the Sea of Okhotsk if his
resources extended to it.

Middendorff was not only an eminent scholar; he was also a
man of great physical energy and a first-class rider and hunter.
After the expedition to Taimyr and Yakutia he went on to the Sea
of Okhotsk. On his way back he traced the course of that section
of the Russo-Chinese frontier which had been summarily indi-

cated in the treaty of Nerchinsk (see above, p. 121) but never marked out on the spot by the Russians. The Treaty of Nerchinsk had left it to the Chinese to put up the boundary marks, but no one in Russia had been sufficiently interested to see if the Chinese had really done it. Middendorff was now able to satisfy himself that the task had been carried out. He saw one of these boundary marks – a stone pyramid with an inscription – with his own eyes, and Tunguse hunters told him of others. In every case the Chinese had put up these marks at the points up to which the tributaries of the Amur were navigable. The frontier thus ran much farther to the south than might have been expected from the wording of the treaty.

Still more important were other observations of Middendorff. He found that the left bank of the Amur was indeed visited by the Chinese but had not been settled by them. It was as good as deserted and the little Gilyak tribe, which lived at the mouth of the Amur, was not under Chinese overlordship; it managed quite happily without any overlord at all. Thus the region on the Sea of Okhotsk between the River Tugur, where the last Russian post was situated, and the mouth of the Amur, was a no-man's-land. Such were the contents of Middendorff's report.

St Petersburg was suddenly struck by the thought that one day there might be a paragraph in the newspapers saying that the Americans or the British had set up a trading post somewhere at the mouth of the Amur and hoisted their flag over it. It was therefore essential at any rate to acquire more precise information about this estuary. Middendorff himself suggested that a secret expedition should sail down the whole course of the Amur to the mouth. The foreign ministry considered this idea too daring. Instead of Middendorff, the Russian-American Company was commissioned to explore the delta of the Amur, to find the mouth and to establish 'whether ships could sail into the river, for this was the question which was important to Russia', as Tsar Nicholas wrote on the report from the foreign ministry. The greatest secrecy was to be observed, and in fact the crew of the brig *Konstantin*, which the Russian-American Company sent to the Amur in 1846 under the command of Lieutenant Gavrilov, smoked only Virginia tobacco, so that the Chinese should take them for Americans.

The instructions given to Gavrilov by the Company gave him so little time and imposed so many restrictions that with the best will in the world he could not carry out his task successfully. The weather was so stormy that he could not pilot his brig through the labyrinth of sandbanks. Nevertheless, he managed to enter the Amur in a rowing-boat. He wrote with perfect truth in his secret report to the managing director of the Company, Baron F. P. Wrangel, that he had been unable to find a channel through the delta of the Amur. The fundamental question thus still remained open. Wrangel thereupon reported to the Foreign Minister, Count Nesselrode, that His Majesty's command had been carried out and it was now clear that the estuary of the Amur was accessible only to flat-bottomed boats. Nesselrode for his part reported to the Tsar that Sakhalin was a peninsula and the Amur had no importance for Russia. Gavrilov's report was thus distorted more and more as it passed from hand to hand. It is not surprising that the Tsar finally decreed: 'The question of the Amur is now closed, since the river is useless.'

So instead of discovering the mouth of the Amur Gavrilov covered it up, so to speak. So far as the various ministries were concerned the question was decided. The only person who did not share this view was Lieutenant-Commander G. P. Nevelskoi, who at that time was at Kronstadt supervising the construction of a small transport in which he was to take a cargo to Kamchatka. He was an educated naval officer, and purely theoretical considerations led him to the conclusion that it was extremely unlikely that a river thousands of miles long, with a basin covering millions of square miles, disappeared into sand just before reaching the coast.

Nevelskoi suggested to his commanding officer, Prince Menshikov, chief of the naval staff, that after unloading his cargo at Petropavlovsk he should sail from Kamchatka to Sakhalin and look for the mouth of the Amur. He was categorically forbidden to do this. Menshikov pointed out that the ministry of foreign affairs regarded the left bank of the Amur as Chinese territory, and that in any case Nevelskoi would not have nearly enough time at his disposal to carry out his project.

Curiously enough, Nevelskoi was not impressed by the weight of these arguments. He took great pains to hasten the building of the *Baikal* and this secured enough time to go on to the Amur after calling at Petropavlovsk. So far as the political argument was concerned, he intended to refute this with the facts. It should be borne in mind that he was doing all this in a police state, in which he himself was less than a tiny stone in a huge military and bureaucratic pyramid.

The sceptical and moody Menshikov, who did not think much himself of the foreign ministry's arguments, had taken a liking to the small, highly-strung seaman. He rejected Nevelskoi's proposals but treated him in a friendly way and, above all, arranged a meeting with Muravyev.

Nevelskoi told Muravyev of his plans and explained to him the importance of the Amur as a traffic artery. He did not need to waste words, for Muravyev already knew much of what he had to say. Muravyev promised to support Nevelskoi and to have the veto on exploring the Amur delta cancelled. However, he did not manage to arrange this at once. The most he could achieve was permission for Nevelskoi to 'inspect' the south-west coast of the Sea of Okhotsk. Only as Nevelskoi was leaving did Menshikov say to him, 'Of course, if you happen to come to the mouth of the Amur, well . . .'

So Nevelskoi set sail in August 1848. Muravyev had already left for Siberia. In Irkutsk he received a ceremonial welcome. But the assembled representatives of the administration were baffled and disappointed, for the new governor behaved in a stiff and haughty way. It was clear at once that he was still influenced by the last inspection and had a 'purge' in mind. He had brought a staff of young, educated officials with him, who all had the 'failing' of not being Siberians. Muravyev confirmed his reputation as a 'democrat' by meeting the political exiles, the Decembrists, socially. They became his first non-official source of information about Siberia. Among them were many clever and educated men. Savalishin, the man who had had plans for California, explained the problems of eastern Siberia to the new governor-general with exceptional clarity.

Gradually Muravyev grew accustomed to his new surroundings, and he soon realized that a matter which had only been mentioned in passing at St Petersburg and dismissed as closed was here the most important, indeed the only theme, namely, the Amur as a Russian river.

THE SAGA OF THE AMUR

Since the time of Poyarkov and Khabarov the question of the Amur had never been forgotten in Siberia. Only in St Petersburg had it been filed away. Russia was chained to the Black Sea and the Baltic. It sought an outlet to the high seas either through the Bosporus or through the Kattegat.

But 'filed away' did not yet mean 'forgotten'. The loss of the Amur had had too serious consequences. It had driven the great wave of colonization away to the north-east, and this movement even struck out across the Pacific towards America. But to hold Alaska and Kamchatka for the future, a better route to them had to be opened up. And to trade with China without an intermediary it was necessary to move closer to China. In addition, there was the old dream of a 'warm land' and corn; probably the idea of revenge for Nerchinsk, too. Everything pointed in the same direction: the Treaty of Nerchinsk had to be revised.

This was the attitude of the Russian 'revisionists' at the time of the Opium War. But the first expressions of 'revisionism' date from much earlier. As early as 1733, only six years after the treaty of Kyakhta had confirmed the provisions of the Nerchinsk treaty, Lorenz Lange, the caravan leader, who had himself played a decisive part in the conclusion of the 'eternal' treaty of Kyakhta, recommended pressing for a revision of the Nerchinsk treaty. His suggestion was that the difficult situation of the Chinese army in rebellious Dsungarei should be exploited and the Chinese government approached with a 'strong proposal' which it would probably accept.

Soon afterwards the Bering expedition made it clear to everyone how terribly difficult it was to reach Kamchatka from Siberia. G. F. Müller knew this perfectly well, for he himself had simply not dared to travel there. On the other hand, Müller did not believe in the north-east sea passage, and quite logically reached the conclusion that the only acceptable route to Kamchatka and the Pacific was down the Amur. The second Bering expedition was not yet over when Müller wrote his first memorandum on the Amur in 1740–1. He compiled this document 'at the personal command of Her Imperial Majesty' Anna Ivanovna. Where the real interest lay can be seen from the contents of this memorandum, which was to form the basis for fresh frontier negotiations with China. With his usual thoroughness Müller begins with a general geographical survey. What he has to say about the Amur is like a hymn to one of the rivers of paradise. 'The Amur,' he writes, 'is convenient for navigation. . . . It has neither cliffs nor waterfalls and is everywhere deep enough for average-sized vessels. . . . The current is very slow . . . its considerable width would also be advantageous for tacking against the wind. . . . The banks are seldom steep . . . abundant woods . . .' and so on. Still more important is the situation of the Amur. It is such that 'it makes everyone wish that Russia could obtain a share in it again or at any rate the right of free navigation to the seas of Kamchatka and Japan. . . . The difficulties of transport between Yakutsk and Okhotsk would be ended . . . intentions with regard to Japan and the hoped-for discoveries in America would be more easily fulfilled, trade with India could be organized and trade with China itself, either by sea or up the River Sungari, would become easier than hitherto.'

Naturally Müller does not fail to mention the legal side of the problem. Right at the start he makes the point that the Treaty of Nerchinsk was concluded under duress and was 'contrary to the universal law of nations'. Russia had been 'deceived and taken advantage of' by China. The time had now come to 'expose the wrong that had been done and press for reparation'.

Müller knew that for all the changes of mood the official policy in St Petersburg was to keep the peace with China. However, in Siberia the Amur idea remained alive and Müller made himself its literary exponent. He took his memorandum on to Lorenz Lange, the deputy governor of eastern Siberia, who agreed with it in all points.

That Müller's attitude was determined not from above but by hints from below, that is, suggestions by the local Siberian administration, is shown by the continuation of the second Bering expedition planned in 1753, in the reign of the Empress Elizabeth. The new expedition was to start from Nerchinsk and 'reach Japan and the American coast via the Shilka and the Amur'. Governor W. A. Myatlev was commissioned to organize it and Peter the Great's old colleague, F. A. Soimonov, was appointed to lead it. The latter was probably the originator of the plan; the concept corresponded exactly to the idea which he had suggested to Peter in 1722.

The plan was not carried out as the Chinese government did not give permission for the expedition to travel through its territory. Nevertheless, Soimonov had investigated and sounded the waters of the Shilka and his report on his findings aroused interest in St Petersburg. When Myatlev resigned his post, Soimonov was appointed governor of Siberia, in spite of his seventy-five years.

The commandant of Selenginsk, W. Jakobi, also made a contribution to the Myatlev–Soimonov plan. In his report of 1756 he recommended assembling a respectable number of troops between Nerchinsk and Selenginsk and only then calling on China to negotiate. If the Chinese rejected the proposal the left bank of the Amur would simply have to be occupied and fortified at strategic points.

So the Amur question was also alive in Catherine's reign. The young empress was not very interested in the river itself, but she was in Russo-Chinese trade. About this time the monopoly in trade with China was cancelled and trade through Kyakhta was declared free, but without any striking results; there were continual disputes about Mongolian border tribes, the Chinese threatened to close the frontier to trade, and soon in fact did so. Just at this time Müller was again asked to compile a memorandum, which he delivered in 1763. It was kept strictly secret and only published in 1882.

This time Müller deals very briefly with 'Russia's right to the Amur and most of Mongolia' and passes straight on to plans for a war with China. His ideas about strategy need not delay us here; what is interesting in his memorandum is his view of what would constitute a desirable frontier with China. Apart from the Ussuri region, which is not claimed by Müller, the frontier which he outlines corresponds almost exactly with the present border between the Soviet Union and China, as drawn after the incorporation in Russia of the 'People's Republic of Tannu Tuva' in 1944. If we include the Soviet protectorate of Outer Mongolia ('The Mongolian People's Republic'), which corresponds completely to Müller's conception, then Russian territorial expansion in the Far East for two centuries was forecast perfectly by a German professor in the Russian service!

Müller's memorandum was certainly read in St Petersburg. We

do not know whether the powerful Potemkin read it too, but the idea of a campaign against China certainly had a place in the great statesman's lively imagination. Catherine's secretary Khrapovitzky recorded in his diary on 13 April 1788 that in a discussion of the Chinese question the Empress said, 'Before the war with Turkey we were on the point of tackling the Chinese question: six regiments stood ready. In the existing European situation this would not have involved us in a general war.' Things had gone as far as that. But in fact Catherine had to take account of the 'European situation' and that is why she clung to the policy of peace with China inaugurated by Sava Vladislavich. So towards the end of eighteenth century the Amur became a distant dream, thought of with longing and resignation.

The dream lived on. 'Alexander's first glorious days', as Pushkin described them, arrived, and the governor and commander-in-chief of eastern Siberia, General von Strandmann, made a concrete suggestion. In 1801 he sent Alexander a memorandum in which he proposed that negotiations should be started with the Chinese about the revision of the frontier and the right to use the Amur as a waterway. 'If they do not agree to negotiations,' wrote the good general, 'then use force.'

Apparently this memorandum had some effect, for four years later a large mission, headed by Count Yuri Golovkin, was sent to China to negotiate. Its outward purpose was to announce the accession of Tsar Alexander to the Emperor of China, but Golovkin's real task was to discuss trade. He was to talk about the opening of Chinese ports to Russian merchant ships, the opening of another Russo-Chinese trading centre besides Kyakhta and finally the question of Russian use of the Amur.

With an enormous retinue and costly presents Golovkin travelled through Siberia and Mongolia – and came to a halt at Urga. Like so many of his predecessors, he wrangled there for months with the mandarins about ceremonial, finally lost patience and returned home without accomplishing anything.

This was a decided setback, which coincides remarkably in time with Resanov's similar failure in Japan. We still do not know the precise reason for it. It is hardly likely that the Chinese knew anything about the growing Russian 'revisionism', for they made no move to fortify the Amur frontier. But the activities of the Russian-American Company must have been known to them, as they were to the Japanese. At that moment Krusenstern and Lisyansky were at anchor in Canton harbour – indeed they were selling furs in the city – and the Chinese mentality may well have interpreted this as an alarm signal. News of similar import certainly reached them from Kyakhta, for the Chinese merchants there were just as interested as their Russian colleagues in the failure of Golovkin, whose aim it was to break Kyakhta's trade monopoly by setting up a second trading centre on the frontier.

However that may be, the failure was extremely painful, for news of both Golovkin's and Resanov's missions had reached Europe, and there were foreigners in Golovkin's suite, the German sinologist Klapproth, for example, 'our little Klapproth, a Chinese incarnate', as Goethe called him. Later on, Goethe heard an account of the trip to China from Golovkin's own lips; he mentions 'the count's intelligent conversation' in his diary on 27 July 1812. The mood in which Golovkin and his companions returned home is shown best by the words of a minor foreign office official called Wiegel: 'Why not build a new harbour at the mouth of the Amur, where there are so many landing places, to replace the wretched ports of Petropavlovsk and Okhotsk? It would be much more useful than our stupid American possessions. . . . There is not one person in Irkutsk, Nerchinsk and Transbaikalia who does not speak of Daurien as of a lost paradise. . . .'

General Pestel seems to have been the only governor of Siberia who was not interested in the Amur. His unfortunate son, on the other hand, the Decembrist, was enthusiastic about it. In his sketch of a new constitution for Russia he demanded the incorporation of 'a part of Mongolia', so that the 'whole course of the Amur' would fall into Russian hands and 'the Russian fleet could be sailed to the Pacific'. Thus both those who saved the throne and those who wished to overturn it were obsessed with the thought of the Amur.

Three years after the Decembrist Pestel had ended his life on the gallows, an escaped convict, the 'Old Believer' Guri Vasilyev, repeated Poyarkov's journey and once more reminded Siberia of the Amur.

In 1808 Vasilyev had been sentenced to hard labour in Siberia. Seven years later he fled to the Amur with two companions and decided to set up a hermitage there for the salvation of souls. At that time the Tunguses and Manchus were in the habit of hunting escaped convicts. The Siberian authorities paid a special reward for every fugitive handed over, so Vasilyev could not stay long in the *taiga*. After a year he and his companions were captured by the Manchus and taken to the Russian frontier.

Two years later Vasilyev fled to the Amur again. Again he was captured and handed over, this time at Nerchinsk. There he received the appropriate number of lashes with the whip – and after three years escaped again. He sailed down the Amur in a small, home-made boat and soon fell into the hands of the Manchus. This time they handed him over to the Chinese authorities at Aigun.

Three years later he ran away from there. Again he built a boat, in which he drifted down the Amur to its mouth and out into the Sea of Okhotsk. He sailed northward along the coast, landed, joined a band of Tunguse hunters and made friends with them. However, in the spring his new friends handed him over triumphantly to the authorities and received their three roubles. This was in 1828.

Vasilyev's adventures were so unusual and his reports so sensible that after a conversation with him the governor-general of eastern Siberia, Lavinsky, sent in a plan for the occupation of the Amur region to the proper authorities in St Petersburg. They replied that things could not be done so quickly and demanded that Vasilyev's statements about the navigability of the Amur should first be tested. In 1832 Colonel Ladyshensky was seconded for this task. He carried out an extensive trip on the Amur and then worked out the details of a military occupation of the Amur territory. Middendorff studied his plan before setting off for the Far East.

NEVELSKOI GAINS A
FOOTHOLD AT THE MOUTH OF THE AMUR

The Siberians did not take long to learn a lesson from the consequences of the Opium War. The British had opened the door to China from the other side. Opium was flooding into China from India, and, more important, tea was going back from China to Europe. If Shanghai and Canton gained control of the tea-trade, that meant the end of the Russian transit trade in tea to Europe.

Russia had to find its own water route to China or else be prepared to lose the trade with China. The greatest power in Siberia were the merchants, wrote Muravyev in one of his first reports from Irkutsk, and they were convinced that the whole future welfare of eastern Siberia depended on a sure and convenient route to the Pacific: 'The use of the Amur as a waterway is a centuries-old dream of all Siberians here of every class, for many of them no doubt only an instinctive dream, but none the less a justified one. . . .'

Considering the conditions prevailing in those days, the reference of the governor-general to the dream of his subjects is surprising enough. Even more surprising, perhaps, is the passion with which he made this dream his own. The man felt that he had been sent by history to accomplish its design. Difficulties did not frighten him; on the contrary, they proved that the work was worth while. For example, the Tsar in St Petersburg was dubious whether Muravyev would go to Kamchatka, for the journey was exceptionally difficult, even dangerous; and that was enough to ensure that Muravyev went.

The route lay down the Lena to Yakutsk; from there Muravyev had to take the Bering expedition's route to Okhotsk, seven hundred miles, partly by boat and partly on foot, across rivers, bogs and mountains. Then there was the sea passage to Petropavlovsk. Muravyev took three months for the outward journey and another three months for the journey back, just to spend two weeks in Petropavlovsk. For the first time a governor of Siberia saw Okhotsk and Kamchatka with his own eyes.

In the Sea of Okhotsk, Muravyev met a large number of British and American whaling ships. He realized that access to the Siberian coast could only be barred from Kamchatka. As soon as he reached Petropavlovsk he drew up a plan for its fortification and promised to send men and guns.

Muravyev spent his evenings at Petropavlovsk in the company of the 'apostle of the Aleutians', the missionary Innokenty, Bishop of Kamchatka and the Aleutians. The friendship between the two men dated from this time.

Muravyev's trip to Kamchatka was the beginning of a new epoch in the sleepy Siberian administration. It recalled the heroic days of Shelikhov and Pronchishchev. Muravyev was accompanied by his young wife, a delicate Frenchwoman from an aristocratic

The Riddle of the Mouth of the Amur.

Lorraine family, whom he had taken from France to Tula and later to Kamchatka.

On the homeward journey Muravyev thought of Nevelskoi, and wondered where he was. Muravyev sailed from Kamchatka to Sakhalin to look for him. He reached the northern tip of Sakhalin and from there sailed to the little harbour of Ayan, where the Russian-American Company had a trading-post. There he met his adjutant, M. S. Korsakov, who had already been looking for Nevelskoi. He had been commissioned to remind Nevolskoi that he was expressly forbidden to look for the mouth of the Amur.

At that precise moment Nevelskoi lay in the *Baikal* at the entrance to the Amur lagoon. This lagoon is really the mouth of the Amur in the wider sense; it embraces the whole expanse of water between the entrance to the Amur and the island of Sakhalin. It forms a whole little sea of its own, with an area of about twelve hundred square miles, full of sandbanks and traversed by invisible channels. For six weeks Nevelskoi and his officers explored the lagoon in small boats. Nevelskoi sailed into the estuary of the Amur and about twelve miles up it; from there he steered south and on 22 July 1849 he reached the spot where the mainland comes closest to the shores of Sakhalin. Instead of the neck of land which Lapérouse, Broughton and Krusenstern had suspected was there, he found a strip of water just under five miles wide and nearly thirty feet deep at the shallowest spot. Exhausted and starving, the little expedition returned to the *Baikal* and set course for Ayan.

Nevelskoi had thus proved that Sakhalin was an island. It is true that he was not the first to realize this, for forty years earlier a Japanese called Mamia Rinzo had been in the Amur estuary and established that Sakhalin was an island. He had even made a map of the Tartar Strait. This map was known to only a few people in Europe and to no one in Russia except Krusenstern; in any case, it was of no value for navigation. The credit for finding, staking out and accurately marking on a chart the navigable channels in both the Amur estuary and the Tartar Strait belongs to Nevelskoi alone.

Before the *Baikal* had anchored in Ayan Harbour Muravyev came out personally in a small boat to meet it. 'Where were you? Where you have come from?' he shouted out from a distance. 'Sakhalin is an island; ships can get into the Amur from both north and south; that's what I've discovered!' replied Nevelskoi enthusiastically.

That was on 3 September. The very next day Captain Korsakov set off for St Petersburg with reports from Nevelskoi and Muravyev. Muravyev laid great emphasis on the service of Nevelskoi; he had carried out his task so well, he wrote, 'that even the immortal Krusenstern and the omniscient Middendorff would have been filled with envy.'

The answer was news from St Petersburg in December that Muravyev's proposals for the fortification and colonization of Kamchatka had been approved and that Nevelskoi had been promoted to commander. Muravyev sent him off to St Petersburg. There, however, the commander was informed that as a punishment for his 'audacity and disobedience' he had been reduced to the ranks. But finally the Tsar himself intervened and at the end of 1849 Nevelskoi was able to return to the east. He was appointed leader of the so-called 'Amur expedition', which was to camp as a sort of trading-post of the Russian-American Company on the coast of the Sea of Okhotsk, trade with the Gilyaks and collect information about the Amur. Nevelskoi was strictly forbidden to venture into the estuary of the Amur again.

These instructions, too, Nevelskoi interpreted in his own way. He arrived at Ayan in April 1850 and sailed from there in the *Baikal* to the Amur lagoon. In a little bay on its northern shore he set up the winter camp of Petrovskoye; and at the end of July he went off to the Amur again. This time he sailed up the river and on its left bank, about sixteen miles from the mouth, he put up a flagpole, on which the Russian flag was hoisted on 1 August. Here Nevelskoi set up a second winter camp, which he christened Nikolayevsk.

News of this act naturally caused great excitement at St Petersburg; the minister for foreign affairs, Count Nesselrode, was particularly disturbed, for in opposition to Muravyev he was concerned to stabilize the border with China. A year previously Lieutenant-Colonel Aghte's expedition had been sent to the Stanovoi mountains for this very purpose. Muravyev had held up this expedition at Irkutsk on his own authority and given it the task of exploring the mineral resources of Transbaikalia. Nevelskoi had also taken possession of the mouth of the Amur on his own authority. The two men had sown a fine harvest, which the ministry of foreign affairs would in the end have to reap.

When Muravyev arrived in St Petersburg at the end of the year he found nothing but opposition – and opposition to the Amur as well. His chief opponent was Nesselrode, the minister for foreign affairs. In the end Muravyev succeeded in winning over to his side the heir to the throne, the man who later became Tsar Alexander II, and this decided the issue. Tsar Nicholas is supposed to have said, 'Once the Russian flag has flown anywhere, it must not be hauled down again.' In February 1851 the Chinese government was informed that the post on the Amur had been set up in the interests of both countries and to prevent the occupation of the region by a third power.

This explanation may have been appropriate for hoodwinking the Chinese about Muravyev's and Nevelskoi's real purposes, but the two men themselves were perfectly conscious that they were gradually drawing St Petersburg into a position from which later on it would not be able to retreat. Once again Muravyev sent Nevelskoi to the mouth of the Amur. At Ayan, Nevelskoi put most of his men and part of his supplies on board the *Baikal*, while he himself and his staff embarked in the decrepit long boat *Shelikov*. His wife, who had come to Siberia straight from a St Petersburg boarding-school for young ladies, accompanied him. Just short of its destination the long boat ran aground on a sandbank and sprang a number of leaks. Lifeboats were launched and a few moments after Nevelskoi and his wife had left the *Shelikov* – they were the last to go – the vessel disappeared beneath the waves.

Nevelskoi naturally had a particular interest in his 'newly-discovered' island of Sakhalin. Soon after his arrival in Petrovskoye he noticed a black button on the clothes of a Gilyak. On closer inspection it turned out to be a piece of coal. 'There are whole mountains of black stones like that on Sakhalin,' the Gilyak asserted. Lieutenant N. K. Boshnyak was immediately sent off to Sakhalin. He quickly explored the northern half of the island and on the west coast he found large deposits of coal; the seams were clearly visible in the steep cliffs.

In July 1852 a Russian warship visited Nevelskoi for the first time; it was the corvette *Olivutza*. Its appearance was extremely significant from a political point of view, but on the other hand it brought a letter to Nevelskoi from the Russian-American Company forbidding him once again to step outside the territory of the Gilyaks. It was true that Muravyev simultaneously sent word that he was going to send another fifty men to reinforce Petrovskoye.

One item of the news brought by the *Olivutza* was really catastrophic. Kashevarov, the representative of the Russian-American Company, wrote from Ayan that he could see no possibility of supplying Nevelskoi with food for the coming winter. Nevelskoi had sixty-four men to look after, far too few for occupying a country and far too many to feed properly. Although Kashevarov later shared his own provisions with Nevelskoi, the latter's men had to suffer hunger. In that winter of 1852–3 Nevelskoi paid for his Amur-obsession with the death of his new-born child and the serious illness of his young wife.

Meanwhile, Muravyev devoted all his energies to bringing the government round to his own point of view. He travelled several times to St Petersburg, where he had to swallow many reprimands which often brought him near to despair. But he showed himself to be a skilful diplomat and no less persevering than Nevelskoi. The balance sheet for 1852 showed Nevelskoi hungry and half-dead, but keeping watch on the mouth of the Amur.

THE TSAR YIELDS

At the beginning of 1852 relations between Russia and Turkey were so strained that the outbreak of war was expected daily. It was an open secret that England and France were behind Turkey. The spectre of a foreign attack on Kamchatka and the Amur estuary seemed likely to become a reality. In March 1853 Muravyev was in St Petersburg again. He had with him a memorandum for the Tsar in which he explained the strategic importance of the Amur, this time in relation to the swiftly approaching war. The conception underlying this memorandum was extremely significant; it formed the basis of Russian policy in the Far East until the fall of the Tsarist régime, indeed right up to the present day. Muravyev pointed to the development of the railways in America as a sign of American expansion and drew the conclusion that sooner or later Russia would have to give up her American possessions to the United States. 'If this takes place peacefully,' Muravyev said, 'we shall gain other advantages from the Americans. . . . Close relations with the United States are important to us, for it seems natural for Russia, if not to own all Asia, at any rate to control the whole far eastern coast.'

The necessity of controlling the Amur was only a logical deduction from these premises. Here, moreover, we have the key to the sale of Alaska, which took place not many years later. Muravyev's whole sequence of thought was adopted and developed by the organizer of the sale, Grand Duke Constantine Nikolayevich, who had taken part in all the consultations about the Amur and had been present when Muravyev made his personal report to the Tsar on 22 April 1853.

This was a great day for Muravyev, for he gave his report to Tsar Nicholas I in the presence of his brother, Grand Duke Constantine, the heir to the throne, Alexander, and the whole anti-Amur clique. All the maps and sketches of the general staff were spread out and personally explained by Colonel Aghte, who had made many of them himself on the spot. Muravyev discussed the discrepancies between the Treaty of Nerchinsk and the actual geographical circumstances in the frontier region. If the course of the frontier was still disputable, it was clear in any case that there was no trace of Chinese sovereignty on the left bank of the lower Amur or on either bank at the mouth. 'So that belongs to us,' said the Tsar, pointing to the area between the River Bureya and the sea. He turned to the minister for war and continued: 'We must make the Chinese aware of that.'

When Muravyev went on to talk about the fortification of the Amur estuary, the Tsar replied, 'That is all very well, but to defend all that I should have to send troops from Kronstadt,' and as he spoke he described a wide circle on the map round Europe and Africa (the Suez Canal did not yet exist). 'That is not necessary, Your Majesty,' said Muravyev, pointing to Lake Baikal and the Amur, 'reinforcements can be sent from here.' The Tsar put his hand on his governor-general's curly head and said, 'Come, Muravyev, you're becoming obsessed with the Amur.'

As a result of the consultation in St Petersburg, Nevelskoi's connections with the Russian-American Company were severed and his enterprise was turned into a government affair under the title of 'Amur expedition'. It was decided to occupy Lake Kisi and De Castries Bay (which Nevelskoi had already done on his own initiative) and afterwards Sakhalin as well.

From St Petersburg Muravyev went abroad on leave and only returned to Russia in October. Meanwhile, Nevelskoi had been active on the Amur. Without waiting for orders from St Petersburg he sent Boshnyak off to explore the Tartar Strait, and in May 1853 Boshnyak discovered 'Emperor Harbour', one of the biggest and safest harbours in the world, which is known today as *Soviet-skaya Gavany* (Soviet Harbour) and is one of the most important Soviet naval bases in the Far East. The modest Boshnyak, who never made much of a name for himself, deserves, with Nevelskoi, the greatest credit for the exploration of Sakhalin and the Tartar Strait.

As a sailor, Nevelskoi realized that Sakhalin had little value without the mainland shore opposite, and so he resolved to advance, at his own risk, as far south as possible. In July he sailed round Sakhalin in the *Baikal* and set up a base on the west coast. Then he occupied Emperor Harbour, that is, he left a small detachment of men there. Meanwhile the St Petersburg decisions had produced results. At the beginning of August one of the Russian-American Company's ships arrived at Petrovskoye with provisions and a few weeks later the steamer *Nikolaus* turned up with a company of soldiers on board.

With this military might Nevelskoi went off to Sakhalin again. On 22 September 1853 he landed in Aniva Bay, put up a flagpole in front of the little fishing village of Tomari, hoisted the Russian flag and proclaimed the island Russian territory. To the Japanese present he handed a written explanation of the situation and when he departed he left behind a detachment of soldiers.

Muravyev received the report of these happenings when he was in St Petersburg. The war with Turkey had just begun and everyone knew that England and France would soon take up arms as well. Muravyev repeatedly drew the attention of the Tsar and the competent ministers to the dangers threatening Kamchatka and all the Russian possessions in the Far East. He eventually emerged victorious from the struggle with his greatest opponent, the minister for foreign affairs. In January 1854, on the authority of the Tsar, he was given the right to negotiate directly with the Chinese government. Simultaneously Muravyev triumphed over the war ministry: the Tsar agreed to ship troops down the Amur! He made only one condition: there was to be 'no smell of powder'.

Muravyev travelled back to Siberia in April 1854, full of energy and new hopes. On the way he stopped at Moscow, where Filaret, the metropolitan of Moscow, gave him his blessing. Archbishop Innokenty was already working hand in hand with him in Siberia, and Innokenty's son, the young priest Gavriil, was serving as chaplain to Nevelskoi's forces on the Amur. Thus Muravyev's alliance with the Church was complete.

IN THE SERVICE OF SIBERIA

A colleague of Muravyev's says in his memoirs that it was only at the start that Muravyev devoted himself with enthusiasm to the internal affairs of Siberia; later on his real attention was given exclusively to the Amur. This verdict is not fair to Muravyev; rather does it reflect a chancellery view of him. In reality Muravyev's home policy cannot be separated from the Amur question. The Amur meant for him the assertion of Russian claims on the Pacific; Siberia was only the hinterland of the Amur, but on the other hand only a well-governed and strong Siberia could realize the possibilities opened up by the Amur. Muravyev put forward this point of view again and again at every opportunity and in the most various connections in both his official and private correspondence.

This double aim can always be discerned in his actions. He set up a number of fresh governorships or administrative districts, including those of Kamchatka and Transbaikalia, and a special captaincy for Kyakhta. In this way he brought the apparatus of government nearer to the populations and control over local officials was strengthened. It was a blessing for remote regions not to have to refer every question to Irkutsk. At the same time the governor of Kamchatka had to look after the defence of the peninsula and the captain of Kyakhta had, amongst other things, to organize the intelligence service in the Chinese frontier regions. As for Transbaikalia, Muravyev wanted understandably to increase his war potential in this region, for he had almost no troops there. To this end he suggested in St Petersburg that the Nerchinsk 'royal serfs' should be converted into Cossacks.

Not every governor would have dared to make such a proposal, for the private interests of the Tsar's family were involved; the 'royal mines' of Nerchinsk and the Altai mountains were the personal property of the Tsar. These mines were worked by convicts and specially 'enrolled' peasants. The latter were thus the Tsar's private serfs. It was particularly unfortunate that the situation of the 'enrolled' peasants was far worse than that of the convicts, for the criminals were settled in Siberia as free men when they had served their sentences, while the peasants had to go on with their slavery until they died.

Muravyev had his way and the Nerchinsk peasants were made into Cossacks in 1851. He thus obtained the soldiers he needed for his plans and at the same time performed a truly humane action: about twenty-seven thousand men in Siberia were released from the worst kind of serfdom ten years before the general emancipation of the serfs in Russia. For active military service Muravyev obtained four thousand healthy young men, to whom any kind of service seemed a blessing after working in the royal mines.

Muravyev could report to the Tsar with a good conscience that the new Cossacks thanked him enthusiastically for his 'mercy'. Now, however, the governor-general himself had to show that his reform had increased, not lowered, the production of gold. Muravyev knew very well that his own position and the fate of his Amur enterprise depended on his ability to demonstrate this. Gold alone could silence his critics. So as soon as he had formed his new Cossack army he put the energetic and indomitable engineer Rasgildeyev in charge of the Nerchinsk mining district and ordered him to raise gold production.

Rasgildeyev did his best. He rounded up all the convicts he could find and sent them to work in the royal mines day and night in two twelve-hour shifts. The results were soon apparent. In 1851 about 70 *puds* of gold were produced and in 1852 about 110 *puds*. In 1853 the privy purse expected 115 *puds*; Muravyev sent 171 *puds* and 17 pounds to St Petersburg.

Rasgildeyev was a good fellow; he had forgotten only one thing – to build warm quarters for the workers and to organize care and medical help for them. About a thousand of his 4,560 convicts died of typhus.

To tell the truth, Rasgildeyev's 'service' owed a good deal to Muravyev's good luck, for just at that time a rich seam of gold was discovered in the famous – and notorious – Kara district. Nevertheless Muravyev enjoyed an undisputed personal triumph, which he knew how to use in the service of his Amur enterprise. For this reason he continued to show a good deal of interest in gold. He was a decent and humane sort of man, and he devoted considerable efforts to lightening the lot of those banished to Siberia, but, like most born leaders, he did not succeed in uniting humanity and productivity. He instructed his friend and assistant, Korsakov, in his managing of the mines, to spare the men, raise production and lower costs. Intelligent though he was, he did not notice that these principles are in practice absolutely incompatible.

The Amur idea had finally matured in Muravyev, and with it the idea of what we should now call an autonomous eastern Siberia. Hence his continual concern to find new mineral deposits. For his patrons in St Petersburg he looked for precious stones; as always, his search was conducted energetically, and again it cost him, against his will, many human sacrifices. For himself, for his Siberia he looked above all for iron. He modernized the old Petrovski ironworks and began to build engines there for the Amur steamers which would soon be needed. He also tried to further geographical research and in 1851 he opened at Irkutsk the east Siberian branch of the Imperial Russian Geographical Society. For all these things Muravyev needed money, a great deal of money. Even in more peaceful times the government would have grudged him money for his 'Amur adventure' and in the tense days before the Crimean War the financial position was even more difficult. In fact, he carried out his plans with scarcely any financial help from the central government. He made economies in the administration and the rest was given to him by the merchants. His relations with the latter are the best proof that he was not a jingoist adventurer, but on the contrary intuitively recognized definite social and economic forces and only seemed to act in an autocratic way because he was serving these forces.

From his first day in Siberia Muravyev was haughty and mistrustful towards the 'shopkeepers and profit-makers'. His pride prevented him from seeking a closer relationship with the 'Siberian rascals' who, as he had so often been told, had succeeded in making every previous governor serve their own interests. However, he very soon saw that the merchants were the only social group in Siberia which had means of its own, knew how to defend its own interests and was even to some extent organized. The greatest power was wielded by the *otkupchiki*, the vodka monopolists; next to them came the gold-mine owners, and after them the wholesale tea merchants. The power of capital became invincible when various interests were united in one person or company, and combinations of this sort lay in the nature of things. For example, a latter-day descendant of the Argonauts, a Greek called Bernard-akis, was both a gold and vodka tycoon; he had collected a large number of gold-mines, but he paid his workers mainly in vodka, which he distilled himself in his capacity as an *otkupchik*, watered down and sold to the workers on credit at prices fixed by himself. When Muravyev decided to put a spoke in this Argonaut's wheel it transpired that he had the backing of a powerful patron, the war ministry, to which he was vodka-purveyor. Furious, Muravyev wrote to his friend L. A. Perovsky, minister for home affairs: 'Bernardakis' power is greater than mine; he can use his power and influence on me, but I can't do the same to him.'

Muravyev did not throw in the towel. He fought on, and even if he did not succeed in getting to the root of the evil he did manage to alter the system by which new gold-mines were shared out and to limit the power of the vodka-distillers. The latter put up a bitter defence and a good deal of informing went on. However, Muravyev's struggle against the millionaires won over their smaller competitors to his side and the latter were in the majority. Muravyev's attitude to the 'shopkeepers' had gradually changed, too. He came to realize that the prosperity of the 'shopkeepers' formed part of his own programme and that if anyone needed the Amur it was in fact the merchants, but for whom his enterprise would have been nothing more than a military adventure. He now began to talk to the merchants in a different tone and they immediately recognized his 'democratic views' and 'liberalism'. He was in fact a liberal in his economic views and had probably adopted some of the ideas of English economic liberalism, which had been championed in Russia at the beginning of the nineteenth century by his great-uncle, Count Mordvinov. The merchants realized that he wanted to open the way down the Amur to China and America for free trade.

It is therefore scarcely surprising that the great majority of the Siberian merchants and even some of the gold-mine owners were captured by Muravyev's enthusiasm for the Amur and stood firmly behind him to the last. It was the 'gold-digger' Solovyev who gave Muravyev half a *pud* of gold (about sixteen pounds) for the exploration of the Amur. The other business men were no less generous. When preparations were being made for the Amur expedition, the merchants of Irkutsk and Kyakhta delivered tea, sugar and meat for the men, and tools and cattle for the first settlers, free of charge. What bound these blunt Siberians to the moody and arrogant general who spoke only French at home and preferred to spend his leave in Marienbad or Paris? The best answer is provided by a poem written by Xenofont Kandinsky, a tea millionaire and an ancestor of the modern painter Vasily Kandinsky. Kandinsky read out this poem at a banquet in honour of Muravyev at Kyakhta in April 1854:

> The red dawn shimmers in the east,
> Siberia gazes full of hope,
> Waiting for you to open
> An outlet for its wealth.

Thus the ambitious general's isolation in his war on two fronts against St Petersburg and Peking was more apparent than real. He had a powerful ally, the growing economic might of Siberia, whose interests he had been called upon to serve by history.

DAURIEN BECOMES RUSSIAN AGAIN

When Muravyev returned to Siberia in April 1854 preparations for the expedition down the Amur were in full swing. The town of Chita on the Shilka had been chosen as the starting point. The sound of axes rang out day and night and the river bank was covered for miles with the ribs of cargo boats. Caravans of camels and horses brought provisions and arms, and whole herds of cattle were driven up. Muravyev directed the work from Irkutsk. He superintended the assembling of the troops and their equipment, and corresponded with the proper authorities in St Petersburg, with the Russian-American Company, with Nevelskoi and with the Chinese authorities. He had already informed the Chinese government of the coming expedition. In his letter he had pointed to the war with England and France, who had both joined Turkey, and gave as the motive for his project the necessity of reinforcing the Russian defences in the Far East. Muravyev did not wait for an answer; he knew that the Chinese had other worries besides the Amur. A few years before, the Taiping revolt had flared up, a revolutionary peasant movement which had affected half China. The Chinese had no troops in the north.

By May everything was ready on the Russian side. The last

banquets took place, the last artillery salutes rang out and the last toast was proposed to 'the man who was carrying out the wishes of Peter the Great'. Trails of fire shot across the night sky over the dark waters of the Shilka – fireworks set off by the energetic Rasgildeyev. Muravyev only gave permission for the display after he had been informed that there was a large gathering of Chinese 'spies' on the opposite bank.

On 14 May the last Mass was said before the Virgin of Albasin. The venerable icon could still remember the prayers of Stepanov and Tolbusin in old Albasin; for the next hundred and fifty years it had listened to the prayers in Nerchinsk Cathedral. Muravyev now vowed to take it back to Albasin.

The expedition numbered about a thousand men, including a detachment of infantry, a hundred Cossacks and a battery of light artillery. Men, cattle and supplies were embarked on ninety flat-bottomed boats and rafts; Muravyev and his staff travelled on board the first Amur steamer, the *Argun*. Although only a small vessel of sixty horse-power, it was the harbinger of the coming technical and commercial age in the Pacific. The merchant Kuznetzov, with whose money the steamer had been built, came himself, and with him sailed mining engineers, botanists, geographers and experts of every kind.

The expedition sailed down the Shilka and into the Amur. On 20 May it stopped at the ruins of Albasin, and eight days later it passed the mouth of the Seya. Farther downstream on the opposite bank lay the Chinese town of Aigun, administrative and military centre of the Chinese Amur province. Chinese officials, who came up in small boats, explained that they had no authority to let Russian troops through. Muravyev explained that he had been dispatched by the Russian Government to defend the mouth of the Amur, whereupon the Chinese asked the general to pass on as quickly as possible. About 180 miles before it reaches the sea the Amur approaches very close to the Tartar Strait. In between lies the little Lake Kisi, which is connected to the river by several arms of water. At this point it is not difficult to reach De Castries Bay, discovered by Lapérouse and christened after the French navy minister. On the shores of Lake Kisi there was already a Russian post. This was the last stopping-place.

From Nevelskoi Muravyev learnt that a whole fleet had collected in De Castries Bay and Emperor Harbour. The frigate

Pallada, under the command of Admiral Putyatin, had sailed from Nagasaki to Emperor Harbour, followed by the steamer *Vostok*. In addition, two freighters had come from Kronstadt with cannon and munitions for Petropavlovsk and also two ships of the Russian-American Company. In the Sea of Japan, British and French warships had been sighted, the base on Sakhalin had already been evacuated and the detachment from Sakhalin was in De Castries Bay. Farther back, in the Amur, lay the flat-bottomed boats carrying the troops. The situation was not very clear, and it was not easy to see what should be done.

Muravyev made a quick decision. He disembarked 350 men and had them taken to De Castries Bay, put on board the two munition ships and shipped off at once to Petropavlovsk. He set up the artillery at Nikolayevsk and at the narrowest spot in the Tartar Strait, divided up the troops and organized communications.

On 10 August Muravyev went off to Ayan, and ten days later he set out for Irkutsk. Meanwhile the troops he had sent arrived at Petropavlovsk, where the little frigate *Aurora* also lay at anchor. The two transports succeeded in eluding the Anglo-French squadron, but one of the Russian-American Company's ships was captured.

Admiral W. S. Savoyko, who had been appointed governor of Kamchatka by Muravyev in 1849, showed that he was a good organizer. Batteries were hastily set up and troops posted at the spots where the enemy might attempt landings. These preparations were not yet complete when hostile ships appeared in the roads; there were seven of them – 204 guns against 57 Russian ones.

After a bombardment on 17 August the enemy decided to land the next day and storm the Russian positions. But fate was obviously on Muravyev's side. An event unparalleled in the history of naval warfare occurred: in the morning, before the battle, the English Admiral Price, commander of the allied squadron, blew his own brains out. He left no letter behind, but the assumption is that his mental depression was caused by his recent lack of success, for he had failed to capture the *Aurora* or to prevent Muravyev's transports reaching Petropavlovsk, and he had wasted a good deal of time. The story was that he had lost faith in his star. The same thing happened, as was learned later, to his successor, the French Admiral de Pointe.

The bombardment lasted another three days and almost all the coastal batteries were silenced. On 23 August (4 September) the allies finally put seven hundred men ashore. The whole garrison of Petropavlovsk, including the temporarily enlisted civilians, amounted to about eight hundred or a thousand men. At the decisive point about three hundred men fought under the personal command of Admiral Savoyko. Although the coastal batteries had been silenced the field pieces were still in action. Muravyev's freshly-created Baikal Cossacks drove the enemy back to the sea with their bayonets; there the British and French embarked in their boats again under cover of the ships' guns. They took their wounded with them, leaving four officers and thirty-four men dead on the field of battle. Four men and a British flag were captured. Russian losses were thirty-one dead and eighty-four wounded.

Three days later the combined squadron weighed anchor and made for the open sea. The unfortunate Admiral de Pointe died on the way before he could set eyes on France again.

After preparations which took the whole winter the second Amur expedition was ready to sail at the beginning of May 1855. It was bigger than the first. Heavy guns were brought with indescribable difficulty from the Urals. As they were being put aboard the boats, the three-ton barrels often broke through the bottoms of the hulls and sank. Forty such guns had to be dispatched, together with ammunition and 6,500 tons of other cargo.

This second expedition started on 14 May, the anniversary of the first. The 125 boats were divided into three groups; instead of his previous single steamer, Muravyev now had two. He himself, accompanied by his wife, sailed with the first group; the second included the Geographical Society's Amur expedition, financed by the already mentioned half *pud* of gold given by the merchant Solovyev. It was led by the well-known geographer, R. Maack. Its splendidly illustrated, four-volume report was published four years later, also at the expense of Solovyev. The first settlers also sailed with the expedition, 481 in number, including women and children.

Events soon showed that the immense difficulties and hardships endured by Nevelskoi and his men had not been in vain. On 8 May a large English frigate and a brig approached De Castries Bay from the south. After an exchange of shots with a small

Russian warship the frigate withdrew to fetch reinforcements. The brig stayed behind to watch the exit from the supposed Tartar 'gulf'. When the British returned a few days later they found the bay empty. In the Sea of Okhotsk, too, the British were amazed to see that Russian ships which had reached the Tartar 'gulf' from the north had suddenly disappeared. They had all withdrawn into the mouth of the Amur. In spite of Muravyev's fears, the British did not find the entrance to the lagoon. So he had won the game. A weak British attempt to land in De Castries Bay was defeated by Muravyev's artillery. By this time Muravyev and his wife and staff were already on the way to Ayan. For this journey he had chartered a small American schooner which had wandered by chance into these waters. A French warship chased him for ten days, but the schooner eluded its pursuers.

In spring 1856 Muravyev was back in St Petersburg. There he heard that the war had ended. No more troops were now needed at the mouth of the Amur than were already there, but the men had to be relieved. Service in the east was no pleasure, and typhus and scurvy had already made their presence felt. So in May 1856 another 110 boats and rafts sailed down the Amur, to take fresh troops to Nikolayevsk and to bring the others back. Muravyev himself went to take a cure at Marienbad. This was the biggest mistake he ever made. It was far more difficult to return home up the Amur than to sail down it. Muravyev had given orders that provisions were to be stored up for the homeward journey, boats full of flour and meat were to be sent down the Amur, and more medical assistance provided. But he only gave the orders; he did not himself supervise their execution.

The troops left Nikolayevsk in the middle of the summer, and made only slow progress. The boats were rowed, towed and poled along – for nineteen hundred miles! Autumn came, the boats were caught in the ice, and the men left them where they were and proceeded on foot. According to official sources 183 men perished on the way, but in Siberia itself the losses were reckoned at two to three hundred men, for many died soon after reaching home. Reports of this incident, enormously exaggerated by Muravyev's former friend, Savalishin, appeared in the Russian and even the foreign press. This was the greatest reverse that Muravyev ever suffered in Siberia.

Society for Cultural Relations with the U.S.S.R.

The River Amur near Khabarovsk. For a long stretch this river forms the boundary between Russia and China.

The Trans-Siberian Railway which links Europe with the Pacific coast.

THE TREATY OF AIGUN

After his return from abroad in August 1856 Muravyev found that the situation in St Petersburg had changed. His most exalted patron, Tsar Nicholas I, was dead, and Muravyev noticed signs of change even at the coronation of the new Tsar, Alexander II; in these 'higher spheres' there are sure signs which the man with experience can spot at once. Muravyev therefore hastened to consolidate his gains in the Amur question. Loyal to his method, he first secured the formation of a new province, the so-called maritime territory, embracing Kamchatka, the Okhotsk coast and the Amur region. This set the seal on the incorporation of the left bank of the Amur. The governor-general of the new province was to reside at Nikolayevsk, which was now mentioned officially for the first time as a Russian town.

The full powers previously given to Muravyev to negotiate with the Chinese remained in force. He also received a fresh decoration, but before he left for Irkutsk he suggested to the Tsar that his successor should be the faithful Korsakov, and the suggestion was accepted without protest. The way was now clear, and Muravyev could bring his great work to its conclusion. In 1857 fresh troops and settlers were transported to the Amur and a line of bases occupied and fortified. An 'Amur Company' was formed; its main interest was gold. In 1857 Muravyev reported enthusiastically to St Petersburg that seven foreign steamers had arrived at Nikolayevsk. In the same year the Russian-American Company used the Amur as a route to Alaska for the first time.

At that time there appeared in Irkutsk the first United States 'commercial agent' for the Amur territory, Major Collins. One can be sure that he received a very friendly welcome. The American suggested the construction of a railway between Irkutsk and Chita. Muravyev immediately recommended the project to St Petersburg, but Siberia had to wait forty years before it was carried out.

The conclusion of negotiations with the Chinese was now an urgent necessity. England and France were in open conflict with China. Canton was already being blockaded and the allies were on the point of invading China from the south. The Chinese had sent no reply to the Russian notes, so the Tsar sent Admiral Putyatin, now a count, who two years before had signed the first trade and frontier agreement with Japan, to China to discuss the question of the Amur.

After initial difficulties, in June 1858 Putyatin concluded a treaty with the Chinese in Tientsin which gave Russia freedom to trade by sea and land. All that was said about the frontier question was that it should be investigated and settled without delay 'on the spot' by representatives of both powers. While this was being committed to paper Muravyev had already done the whole job 'on the spot'. At the beginning of 1858 he had informed the Chinese that, as soon as the Amur was free of ice, he intended to travel to Nikolayevsk and would discuss all disputed points on the way.

In April he crossed the frozen Lake Baikal and in May sailed down the Amur. By that time he already possessed a proper fleet, and his cutter was escorted by two gunboats.

On 11 May he anchored off the left bank of the Amur and proceeded to Aigun with his diplomatic adviser (Perovsky, the representative of the foreign ministry), an interpreter and a small suite. There the 'Dsan-Sun' (commander-in-chief), Prince I-Shan, was waiting for him. The negotiations began the next day, after the usual ceremonies. Muravyev stated the Russian point of view briefly and concisely. He pointed to the absolute necessity of making the Amur the frontier in the interest of both countries. The present situation forced this solution since England was at war with China and her fleet might occupy the mouth of the Amur and the neighbouring shores at any moment. To prevent the British doing this Russia needed the backing of a treaty with China.

The Chinese replied by referring to the Treaty of Nerchinsk and repeated the arguments which they had already unfolded to Putyatin and forwarded to St Petersburg.

The session went on with argument and counter-argument for four full hours until it was adjourned at Muravyev's suggestion and its continuation postponed until the next day. Before the two sides parted Muravyev handed the prince a draft treaty.

Muravyev did not attend the sessions that followed. The negotiations were conducted according to his instructions by Perovsky. When it was clear that the Chinese were not going to abandon their position Perovsky brought up his heavy artillery. In Muravyev's name he rejected the appeal to the Treaty of Nerchinsk, in negotiating which the Chinese had broken their word and brought up a whole army instead of the agreed retinue. Contrary to the treaty, the Chinese had exacted tribute from tribes living inside the Russian frontier; the Chinese had recently plundered a Russian settlement and thereby dishonoured the Russian flag; and it was only the Tsar's love of peace that had preserved the old friendship between the two empires.

In the end the Chinese gave way and agreed to conclude a treaty. They really had no other course open to them, seeing that they did not have one serviceable cannon in the Amur region, the emperor's throne was tottering under the blows of the Taiping revolt and Canton was occupied by the British and French. More-over, it should not be forgotten that the left bank of the Amur had no economic importance at all for the Chinese and had been settled neither by them nor by the Manchus. On the other hand, it was plain to see that the Amur was vitally important to Siberia, and the Chinese were conscious of this. No state can keep what it cannot use. Muravyev showed that he was acting honestly about this by recommending the peaceful surrender of Alaska. The Russian government soon actually made this surrender and thus applied the same principle to itself in the case of Alaska as it had applied to China in the case of the Amur.

When it came to drawing up the treaty Muravyev did not argue about details with the Chinese. They did not wish to use the word 'border' with reference to the Amur; Muravyev let them have their way. 'The left bank of the Amur from the River Argun to the mouth belongs to the Russian Empire,' says Article I of the final text, 'but the right bank to the mouth of the Ussuri belongs to the Chinese Empire.' The land between the Ussuri and the sea was to be the common property of both empires 'until the establishment of the border there'. In addition, it was laid down that only Russian and Chinese vessels should be allowed to use the rivers Amur, Sungari and Ussuri, and further that in the interests of reciprocal friendship the subjects of both empires should be permitted to trade, that both governments should protect merchants and precisely observe all the provisions of the treaty for ever.

The treaty was signed the next day. After each side had pre-pared two copies, Muravyev in Russian and Manchurian, I-Shan

in Manchurian and Mongolian, the two men exchanged them,
embraced each other and parted.

A companion of Muravyev's describes in emotional language
how two hours later the little general stood in the middle of his
cabin in a white linen tunic, a glass of champagne in his hand, and
dictated his famous Order of the Day to the Army and Navy in
the Far East. It began with the words: 'Comrades! Our efforts
have not been in vain. The Amur now belongs to Russia. The
Holy Orthodox Church prays for you. Russia thanks you!'

The Church was in fact represented on Muravyev's staff in the
person of Archbishop Innokenty. On the following day they all
went to the mouth of the Seya, where there was already a small
Cossack settlement. There Muravyev laid the foundation stone
of the cathedral of the Assumption, in Russian *Blagoveshchenye*,
whereupon the settlement was renamed and proclaimed a town.
Curiously enough, the place still bears its ecclesiastical name of
Blagoveshchensk today. Its cathedral shelters the holy icon of the
Virgin of Albasin.

Muravyev then sailed down the Amur for the third time. On the
way he founded new bases and settlements, among them one which
he named Khabarovsk – the modern city of Khabarovsk at the
confluence of the Amur and the Ussuri. He also visited Nikolayevsk, where there were already nearly two hundred houses. But
Nevelskoi was no longer there. Muravyev knew the value of his
services and had often given him credit for them both publicly
and privately. But Nevelskoi was self-willed and stubborn, like
Muravyev himself, and the Amur became too small to hold both
of them. When Nevelskoi was promoted to rear-admiral, Muravyev appointed him to his own staff in Irkutsk. Nevelskoi took the
hint and soon obtained a transfer from Siberia.

On the way back from Aigun Muravyev met boats and rafts
loaded with soldiers, settlers, guns and supplies. He was greeted
by those who lived on the banks of the river and walked through
triumphal arches. In Irkutsk, letters, addresses and telegrams
came flooding in to him from every corner of Russia. From St
Petersburg came the news that he had been promoted to general
of infantry and made a count. At the Tsar's wish he added
'Amursky', that is 'of the Amur', to his name. But he himself knew
that the Amur story had not yet reached its end. On the way to
St Petersburg he had heard that a fortnight after the signing of the

Treaty of Aigun Count Putyatin had also signed a treaty in Tientsin, which, as we know already, opened China to Russian trade but represented no progress in the Amur question. When he signed it Putyatin knew nothing about the Aigun treaty. However, Muravyev had already made Nevelskoi's favourite idea of 'a Russian Ussuri territory' his own. Nevelskoi had explained to him that Nikolayevsk did not solve the problem of a Far Eastern naval base, for the Amur estuary was frozen over for more than six months of every year. A harbour that could really be used all through the year would have to lie farther south, and for that the Ussuri territory was needed. At a fresh conference in St Petersburg Muravyev asserted that the Emperor of China, pressed on all sides, would shed no tears for the forests of the Ussuri.

The twenty-eight-year-old General Ignatyev was sent to China to carry out this plan. He arrived at Peking in September 1859 and started negotiations, which were to be extremely complicated and tedious. Although the Chinese had already told Putyatin that the emperor had ratified the Treaty of Aigun, they now tried to interpret it differently and even to declare it invalid. Meanwhile, however, Muravyev, basing his action on the Tientsin treaty, sent a military commission to the Ussuri region which marked out the new frontier; he also sent settlers there right away.

In May 1859 Muravyev travelled down his beloved river for the fourth time. He sailed round the coast of the Ussuri region and in a big bay at its southern end, which he christened after Peter the Great, he chose the site for the future port of Vladivostok. The first Russian settlers arrived there the very same year.

Muravyev went on to Japan and discussed the common ownership of Sakhalin agreed by Putyatin in 1855. Then he proceeded to the Gulf of Chili and from there sent to Ignatyev a map of the Russian-Chinese frontier; the Amur and Ussuri regions were marked in the same colour as Siberia.

By that time there was a regular war in progress between China on the one hand and Great Britain and France on the other. The diplomatic corps left Peking; Ignatyev alone remained behind with a few colleagues and fourteen Cossacks. Tough, optimistic and undismayed, he continued to negotiate with the Chinese. When the allied forces besieged Peking in October 1860 the emperor fled to Mongolia, and the reins of government were taken over by his younger brother. The latter asked Ignatyev for his advice and his services as a mediator. Ignatyev provided both and saved Peking from a bombardment. As his thanks, he received on 2 (14) November 1860 an agreement signed by the emperor's brother, Kong Sin-fan, confirming the treaties of Aigun and Tientsin and establishing the border between Russia and China on the basis of Muravyev's map. Muravyev's work was thus put into legal form and the Ussuri region was now Russian.

SIBERIA ACQUIRES A MEANING

For all his successes, Muravyev was not just lucky. He had shown his capabilities in the Crimean War. That his defence of the east was brilliantly successful was the result of his vision and determination, that is, the two qualities which the supreme command in the Crimea lacked completely. However, in the national consciousness the Far East was overshadowed by the Crimea; the Amur, Sakhalin and Kamchatka became matters of secondary importance.

This attitude explains the under-valuation of Muravyev by public opinion and the press. But how was it that the ruling circles, the Tsar and his closest advisers, did not make more use of such a man's service? The answer is that he was far too independent and fond of acting on his own responsibility. He was pursued by envy and slander, like all those with minds of their own who were not prepared to toady.

Things finally reached the point at which the best way of demonstrating one's loyalty was to slander Muravyev. For example, the politically suspect A. P. Shchapov, a Siberian patriot and the proponent of cultural autonomy for Siberia, wrote a letter of self-justification to the Tsar in which he said that Muravyev was quietly thinking of making himself Tsar of Siberia.

Shchapov wrote this from prison; the unhappy, broken man felt justified in using any means to help himself. But the Tsar read this letter just when Muravyev had left Siberia for good and rumours were current in the capital that he would soon be appointed viceroy of the Caucasus or Poland.

In fact, Muravyev never received another appointment. He went to Paris and spent the rest of his life there. From there he followed developments in Siberia and they gave him little pleasure.

Soon after his departure colonization of the Amur and the Ussuri came to almost a complete halt. Then came the revolt of the Polish exiles. This unfortunate incident damaged not only the exiles but also Siberia as a whole, for after it the government decided to tighten the rein. Plans for railways were postponed indefinitely.

Muravyev died in Paris in 1881. The founder of Vladivostok found his last resting-place in the cemetery of Montmartre.

As one of Muravyev's biographers writes, his character has always provoked 'very different estimates'. In fact he was re-proached for many things, especially his autocratic ways. The story went all round Russia that Muravyev had had a village head-man whipped because he had collected 'voluntary contributions' for a present for Muravyev.

The criticism was not without foundation. Prince Kropotkin, famous later as a geographer and anarchist, who went to East Siberia in 1862, praised Muravyev as 'an outstanding man' but considered him 'at heart a despot, like all men of action who have been taught to govern'.

All the same, this despot stamped his administration with a humanity unknown in Siberia before his time. His humane and generous treatment of the Decembrists has been described by those men themselves. While Dostoyevsky, a minor offender, languished in the 'House of the Dead' in West Siberia, Petra-shevsky, the most important prisoner, who had been lucky enough to be sent to East Siberia, lived in complete freedom at Irkutsk under the eyes of the 'despot' Muravyev. It also says a good deal when a Polish writer records that after Alexander II's coronation amnesty Muravyev freed all the exiled Poles 'against the secret wishes of the government in St Petersburg'.

Nor should we forget Muravyev's efforts to 'clean up' the Siber-ian administration. According to Kropotkin, 'In 1862 the senior members of the Siberian bureaucracy were far more educated and in general far better than those of any province of European Russia.' With their chief, his colleagues also fought against that old Siberian evil, the *vsyatka*—the palm-oil or bribe. A quarter of a century later the colonists in eastern Siberia told the deported writer W. G. Korolenko that there had been no bribery in Muravyev's time.

Muravyev was sharply criticized for colonizing failures. There were certainly failures, but Muravyev personally was far less to blame than reports claimed. He knew that the future of Siberia depended on the success or failure of the colonization programme. He sent quite a large body of settlers down the Amur with the second batch of troops.

Things were often done in a patriarchal, despotic, typically Muravyevian way. Once he was sending a group of convicts as colonists to the Amur. At the last moment, just before they embarked, the 'colonists' pointed out that they would not be able to keep house in their new homes without women.

Muravyev immediately sent for all the available female convicts, organized about a hundred couples and declared them legally married on the spot. He wished them luck, gave them a fatherly word of advice, and warned the men to treat their new wives kindly.

'I saw these colonists ten years later,' writes Kropotkin. 'Their villages looked poor, for they had to win the ground from the virgin forest, but in the circumstances this colony was by no means a failure and the "marriages à la Muravyev" were just as successful as most normal marriages. Bishop Innokenty, a kind-hearted, intelligent man, retrospectively legalized these marriages and the children that sprang from them.'

It can be said in Muravyev's favour that he devoted more attention to the well-being of his colonists than any Siberian governor before him. He never forgot the peasants after they had been settled somewhere; he always did whatever he could for them. He dreamed of free colonization; he wanted to attract settlers by giving them religious and economic freedom. But St Petersburg would not even discuss these dreams.

For he did dream, like so many men of action. He took care not to speak of it, for it was dangerous to be considered a dreamer in Russia in those days, and in any case unfitting for a governor-general. Nevertheless we possess several documents which give us an insight into the atmosphere round Muravyev during his last few years in Siberia. They are letters which Mikhail Bakunin – another famous exile – wrote from Siberia to his friend Alexander Herzen.

An anarchist and revolutionary, better known in Europe than in Russia, after eight years of involuntary residence in Prussian and Russian fortresses, Bakunin was deported to Siberia, where he arrived in 1857. He was a scion of the old Russian landed aristocracy and a nephew of Muravyev. Soon he was quite at home in his house. The letters which Bakunin wrote at this time contain not only a character-study of Muravyev but also many thoughts about Siberia; which originated from Bakunin and which from Muravyev it is difficult to say. One thing is certain: these ideas were discussed in Muravyev's study, as Kropotkin confirms.

Bakunin is full of enthusiasm about Muravyev; it seems a little odd when this participant in the First International, who personally discussed problems of world revolution with Marx and Proudhon, portrays the Siberian 'satrap of the Tsar' as 'one of the best and most useful men in Russia'.

Still more interesting to us are Bakunin's explanations of the economic and political problems of Siberia. 'The possibility and necessity of importing foreign goods up the Amur have already been demonstrated,' writes Bakunin. The resources of Siberia are vast – precious metals, especially gold, 'splendid iron ore', then furs, hides, wood, the coal of Sakhalin and heaven knows what else. The Far East must be colonized – and no one understood that better than Muravyev, who showed tolerance to all religious non-conformists and in this way was always attracting fresh settlers. 'What need one say about the political significance of a huge, newly-acquired territory which has a mild climate and fertile soil, is enclosed by two mighty, navigable rivers and is connected to the Pacific, the Mediterranean of the future! Through the Amur Siberia has for the first time acquired a meaning, for through the Amur it was linked to the Pacific and is no longer a wilderness without an outlet.' 'The Slav Russian Empire now stands on the Pacific, and an alliance with the United States, previously a Platonic idea, now becomes a reality.' 'Thanks to the Amur we can now maintain a powerful fleet in the Pacific instead of toys in the Black Sea and the Baltic: Siberia was transplanted by Muravyev to another site; it is coming closer to America and Europe than to Russia, it is being ennobled and humanized. Siberia – a blessed country of the future, a land of renewal!'

Müller, Jakobi, Soimonov, Sarychev, Mordvinov had all had the same dream; only they could not write so well.

VII

THE END OF RUSSIAN AMERICA

◆◆◆◆◆

GOLD AND MORMONS

WE CAN hardly imagine today the excitement which Muravyev had caused in Siberia. People there not only hoped for a free path into the golden paradise of China; they also believed that the age of 'great reforms', which had already started in Russia, had now arrived for Siberia as well. The new governor-general's chief of staff, young General Kuckel, planned with his adjutant, Prince Kropotkin, all kinds of changes: administration, prisons, deportation, economy, all were to be fundamentally reformed. These projects ended with Kuckel's arrest and dismissal.

But surely Siberia, Bakunin's 'glorious Siberia', and the myth of a 'Slav empire on the Pacific' were still there? No, the myth had been exploded; in 1867 Alaska was sold. This was a lesson to all foolish dreamers.

It is difficult to say who was ultimately responsible for the sale of Alaska. As early as 1845 Secretary of State R. Walker had suggested to the American president, James Polk, that he should bear in mind the possibility of acquiring Russian America for the U.S.A., but at that time American eyes were fixed on the southwest.

Only a relatively small circle of men connected with the fishery companies in California were interested in Alaska at that time. Circumstances were different on the Russian side. Before the Crimean War the representative of the Russian-American Company in San Francisco learnt of supposed aggressive intentions by the Hudson Bay Company. With the help of his American friends he formed a company and concluded a sham contract with it for the sale of all the Russian possessions for seven million dollars. If the British ever attacked Alaska this company was to seek protection for its rights from the American government.

This fictitious contract later seemed to many people naïve and valueless, but the directors of the Hudson Bay Company took it very seriously. They probably knew that the Russian government would rather hand over its American possessions to the Americans than to the British. The British for their part therefore suggested the neutralization of Alaska and an agreement to this effect was signed in London in 1854.

Russian America was thus protected, and there was no need for a fictitious sale. But the incident was not forgotten, for soon afterwards Marcy, the Secretary of State, and Gwin, the senator for California, asked the Russian ambassador, Baron E. von Stoeckl, what truth there was in the rumours that the Russian government intended to sell Alaska. Stoeckl replied that the Tsar had no such intention. But he himself did have such an intention, and his reports to St Petersburg found a hearing with the Tsar's brother, Grand Duke Constantine Nikolayevich.

When the Crimean War ended the Russian Black Sea fleet had been annihilated. So the Grand Duke, as admiral-in-chief of the Russian navy, had no illusions about Russia's sea power. In confidential letters to members of the government he was always referring to the impossibility of protecting 'our colonies'. He first made the suggestion that Alaska should be sold to the United States in a letter to Prince Gorchakov, the minister for foreign affairs, in March 1857. Gorchakov was apparently by no means enthusiastic about the proposal and was certainly not going to hurry to get rid of Alaska at any price. He commissioned Stoeckl to sound the American government. But in Stoeckl's eyes the matter was already settled; he was continually advancing fresh arguments in favour of the sale. Among other things he reported rumours that the Mormons meant to emigrate to Alaska, a move which would probably cause all kinds of trouble. But only after the Tsar had judged Stoeckl's arguments sufficiently weighty did Gorchakov commission him to suggest tactfully to the government in Washington 'that, if the conditions were satisfactory, Russia might be induced to part with Alaska.'

The meaning of 'satisfactory' in this context had already been decided by the foreign ministry in consultation with the managing director of the Russian-American Company, Baron F. P. Wrangel. The Company's dividend at that time was equivalent to 4 per cent interest on a capital sum of 3,721,400 roubles, and this was the amount which Wrangel had fixed as the selling price for the shareholders; he proposed the same sum as compensation for the treasury. The total selling price was therefore to be 7,442,800 roubles, or rather more than five million dollars at the current rate of exchange.

It was often said afterwards that the Russians acted like simpletons and sold Alaska without realizing the value of its mineral resources, especially its gold; this was supposed to lend the transaction a somewhat piquant flavour. In reality just the opposite was the case, which makes the whole thing even more piquant. The Russians hastened to make the sale precisely because they were perfectly aware that gold and other minerals were to be found in Alaska. The Russian-American Company had every reason to conceal its knowledge of these deposits because it was bound to fear that if the gold-hungry government found out about them it would immediately withdraw the Company's monopoly rights. It was only in 1862, when gold was discovered in the River Stikine in British Columbia, that the Company admitted that there was gold on the Russian side of the border as well. However, to the Russian government gold meant much the same as Mormons – colonization of Alaska from the United States without any possibility of colonization from Russia. Thus for St Petersburg gold formed the final incentive to get rid of Alaska.

The Russian-American Company's third charter period expired in 1862. The charter was not renewed. The administration of the colony was handed over to a government commissioner and there was then nothing to hinder direct negotiations. They were held up only by the outbreak of the American Civil War. Russia was now able to show her gratitude for America's friendly attitude during the Crimean War. Russia took the side of the North while England and France supported the Southern states. Russian diplomacy exerted itself to prevent the secession of the Confederacy and to preserve the unity of the United States. At the end of September 1863 five Russian warships entered New York harbour and a month later a squadron of six anchored off San Francisco. These incidents provoked immense enthusiasm in America.

HOW ALASKA WAS SOLD

American interest in Alaska had begun during the presidency of James Buchanan, the last president before the Civil War. In 1860 an unofficial offer of five million dollars was made. Stoeckl advised acceptance, but Gorchakov was against it and recommended further negotiations. With the end of the Civil War and the election of Andrew Johnson as president, the negotiations entered the decisive stage and were taken over by Secretary of State William H. Seward.

The last conference on the Russian side took place in St Petersburg on 16 December 1866; Tsar Alexander II presided over it. Those present were Grand Duke Constantine Nikolayevich, Gorchakov, the navy minister, the finance minister and the ambassador in Washington, Baron Stoeckl, whose ideas were thoroughly discussed. His argument was that Russia was not in a position to defend Alaska; in the Crimean War the colony had been retained only as a result of its neutralization, a favourable situation which would probably not recur since the Americans felt cramped in their present frontier and were already looking northwards (Mormons! Gold!).

Stoeckl's case was supported by everyone present from the point of view of his own department. The navy minister pointed to the weakness of the Russian fleet in the Pacific, the finance minister confirmed that the Russian-American Company was bankrupt. The Grand Duke also advanced a fresh argument, the necessity of concentrating all Russia's strength on the continent of Asia. Apparently this argument impressed Gorchakov; nevertheless, he was still not inclined to hurry. However, both the Tsar and the Grand Duke here spoke in favour of selling Alaska and Stoeckl therefore received corresponding instructions.

Returning to America, he began to push the negotiations on energetically. Seward had long been ready for the deal; for him it was only a question of the price. He offered five million dollars and Stoeckl asked for ten. When Seward was ready to pay seven million, Stoeckl demanded that the buyer should also take over all the debts and obligations of the Company. This forced Seward to add another 200,000 dollars at the last moment. Stoeckl wired the conditions to St Petersburg over the newly-opened Atlantic cable. Assent was received four days later.

The actual conclusion of the transaction was later described by Seward's son Frederick in his memoirs. On the evening of 29 March, as Seward was playing cards in the family circle, the Russian ambassador visited him unexpectedly. 'My government has cabled the answer,' he said. 'The Emperor has given his assent. If you like, I'll call on you in the morning and we'll conclude the agreement.' With a friendly smile Seward pushed the table away. 'Why wait till tomorrow, Mr Stoeckl,' he replied, 'we can do it tonight.'

The surprised secretaries were summoned, Frederick Seward was commissioned to fetch the president of the Senate's foreign affairs committee, and Stoeckl sent for his colleagues.

At midnight the whole gathering went off to the State Department and there at four o'clock in the morning the fair copy of the treaty was signed by Seward and Stoeckl. A few hours later the President laid the document before the Senate. Ten days afterwards the treaty was ratified by the Senate and on 15 May Stoeckl was in a position to announce its ratification by the Tsar.

Although the purchase price had not yet been paid, the handing-over of Alaska was not delayed. It took place on 18 October 1867 on Baranov Island (Sitka). The ceremony was a very simple one: one company of soldiers took part on each side. Captain Alexey Pechurov ordered the Russian flag flying in front of the governor's residence to be hauled down and, turning to the American commissioner, General L. H. Rousseau, announced that the Russian possessions in America had been handed over to the U.S.A. Rousseau declared the transfer completed in the name of the U.S.A. Military bands played the two national anthems, the Russian shore battery and the American ships fired a salute, and the Stars and Stripes were run up the flagpole.

There was still one last obstacle to be overcome and that turned out to be the most difficult. The purchase price had been ratified by the Senate, but the money had to be voted by Congress. And at this point there was opposition, strongly supported by the press.

Public opinion was angry that the negotiations had been conducted in secret. People suddenly found themselves confronted with a *fait accompli*. The presidential elections were not far off and the opposition was naturally unwilling to let go of such a promising

piece of propaganda material. The worst of it all was that the majority of Americans had not the faintest idea of Alaska and its treasures. In numerous caricatures and lampoons Alaska was described as
'Seward's icebox', 'Walrussia' or 'Johnson's Polar Beargarden', and
the transaction was soon known to every child as 'Seward's folly'.

But Seward did not allow this to worry him. His answer to these
attacks was energetic propaganda on behalf of Alaska. His supporters spoke and wrote about the mineral resources of 'Russian
America', about the rich fishing-grounds, the valuable furs, the
copper and gold. They exerted themselves to convince the public
that the money had not been thrown away. To Congress and the
Senate, however, Seward put another argument: the thanks they
owed the Tsar for his support during the Civil War and the impossibility of offending him by refusing the 'icebox'. Today, when
the yearly income in fish, metals, wood and furs amounts to almost
twenty times the purchase price of Alaska, it is difficult to com-
prehend that at that time people were able to regard the seven
million dollars as almost a present to the Tsar in return for the
friendship he had shown to the U.S.A.

Congress delayed so long that the affair finally threatened to
turn into a large-scale political scandal. More than a year went by
between the signing of the agreement and the voting of the money.
The Americans were in full control of Alaska and the money had
still not been paid. The situation became extremely critical, and
while Seward went on talking, Stoeckl finally succeeded, with the
help of R. Walker, the old protagonist of the Alaskan idea, in giving some newspapers and influential congressmen a 'financial
interest' in the matter. The biggest sum, thirty thousand dollars,
was received by the publisher of two influential newspapers, which
became enthusiastic supporters of the purchase overnight.

What really induced the American government, or rather
Seward and President Johnson under his influence, to acquire
Alaska against the will of the whole country? The reasons are laid
down in the report of 18 May 1868 by the foreign affairs committee of Congress. This report recommends the voting of the
purchase price and adduces as its main argument the friendship
with Russia. This argument was also in the forefront of Seward's
propaganda. But obviously that was not the decisive factor for
Seward himself; no politician risks his whole career for a 'friendship'. It is not surprising that Seward's motives were until recently

'not clear' even to the Dictionary of American Biography. The American Air Force General W. Mitchell's explanations were not 'clear' in 1935 when he declared to the military affairs committee of Congress that Alaska was 'the most important strategic place in the world. . . . In the future . . . whoever holds Alaska will hold the world.' It looks as if some members of Congress were clearer in 1868, for in the same report it is pointed out that the occupation of the north-west coast of America by an unfriendly nation (obviously this referred to England) must be prevented. Furthermore, trade with China and Japan was mentioned and also the task of creating 'new economic interests' in the Pacific, which were necessary for 'the supremacy of our Empire' both on the sea and on land. Thus for the initiated it was already a question of the same 'supremacy' over the Pacific whose connection with the control of Alaska and the Aleutians only became clear in the light of the 'global strategy' of the Second World War.

As a biographer of Seward writes, the latter was 'an expansionist both by temperament and by conviction'. His political views were formed in the period of the American advance southward and westward. Twenty years before the purchase of Alaska, when the advocate of the occupation of Texas first coined the catchphrase 'Manifest Destiny' ('our Manifest Destiny to overspread the continent allotted by Providence', as a leading article in a newspaper put it), Seward had predicted that in time Alaska would become an outpost of the U.S.A. in the north-west. In Seward's imagination 'the waves of the American population broke on the ice barrier of the north'. Seward remained true to the idea of the 'Manifest Destiny' when he had become the director of American foreign policy. He continued to look for bases for American seapower both in the north and in the south. He dreamed of occupying San Domingo, he wanted to acquire Greenland and somehow or other to extend American domination over the Hawaiian Islands. When he visited Alaska in 1869 he made a real pioneer's speech in Sitka. Closer acquaintance with Alaska, he said, had convinced him of the truth of the theory that 'the waters of the earth harbour more food than the dry land'. Today everyone knows that the real 'gold' of Alaska is the salmon.

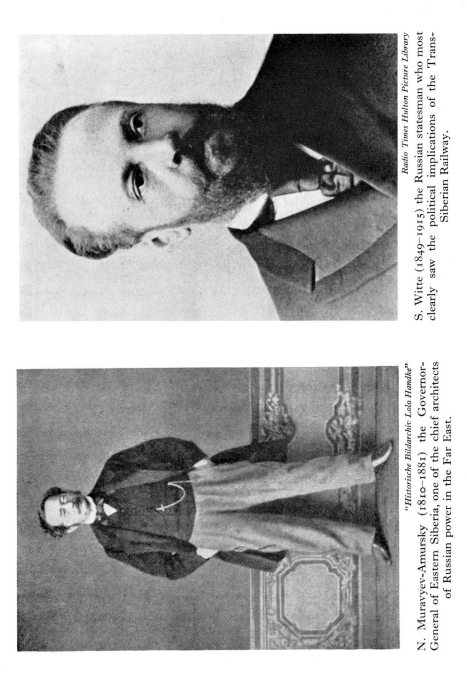

N. Muravyev-Amursky (1810–1881) the Governor-General of Eastern Siberia, one of the chief architects of Russian power in the Far East.

S. Witte (1849–1915) the Russian statesman who most clearly saw the political implications of the Trans-Siberian Railway.

The diamond town of Mirny in eastern Siberia. Many important towns
in Siberia have been founded by mineral-prospectors.

Kuznetsk steel mills. A railway links the coal region of Kuznetsk with
the iron region of Magnitogorsk producing a formidable nucleus of heavy
industry in what used to be barren steppe.

AND WHY

We have seen that the inner motives for government actions could not be appreciated by the people as a whole even in democratic America. As for Russia, the government did not even attempt to keep public opinion informed. Russian motives for the sale of Alaska are only to be found in official documents and private letters. They can be divided into three groups. The first is based on the recognition of the complete bankruptcy of the Russian-American Company. It was for Russia, not the U.S.A., that Alaska was a 'folly' and an 'icebox'. This fact is not in itself unusual; from the history of other countries we know of many colonies which brought only losses. The reason why the Alaska pill was a particularly bitter one for Russia to swallow was that not only the navy but also diplomacy had admitted in advance its inability to hold on to Alaska. When the sale of Alaska was made public, criticism was therefore directed mainly against Russian diplomacy. That a military defence of Alaska was impossible was quite plain; but why should it be impossible by political and diplomatic means?

Theoretically the criticisms were perfectly justified; but the question, once posed like this, had to be thought out to its logical conclusion. Alaska could perhaps have been retained with the help of skilful diplomacy, but only on condition that foreign capital was allowed in freely, for Russia in her weakened condition was not at that time in a position to keep for herself assets which she could not exploit – the discovery of gold had shown that clearly. But the activity of foreign capital in Alaska demanded the presence of a certain amount of Russian capital as well, enough to collaborate if not to compete. Economic compulsion was at work here, for economically Alaska was dependent on America; political and economic supremacy in the Pacific belonged to the British and Americans, not the Russians. But the requisite Russian private capital was lacking. In these circumstances no diplomacy in the world could retain the colony for Russia.

The second group of arguments concerned a very sensitive point in international politics. By handing over Alaska to the U.S.A. the Russian government hoped to separate England and America, which in turn should automatically lead to a closer relationship between the United States and Russia. Russian diplomacy had made this train of thought its own. Even thirty years later, during the international developments over Manchuria, Count M. N. Muravyev, the Russian foreign minister, wrote to the ambassador in Washington, Count Cassini: 'The fact that in 1867 we handed over Alaska to America for a very small sum shows how well disposed we have been to an increase in the power of the U.S.A. as opposed to similar aims on the part of England.'

The idea was that Alaska was bound almost in the nature of things to keep the U.S.A. and Great Britain apart for ever. The foreign minister, Muravyev, clung to this traditional conception even when it was already clear that the two Anglo-Saxon Powers had united to resist the new Russian claims in the Pacific. The theory of the 'irreconcilable opposition between British and American imperialism in the Pacific' persisted with amazing obstinacy as an axiom of Soviet political thinking right up to the Second World War!

The effort to weaken England and to win an eventual ally in the United States was connected with the last and decisive reason for the sale. In the same year, 1860, as Stoeckl began negotiations about the sale of Alaska, Count Muravyev-Amursky founded Vladivostok. As we indicated above (p. 261), the same Muravyev had suggested to Grand Duke Constantine Nikolayevich with some emphasis as early as 1853 that Russian strength should be concentrated in the Asiatic continent and Alaska handed over voluntarily to the U.S.A. It was also Muravyev-Amursky who began the new Russian advance in the Far East which brought up the question of central Asia.

This movement towards central Asia corresponded to the old Russian striving for 'natural frontiers' in the south-east which Ivan the Terrible had begun and Peter the Great had continued. In the sixties of the nineteenth century this old urge received a powerful economic stimulus, which curiously enough originated in America. At that time the most highly developed industry in Russia was the textile industry, which obtained its cotton almost exclusively from America. The American Civil War interrupted the flow of raw materials, and the Russian factories only just managed to survive the crisis by means of small imports of cotton from Turkestan. If the government sent its troops, behind whom travelled the Moscow textile experts, to central Asia, it was sure of the support of all patriotic Moscow and hence of all Russia. But St Petersburg also knew that for England the conquest of Turkestan meant a 'threat to India', and an answer to that would not be long in coming. There had therefore to be a clarification of issues with England. So it seems to have been no coincidence that the Stars and Stripes fluttered out over Alaska in the same year that the provinces of Turkestan and Semirechensk were formed. Gorchakov, who had wavered some years before, now declared that he was ready 'to take his share of the responsibility for the sale of Russian America'. It is permissible to say that Russian America paid for Russian Asia.

VIII

THE MYSTERIOUS
ISLAND OF SAKHALIN

RESANOV'S UNSUCCESSFUL MISSION

AFTER THE loss of Alaska the occupation of Sakhalin in 1875 passed without arousing any attention. The 'prisoners' tales' of 'falcon island', as Sakhalin was called by its involuntary residents, had not yet reached Russia, and Sakhalin had no myth of its own. Without a myth distant islands are forgotten.

That is understandable. The Kuriles were of interest to Russia because they lay on the way to Japan. But Sakhalin did not lie on the route to anywhere and so remained outside politics to the Russians. As we shall see in a moment, this was a fateful mistake.

Little was known about Sakhalin at all. As late as 1865 the surrounding region was described by the German geographer Oskar Peschel as 'a mysterious corner of Asia'.

Before Nevelskoi's time people in Russia had thought more about Japan than about Sakhalin. Peter the Great had been interested in Japan and the interest continued to grow. The first contact with Japan through Spangberg and Walton in 1739 was a purely exploratory trip, but forty years later Antipin and Shebalin were commissioned to initiate trade relations. They accomplished nothing although, in accordance with their instructions, their visit was conducted 'with courtesy, charm and good manners'.

In 1783 a Japanese ship was wrecked in the Aleutians. Of the crew of seventy only nine were saved, and in 1786 these nine were taken to Kamchatka. Two years later they were seen in Nishne-Kamchatsk by Jean de Lesseps (the uncle of the constructor of the Suez Canal), who had been sent through Siberia by Lapérouse with a report for Paris. They were taken to Irkutsk. Erik Laxman, Baranov's old comrade, got one of the Japanese, a merchant called Kodoi, to draw a map of Japan and took Kodoi with him to St Petersburg. At Laxman's suggestion Catherine II gave orders for the Japanese to be taken home. The Russian expedition was to make use of this opportunity to start negotiations in the name of the governor of Siberia about 'friendship and commerce'. An Irkutsk merchant was to take some goods with him, sell them to the Japanese and to buy Japanese goods in exchange. Shebalin, who knew the Kuriles, was entrusted with this task.

As we can see, the Tsarina went to work cautiously; obviously she was aware of the Japanese mistrust of foreigners. Lieutenant Adam Laxman, Erik's son, was appointed leader of the expedition. He left Okhotsk in September 1792 and sailed to Hokkaido. He had to lie at anchor in a little bay on the north coast for eight months before he was taken to Matsumaë, the residence of the Daimyo. Continually watched and spied upon, he conducted negotiations with the Japanese representatives, who were polite, but formal and mistrustful. At first they would not even accept their returning fellow-countrymen; they finally did so, but without a word of thanks. Shebalin was forbidden to trade. However, before he departed Laxman was given a document in which the Japanese emperor gave his permission for another Russian ship to visit the port of Nagasaki. There was no word about regular trade relations, but the granting for the first time of permission for a Russian visit did constitute a valuable sign of progress.

That was what St Petersburg thought, too; after his return Adam Laxman was promoted and both father and son received decorations. Encouraged by this success, Erik Laxman immediately began to make preparations for a fresh expedition, in which Grigory Shelikov, as a business expert, was also to take part. But the uncertain situation created by the French Revolution and the death of Catherine prevented the Russians from taking advantage of the Japanese invitation. The opportunity was lost. It was not until twelve years later that the government decided to send a plenipotentiary to Japan with Krusenstern's expedition round the world. Nikolai Petrovich Resanov was to make up for lost time.

He took costly presents with him and a letter from the Tsar to the Mikado, but he received only a very cool welcome. He had to spend six months in Nagasaki, from 25 September 1804 to 6 April 1805, and was received by no higher officials than the provincial governor and the representative of the Shogun (hereditary commander-in-chief and virtual ruler).

This treatment naturally affected Resanov's nerves, especially as he had arrived in Japan in a low mental state. He was depressed when he started the voyage, for his wife, Shelikov's step-daughter, had just died, and on the way he received such unfriendly treatment from Krusenstern and his officers that for a time he had to break off all relations with them. Krusenstern was angry because Resanov, instead of himself, had been made the head of the expedition. We do not know of any indiscretions committed by Resanov in Japan. Krusenstern later said that Resanov had allowed himself to be humiliated by the Japanese by consenting to sit on the floor bare-footed in front of the Shogun, but it should be remembered that it is still the universal custom in Japan not to wear shoes indoors. As for sitting on the floor, none of Resanov's colleagues was with him at the audience. According to Resanov's own report, he had sat in an armchair. It is worth noting that Krusenstern only made his disclosures after Resanov's death, when the latter could no longer reply.

We mention this episode because it aroused attention in Europe at the time. At the beginning of the nineteenth century foreigners had to put up with a good deal in Japan. Krusenstern himself saw how van Doeff, the famous director of the Dutch trading settlement in Nagasaki, stood bowing for some minutes before a low-ranking Japanese official. Such officials searched the Dutch ships and houses with sticks in their hands. The Dutchmen were not allowed to hold religious services and had to work on Sundays. As a modern writer says, 'Calvin would turn in his grave if he knew what his followers had to put up with in Japan in the eighteenth and early nineteenth centuries.'

In spite of his long wait Resanov did not lose hope and he was thunderstruck when he received from the Japanese a letter which expressed thanks for the gifts, but explained that gifts had to be answered with gifts and these had to be handed over by an ambassador, which was impossible, since Japanese laws forbade any foreign travel. For this reason the Emperor of Japan could not accept the Tsar's gifts. Russian ships were in future forbidden to come to Japan; if the Russians wanted to trade, they could do it through the Dutch.

To understand this document we must go a little further back in history. Since 1638 Japan had been closed to all foreigners except the Dutch merchants. Even the Dutch could visit only Nagasaki, where they had a trading post on the island of Deshima. They worked and lived under a supervision which differed little from that in a prison, but all the same they held a monopoly in trade between Japan and Europe and until the 'opening' of Japan in 1854 they were the only Europeans there. Moreover, they were the only links between the outside world and the Japanese government; if the latter was forced to make contact with foreigners it was accustomed to call on the services of Dutch interpreters.

The Dutch had driven the Portuguese out of Japan and subsequently guarded their monopoly carefully by keeping their competitors out. To counter British attempts to obtain closer relations they continually reminded the Japanese of India's fate. The most effective argument against Japan's northern neighbours was provided by the activities of the Russian-American Company. The Dutch were excellently informed about everything; they knew that Resanov was the head of the Russian-American Company; like all the other colonial powers, Holland had been officially informed of his mission. It therefore seems to be quite wrong to seek the reason for Resanov's failure, as some writers do, in his supposedly undiplomatic behaviour; the real reason was not Resanov's diplomacy, but that of the Russian-American Company, whose statute had meanwhile proclaimed it the ruler of the Kuriles. This was the cause of the Japanese disquiet, which the Dutch found it easy to keep alive.

A REPRISAL AND ITS CONSEQUENCES

What was Resanov to do? Unfortunately he felt that he had to do something. There could be no mistake about the extent of his diplomatic defeat; all the European newspapers had described it. He took the view that he could not let the insult go unanswered, and in retaliation he determined to drive the Japanese out of the Kuriles and Sakhalin. The Kuriles he regarded in any case as the property of the Russian-American Company; and Sakhalin was now to be incorporated in the Russian empire as a reprisal.

Resanov came to this decision after his American trip quite independently and without the knowledge of the government in St Petersburg, and he must bear the historical responsibility for it. It is difficult to say whether or not the idea of a reprisal was suggested to him by anyone; only Baranov and Krusenstern would come into question. Baranov was not very interested in Japan, and as for reprisals, he did not take them even against the Indians. Krusenstern on the other hand was an open advocate of the occupation of Sakhalin and the ejection of the Japanese. He recorded this idea in his journal, backing it with economic, political and strategic motives which he almost certainly explained to Resanov when the two of them visited Aniva Bay.

The reprisals were entrusted by Resanov to Lieutenant Davidov, who carried them out with his inseparable companion and friend, Lieutenant Khvostov, in 1806 and 1807. The two lieutenants appeared off the islands of Iturup and Urup in the little frigate *Juno* and destroyed some fishermen's huts. A few shots were fired in the process. Then they occupied a Japanese settlement on Sakhalin and handed the Japanese a paper which said in Russian that from then onwards Sakhalin formed part of the Russian empire. In connection with this episode an Ainu village headman was given 'a silver medal on the ribbon of Vladimir'.

Not satisfied with this, Davidov also put ashore the first Russian settlers in Aniva Bay, five sailors, who were to await the arrival of Russian ships. They were simply forgotten. When Lieutenant Boshnyak came to Sakhalin in 1852 on Nevelskoi's orders, the natives gave him a few yellowed pages from a psalter, on which was written: 'We, Ivan, Danilo, Pyotr, Sergei and Vasily, were landed by Lieutenant Khvostov at the village of Tomari-Aniva on 17 August 1805, and after the arrival of the Japanese in 1810 we went off to the river Tym.'

All this was soon forgotten in Russia, but not in Japan. Public opinion there, already disturbed, reached a state of great excitement, which was increased still further by another incident. A year after Resanov's reprisal the English frigate *Phaeton* sailed into Nagasaki harbour, took a Dutch interpreter prisoner and forced the authorities to hand over provisions by threatening to bombard the city. People in Japan now felt that they were a prey to attacks from every side. The nationalistic publicist Hirota devoted a whole book to the description of 'the barbarous deeds of the Russians'. Scarcely had the excitement subsided when Krusenstern's *Voyage round the World* was translated into Japanese and every reasonably educated person could read the details of his plans for Sakhalin. All these things were mentioned by every anti-Russian publication right up to the time of the Russo-Japanese war.

The first to suffer the consequences of the unfortunate reprisal was Captain W. M. Golovnin, who came to Kamchatka in 1809 in the corvette *Diana* and from there was ordered to the Kuriles to make charts. When he approached the island of Kunashiri to take on board water, he was lured to the coast by the Japanese and he and his six companions were taken prisoner. They were not treated in a particularly friendly way. They tried to escape, but after a long chase they were all captured again, exhausted and hungry, and thrown into prison.

Golovnin learnt Japanese from the interpreter and was thus able to pick up all kinds of information during his long imprisonment. The Japanese told him, amongst other things, how they had been informed by the Dutch that the Russians intended to divide Japan between themselves and the British and to force the people to adopt Christianity. The prisoner was also visited by Mamia Rinzo, who made no secret of his hostile attitude. It was really hardly surprising, for Golovnin tells us that on Iturup the explorer of Sakhalin had been wounded by a Russian bullet 'in the soft part of the posterior'.

But even in this rather depressing situation Golovnin retained his talent for observation and objective political judgement. One hundred and fifty years ago this Russian officer, who had gone through so much in Japan and only escaped death by a hair's breadth, wrote this about the Japanese: 'If this numerous, clever, sensitive, receptive, patient, industrious and talented people were granted a ruler like Peter the Great, he would not take long, with all Japan's natural resources, to bring the country to the point where it could dominate the whole eastern ocean. ... Deeply rooted as the Japanese aversion from everything foreign may be, they could perfectly well decide one day to introduce European knowledge and science. ... Attacks by neighbours might suggest the construction of ships of their own, these ships could develop into a fleet and the success of this measure might well lead them to adopt other 'enlightened' methods of ours for the extermination of the human race; teachers enough would come from all over Europe if the Japanese only invited them. For this reason it seems to me that we should not provoke this just and honourable people. ... '

Only after two and a half years were Golovnin and his companions released by the Japanese, after repeated visits by Russian warships and the condemnation of Resanov's reprisals by the

Russian government. Probably the Japanese did not want to go too far and provoke fresh and perhaps more serious reprisals. So the mysterious island became a real, if still invisible, political factor in the Far East.

WHAT THE JAPANESE WERE THINKING

Even after Golovnin's warning the Russians could not understand the real reasons for Japanese hostility, and right to the end they regarded it only as 'a cunning flight from the scourge of civilization' as the novelist Goncharov wrote in 1853 on board the frigate *Pallada* in sight of the Japanese coast. No one had the slightest suspicion that the Russian advance from Kamchatka down the Kuriles in the direction of the northernmost Japanese island of Hokkaido (known in those days as Jedzo or Jesso) was felt in Japan even in the eighteenth century as an immediate threat. To the Japanese, however, Jesso formed a direct continuation of the Kurile chain; it was regarded as its most southerly member. Russian visits to Jesso were viewed as reconnaissance and preparations for the occupation of this unprotected and thinly populated frontier territory. It amazes us to read today in the Japanese historian Y. S. Kuno that it was not England or America, as is generally assumed, that awoke Japan from her long sleep, but Russia — a view, by the way, which was expressed a hundred years ago by Franz von Siebold. But Siebold meant it in another sense; in his eyes Russia and Holland deserved most of the credit for opening Japan to international trade. The modern, Americanized Japanese, Kuno, on the other hand, sees things in a different light. He says that for nearly a century and a half Russia was 'a nightmare to the people and to the government'!

There is no doubt that the Russian question was at the centre of all political discussions in Japan; it was the decisive factor in the dispute between the advocates and opponents of the 'opening of the doors', between the liberals and the conservatives. In the eighties of the eighteenth century, that is, in the time of Catherine II, the political writer Heisuke Kude took the view that the Europeanization of Japan was the only way to ward off the danger from the north. The historian Riken Nakai, on the other hand, suggested evacuating the island of Jesso completely, converting it into a no-man's-land and thus creating a buffer between Japan and Russia. A third writer of the same period, Seiyo Habuto, wanted on the contrary to colonize and fortify Jesso.

At the beginning of the nineteenth century opinions were still more sharply divided. Genpaku Sugita advocated closer relations with Russia and the conclusion of a trade treaty; Toshiaki Honda and Soin Yoshida supported the idea of an effective aggressive policy against Russia; and Sanai Hashimoto posed for the first time the fundamental question, should Japan seek the friendship of England or Russia? After China had been forced by England to permit the import of opium, Sanai gave up the idea of friendship with England; he chose Russia.

Soin and Sanai had to pay for their rather too free expressions of opinion with their heads. Both were executed, Soin at the age of twenty-nine, Sanai at the age of twenty-five. Yet to these two young men can be traced the two main political currents in the growing power of Japan; at the beginning of the twentieth century, before the Russo-Japanese war, Sanai's policy of reconciliation was represented by the older politicians, and the irreconcilable attitude by the younger generation.

No one in Russia had ever suggested the occupation of Jesso or thought of an attack on Japan. But on the Japanese side a programme of expansion against Russia had long been developed. The Russians were quite unaware of this. The above-mentioned Toshiaki Honda (1744–1821), who may be regarded as the herald of Japanese power politics, had conceived the following imaginative plan. First of all Japan was to occupy Jesso and with the help of the 'immense deposits of gold and silver' there become the richest country in the world. The next step would be to take Sakhalin and the Kuriles and drive the Russians out of Kamchatka, whither the capital of Japan was to be moved. Honda also recommended building a big town in Sakhalin; the climate was favourable in both cases, he said, for Kamchatka lay no farther north than London and in Sakhalin one could choose a site on the same latitude as Paris!

Soin's programme looks rather more realistic. It was drawn up four decades later and contains no geographical peculiarities. Soin, too, wanted to start with the occupation of Jesso, Sakhalin and Kamchatka, but his next steps were the establishment of a protectorate over Korea and the conquest of Manchuria as a basis for the foundation of a Japanese empire on the mainland. Formosa and the Philippines were to form the succeeding stages.

After his execution Soin was deified and added to the pantheon of national heroes as 'Father of the new Japan'. At the period of Japan's greatest successes in the Second World War his programme was more than fulfilled.

PUTYATIN OPENS JAPAN TO RUSSIA

Such was the mood in Japan round the middle of the nineteenth century when the Russians made a last attempt to gain entry to Japan. For this purpose the Russian government sent Admiral E. W. Putyatin to Japan, the Putyatin who thirty years before had rejected Savalishin's fantastic Californian plans and in 1858 was to conclude the Treaty of Tientsin with China. Putyatin arrived at Nagasaki on 10 August 1853 in the frigate *Pallada* and accompanied by three other ships. The Dutch had instructed their Japanese friends a few weeks earlier of the coming visit by a Russian naval squadron, and the Samurai and their followers round Nagasaki were mobilized to repulse the Russians if need be. Every move of Putyatin's squadron was watched. Goncharov, who took part in the expedition as Putyatin's secretary, relates how surprised he was to meet the 'half-savage son of nature' who had pulled his rickshaw in Singapore as a servant in the hotel at Shanghai. 'How did you get here? What are you doing here?' Goncharov asked him. 'Oh, I'm only a merchant,' was the reply. Goncharov saw at once that the 'half-savage son of nature' was lying, but it escaped the Russian gentleman's notice that he was probably not so savage at all.

The negotiations went on for a long time and were accompanied by many critical incidents. When the Crimean War broke out, the presence of Anglo-French squadrons in the Far East made Putyatin's position very dangerous. Several times he left Japan temporarily; on one occasion he sailed to China, on another to the Philippines, and finally he went to the Tartar Strait, where the frigate *Diana* from Hawaii, under the command of Captain S. S. Lesovsky, was waiting for him. Putyatin returned to Japan in the *Diana* and anchored at Shimoda. In December 1854, during a terrible earthquake, the *Diana* was so badly damaged that it had to be lightened and the guns put ashore. When it was being sailed to another harbour for repairs it started leaking in the rough seas and sank off the cliffs at the foot of Fujiyama.

One can imagine the painful feelings of an admiral cast ashore, an ambassador cut off from his native land. However, Putyatin did not lose heart; his behaviour was clever and discreet. Nevertheless, he could scarcely have carried out his mission so successfully if the Japanese government had not been so hopelessly weak at that time; it had no army, no fleet and no money, and was being hard pressed by the Americans. Six months before Putyatin's arrival Commodore Perry had appeared off the coast of Japan with a squadron of warships and on 31 March 1854 he signed a treaty of trade and friendship with the Japanese government. When the British Admiral Sir James Stirling also concluded a similar treaty shortly afterwards the way was clear for an agreement. In January 1855 Putyatin was able to sign the first Russo-Japanese treaty at Shimoda.

The three powers had thus acted, if not in concert, at any rate more or less simultaneously, and this lent particular force to their demands. But this was true only of trading facilities; Putyatin had also to settle the question of Sakhalin, and here the situation was different. In any anti-Russian action the Japanese could count on the support of Britain.

Stirling was a man of broad vision and full of high-flown ideas, a typical representative of nineteenth-century British imperialism. He had recognized the importance of Manchuria as the key to the control of the Far East and to 'the defence of China and India' against Russia. For him Russia was the enemy in the Far East as well as in the Near East. But he was no man of action. In practice, Stirling showed that he was not big enough to handle the situation, and did not manage either to sink Putyatin's ships or to obtain better terms than he did. On the contrary, the treaty concluded by the powerless, shipwrecked admiral on behalf of Russia was more favourable than the one obtained for England by the admiral who ruled the sea. Three Japanese ports were opened to Russian and American ships, but only two to British ships.

Putyatin also had the Sakhalin problem to solve. From the start he did not deny that Japan had certain claims to Sakhalin and to some of the Kuriles, but he energetically rejected Japanese suggestions that Sakhalin should be divided along the fiftieth parallel. In the end the following agreement was made: in the Kuriles, Urup and all the islands to the north west to Russia, Iturup and the islands to the south of it went to Japan. 'So far as Sakhalin is concerned,' said the second article of the treaty, 'it remains, as before, undivided and the joint property of Russia and Japan.'

In this way almost the whole Kurile chain passed into the legal possession of Russia and the Russian claim to Sakhalin was recognized as just as well-based as the Japanese claim. Putyatin had every reason to be satisfied, but he still had one problem to solve: how to get back safely to Russia. He had lost the *Diana* and the British and French were keeping watch for him on the high seas. Thanks to generous help from the Japanese, who put at his disposal everything he needed to build a ship, Putyatin accomplished this task successfully as well. The newly-built schooner *Heda*, with Putyatin, seven officers and fifty sailors on board, sailed to the Amur, and the party reached St Petersburg safely via Irkutsk. A second group of eight officers and a hundred and fifty sailors under Captain Lesovsky also reached the Amur in a chartered American ship. A third ship, chartered from the Germans, was caught by the British in the Sea of Okhotsk. This small success by the British Far Eastern fleet, which otherwise had accomplished little, could not seriously affect the balance-sheet of Putyatin's mission. The admiral and diplomat was rightly made a count on his return to St Petersburg.

In concluding his agreement Admiral Stirling had not omitted to warn the Japanese government of Russian 'territorial aims'. This formed the introduction to a long series of efforts by British diplomacy which finally culminated in the Anglo-Japanese alliance of 1902.

It soon became evident that the Sakhalin problem had by no means been resolved in 1855. The Shimoda treaty had recognized the sovereignty of both countries over Sakhalin, but had made no arrangements at all for a joint administration. The result was a curious 'open door' régime; the subjects of two different states were to be ruled in the same piece of territory by their respective authorities according to their own laws. The situation remained the same after the Russo-Japanese convention of 1867.

Naturally this position was only tolerable so long as neither side made serious attempts at colonization. As soon as such attempts started it became clear to both sides that the island would have to be divided. In the 'seventies the Japanese made themselves felt only in the southern half of the island; they fished, bought furs from the Ainus and collected seaweed on the shore. In the northern half of Sakhalin, on the other hand, Russian deportees were settled; they had been sent there in 1869. On the north-west coast settlements, prisons and military posts arose; in Due a private company, which was allowed to hire the convicts as a labour-force, mined coal. So in the north the island was predominantly Russian, in the south Japanese, and this gave rise to the belief that Sakhalin had been divided between Russia and Japan in 1855; even Russian diplomats believed this.

Joint Russo-Japanese sovereignty over Sakhalin came to an end in 1875, when a new treaty gave the whole of Sakhalin to Russia and all the Kurile Islands to Japan. This time, too, no one in Russia noticed what kind of a change this meant somewhere 'at the end of the world'. When the draft of the treaty was being drawn up nobody in the foreign ministry knew how many of the Kurile Islands Russia had really owned up till then. Anton Chekhov, who visited Sakhalin in 1890, thought that the Treaty of Shimoda had given all the Kurile Islands to Russia. No one in Russia at that time worried about this 'mysterious Asiatic spot'. No one could guess how much blood was to be spilled there in days to come.

IX

INTERLUDE
AND GREAT ENDEAVOURS

———◆·◆◆◆———

WRANGEL ISLAND

The acquisition of Sakhalin in return for the Kuriles was not a bad deal from the economic point of view, but from the political and strategic angles it seemed a pure loss. The Kuriles cover the approach to the Sea of Okhotsk; without them the whole east coast of Siberia lay open to an attack from the sea. Alaska had been handed over to America, the fortress of Petropavlovsk demolished and the Kuriles given away to Japan. From the sale of Alaska to the acquisition of Sakhalin it had been one long series of retreats resulting in renunciation of the Pacific.

This renunciation was bound to diminish interest in the north-east sea passage. Yet, in fact, never was so much attention given to it in Russia as in the second half of the nineteenth century. We shall see that in a moment from the history of another 'mysterious island'.

Among the many variants of the legend of a 'great land' opposite the north-east coast of Siberia the one that attracted most attention in the second half of the last century was the rumour of the so-called 'Andreyev Land'. News of it had been brought by Sergeant Stepan Andreyev, who was supposed to have sighted it in 1764 from one of the Bear Islands, which he had discovered.

Of those who searched for this land the most important was Lieutenant Baron F. P. Wrangel, a pupil of W. M. Golovnin. In 1820 he was given the task of exploring the Arctic coast to the east of the mouth of the Kolyma. He was to establish 'once and for all' whether or not Siberia and America were joined together.

In the years 1820–3 Wrangel mapped the east Siberian coast and three times from different spots he tried to reach the mysterious island across the ice, but did not find it. He finally returned with the conviction that 'Andreyev Land' did not exist, but that farther to the east there was an island, which the Chukchas had described

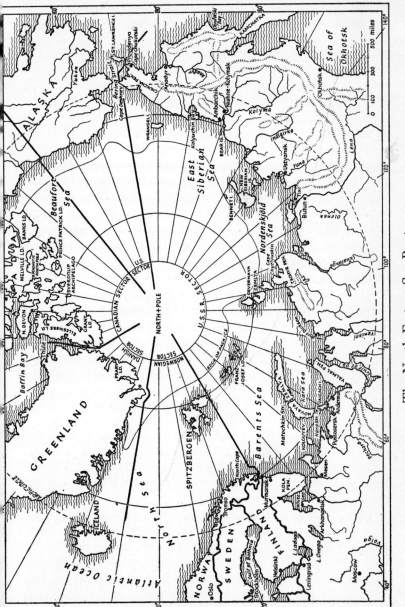

The North-Eastern Sea Route.

to him. Wrangel showed the position of this supposed island on one of the maps he made, and many years later it turned out that his estimate corresponded almost exactly with the facts. Wrangel thus strengthened the supposition of G. A. Sarychev, who thirty-five years earlier had postulated the existence of an island – this island of Wrangel's – on the basis of the changing level of the sea and the configuration of the ice.

So now there was a map of the island, but no one had so far seen it. The first man to succeed in doing so was an Englishman, Captain H. Kellett, who had sailed north-west from the Bering Strait in summer 1849 while looking for Sir John Franklin's expedition, which had disappeared. Kellett first discovered a small island which he christened Herald Island after his ship. He also hoisted the British flag on it. To the west of this little island could be seen the outlines of a 'big land'. This 'land' was Wrangel Island.

In August 1867 the American whaler Thomas Long came across land which was not marked on his chart. He realized at once that this was the 'land' whose position had been fixed forty-five years before by Lieutenant Wrangel. By this time Wrangel had a world-wide reputation. He had governed the Russian possessions in America for a time, then became managing director of the Russian-American Company and later Navy Minister. Long found the 'land' in the year of the sale of Alaska, when the Americans were well disposed towards the Russians. He gave the 'land' Wrangel's name and turned round without landing.

Nine years later, in 1876, the Russian clipper *Vsadnik* tried to reach the island but could not get through the ice.

An American captain called G. W. de Long was the third to sight Wrangel Island, in 1879, when the current drove his *Jeannette*, which was locked in the ice, from the Bering Strait into the Arctic. Two years later the ship was crushed by the ice; the crew reached the Siberian coast and perished there.

The first landing on Wrangel Island was made in August 1881 by Captain C. L. Hooper, who was looking for the *Jeannette*. Hooper only remained on the island for six hours, but thirteen days later a second American rescue expedition led by Lieutenant Berry arrived, traversed the island and hoisted the American flag. That is the end of Wrangel Island's history in the nineteenth century.

PIONEERS OF THE KARA SEA

If the government's interest in Arctic problems waned, that of the Siberian merchants remained strong, but it veered now from the east to the west. There were no railways in Siberia. The only outlet for heavy loads was via the northern ocean, to which two rivers led, the Yenisei and the Ob. Both flowed into the Kara sea, which was considered unnavigable because of the ice.

Curiously enough, this reputation still clung to it long after the Russians had sailed through it. In 1734 and 1735 Lieutenants Malygin, Skuratov and Sukhotin sailed from the mouth of the Pechora to the mouth of the Ob and then upstream to Beryesov. These young officers were thus the first to conquer the Kara Sea.

In the eighteenth century Russian whale and seal hunters not only went to Novaya Zemlya, they also sailed into the Kara Sea and in 1760 one of them, Sava Loshkin, even circumnavigated Novaya Zemlya. But no one was able to repeat the heroic achievement of Malygin and his comrades, not even the government expeditions of 1807, 1819 and 1821–4. The polar explorer P. K. Pakhtusov also failed to do so when he investigated Novaya Zemlya and in particular the Matochkin Strait in 1832 and 1834 on behalf of the merchants of Archangel.

What the merchants wanted to open was kept unaccountably shut by a scholar. In summer 1837, K. E. von Baer visited Novaya Zemlya. He pronounced the Kara Sea ice-bound and inaccessible. As a result, in the next thirty years no one could bring himself to peer into the Kara ice-box.

Baer's verdict was refuted by Norwegian whalers from Tromsö. As the catches on the shores of Greenland and Spitzbergen grew smaller and smaller, they sailed farther east, first to Novaya Zemlya and later past it into the Kara Sea. In 1869 about twenty-five Norwegian whalers were at work there; they were joined by an eccentric English sportsman, who accounted for 48 whales and 14 polar bears.

In Russia nothing was known of this invasion at first, for the Norwegians did not discuss their trips with anyone. However, in 1869 the Norwegian, E. Johannesen was given a silver medal by the Swedish Academy for sailing through the Matochkin Strait into the Kara Sea and back through the Kara Strait, and everything became known. The Imperial Russian Geographical Society put a plan before the government for an expedition to the Kara Sea, but the finance minister refused to grant thirty thousand roubles for it.

Only one man at that time obstinately persisted in exploring the Kara Sea, the Siberian merchant M. K. Sidorov. Back in 1859 he had suggested sending an expedition to the mouth of the Ob. He had shares in a big timber enterprise there. He was the first to export timber from Pechora, he was the first to extract graphite from the River Kureyka in Siberia, and he also discovered and began to exploit gold deposits in the basin of the Yenisei. He had long been trying to awaken interest in Siberia; he wrote about it in Russian and foreign periodicals and took part in international congresses and exhibitions.

People in the West, too, were thinking about the Kara Sea. In 1871 Nordenskiöld, at that time a well known polar explorer, told Prince Kropotkin in Stockholm of his plan to sail up the Ob and Yenisei. An English merchant seaman, Captain Joseph Wiggins, had the same idea.

He was an idealist, a pious ascetic of the British merchant service. To him it was 'a crying shame' that England had not yet fulfilled her holy mission and found a sea-route to Siberia. He did not believe that the Kara Sea was impenetrable; he had heard that 'Kara' was the Tartar word for 'black', and thought that only a sea whose waters looked dark amid the arctic ice could be called 'black'. He corresponded with Dr. August Petermann, a tireless propagandist for the Kara idea, who confirmed this supposition. Wiggins used his savings to equip a little steamer and in 1874 set out from Dundee for the mouth of the Ob, which he reached. However, he did not succeed in finding the channel and could not look for it any longer because his crew demanded to go home. So he turned back.

He had no more money, so he collected it wherever he could, gave lectures and spread his ideas with the help of the Y.M.C.A. In 1875 he set out for Siberia again in a 27-ton fishing vessel, but got no further than Kolguyev Island. This failure went unnoticed; it was drowned in the noise of the tributes to A. E. Nordenskiöld.

Nordenskiöld was a lone wolf like Wiggins. When he set about putting into effect his Siberian plan he already enjoyed considerable fame as a scientist and had everything he needed at his disposal thanks to the Gothenburg merchant Oskar Dickson. He had a far better knowledge than anyone else of the literature on the Siberian Arctic, including Russian works, for he was a Finn by birth and could read Russian easily. He could also speak it a little. Nordenskiöld left Tromsö on 8 June 1875 in the Norwegian sailing ship *Pröven*; the captain and crew were Norwegian whalers. On 15 August he anchored in the peaceful bay of a little island on the north-east coast of the Yenisei estuary. He christened the island Dickson.

The *Pröven* turned back, but Nordenskiöld himself sailed on in an open boat southward up the Yenisei. On 31 August he sighted the river steamer *Alexander*, which took him on to Yeniseisk. Nordenskiöld had thus travelled by water from Norway to the heart of Siberia, to a spot where, as the Siberians used to say, you could touch China with your hand. The ovations began on the Yenisei and his journey to European Russia turned into a triumphal progress. The Siberian merchant Sibiryakov, who had not yet met Nordenskiöld, declared himself ready to give him financial support in his further enterprises.

The name Sibiryakov indicates this man's Siberian origin. He belonged to a famous merchant family; in 1774 his great-grandfather, Mikhail Sibiryakov, had built a factory to smelt silver at Nerchinsk and was reckoned to be the richest man in Siberia. His grandfather, Mikhail II, controlled the whole salt trade of east Siberia and had been mayor of Irkutsk.

Alexander Sibiryakov was born in 1849 and grew up in Siberia. He had gained an engineering degree at the technical high school in Zürich and thoroughly understood all the economic and technical problems of his age. He believed that the central economic problem of Siberia was that of a traffic artery. Like his brother Innokenty, he shrank from nothing where the development of Siberia was concerned. Innokenty financed the expedition of the ethnographer G. N. Potanin to Mongolia and China; Alexander spent 170,000 roubles on the first university in Siberia, at Tomsk. At his own expense Alexander had built the 'Sibiryakov road' through the Urals; along it his wheat travelled from the Ob to Pechora and thence abroad. In the 'eighties his steamers plied on the Angara, the Yenisei and the Ob. He personally investigated the road from Yakutsk to the Sea of Okhotsk and also tried to sail from Norway to the Yenisei, but lost his ship and only just escaped with his life. Together with Dickson, he financed Nordenskiöld's second Siberian expedition.

Today, when there are motor cars of two hundred horsepower on the market, it is amazing to read that the four-hundred-ton steamer *Ymer*, in which Nordenskiöld travelled to Siberia in 1876, had an engine of only forty-five horsepower. But it was enough to take him from Tromsö to the mouth of the Yenisei in three weeks. This time Nordenskiöld took a quantity of, so to speak, 'symbolic' goods with him, in order to show the practical importance of his expedition.

The sea route to western Siberia had been opened.

But where was Wiggins, the pioneer? He was in England, making preparations for a fresh expedition. He had finally obtained financial support; an English Maecenas had given him a thousand pounds, and he received another thousand from – Alexander Sibiryakov. In September 1876 Wiggins sailed into the Yenisei in the *Thames*. There he was to take on board a cargo of Sidorov's graphite, but as the freight was late in arriving, Wiggins left the *Thames* there for the winter and went off himself to St Petersburg.

In the following spring he returned to the *Thames* and started off home, but the steamer ran aground on a sandbank and Wiggins finally had to sell it to a group of Irkutsk merchants. He acquired a Russian schooner and asked his crew to sail it home with him, but the sailors preferred to go home by land.

This refusal seems strange at first sight. Wiggins was an excellent seaman and a good fellow. But virtues always cause trouble when they are exaggerated. Wiggins himself was a strict abstainer and his sailors, too, only got tea!

With a broken heart but, like Job, not complaining, Wiggins sold his schooner to Sidorov. Sidorov renamed it *Morning Glow* and next year this Yeniseisk-built vessel sailed under the command of the Russian captain Schwanenberg with a cargo of Sidorov's graphite to Gothenburg, from there through the Göta canal to Stockholm and finally, escorted by a Russian gunboat, to St Petersburg.

Wiggins chivalrously applauded this success; it showed that he had been thinking along the right lines. In the ten years between 1877 and 1886 twenty-seven steamers were dispatched from

Europe to the Ob and the Yenisei. Only twelve succeeded in completing their voyages, among them one commanded by Wiggins, who in 1878 sailed to the Ob and brought back a cargo of Siberian wheat to England. But this success was put in the shade by another, much greater one.

NORDENSKIÖLD'S EPOCH-MAKING VOYAGE

Nordenskiöld and Wiggins are like the two heroes in Pushkin's little play *Mozart and Salievi*. One was destined for 'trouble, prayer and zeal', the other for great deeds accomplished apparently without effort. How easy and perfect, how Mozartian – if this term is appropriate – Nordenskiöld's achievements seemed to the world. He himself felt this, as is apparent from the words he addressed to his companions to calm them when they were upset at having to winter where they were: 'It is really a good thing . . . otherwise no one would appreciate what difficulties we had to contend with.'

There were no difficulties about the preparations. His new expedition was arranged one evening in January 1877 at a dinner in Stockholm Castle, when King Oscar II and Dickson, who was one of the guests, declared themselves ready to finance a voyage to the Bering Strait. Nordenskiöld then made known the name of the third Maecenas, Alexander Sibiryakov. These three men contributed the same amounts (Sibiryakov's share amounted to 110,000 crowns), and in addition the Swedish Navy provided Nordenskiöld with some of the provisions, medical stores and coal he needed. The expedition was organized on a big scale. Nordenskiöld himself and his scientific staff sailed in the 357-ton, sixty-horsepower steamer *Vega*, which was commanded by Captain Louis Polander. Altogether thirty people travelled in the *Vega*, including Sibiryakov's Russian representative. The *Vega* was accompanied by another three ships, which belonged to Sibiryakov and were under Russian command: the steamer *Fraser*, with freight for Siberia, and the sailing-ship *Express*, with coal for the expedition, both bound for the Yenisei, and the steamer *Lena*, with a cargo for eastern Siberia.

Apart from the wintering of the *Vega* in the East Siberian Sea, the whole extremely complicated expedition went off with the precision and elegance of a naval review. The *Vega* and *Lena* left Tromsö on 21 June 1878; the *Fraser* and *Express* had sailed earlier. All four ships anchored in Dickson Bay on 6 August. After transferring the coal they did not need to the *Vega*, the *Fraser* and *Express* sailed to the Yenisei, loaded corn and other Siberian products and then delivered these cargoes to Hammerfest.

The *Vega* and *Lena* steered east. On 19 August they anchored off Cape Chelyuskin. On 28 August the two ships parted at the mouth of the Lena; the *Lena* sailed southward up the Yenisei and unloaded her cargo five weeks later at Yakutsk.

The *Vega* went on alone. The struggle with the ice became more and more difficult and at the end of September Nordenskiöld was forced to make up his mind to winter in Kolyuchin Bay, about a hundred nautical miles west of Cape Deshnev.

On 18 July 1879 the *Vega* weighed anchor and two days later sailed through the Bering Strait. The question of the north-east passage to 'Cathay' and India had been solved by Nordenskiöld – 354 years after it had been posed by Dimitri Gerasimov, 325 years after Willoughby and Chancellor had made the first attempt to solve it, and 150 years after the Great Northern Expedition. Nordenskiöld himself recognized that the achievement had only been made possible by technical progress in the form of the steam engine. The sober Müller had been perfectly right: in his time, for sailing ships, the task had been impossible.

But that is not the end of the story of the Kara Sea. Wiggins did not abandon his ideas. In 1887 he sailed in the steamer *Phoenix* with a cargo of salt from England to the mouth of the Yenisei. From there he took the *Phoenix*, a 273-ton steamer, up to Yeniseisk, piloting her round all the sandbanks and rapids fifteen hundred miles up a river in which there was not a single buoy or light. The next year the *Phoenix* took a cargo back to England.

Wiggins had his triumph six years later. By that time the Trans-Siberian railway was being built. In spring 1893 Wiggins received a telegram from St Petersburg which said, 'Can you carry 2,000 tons of railway lines by sea to Krasnoyarsk?' 'Twenty thousand if you like,' Wiggins wired back.

The very same year he sailed with a whole flotilla to the mouth of the Yenisei. The flotilla was led by the *Orestes*, a 2,500-ton steamer, the first proper ocean-going cargo ship to cleave the waters of the Kara Sea. In her wake steamed two smaller English vessels and three little Russian steamers destined to ply on the Yenisei.

Nineteen years of 'trouble, prayer and zeal' ended in a brilliant success. Everybody saluted Wiggins as a hero. The Royal Geographical Society in London gave him a golden chronometer. The Imperial Russian Geographical Society in St Petersburg honoured him with a banquet, at which Wiggins sat between two grand dukes, surrounded by the most important representatives of science, and by ministers, admirals and ambassadors. At the request of the Tsar the ministry of marine presented him with a silver punch-bowl, suitably inscribed, twenty-five goblets and all the usual accessories. Unfortunately in all his sixty-two years Wiggins had never allowed a drop of alcohol to pass his lips!

Many years went by. The Trans-Siberian railway had long been completed, and Nordenskiöld and Wiggins were both dead. In Russia the Soviet régime had taken over the legacy of the Tsars. Then one day in 1920 the Swedish consul in Nice informed his government that he had by chance come across a Russian refugee, an old man, living in extreme poverty. His name was Alexander Sibiryakov.

The news caused a considerable stir in Sweden. On 18 January the three biggest parties proposed to parliament that Sibiryakov should be granted a pension for the rest of his life. The reason adduced was that Sibiryakov had unselfishly supported an enterprise that had considerably enhanced Sweden's reputation throughout the world. The speakers used phrases such as 'national debt of thanks' and 'duty imposed by honour'. They all emphasized that when Sibiryakov gave his support to Nordenskiöld he had sought no personal advantage for himself.

This attitude bears witness to the nobility of Sweden's parliamentary representatives and does credit to the whole Swedish people, but it is partly based on a misunderstanding. When Sibiryakov supported Nordenskiöld he was certainly far from thinking of any advantage to himself. When Nordenskiöld was wintering in the Arctic and fears were expressed for his safety, Sibiryakov cabled to a steamer in Japan and sent it to look for him. There could be no question of any 'advantage' here. All the same, Sibiryakov's attitude was not dictated solely by the interests of Swedish science; he knew that above all the interest of Siberia and Russia were at stake. It was not Sweden that needed the northern sea-route, but Russia. Sibiryakov let Sweden have the honour and glory, but the economic future he kept for himself.

Sibiryakov died at Nice in 1933 at the age of 84. This great man, too, the only hero of Siberia in the dark days after Muravyev who was capable of a historical gesture which the Tsar had neglected to make, found his last resting-place in French soil. The burial-plot and the funeral were paid for by the Swedish consul.

A RICH BUT NEGLECTED REGION

During the reign of Alexander II and most of that of Alexander III Russia to some extent forgot Siberia. Alexander III saw this when in 1886 he replied to a report from Count A. Ignatyev, governor-general at Irkutsk, with these words: 'How many reports from Siberian governors-general have I not read already, and I have to admit with shame and grief that until now the government has done almost nothing to satisfy the requirements of this rich but neglected region. It is time, high time.'

Everyone knew that this was the truth. A certain amount of progress had of course been made. In 1875 at the mouth of the Yenisei, Nordenskiöld had met a steamer: there were some dozens of such steamers at that time on the Yenisei and the Ob. Wiggins spent the Christmas of 1877 in a private house in Krasnoyarsk which had electric light, and there were not many houses like that in Moscow itself at that time. But these were isolated achievements and in any case the government had nothing to do with them. The Siberian economy was not moving forward properly; it was stagnant, indeed in some respects it was slipping backwards. This was true especially of forestry. The forests were simply regarded as inexhaustible. The old law allowed all inhabitants of Siberia 'to use the forest for their needs free and gratis'.

When the forestry board was set up in West Siberia in 1884, it resolved at once to combat the plundering of the forests. It entrusted the 'protection of the forests' to the settlers, with the opposite result, as can be imagined: they did not protect the forests, they felled them. In 1869 some limited company or other received a concession for the free and unlimited exploitation and export of the woods on the rivers Ob and Yenisei and their tributaries, that is, in practice, in the whole of western Siberia. The result of this kind of 'forest protection' was that the woods on the banks of the most important rivers of western Siberia disappeared 'almost completely', as an official report puts it. Obviously there were still plenty of trees in Siberia, but fewer and fewer of them were in spots where they could be conveniently felled and exported.

The fur-bearing animals were also ruthlessly exterminated. Furs had once been one of old Moscow's most valuable assets; indeed it is true to say that they had been the main reason for the conquest of Siberia. These animals were still plentiful. In the eighties of the nineteenth century over the whole of Siberia twenty thousand sables, twenty to twenty-five thousand ermines, about twenty thousand red foxes, and over two thousand blue foxes and otters were slaughtered every year. Squirrels were killed by the million. Silver foxes were already becoming rare but there were still plenty of bears, wolves, minks, pine-martens, lynxes and cats. The hunters of the Ussuri region even used to deliver a few dozen tiger- and leopard-skins every year. Furs were convenient and popular goods for smuggling out of eastern Siberia into China.

No one thought of protecting the fur-bearing animals; but in any case such protection would have been impossible to organize in the tundra and the *taiga*. Even where it could have been arranged it was neglected; the truth was that fundamentally the authorities sanctioned this wholesale destruction. In 1871 the sea-otter hunting in the Commander Islands was rented to the American firm of Hutchinson, Kohl and Co. A year later this firm became the Alaska Commercial Co. and now received from the American government the concession to catch sea-otters in the Pribylov Islands. The Americans were thus working in both Russian and American territory, but on quite different conditions. On the American side the size of the catches was limited; on the Russian side the company was allowed to catch all it could. The Russian treasury received a yearly rent of five thousand roubles and two roubles for every skin; the American government was paid a rent of fifty-five thousand dollars and $2·62\frac{1}{2}$ per skin. When the lease ran out in 1891 the concession was granted to a Russian company, and although the catch was now restricted the receipts of the Russian treasury increased fivefold. It was the beginning of a new epoch.

The general impression left by Siberia in the second half of the nineteenth century is one of over-exploitation and maladministration. The reports of the finance ministry are quite frank about it. The 1893 report notes a decline in the number of fish caught as a result of over-fishing and also emphasizes the poor state of the cattle-raising industry. 'The cattle are small,' it says, 'fairly thin and give only a poor yield of milk. The horses are moderate; they have plenty of endurance and they are swift, but they are not strong. The sheep are all of a very poor breed.' Such was the balance sheet at the end of the century; yet many parts of Siberia, as the Decembrists had noted, provided ideal conditions for cattle-rearing.

Industry was very backward. Although the presence of huge deposits of coal in the Kuznetsk basin had been established in the eighteenth century no one had made any attempt to exploit them. In the whole of Siberia the only place where coal was produced was Sakhalin. The emancipation of the serfs, which deprived the royal mines of their free labour, dealt a heavy blow to the Altai works; the production of copper and silver declined rapidly. As for iron, there were only twelve small ironworks in the whole of Siberia; their total production was estimated at 571,000 roubles – about ten kopecks per head of the Siberian population.

Only gold production was increasing. From 1850 to 1860 the average yearly output was 22,000 kilogrammes, or about 86 per cent of the figure for the whole of Russia. It was realized in the 'seventies that gold was to be found in literally every river of East Siberia. In the Nerchinsk district and in the coastal regions progress was slow, but on the Amur a real California came into being. Gold had been discovered there in 1859 by the engineer N. P. Anosov, Muravyev's collaborator. After Muravyev's departure Anosov left the public service but continued to prospect for gold on behalf of the financier Bernardakis. For twenty years he lived the life of a gold-prospector and hunter and during this period he discovered three of the richest deposits of gold as well as innumerable smaller ones.

Work began in 1868 on the deposits found by Anosov between the Amur and the Seya, and in the very first year eight hundred kilogrammes of gold were produced. By law all precious metals had to be sold to the government. In 1890 seven thousand eight hundred kilogrammes were delivered from the Amur alone, but nearly as much went over the border every year illegally to China.

So much for the economy. But the most valuable economic asset is undoubtedly man himself, and here the position was worst of all. Siberia was still far too thinly populated. There were far too few colonists to develop the country's natural resources, and the solution of this problem was farther away than ever in the second half of the nineteenth century.

There is a widespread misconception – even in Russia – that Siberia was settled mainly by deportees. It is not difficult to see how this view arose. The fate of the exiles fascinated every observer. There were important people among them and not only their personal destinies but also their supposed crimes were highly dramatic. Prisoners of war of every nationality, Polish, Ukrainian, Caucasian and other rebels against the Tsarist régime, innumerable Russian fighters for freedom were all sent to Siberia, and although Tsar Alexander III had described the exiles as 'the dregs of Russia' the people who lived with them in Siberia had the greatest respect for these 'criminals'. The writer Korolenko once even heard an offended Siberian say to an exile, 'And you call yourself a criminal. . . .'

On the whole the influx of political and criminal elements had little effect on the settlement of Siberia. Apart from the 'Old Believers', who had in fact provided the best material for colonization, the rest were incapable of adapting themselves to this harsh land and an enormous number of people simply disappeared without trace. This had struck Speransky, who had written to his daughter a hundred and thirty years earlier: 'You must not think that Siberia is peopled by exiles and criminals. You hardly notice them; they are just a drop in the ocean.' At the end of the nineteenth century the deportees formed no more than five per cent of the population of Siberia.

Apart from deportation there was also a milder kind of compulsory settlement, the so-called 'official' colonization. This included the settlement of farmers, transport workers, Cossacks and the peasants 'enrolled' to work on royal property. Although only a proportion of all these people had taken root in Siberia, they were nevertheless very important and without them Siberia could not have been held and administered. All the same, the core of the colonization was provided not by deportation or 'official' resettlement, but by free colonization, which did not worry much about official regulations. It is thanks to this that by the end of the eighteenth century there were over a million Russian settlers in Siberia.

In the early years of the nineteenth century two thousand people at the most crossed the Urals every year; when Speransky managed to get the regulations eased in the twenties the numbers rose to about ten thousand a year, and in many years considerably more. After the liberation of the peasants in 1861 the government began to waver again. In 1865 the royal lands in the Altai were released for settlement and a mass of colonists, mainly from the Ukraine, streamed there at once. Then the government grew anxious again and for five years – 1874 to 1878 – stopped 'official' settlement completely, just at a time when population pressure from Russia had been powerfully increased by the emancipation of the serfs.

The government could naturally see the senselessness of this measure, but Russian landowners put up energetic opposition to the departure of landless and unemployed peasants to Siberia since they naturally provided the cheapest labour force available.

Only in the 'eighties, when it had begun to be clear to everyone that the development of a village proletariat constituted a serious danger to Russia, did the government open the flood-gates again. The laws of 1881 and 1889 opened Siberia to colonization again and provided assistance for new settlers. In 1887 twenty-five thousand people crossed the Urals, in 1888 thirty-six thousand, in 1889 forty thousand and in 1892 as many as ninety-two thousand. By that time the population of Siberia was about five and a half million.

The non-Russian natives formed less than ten per cent of this number and even this percentage was only reached thanks to the relatively numerous Tartars, Kirghiz, Kalmucks and Mongols of the steppes and Transbaikalia. In the vast remainder of Siberia the natives were hardly noticeable. Siberia was Russian, but even with the Russian settlers there were still far too few people in it – about half a person per square kilometre!

It is true that this 'half person' was not static or passive. Many thousands of people were continually moving around Siberia: escaped convicts, independent emigrants and vagabonds of every kind. They might suddenly coalesce somewhere in a conspiracy and then the old Siberia would come to life again, elemental, uncontrolled and intoxicated with its own vastness. Its vitality was inexhaustible.

In 1883 gold was discovered by Russian prospectors on the Sheltuga, on the Chinese side of the Amur. In the course of a few months a horde of people streamed there; contemporary sources speak of six to twelve thousand. No one knew the precise number, for the 'Sheltuga Republic' had every reason to avoid censuses. It consisted of wandering Siberians with an admixture of Chinese and Manchus; Amur Cossacks also made guest appearances from time to time. This throng of people organized its own state, with an administration, police, a budget and a 'government' of elders. There were courts of law as well; they were strict, but swift and just.

This episode reflects the many-sidedness of Siberian history: the 'elemental expansion' eastwards, the survival of the fittest and the economic exploitation of new territories. The 'Sheltuga Republic' did not recognize Chinese sovereignty and it succeeded several times in repulsing Chinese military units, until in 1886 a whole army was dispatched against it and hunger forced it to submit. The whole Russian population crossed the Amur to the Russian side and was lost again in the vast expanses of Siberia.

X

THE RAILWAY SETS THE PACE

———◆◆◆———

THE DECISION
TO BUILD THE GREAT RAILWAY

ALL THE problems of Siberia – economy, colonization, defence –
met in the nineteenth century. They all began and ended with the
question of communications. Anyone should have been able to
see that. Muravyev was the first to demand railways for Siberia. In
1857 he enthusiastically recommended the plan of the American
Major Collins, who had suggested building a railway from Chita
to Irkutsk.

Collins was not the only one to be inspired by the occupation of
the Amur region. At the same time an Englishman called Dull
turned up at St Petersburg with a suggestion for a horse-tramway
from Nishni-Novgorod to the Pacific!

There was no lack of ideas among the Russians themselves. In
1858 a St Petersburg business-man called Sofronov put forward
a plan for a railway from the Volga to the Amur and soon the
government was overwhelmed with petitions from private individuals, learned societies, towns and the business communities of
Russia and Siberia. There might perhaps be some doubt about the
profitability of a railway from the Urals to the Pacific, wrote the
merchant, but an 'iron road' to West Siberia would involve no
risks at all.

Why, then, it may be asked, did the government not build this
railroad, for which everyone was literally praying? For the same
reason that it put the brake on the settlement of Siberia. This
railway would have caused the emigration of workers from European Russia and brought the price of land down. It would also
have made possible the import of wheat from Siberia and forced
the price of wheat down.

However, no one can resist vital forces for ever. By the end of the
'seventies, Possiett, the minister of transport, was himself demand-

ing a railway to West Siberia. Shades of an agrarian revolution were rising before the big landowners and they began to understand that it might be better to let 'restless elements' go off to Siberia. But more important than anything else was the rise of a new power, industry. Industry shrieked for a Siberian railway. To start with, it wanted to earn profits by building it. Furthermore, it was directly interested in lowering the price of wheat so that workers' wages could be kept down. Finally, industry was keen on the colonization of Siberia because it wanted Siberia as a market; Siberia was to provide raw materials and then buy the finished products.

The gateway to trade with Siberia was Nishni-Novgorod. The representatives of Russian commerce, who gathered there in 1889 for the usual annual fair, demanded the construction of an 'iron road' across Siberia to the Pacific. 'This railway,' they wrote, 'will have tremendous importance for Russia and give a considerable stimulus to Russian industry.'

Really all that remained to be done was to hasten the building of the railway, for the plan had been decided on in principle four years earlier when Possiett himself had suggested building a line to Vladivostock. The council of ministers had passed the plan and it was now up to the Tsar to give final permission. It might be necessary to wait a long time for that, for there was no money available for this gigantic project.

But contrary to all expectations Alexander III pronounced himself in favour of the enterprise, for just at that time political considerations joined the economic ones.

We know already that the policy of 'concentration of strength on the continent of Asia' had caused, as was foreseen in Russia, disquiet in England. Every move of Russia in Asia was regarded as a threat to India. Admiral Stirling even saw a threat in the arrival of Russia on the Amur. The publicist Thomas T. Meadows, now forgotten but famous in his day, wrote in 1856 of the coming 'Russian Alexander', who would conquer China, destroy the British Empire and reduce the whole world to subjection. The pathetic cries of alarm uttered by the British press seemed to have received some justification when in the 'eighties Russia reached to the Afghan border in Turkestan. In 1884 the famous 'Afghanistan incident' took place. A detachment of Russian troops took possession of a disputed point on the frontier. When they were attacked by the Afghans, who were acting on British instructions, the Russians defeated them and scattered them. Gladstone told parliament that war with Russia was unavoidable. Only Bismarck's refusal to support the British prevented a war between Great Britain and Russia.

In Russia, too, it was realized that further clashes with England were bound to occur. It seemed obvious. It was the age of 'the division of the world', of imperialism. People and things knew their place and stayed in it. In England Whigs and Tories alternated with each other in holding power, Germany was ruled by the Iron Chancellor and on the throne of Russia sat that giant, Alexander III, who held the view that Europe could wait just as long as the Tsar of Russia cared to slumber. Where would the blow from England fall? Probably where Russia was weakest, in the Far East.

There, in Korea, the interests of the great powers clashed. For Japan and Russia this country was very important strategically and politically. In particular, it offered Russia an opportunity to gain her long-denied ice-free harbour. The attempt to acquire it was made in 1885, but it was frustrated by the British, who occupied a small island in the entrance to the Korea Strait and evacuated it only when Russia abandoned her project.

Once again Russia's weakness in the Far East when she clashed with a power that ruled the sea was made painfully obvious. In 1886 the Canadian Pacific Railway was completed and this meant a strengthening of Great Britain's position in the Pacific. In the same year the governor-general of the Far East, Baron von Korff, and his colleague at Irkutsk, Count A. Ignatyev, both declared that the defence of the Far East would be impossible unless it was swiftly linked with the mother country by a railway. So the railway was now demanded by the minister of foreign affairs as well.

On 29 March 1891 it was proclaimed that the Tsar had decided to build a railway from the Urals to Vladivostok. Nicholas, the heir to the throne, was ordered by his father to lay the first sleeper at Vladivostok.

The twenty-three-year-old heir was engaged at the time on a foreign tour in order to gain 'a thorough political education'. Today this trip seems like a mysterious hieroglyph foreshadowing the fate of the last aristocratic ruler of Russia. When Nicholas was visiting a Japanese town near Kyoto and driving in a rickshaw between two lines of policemen, one of them attacked him and wounded him in the head with his sabre. At his trial the man said that he was a Samurai and had no associates.

'What provoked him to his abominable deed?' asked the official Russian account of Nicholas's trip. 'Hatred of the Russians? That is excluded, for there is no such thing in Japan.' This was another example of the old Russian complacency and blindness where Japan was concerned. It occurred to no one that the Samurai's hand had risen from the depths of Japanese history, from a hundred and fifty years of fear and hostility.

From Japan Nicholas travelled to Vladivostok and from there, after he had solemnly inaugurated the construction of the Ussuri railway, through Siberia to St Petersburg. He had learned to know Siberia and always retained a feeling of special attachment to this land. His personal fate, the fate of his dynasty and the empire, was linked then to the Far East and Siberia.

The year of his return, 1891, is remembered in Russia because of the terrible drought and famine. But in Siberia the harvest had not failed, and it now became apparent that without a railway wheat could not be brought from there to European Russia. Throngs of hungry peasants moved towards the east; if only there had been a railway! Everyone was calling for it now.

The project was now pushed forward energetically. Crowds of engineers and experts of every kind had already been sent to Siberia; complicated questions of finance, organization, and the ordering and transport of material had now to be solved. Everything went off smoothly, everything was directed by the powerful will of a man with a genius for organization, Sergei Yulyevich Witte.

WITTE AND THE SECRETS OF THE EAST

At that time Witte was forty-two. He was a newcomer to St Petersburg and people looked at him askance; he was regarded, in the Russian phrase, as 'a man of no birth or breeding'. This reputation was assisted by his gruffness, his bad manners and his massive and uncouth appearance. In fact he was by no means a man 'of no breeding'. His father had a good position in the Caucasus and the Witte family belonged to the highest circles of the Tiflis bureaucracy. His mother was the daughter of the well-known military writer General Fadeyev, whose wife was by birth a Princess Dolgorukov. So the blood of one of the oldest Russian noble families flowed in Witte's veins. However, there was nothing of the Russian aristocrat about him. Although he emphasized at every opportunity that his father had belonged to 'an aristocratic Baltic family', the nobility was pretty dubious; it had been a reward for services rendered. A man with a German name but no 'von' was regarded in St Petersburg simply as a German colonist. People of the sort were well known in Russia. They were excellent farmers and industrialists, and reliable officials, but a crude, unimaginative and philistine lot. Witte was a typical example, although he was half-Russian, belonged to the Orthodox Church and even had blue blood in his veins.

The only asset he possessed for a career in the capital was his knowledge of French; he had not bothered to learn German. That he had a mathematical degree from Odessa University and had displayed outstanding ability in gaining it interested no one. At the end of his university course Witte joined the staff of the railway. He began by selling tickets, transferred to the goods department, became assistant station-master and finally station-master. His superiors knew that he did not live for the job but simply wanted to study the railways, and everything went smoothly. After only a few years he knew more about railway fares and freight rates than anyone else in Russia. He had written a whole book on them.

He showed his talent for organization during the war with Turkey in 1877-8 when he organized the dispatch of the Russian troops and reinforcements to Roumania. His work did not pass unnoticed and he gained further promotion. After a few years he was manager of the South-Western Railway.

On the occasion of a royal railway journey he arranged for the Tsar's train to travel more slowly on the stretch of line under his jurisdiction than on the others. This caused dissatisfaction.

The Tsar remembered this incident when two months later on a neighbouring line the imperial train was derailed at full speed. The royal family was in the dining-car. The athletic Tsar held up the roof of the carriage with his back. Witte was ordered by telegram to take part in the inquiry into the accident. Soon afterwards Possiett, the minister of transport, and a number of high officials had to resign.

Witte went on with his work. The line which he managed became one of the few which made a profit. Soon he was given the task of drawing up fresh fares and freight rates which were to produce a dividend for the other Russian lines.

This was all the more unusual since Witte was not even a government official; he was employed by a private company. When he was offered a senior post in the ministry of transport he declared quite openly that on the railway he could do what he liked and received a salary of fifty thousand roubles into the bargain, while in St Petersburg he would be a mere civil servant with a salary of eight thousand roubles.

The answer he received was that the Tsar wished him to take the post, and that in addition to his official salary he would receive another eight thousand roubles from the privy purse.

In the whole history of Russia there had been no other example of a deal like this. But that did not bother Witte: it was not for nothing that he had studied and begun his career in Odessa, a city whose inhabitants were known for their commercial talent and bad manners.

Besides, he was in fact making a financial sacrifice. He assented because his ambition and lust for power had been sharpened. In February 1892 he was entrusted with the direction of the ministry of transport. Six months later he was finance minister.

He had no systematic programme at that time. One thing he did know: Russia was enormously big and rich, and for its economic development railways had to be built and industry encouraged. He was a disciple of the German economist List, on whom he even wrote a pamphlet. It was List who made him realize the importance of protective tariffs and railways for the development of a country's economic resources.

When he became a minister, the question of the Trans-Siberian railway had already been decided and the Ussuri line was already being built. The Tsar asked him to 'push on with this affair'. That was all he was waiting for.

The most important thing here was speed. Witte suggested setting up a committee to direct the construction and giving it the power to make laws. Usually it took the state council years to decide on laws; now everything was settled in a few days. The Tsar asked who was to be chairman of the committee. 'The heir to the throne,' replied Witte. 'But he's only a boy; he doesn't know anything at all,' said the Tsar. 'Precisely, Your Majesty, he must learn.' The real leader of the committee was naturally Witte. He could control the committee anyway because he had the keys to the treasury in his pocket. The committee always had money at its disposal. The financial tricks he sometimes had to resort to he described later himself.

As List's disciple he had of course soon grasped the connection between railways and national policy. Now, at the fount of all power, he became thoroughly acquainted with these links. The railways were the state's nervous system. Every terminus opened up a new area. Every end was a new beginning.

The perspectives opened up by the new Siberian railway were described by Witte in a memorandum handed to the Tsar in November 1892, three months after his appointment as finance minister. It began with the importance of the line for Siberia and Russia: it would exercise a beneficent economic effect not just for hundreds of miles, but for thousands, since it would connect up all the navigable rivers of Siberia. It would lend an impetus to the exploitation of Siberian mineral resources and to the development of industry, and it would put fresh life into commerce. But its most important effect would be to assist colonization, which would be a blessing for European Russia since it would reduce over-population there and lessen the danger of an agrarian revolution.

Naturally for some time the railway would not show a profit. But can one, wrote Witte, look at a national undertaking from the point of view of dividends alone? The Trans-Siberian railway would not only link Russia to Siberia, it would also link Europe to the Pacific and eastern Asia. It would open 'a new path and fresh horizons not only to Russia, but also to world trade'. The Trans-Siberian railway would enable Russia to take part in the struggle for the Pacific and open the markets of China and Japan to her merchants. At the same time the line would also increase Russian power in the Far East. It would strengthen ties with Russia's neighbours and perhaps also with the United States. It would assure the Russian fleet of all the supplies it needed in Far Eastern ports, and this fleet could be significantly strengthened.

These ideas were not new, but they corresponded to the new mood in St Petersburg, where people were beginning to immerse themselves in the 'secrets of the East'. A cousin of Witte's, Helene Blavatsky, a well-known theosophist who had settled in London, published her fantastic accounts of her travels in India in Moscow newspapers. Witte was surprised that even clever people could enthuse over her effusions, but he himself did not avoid the company of the St Petersburg specialist in 'secrets', a 'doctor of Tibetan medicine' called Badmayev.

Through this 'doctor' Siberia once again sent its mysterious fluid to the throne of the Tsars. Badmayev was a Buryat from Transbaikalia. He had studied at Irkutsk and then at the Oriental faculty of St Petersburg university. He had become a lecturer in Mongolian and began to treat sick people 'in accordance with Tibetan methods'. He did not talk about Asiatic secrets, as Madame Blavatsky did; he possessed them himself, and this awoke the curiosity of some big names; and where there are big names there is usually big money.

Witte describes Badmayev in his memoirs as a clever man, but a charlatan and intriguer. But to start with he had clearly taken a different view of the man. Two months after Witte had handed his memorandum to the Tsar he gave him a memorandum compiled by Badmayev. At that time the question of the eastern section of the Siberian railway had not yet been decided. Badmayev asserted that the section from Baikal to Vladivostok was of secondary importance; first, the line from Baikal to the south should be built, deep into the Chinese province of Kansu, which was next to Tibet. Badmayev offered to engineer there, with the help of his Buryat agents, a rising of the local population, which, so the 'Doctor' maintained, would demand to be annexed to Russia.

Witte had added his own remarks to this memorandum. He does not mention them in his memoirs; they were only found later. Witte was not of the same opinion as Badmayev; he continued to regard the link with Vladivostok as the most important task. But he considered that Badmayev's idea of branch lines on Chinese territory should be taken seriously. Its realization could lead to Russia's playing a dominant rôle 'from the shores of the Pacific and the slopes of the Himalayas' not only in Asiatic questions but also in European ones.

The Tsar declared that Badmayev's ideas were fantastic and refused to believe that they could be put into effect. Soon Witte realized too where the 'leap on to the peaks of the Himalaya' might lead, but he had to pay for his enthusiasm for the Himalayas. Badmayev had turned to the Tsar with the request for a loan of two hundred thousand roubles to start some enterprise or other in Transbaikalia which would contribute to 'the end in view'. Witte was most unwilling to part with the money, which would clearly not be paid back, but it was he who had passed the memorandum on to the Tsar and to his irritation he had to pay out on direct orders from above.

He dismissed the Tibetan doctor's fantasies from his thoughts, but the idea of a branch line on Chinese territory remained at the back of his mind and, once having taken root there, called out for action.

WITTE BUILDS
THE TRANS-SIBERIAN RAILWAY

In St Petersburg ideas seethed, in Siberia the work went forward. Some ten thousand settlers crossed the Urals and parties of engineers, topographers and surveyors streamed over the proposed route. Temporary lines were laid and landing-stages built on the rivers. Russian firms had already received orders for rails, locomotives, rolling stock, steamers and sleepers. It turned out to be impossible to manage completely without making any purchases at all abroad, but these foreign purchases formed an insignificant proportion of the total orders and almost all the money spent on the railway remained in Russia.

The golden rain made Witte the most popular man in the country. The industrialists were just as intoxicated by the new ideas as Witte himself, Tsar Alexander and Crown Prince Nicholas. Every engineer felt like a fresh Yermak and set about conquering Siberia anew.

The political clouds were beginning to gather and the new war minister demanded speed. Witte himself liked a lively tempo and so did the new minister for transport, the 'American', Prince Khilkov. A lordly aristocrat, Khilkov had gone to the U.S.A. as a young man and, starting as a stoker, had learned all there was to know about railways. This American training now paid a dividend. First-class engineers, industrial organizers, experts on land-settlement and learned agronomists all suddenly appeared from nowhere. Tsar Nicholas I had always said that he could never find the 'right men', but Alexander III and Witte were able to lay their hands on as many as they wanted.

To hasten the construction of the railway it was decided to reduce technical requirements to a minimum, to build only a single track and to lay lighter rails than were usually employed in Europe and America. It was clear that everything would soon have to be replaced, but no one was willing to wait.

Construction began simultaneously at five different places. The western section from Chelyabinsk to the Ob was relatively easy to build since it ran across a plain and through partly inhabited regions. On the other hand there were no stones there at all and they had to be brought up by river from five to six hundred miles away. In many places there was no sand, and the wood for the sleepers had to be fetched from European Russia, the Altai and the remotest tributaries of the Ob.

The farther east the line progressed, the more difficult its construction became. The stretch from the Ob to Irkutsk led mainly through the *taiga*. There was more than enough timber here, but the very severe climate, with masses of snow in winter and floods when it thawed in the spring, stopped the work regularly for six months at a time. In addition, the terrain was becoming more hilly and the excavating work more complicated, especially as the ground was always frozen. But the chief difficulty was shortage of labour, and this grew steadily worse as the line went farther. All the craftsmen, the foremen and even a large proportion of the unskilled labourers had to be brought from Russia, and consequently there were about thirty thousand men to be fed and housed.

Among them there were convicts and exiles. They were all paid for their work. The convicts lived apart and under guard, but under the same conditions as the free workers. They had all been told that when the work was completed their sentences would be cut by a third or a half.

The work as a whole was organized by the treasury, but individual projects were handed over to private contractors. Their participation was part of the programme for the industrialization of Siberia. However, very few private firms took part in the construction of the central and eastern sections. Seventy per cent of the whole task had to be carried out by the government.

The most difficult stretch turned out to be the section beyond Lake Baikal, especially the part that ran through the valley of the Shilka. In 1897 a flood caused by torrential rain carried away about sixty miles of completed track, including a number of bridges and viaducts.

Nevertheless the speed of construction beat all previous records. The two-thousand-mile stretch from Chelyabinsk to Irkutsk was due to be finished in 1900, but it was actually opened to traffic in 1898. The Ussuri line was opened as early as 1894. The seven-hundred-mile section from Lake Baikal to Sretensk was built in four years and opened in 1900. In that year it was possible to travel from Moscow to Sretensk without changing, although there were gaps in the line round Lake Baikal; the trains were ferried across the lake by two steamers.

So the only stretch between the Urals and Vladivostok which still had to be built was the section between Sretensk and Khabarovsk. These two places are linked by the Shilka and the Amur, but the connection is not a very good one as both rivers freeze over in winter. Nevertheless the construction of this section was postponed to the future. Vladivostok was to have another link with the Trans-Siberian railway which was not only shorter and more convenient but would also, in Witte's words, 'mark the beginning of a new epoch in the history of the nations.'

Meanwhile the Siberian railway grew, and so did Witte's stature. His unparalleled energy and toughness, his decisiveness and his readiness to go the whole hog all made him into a personality among ministers who were just colourless officials. 'At last we've got a lobster among the oysters,' said one diplomat with a reputation as a gourmet. He soon put his signature on a series of important political actions, among them a customs war with Germany, which he ended in 1894 with a compromise favourable to Russia. This was a personal victory which was talked about all over Europe. Bismarck asked the Russian ambassador who the new star was.

In the following year he made the sale of spirits a government monopoly in Russia. The reign of the *otkupchiki*, the private concessionaires whom Muravyev had hated so much, had at last been ended.

Witte's critics asserted that he was turning Russia into a nation of alcoholics, but this was not true. Apart from the fact that the idea was not his own but had been forced on him by Tsar Alexander, Witte's intention was to secure control over the consumption of alcohol and at the same time to give the state the income from its sale. With the help of this income the state was to combat the misuse of alcohol.

Next, in 1897, came the introduction of the gold standard in Russia. This reform made it possible to stabilize the budget, and its beneficent results were obvious, but there was agitation against it at once, fomented by the big land-owners, for whom it was more profitable to pay their labourers with paper roubles and sell the wheat abroad for jingling coins.

Witte's reforms did perceptible damage to the interests of the aristocratic landowners and he was never forgiven for this, in spite of all the efforts he made not to ruin the nobility. To be sure, he was not inspired by the sight of 'aristocratic country homes'; his enthusiasm was reserved for industries, banks and railways. He found the patriarchal and conservative landowners comical and boring; the people he liked and found interesting were business-men, bankers and capitalists. He understood their love of money and their cynicism did not bother him. 'Witte tries to bribe every-one in one way or another and to squeeze all he can out of them,' wrote the publisher Suvorin, editor of the influential paper *Novoye Vremya*. 'Witte despises us all,' said the minister Khilkov, 'be-cause he knows that he can buy any of us.' These assertions were not far from the truth. Witte himself later told how everyone from minor officials to grand dukes crept before him for money.

He was certainly a capitalist by temperament. His critics con-sidered that his methods were 'rootless' and 'inorganic', but it was this capitalist who first saw the colonization of Siberia as a national task and one for the government. In trying to carry it out he acted far more 'organically' than the Russian landowners. Witte linked the colonization to the building of the Trans-Siberian railway. Siberia had been opened to colonists in 1889; the Siberian Com-mittee took over the organization of the settlements and gave the emigrants assistance. In 1897 a 'settlement board' was set up, an official institution with the character of a ministry. Finally the Ural 'sluice' was opened. In 1891–2, after two years of famine, 180,000 people moved across into Siberia; in 1895 it was 120,000 and in 1896 as many as 200,000. In the twenty-five years from 1860 to 1885 about 300,000 people had moved to Siberia, in the next ten years 370,000 and in the five years from 1895 to 1899 the number was 820,400. Siberia was at last beginning to fill up.

Witte was continually reproached with introducing state capitalism into Russia, and wanting to make 'the all-powerful state', as a pamphlet put it, 'the owner of all the country's wealth'. In reality he favoured private capital and considered that Russia's weakness lay precisely in the under-development of private capital. The American diplomat A. D. White once said that he understood why the state was building the Trans-Siberian railway – 'it's cheaper'. 'I doubt that,' replied Witte, 'but I would pay private firms even more if they were capable of doing the job.' There was only one real capitalist in Russia, the state, and in Witte's opinion it had had to carry private enterprise along with it. Here lies the reason for the ambiguity of his policy: this same White also considered that Witte's only fault as a statesman was his desire 'that everything should be done by the state'.

Witte did not want the state to do 'everything', but he did take the view that the great projects could not be carried out without the state, and great projects were necessary because the state was great. The Russian empire had to be great or else not exist at all.

'Capital, more capital,' he was always repeating, and at the first opportunity he began to pump foreign capital into Russia. He was a master at securing foreign loans, the greatest expert at it ever known in Russia. He was in personal contact with financial kings like Mendelssohn and Bleichröder in Germany, Rothschild in Paris and Morgan in America.

When his enemies spread the rumour that he had 'put aside half a million', he only shrugged his shoulders. If he had wanted to 'put something aside', he could probably have made it much more and done it quite openly: he would only have needed to leave the public service and to take up an appointment in a bank.

He was attacked unmercifully in St Petersburg; the utterances of contemporaries about him are an astonishing mixture of malice and stupidity. By the end of the century he had grown into a demonic figure. His first wife was dead; people asserted that he had poisoned her. He became the most hated man in the capital. To the court he was an upstart, to the civil service an outsider and to the patriotic press a non-Russian. But he was indispensable.

This uncouth and prosaic man seemed demonic because he was incomprehensible to his contemporaries; he was not in harmony with his age. He would have fitted better into the epoch of the 'managerial revolution'. He was a mathematician, a politician and a financial expert, but by temperament he was and always remained an engineer and a manager. Railways and 'industrial giants' were his ruling passion. His favourite occupation was planning on a large scale in space and time. It is not difficult to recognize in these characteristics a reality that is very near to us.

In Russia it had been rightly assumed that the Trans-Siberian railway would cause disquiet among those powers interested, but as usual least thought had been devoted to Japan. The Japanese, however, knew that the Russians needed an ice-free port on the Pacific and that when the steel serpent reached the Amur it would certainly turn south. Where would it strike? In Korea, or still further to the south? In either case Korea would be lost to Japan, and that could not be permitted. Korea was not only, to use the conventional phrase, 'a pistol pointed at Japan'; it was also the bridge for future Japanese expansion in Asia. We know the place occupied by Korea in the plans of 'greater Japan'. In 1876 Japan had opened Korea to international trade and she already had important commercial interests there.

Korea was not yet Japanese, but the Japanese were trying to prevent it becoming Chinese. In 1885 Japan and China agreed not to send troops to Korea without letting each other know first.

In spring 1894, when the construction of the Trans-Siberian railway was already under way, a rebellion broke out in South Korea. At Seoul's request, the Chinese sent troops to Korea. They informed the Japanese, but at the same time described Korea as owing allegiance to themselves. The Japanese protested, but another detachment of fifteen hundred men was dispatched from China. The transports were sunk by the Japanese, who thus started the war 'for the independence of Korea'.

The small but splendidly disciplined and equipped Japanese army defeated the Chinese in no time. The Japanese occupied the peninsula of Liao-Tung and Port Arthur, and also Wei-hai-wei. At the end of March the peace negotiations began in the Japanese town of Shimonoseki. After a few days it became known that Japan was demanding the recognition of Korea's independence and the cession of Liao-Tung and Port Arthur.

At St Petersburg consultations had been in progress since January under the chairmanship of the Tsar's uncle, Grand Duke Alexei Alexandrovich. Tsar Nicholas, the Grand Duke and the foreign minister, Prince Lobanov-Rostovsky were all inclined to come to an agreement with Japan. However, at the same time the German and French governments were asked if Russia could count on their support if she decided to intervene in the Far East. When affirmative answers had arrived from both Berlin and Paris, Witte stepped forward to express his opinion.

He put the question in his usual incisive way. 'The war,' he said, 'is the consequence of our starting to build the Trans-Siberian railway. It was waged against Russia, not against China. We can let Japan have everything except the Liao-Tung peninsula, which is a gateway to Manchuria. To hand over Liao-Tung to the Japanese would mean waging a war against them in a few years' time when they have dug themselves in there. Therefore an ultimatum must be delivered to Japan and, if necessary, backed up by a bombardment of Japanese posts. We shall appear in the rôle of saviour of China, who will appreciate our services and later agree to a friendly alteration of our frontier.'

The author of the intervention was thus Witte, and his resolution was crowned with complete success. The ultimatum was delivered after the peace treaty (in which China accepted all Japan's demands) had been signed on 17 April 1895, at Shimonoseki. With the support of France and Germany, and in the name of China's inviolability, Russia forced Japan to hand back Liao-Tung – and this after the whole of Japan had already celebrated the great national victory!

This was a blow to Japan's pride like the one which Russia had to accept at the Congress of Berlin in 1878. And just as Russia then turned away from her old German friend and threw herself into the arms of France, so now the Japanese transferred all their hopes to England. It is interesting to note that only one man had foreseen this, Grand Duke Alexei, who according to Witte 'had no statesmanlike ideas and indeed no ideas at all'. That was the usual opinion of the frivolous Admiral of the Fleet. Yet it was he who said at the decisive conference: 'Russia will make Japan into an eternal and a strong enemy, who is bound in the nature of things to make common cause with England.'

But Witte did not believe in the strength of Japan and was convinced of the possibility of a friendly penetration of Manchuria. 'Grateful China' would have to agree to it.

The other participants in the intervention were also thinking of 'gratitude' from China. Kaiser Wilhelm II wrote a few days later to Nicholas that Germany wanted a port on the East China coast, 'somewhere where it does not interfere with you'. France started negotiations with China about railways and mines in the south.

GRATEFUL CHINA

When Witte spoke of 'the gratitude of China' he did not have territorial gains in mind but the construction of a railway through Chinese territory. The Sino-Japanese war had shown how necessary a rail link with Vladivostok was. Haste had to be made with this. The proposed section on Russian territory, along the Russo-Chinese frontier, presented exceptional technical difficulties and could therefore not be built in a short space of time. A line straight across Manchuria, on the other hand, would be not only much easier to build but also five hundred miles shorter.

But China's agreement had to be secured. An opportunity to influence the Chinese government in this direction was provided by its difficult financial situation. China had to pay Japan an indemnity, but as usual she had no money. The British had already offered a loan, but Witte did not waste any time either. His name already carried such weight on the Paris stock exchange that in an exceptionally short space of time he was able to arrange a loan to China which was guaranteed by Russia. So China received from Russia a loan of one hundred million gold roubles on very favourable conditions.

After the negotiations with the consortium of French banks had been concluded Witte carried out his 'coup'. He suggested converting the deal into permanent co-operation in the Far East and founding a 'Russo-Chinese', that is, in reality a Russo-French, bank. Five-eighths of the capital was to be provided by the French and three-eighths by the Russian government, but five of the directors were to be Russians and only three French.

The banks accepted the suggestion. They realized that Witte was inviting them to begin a new chapter of history in the East; the chapter would be written by the Russians, the Chinese and perhaps also the Japanese, but the fees would fall into the pocket of French bankers.

Once again the 'irony of history' became apparent. The

Sino-Japanese war was short and the Japanese had paid for it almost entirely out of savings. Now, thanks to Witte, they received 364 million yen, an enormous sum for those days; in 1893 the whole Japanese budget amounted to only 84 million yen. The Japanese parliament voted without delay a seven-year armament plan. Witte was arming Japan for the coming war with Russia.

The first Russian request for a railway concession was rejected by Peking. Witte increased the pressure and the Chinese gradually realized that interest was already falling due on the 'debt of gratitude'. When the Chinese government heard of the approaching coronation of Tsar Nicholas II, it decided to send as its representative the highest dignitary in the empire, Li Hung-Chang.

Li was seventy-three at that time, and he had a world-wide reputation. He was an extremely well educated man by Chinese standards and belonged to the élite of the Mandarin class. He had begun his career during the struggle against the Taiping. He fought with General Gordon, freed Nanking from the Taiping and was rewarded with the governorship of Kiangsu province and the yellow coat. His whole life was spent in the service of the Chinese Empire. He suppressed revolts, strengthened China's military power and secured foreign capital for the construction of railways and the development of industry. All this reminds us of Witte's programme.

For many years Li had been combating Japanese attempts to control Korea. To this end in 1885 he had signed the Korean treaty with Prince Ito. When the war with Japan was lost, he was sent to save whatever could still be saved and signed the Treaty of Shimonoseki with this same Ito.

Li Hung-Chang was often reproached in China for his friendly attitude to Russia. Shimonoseki had shown that he was right, Russia had saved Liao-Tung for China. In spite of the loss of the Amur region and the building of the Trans-Siberian railway, Li Hung-Chang considered the danger from Russia less than that from Japan. He was also ready to modernize the Chinese economy with the assistance of Russia.

Witte made every effort to give Li a fitting welcome. A Russian steamer was sent to meet him at Port Said, and at Odessa he was greeted like a reigning monarch with a guard of honour. A special train took him to St Petersburg and there he met Witte. 'I have had the opportunity,' wrote Witte, 'of meeting many statesmen whose names will go down in history, and I rank Li Hung-Chang very high among them. He was a really distinguished statesman.'

The negotiations began with a reminder by Witte of Russia's attitude during the Sino-Japanese war. Russia had always remained true, continued Witte, to the principle then enunciated of the inviolability of China. But to enforce this principle Russia had to be strong in the Far East, and for that she needed a direct line to Vladivostok through Manchuria. Such a railway would be economically advantageous to both China and Russia, and would probably be accepted without demur in Japan because it would offer advantages to her too.

Li Hung-Chang made all kinds of objections, but Witte soon saw that he would agree when he found that this was the Tsar's wish.

The negotiations were quietly continued in Moscow during the coronation festivities and on 22 May (3 June) 1896 the treaty was signed. It was a defensive alliance: in the case of Japanese aggression both sides promised to support each other with all their military and naval forces. To facilitate the movement of Russian troops to the Far East, the Chinese agreed to the construction of a railway through Manchuria, but the railway was not to be made the excuse for the infringement of China's sovereign rights.

The concession was granted not to the Russian government but only to the Russo-Chinese bank. However, this bank was identical with the Russian ministry of finance, and a formality of this sort could not hold up the march of events. Three months later the contract for the construction of the railway was signed by the Chinese government and the Russo-Chinese bank.

The building and management of the new line were entrusted to a special company all of whose shares were held by the Russian government. While the other Chinese railways had the narrow European gauge, the new line was to employ the Russian broad gauge. It was exempt from all Chinese dues and taxes. The company received the right to take over the land on each side of the track for its own purposes and also to maintain troops to police and protect the line. In this way Chinese sovereign rights were formally recognized but in practice an undefined strip of territory passed into Russian hands. China was given the right to buy the railway after thirty-six years, but in that case would have to pay the cost of building it together with all the interest that had accrued. It was extremely unlikely that China would ever be in a position to do that. Otherwise the contract was to be valid for eighty years.

A few days after the conclusion of this treaty an agreement with Japan was signed in Moscow giving both powers equal rights in Korea. It is interesting to read today that the Japanese plenipotentiary raised the idea of dividing Korea along the thirty-eighth parallel.

Soon afterwards a Korean delegation appeared in Moscow and asked for assistance. It was granted a loan and a Russian financial adviser. The latter was dispatched a year later, and simultaneously a Russian military mission arrived in Korea.

Although the Russo-Chinese agreement was kept secret the rumours of a military alliance put the European press into a ferment. Soon people began to whisper that Witte had bribed Li Hung-Chang. The suggestion was not without foundation.

Witte had taken steps in advance to 'prepare' Li Hung-Chang. In Peking a way had been found to his financial adviser, a 'Russian subject' by the name of Groth. Li Hung-Chang was accompanied from Port Said to St Petersburg by Prince Ukhtomsky, a friend of Badmayev's and a specialist in the handling of eastern notabilities. Li was also accompanied on his journey by his son, a worldling well known for his greed. The old man had been given to understand through these three persons that the Russian government understood perfectly well what difficulties and perhaps also expenses the trip to Russia must have cost him; it also realized that he might need means in China to close the mouths of his critics.

Li Hung-Chang never made the slightest reference himself to his expenses, but those around him spoke of Russian 'good will', and apparently he made no objections. Anyway, somehow or another it was conveyed to him that he would receive three million roubles, the first million of them after the contract was signed. Li did not receive either a written or even a verbal promise from Witte; for form's sake an internal record of the decision to pay him the money was made in the finance ministry after the signing of the Russo-Chinese treaty.

So money was involved. Does this diminish the stature and the tragedy of the last Confucian paladin, who together with Witte had conjured up spirits which later on neither of them would be able to control? Li was an Asiatic and always behaved like one. At the time of the suppression of the Taiping he had committed a breach of faith by putting to death some leaders of the rebellion who had surrendered on General Gordon's word. He denies this in his memoirs, but not very convincingly. When he visited the trade fair in Nishni-Novgorod he stopped in front of a display of precious stones, asked for an enormous sapphire or emerald to be taken out of it and put the stone in his pocket, saying as he did so, 'I'll take it with me as a souvenir'. When he was in Paris he was portrayed in a comic paper as a usurer to whom a poor devil had pawned a pair of old trousers. Li was asked if he wanted to prosecute the editor. 'Why should I?' he replied, 'I laughed myself.' He could not have appeared in court for he did in fact own innumerable money-lending establishments in China. While he was viceroy and the highest official in the empire he lent money to various Chinese provinces and even to the imperial court at high rates of interest, and no one was surprised. He was the richest man in China and it is incomprehensible that he should have accepted one of Witte's notorious bribes. It must remain an 'Asiatic secret', like the emerald he took with him as a memento.

Witte and Li resembled each other more than they themselves realized. Both served dying régimes, both tried to prolong these régimes' lives by injecting the blood of capitalistic civilization into the veins of feudal states, and both fought against the inexorable march of events. A remarkable parallelism can be observed between Russia and China, too. The Romanov dynasty came into power in Russia almost at the same time as the Manchu dynasty in China; the Russian explosion of power under Peter the Great coincided with a similar expansion in China under K'ang-hsi; and two hundred years later the two empires inclined their branches towards each other like two old trees with withered tops.

PORT ARTHUR AND THE RAILWAY

This time the appetite came before eating. The East China Railway existed as yet only on paper, but St Petersburg was already thinking of a branch to the south, to the Yellow Sea or even Peking.

This idea was the logical consequence of political and economic developments. For three centuries Russia had sought a land-link with China. For two hundred years Siberia had been moving south from Kamchatka in search of an ice-free port. Now, equipped with the technical means and the capital, Russia felt herself within reach of both goals.

Even during the negotiations with Li Hung-Chang Witte had turned the conversation on to a branch of the future Manchurian railway, but Li had not agreed to the Russian broad gauge. Witte had not pressed this subject any further at the time, but a year later he decided to try again. He sent Prince Ukhtomsky to China, officially to take presents from the Tsar to the emperor of China, but really to hand over the promised million to Li Hung-Chang. Ukhtomsky was to try to obtain a fresh complementary concession for the southern branch line. 'The old man', as Ukhtomsky called him in his letters, took the money but refused the concession.

The avalanche of events had already started to move and the further things went the clearer it became that Witte had lost control of them. In 1897 two German Catholic missionaries were murdered on the Shantung peninsula. As we already know, since the Treaty of Shimonoseki Kaiser Wilhelm had been toying with the idea of a naval base in eastern China. When he visited St Petersburg in 1897 he touched on this subject again. The murder of the missionaries was taken by Wilhelm as an invitation to action. He asked in a telegram if the Tsar would raise any objection to the occupation of the port of Kiao-Chow by the German fleet. Nicholas replied that he could neither agree nor disagree, since Kiao-Chow had never been occupied by Russia.

In other words, Nicholas did not object, and on 14 November 1897 a German naval squadron occupied Kiao-Chow, where the fortress of Tsingtan was later built. Li Hung-Chang sent a despairing S. O. S. to St Petersburg.

Ten days later there was a conference presided over by the Tsar at which the new foreign minister, Count M. N. Muravyev, suggested occupying without delay Port Arthur and the neighbouring harbour of Talien-wan on the Liao-Tung peninsula.

There was logic in this proposal too. After Germany had seized Kiao-Chow it became necessary either to demand that she withdraw in the name of the inviolability of China or else to follow her example. In fact the Tsar had already given his assent, and the fact that Kaiser Wilhelm had acted first took some of the sting out of the Russian action, for Germany too had proclaimed the inviolability of China at Shimonoseki.

It was petty logic, worthy of a diplomat or a bureaucrat but not of a statesman. Witte said as much. He protested as strongly as he could. He reminded his listeners of the principle of the integrity of China on which all his agreements with Li Hung-Chang had been based, and he asserted that action by Russia would make war with Japan inevitable. Germany should be called upon to evacuate Kiao-Chow, a Russian squadron should be ordered there and not withdrawn until the Germans had departed. Witte even sent the Kaiser a telegram, in which he begged him to be content with compensation and to evacuate Kiao-Chow.

But the Germans stayed in Kiao-Chow and on 15 December a Russian squadron sailed into Port Arthur harbour.

Only a day earlier Li Hung-Chang had asked St Petersburg again for a big loan. Witte agreed, but demanded the concession for a branch line to the Yellow Sea with the right to use a Chinese port on this sea. Thus, unlike Muravyev, Witte did not want a military occupation of Port Arthur; he demanded only the right to build and use a railway. There was a formal difference here, but it cannot have seemed an essential one to the Chinese for Russian warships already lay at anchor in Port Arthur roads. It is hardly possible that Witte did not see this, but the question had already been decided by the young Tsar, 'eager for fame, successes and victories', as Witte himself put it. He had already reached the point where he ought to have resigned, but it was difficult for him to make this decision at the very moment when the work he had begun assumed global dimensions and only he could bring it to a successful conclusion. Moreover, behind him stood the French banks, which were also eager in their own way, for 'successes and victories'. Whatever happened he could not betray their trust.

The negotiations in Peking and Port Arthur were protracted and while they went on the landing parties of troops remained on board their ships. Spring came and the impatience of the military increased. Every day the danger of a landing without China's agreement grew more acute. Witte turned again to his magic golden talisman. Once again Li Hung-Chang and another official were promised substantial sums of money.

In March 1898 the convention between Russia and China was signed. The southern part of the Liao-Tung peninsula, with Port

Arthur and Talien-wan, was leased to Russia for 25 years and she also received the exclusive right to build a branch of the Manchurian railway to it. Port Arthur was to be made into a naval base and Talien-wan was to become a free port for merchant ships of all nations.

All these questions were settled not by Witte himself, but by the foreign ministry working in close contact with him, and Witte could only rejoice at them, as he told Muravyev. But his joy did not last long. A few days after the conclusion of the treaty with China an agreement with Japan was signed by which Russia abandoned the complete economic control of Korea to Japan. Great Britain, too, had demands to make. The Boer War was already approaching and her relations with France were strained; she therefore contented herself with protecting her economic interests. In 1899 Russia undertook to demand no concessions for railways south of the China Sea, and Great Britain in return promised to build none to the north of it.

Furious work was going on in Manchuria at this time. Steel ribbons were already snaking from the Ussuri railway to the Chinese frontier, southward from the Trans-Siberian line and both eastward and westward from Harbin, which was to be the most important junction on the new railway. At this point it crossed the river Sungari. A branch line from Harbin was to lead south to the Yellow Sea. The construction of this stretch began in 1899. Work was started at five different spots simultaneously. The western part ran through the deserts of Mongolia; indeed over its whole length the line passed through only five towns. Rivers and mountains had to be traversed and eight tunnels built, including one two miles long through the Great Chingan. Materials were brought from all directions; by railway from Vladivostok and Siberia, by river down the Amur and the Sungari, and later from great yards set up at Port Arthur and Talien-wan. At Witte's suggestion Talien-wan was given the Russian name 'Dalny' ('in the distance').

Not only were rails laid; towns and harbours were built. The dirty little Manchurian village of Harbin soon became a dirty big city. At Port Arthur and Dalny docks, barracks, magazines and houses were constructed. The East China Railway Company, which had also obtained the South Manchurian concession, suddenly acquired thirteen ocean-going steamers and a number of river steamers. To protect the railway a special defence corps of about five thousand men was organized and the labour force itself numbered more than sixty thousand men.

All this work was directed by Witte, who must have been an organizing genius. He simultaneously controlled the finances of a huge empire, its whole railway system, its economic policy and its industry. He founded institutes of technology, built ice-breakers for the Arctic sea route, supervised the settlement of Siberia and the vodka monopoly, commissioned scientific inquiries and travelled continually all over Russia. Today we know a great deal about him, including things which he had no inclination to relate himself. Like other men, he could be weak and inconsistent, he clung to power and he often acted contrary to his own convictions. Cynically he asserted that gold was filth with which he had dirtied his fingers, but he went on dirtying them. Yet he served his country and his Tsar, and in throwing the whole weight of Siberia against China he was anything but a servant of the French bankers. He certainly took more account of their views than of those of his fellow ministers, but Witte's Far Eastern policy sprang from his own ideas, which in turn were the product of the internal condition of Russia. He had realized at the beginning of the 'nineties that any economic progress in Russia was impossible so long as the peasants had no rights of their own and were economically tied to the village community, the *mir*. The most pressing task was to free the peasants from the yoke of the village and to clothe them with all the rights of an economically free individual. In 1898 Witte wrote a letter to the Tsar in which he literally begged him to tackle this problem.

In this letter Witte suggested the land reform which was undertaken after his resignation – and much too late – by Stolypin. For this the Russian monarchists called Stolypin – after the Revolution! – a statesman of genius, yet they had spurned Witte's proposals and the Tsar had not even replied to his letter.

Nevertheless, Witte clung to his ideas and took the view that the great reform was bound to come sooner or later. This reform, that is, the creation of a class of small landowners, would be bound to drive large masses of the landless proletariat out of the villages and only industry would be in a position to absorb this proletariat and to render it more or less harmless. Industry had therefore to be developed by every possible means. But as the Russian home market was small, additional markets had to be found. These markets were obviously to be found in the East, where Russian industry could compete with European industry. But in the east lay China.

STORM OVER MANCHURIA

By the summer of 1900 the Manchurian railway had attained a length of eight hundred miles and was already beginning to alter the face of Manchuria. The first Chinese settlers were already being attracted by it; round every station there were Chinese shops, vegetable gardens and fields of crops. The Russians on the other hand were having a bad time; the climate was considerably worse than the one to which they were accustomed in Siberia, where such heavy rain and hurricanes were unknown. The Chinese coolies brought with them not only manpower but also typhus, cholera and the plague.

Neither monstrous weather nor epidemic could halt the work, but it was brought to a standstill by political events. In 1899 the Boxer rising broke out in North China and altered the whole situation.

'Boxer' was the European term for the rebels, who called themselves 'the fist of higher justice'; the fist's task was to deal a knockout blow to foreigners in China. The movement began with the slaughter of Chinese Christians, continued with the murder of missionaries and in the summer of 1900 developed into an open rebellion which embraced the whole of North China. Everywhere Chinese troops joined the rebels, the mandarins supported them and even the Dowager Empress sympathized with them. Li Hung-Chang had by this time been removed from the scene. In June 1900 the secretary of the Japanese embassy was murdered, and soon after that the German ambassador, Freiherr von Ketteler. Peking was in the hands of the rebels and the diplomatic quarter was besieged. A British attempt to reach Peking from the coast failed. Germany dispatched an expeditionary corps under the command of Field Marshal Count Waldersee, but it had a long way to come.

Witte did not want to see his Chinese policy ruined by collaboration between the British and the Japanese. He did not want to send any troops to China and it was only on the insistence of the new war minister, Kuropatkin, that a small Russian detachment was dispatched there. After the capture of Peking and the arrival of the German expeditionary corps the Russian troops left Peking and took no further part in the punitive and pacifying operations.

The Boxers themselves forced Witte to change his policy. The revolt spread to Manchuria and uncontrolled destruction of the railway began. Manchurian and Chinese bands burned down stations and goods depots, sank Russian boats on the rivers and destroyed everything they could lay their hands on. Long caravans of Russian refugees, including women and children, wound through the Manchurian steppes to the Amur. The Russian authorities started to eject the Chinese from the left bank of the Amur. In Blagoveshchensk the infuriated mob attacked the Chinese quarter; the Chinese escaped in boats or else tried to swim the river, hundreds of them perishing in the process.

Two or three months later only about two hundred miles of the eight hundred miles of track were undamaged. The local authorities begged for help. Witte himself now demanded that Russian troops should march into Manchuria. Russian detachments arrived from all directions and soon all the strategic points were occupied.

Russia could now no longer hold aloof from the united front against China and a Russian representative took part in the international negotiations about compensation for the Boxer rebellion. As usual the Chinese summoned Li Hung-Chang to save what could still be saved. He had recently begun once more to exercise some control over China's policy and Witte started separate and secret negotiations with him. After all he was an old friend, who moreover was still waiting for his two million roubles. But although he was glad to accept small advances of money, he had his own Chinese policy. He prolonged the negotiations, sometimes agreeing and sometimes objecting, and meanwhile gradually let the British know that his Russian 'friend' had demanded that the doors of Manchuria, Mongolia and Sinkiang should be closed to all except the Russians. However, the principle of the 'open door' in China had been demanded with some emphasis a year before by the U.S.A.

The final agreement about the 'Boxer indemnity' was signed in Peking in September 1901. Altogether China had to pay 450 million taels, about 29 per cent of them – a sum of 184 million gold roubles – to Russia. Witte let it be known in Peking that payment could take the form of 'favours' to Russia. He was already negotiating with Li Hung-Chang's successor, for the old man had died in 1901 without receiving his millions. The old Dowager Empress, who had tormented her paladin his whole life long with her feminine moods and knew all about his private deals, wept bitterly when she heard of his death.

Witte was still carrying on the negotiations in February 1902 when simultaneously, and obviously by prior agreement, three diplomatic actions struck like bolts from the blue. The United States demanded once again that the principle of the 'open door' should be preserved in China, a few days later the Chinese government announced that it had rejected Witte's demands and the very same day the Japanese ambassador brought the news of the conclusion of an alliance between Japan and Great Britain.

Generations of English representatives in Japan had worked for closer relations between the two countries and at the end of the nineteenth century Lord Curzon, an irreconcilable opponent of Russia, had adopted Admiral Stirling's thesis that the fates of Korea and Manchuria were closely linked to that of India. After the occupation of Port Arthur by Russia the idea began to take root that only Japan was in a position to check Russian expansion in the Far East. England's economic interests were not threatened – north of the great wall of China they were slight – but Russia's ice-free harbour on the Pacific could become dangerous.

The terms of the Anglo-Japanese treaty were perfectly clear. Its purpose was 'to safeguard the integrity of China and Korea' and 'to secure equal opportunities for the trade and commerce of all countries'. If either country was involved in a war with another and a third power intervened against it, it was entitled to call for the support of its partner.

It was no longer possible for Russia to exert any further pressure on China. That would have meant war with Japan, behind whom stood England and eventually America. A few weeks later, on 8 April 1902, an agreement with China was signed by which Russia undertook to withdraw all her troops from China in three stages. Witte insisted to the Tsar that this agreement must be observed punctiliously; he was reckoning on Manchuria's finally being opened to everyone. This new programme signified a renunciation and a defeat, but it also took account of the balance of power in the Far East. If it had been carried out there might have been no Russo-Japanese war. But Witte was unable to execute his plan because the control of Far Eastern questions had slipped from his grasp.

Witte had noticed for some time that he no longer enjoyed the Tsar's confidence. 'He does not talk to me any more,' wrote Witte in 1901. 'I say what I have to tell him and that's all. He is in an excited state; ideas of some kind or another are seething inside him.'

Nicholas II was by no means fitted by temperament for ruling. He lacked the most important qualities, a firm will and the capacity for trusting others. Kuropatkin once said to him, 'After my resignation your Majesty's trust in me will increase.' 'Curious as it may seem,' replied the Tsar, 'you are probably right.'

Nicholas knew his own weakness and the striving to show that he could decide for himself was perhaps one of his most striking characteristics. As usual 'independent' decisions were whispered in his ear by people for whose advice he had not asked. That is understandable from a psychological point of view. If he followed private advice he did not cease to be an autocrat; his independence was – supposedly – only impaired by accepting the advice of his ministers. We know from his correspondence with the Tsarina how often she demanded that he should 'show that he knew how to rule', that is, do what she and her friends wanted him to.

Moreover Nicholas was 'a Far Eastern specialist', and no less a person than the Kaiser told him that he was destined to play a special rôle in that part of the world. Wilhelm II certainly influenced him in this connection, even if too much importance is usually attributed to this influence. The mistrustful Nicholas was perfectly well aware that Wilhelm's flattery and advice were largely dictated by self-interest, and was very upset when after the meeting at Reval in July 1902 the Kaiser, from his yacht, signalled a greeting 'to the Admiral of the Pacific from the Admiral of the Atlantic'. Nicholas had no interest in uniforms and he never thought of himself as an admiral. Far worse, however, was the appearance of 'private' Russian advisers as well.

At the time when Russia was still strong in Korea a Vladivostok merchant called Brinner had been granted a concession to fell timber on the left or Korean bank of the Yalu. Brinner did not have great means at his disposal and sold the concession to the former consul in Korea, Matyunin. The latter was a 'society' man and discussed the matter with his old school friend, the retired colonel and businessman Vonlarlarsky. The colonel conferred with a regimental colleague by the name of Besobrasov, and he in turn was able to speak about the affair to the Tsar himself since he was a friend of the Tsar's nephew, Grand Duke Alexander Mikhailovich, and other people close to the throne.

Besobrasov was soon seeing the Tsar almost every day and the Yalu concession was acquired by the Tsar as his own personal property. This was the ultimate source of all the evil that followed. Nicholas was, naturally, not attracted by the prospect of wealth; what attracted him was 'the advantage of the state'. Besobrasov next proposed that the concession on the Korean bank of the Yalu, now known as the 'East Asiatic Company', should be complemented by one on the Manchurian bank; the Yalu valley would then become 'a strategic bar' against Japan.

However, a concession on the Chinese bank could be granted only by the Chinese government, and all paths to the latter were barred by Witte's agents. Witte did what he could and the Besobrasov group did not obtain a concession on the Manchurian bank. It was not until 1903 that it began to fell trees on the basis of an arrangement with the local Manchurian authorities.

Witte opposed these operations, in Manchuria through the Russo-Chinese bank and in St Petersburg with the help of Kuropatkin, the war minister, and Lamsdorff, the foreign minister. The Tsar retreated before this united front; he was even willing to dissolve the East Asiatic Company. But when he was pressed from the other side he retracted his decision and at the beginning of 1903 ordered Witte to pay the new company two million roubles out of government funds. Witte had to clench his teeth again and give instructions for the money to be handed over. It melted away more quickly than snow in the spring sunshine.

Gold gave Besobrasov new energy. Somewhere on the Yalu trees were felled under the protection of Cossacks; most of them rotted where they fell, but in Manchuria 'suitable properties' were acquired, a colliery, a power station and various other things. The Russian troops were still in Manchuria. Russia had promised to withdraw them, but Besobrasov advised the Tsar not to do this but on the contrary to stand firm on the Yalu, to demand fresh concessions from the Chinese and in no circumstances to let other powers into Manchuria. He recommended 'a strong line' in Korea and advised 'isolating Japan from all other powers except England, who will not help her'.

The supposed political acumen behind this advice made such an impression on the Tsar that in May 1903, to everyone's surprise, he appointed Besobrasov secretary of state, which corresponded more or less to the position of minister without portfolio. It was clear that the new secretary of state's portfolio would be the Far East. In practice that meant the end of Witte's rôle. He could still put the brake on this or that, he could raise objections, but the one thing he ought to have done – resign – he unfortunately did not do.

JAPAN ATTACKS

Nicholas understood the language which Besobrasov talked and was sympathetic to his ideas. Besobrasov ruled the roost and decided Russian policy in the Far East. In August 1903 a decree of the Tsar created a governorship of the Far East, including the Amur region and the territory leased on the Liao-Tung peninsula. The governor was responsible directly to the Tsar and he was given the right to conduct diplomatic negotiations with foreign powers.

This was such a senseless act that one would be tempted to regard it as conscious provocation if it did bear all the marks of Besobrasov's conscientious work. The Tsar was treating the leased piece of Chinese territory as if it were a province of Russia; moreover, the governor received command of all the armed forces in the Far East and the right to conduct a foreign policy without reference to the ministry of foreign affairs! And the man who was appointed the Tsar's deputy in the Far East was Admiral Alexeyev, who owed his career to the patronage of one of the Grand Dukes and understood just about as much about politics as Besobrasov. The Tsar had made this choice quite 'independently'; Witte, Kuropatkin and Lamsdorff learnt of the appointment through the morning papers.

The same day the Japanese ambassador in St Petersburg handed over a note from his government suggesting discussions on Far Eastern problems.

The moment of decision was clearly approaching in the East and both sides were preparing for it. Japan was feverishly strengthening her fleet; Russia was hurrying to fortify Port Arthur and to complete the Manchurian railway system. By August 1903 the job was done: the railway connected Russia with Vladivostok and Port Arthur. But Russia's preparations there were not complete; Dalny was not the only place that was 'distant'; so was Port Arthur and the whole of Manchuria. 'The elements, the distances, the oceans and the seas' were against Russia, wrote Witte and recommended far-reaching concessions to Japan. For Japan there was no sense in waiting until Russia had dealt with the 'elements and distances'.

Nicholas did not want the war; he feared it. Perhaps he had a presentiment of its fateful significance for him and his house. He wanted to gain time and believed that the Japanese would not fight for Manchuria, as indeed they told Kuropatkin when he arrived in Tokyo for the discussions.

What were the reasons advanced by Witte and even by Kuropatkin himself with some reservations for giving way to Japan? They not only spoke of Russia's military weakness but also said that a war would not be popular, that the people would not understand it. But on the other hand the new minister for home affairs, Plehve, took a different view. He pointed to the fact that a revolutionary mood had developed among the people which a 'small victorious war' would dissipate at once. For the same reason Besobrasov too recommended 'firmness and consistence'.

It was impossible to reconcile these opposing views; one side had to yield. The Tsar as good as dismissed Witte by appointing him to a post which carried no weight or influence.

The 'strong line' was soon in evidence in Manchuria. Two-thirds of the Russian troops had already been evacuated and in October 1903 the last contingents were due to leave Manchuria. But the evacuation was postponed, although all was quiet in Manchuria. That was just what London and Tokyo had been waiting for: the Russian government was not keeping its promise.

The negotiations were continued, every single question was referred to Alexeyev. Time went by and the Japanese grew more and more impatient.

It is never good to prolong negotiations, but the Russian government was confronted with some difficult decisions and the

Japanese made no effort to facilitate them. They did not try to find a peaceful solution. Severely as the Tsarist policy must be condemned, it is impossible to agree with the Encyclopedia Britannica when it says that 'Japan gradually reduced her demands to a minimum, but Russia made no concession of any importance'. In reality the opposite was the case. The Japanese put forward demands which they knew very well the Russian government could not accept. Russia was to recognize Japan's full authority over Korea, while Japan was only willing to allow Russia certain railway interests in Manchuria. Moreover, Japan wished to build a railway on her own account straight across Manchuria from Korea to Japan, and this would damage Russia's railway interests. Russia's proposal that Korea should be neutralized from a military point of view was rejected immediately. No government could have accepted these demands in the way they were presented. In St Petersburg conference followed conference. The telegraph wires hummed and the Japanese intelligence service reported every movement of Russian ships to Tokyo. The British firm of A. Gibbs bought new, Italian-built cruisers from Chile and the Argentine for Japan, and preparations were made in London to float a Japanese war loan. English newspapers warned Japan to be on her guard against a sudden attack by Russia.

When it finally became clear that Japan would not agree to any compromise, Nicholas told his ministers that a war was impossible. On 6 January 1904 the Russian ambassador in Tokyo, Baron Rosen, informed the Japanese government that Russia was willing to open the door to Manchuria on condition that Japan agreed to a neutralization of Korea. This decided the main question at once and it seemed that nothing could now prevent agreement.

After a few days Japan replied that there could be no question of conditions; its decisions were final and it awaited a swift answer.

At St Petersburg everything had already been decided. It was only a question of drafting the reply which was to recognize all the Japanese demands. The Russian reply was telegraphed to Baron Rosen in Tokyo on 3 February, but the Japanese telegraph office held it back and only released it on 7 February. Meanwhile on 5 February the Japanese instructed its ambassador in St Petersburg to break off the negotiations 'in view of their futility'.

On 6 February the Japanese consul and the whole Japanese colony left Port Arthur. Admiral Alexeyev, the viceroy of the

Tsar and defender of Russia in the East, was busy at this time with the preparations for some family celebration, which took place on the evening of 9 February. All the senior officers were ashore as the viceroy's guests. In the outer harbour lay the Russian battle-cruisers, brilliantly illuminated but without any steam. A squadron of Japanese destroyers with navigation lights turned off sailed right up to them and attacked them.

The prophecy of the British press had been fulfilled; the war began with a sudden and unannounced attack. But it was not Russia that attacked Japan; Japan attacked Russia, after all her demands had been granted. The British press pointed out that international law did not require a formal declaration of war. The Japanese had noted this point, and, still in full accord with international law, thirty-eight years later they destroyed the American fleet at Pearl Harbour.

XI

THE FAR EASTERN DRAMA

WAR

As the experts had predicted, the war provoked no patriotic feelings in Russia. The educated condemned it and the people as a whole did not understand it. Moreover, it demanded a complicated amphibious strategy which was certainly beyond Besobrasov and Alexeyev.

Yet the situation did not seem hopeless. There were about 100,000 men in the Far East, while the Japanese had no troops at all there. The Japanese fleet was stronger than the Russian fleet, but the superiority was not overwhelming since the Japanese had to transport troops to the mainland and to keep them supplied. Control of the sea was a question of life and death to the Japanese; hence their attack on Port Arthur.

The calculation turned out to be a good one. The day after the attack the cruiser *Varyag* and the gunboat *Koreetz* scuttled themselves in the Korean harbour of Chemulpo after a fight against long odds, and the severely reduced Russian squadron was now blockaded in Port Arthur.

The situation on the mainland, too, was thereby swiftly transformed. To fetch troops from Japan only a few days were needed; but troops from Russia had to travel five thousand miles on a single-track railway. By the end of April the Russians no longer enjoyed numerical superiority.

The commander-in-chief of all the Russian forces was at first Admiral Alexeyev, to whom General Kuropatkin, the commander of the land forces, was subordinate. Kuropatkin saw that the Russian position on the narrow peninsula of Liao-Tung was untenable. He wished to retreat and to give battle further inland. But Alexeyev demanded that Port Arthur should be defended. The Japanese attacked from Korea and threatened the Russian flank. Kuropatkin had to split up his forces.

Alexei Nikolayevich Kuropatkin had won his reputation in the campaign in Central Asia and in the war against Turkey, in which he had been seriously wounded. He wrote various works on geography and military history. His book on East Turkestan had been highly praised. He was a brave officer but lacked the essential qualities of a great army commander. A by no means stupid journalist once said of him: 'What kind of a general can a man be who only drinks soda-water?'

Only one of the senior officers seems to have been suited to his task, Admiral S. O. Makarov, who took over command of the Far Eastern fleet a month after the beginning of the war. With his arrival at Port Arthur the passive waiting in harbour came to an end. In the space of a month Makarov led his squadron out to sea five times. He had waited only for the repair of the damaged ships. In April 1904 he put to sea for the sixth time. On the way back to harbour his flagship, the battle-cruiser *Petropavlovsk* hit a mine and blew up. About six hundred men perished with Makarov, including his whole staff and the painter Vereshchagin. Another battleship also hit a mine and was seriously damaged.

In Korea the Japanese had by this time landed a whole army, which soon crossed the Yalu. Simultaneously Japanese troops were put ashore on the Liao-Tung peninsula. Dalny was evacuated without a fight and the Japanese now had an excellently equipped harbour at their disposal.

Port Arthur was poorly fortified on the land side. The fortifications were due to be completed by 1909. Of the twenty-two forts planned, only seven were more or less ready and the commandant, Stössel, had less faith in his fortress than anyone.

From June onwards Port Arthur was left to its fate. The Russian army retreated to Liao-Yany, where there was a battle in August. In individual sectors the Japanese were not merely repelled but defeated, but at the decisive moment suddenly everything went wrong.

Two months went by before the Japanese arrived at the new Russian defence line on the River Shaho. In his order of the day Kuropatkin declared that the retreat was now over and promised to advance. But once again, when victory was almost in his hands, he gave the order to retire.

Immediately afterwards he was appointed commander-in-chief of all forces. He pulled the army back to Mukden. It was still perfectly capable of fighting. Everyone was struck by the fact that not once had the victorious Japanese been in a position after winning a battle to pursue the Russians. On each occasion the army gained a breathing-space during which fresh forces arrived from Russia. And it was already known that a powerful squadron was on its way to Port Arthur from the Baltic.

Except for Stössel no one in Port Arthur regarded the situation as hopeless. Makarov's successor, Admiral Witthoff, led his squadron out to sea in August and took up the struggle with the main Japanese forces. Witthoff himself was killed, some of his ships had to take refuge in neutral harbours and the rest returned to Port Arthur. The Far Eastern squadron had for all practical purposes ceased to exist. A considerable proportion of the crews was disembarked.

After the first, unsuccessful attack in August the Japanese brought up their heavy howitzers and pounded the last Russian concrete block-houses to rubble. The two front lines drew nearer each other, the infantry dug itself in and there were daily bayonet skirmishes. General Kondratenko was the heart and soul of the defence. He came to the conclusion that peace would have to be made before the fall of Port Arthur and suggested to Stössel that he should tell St Petersburg as much. However, it was all right for Kondratenko, who had led the infantry personally in bayonet charges, to make such a suggestion, but not for Stössel, who had avoided such things.

The second attempt to storm Port Arthur was beaten off at the end of October under Kondratenko's leadership with heavy losses to the Japanese, but the besieging army was continually reinforced.

The third attack lasted ten days and ended with the capture by the Japanese of a dominating position, 'Hill 203'. From this point the Japanese heavy artillery began to shell the inner harbour, where the last Russian ships provided motionless targets.

On 15 December Kondratenko fell on the field of battle and Stössel made preparations for surrender, which took place on 20 December 1904 (2 January 1905).

It transpired later that Port Arthur could have held out for much longer, since the garrison had sufficient food and munitions. This news caused bitterness in Russia. Stössel was court-martialled and condemned to detention in a fortress. The fact remains that Port Arthur was able to hold out for seven months, although the defence had been mainly based on primitive earthworks. Singapore, built up for ten years, and defended by a garrison of sixty thousand men, surrendered to these same Japanese after a fortnight.

The defeats in Manchuria had already caused discontent and hatred for the Tsarist régime in Russia. Strikes broke out everywhere and revolutionary parties resorted to terrorism. When Port Arthur was still holding out, Plehve, the protagonist of 'small victorious wars' was blown to bits by a bomb. Three weeks after the fall of Port Arthur, on Sunday 9 (22) January, huge crowds of workers who had marched to see the Tsar with a petition were welcomed with rifle fire from troops. Hundreds of people were killed. Three weeks later the Grand Duke Sergei Alexandrovich, the Tsar's uncle, was killed by a bomb.

Soon after this the two huge armies met in battle at Mukden. The battle went on indecisively for three weeks, the Japanese took Mukden, but the Russian army was able to withdraw again.

The squadron sent from Russia to relieve Port Arthur was sailing at this time through the Indian Ocean. Its commander, Admiral Roshestvensky, was known as a strict but intelligent officer. It is difficult to understand how he can have brought himself to lead a squadron whose eventual fate was obvious to all. 'If he succeeds in reaching even Singapore,' said the Italian military attaché on Kuropatkin's staff, 'you can set his name beside that of Nelson.'

The squadron left Kronstadt in the middle of October 1904. It sailed round Africa, and the whole voyage took seven months. Morale sank lower and lower. At Madagascar the crews learnt of the fall of Port Arthur, in Chinese waters of the loss of Mukden.

The squadron's destination was now Vladivostok, and everyone expected that Roshestvensky would sail to the east of Japan. Instead, he steered for the Strait of Tsushima, where his way was barred by a Japanese fleet operating from nearby bases and familiar with these waters.

The collision took place at the end of May 1905 and lasted three days. One Russian ship after another was riddled with shells, capsized, blew up and sank. Roshestvensky, seriously wounded, was transferred from the flagship *Suvorov* to a torpedo-boat, and from this to another one, which surrendered two days later.

Riddled with shells and on fire, the *Suvorov* was still firing as she sank.

Admiral Nebogatov, who had taken over command, had four seriously damaged battle cruisers and one light cruiser left. The Japanese began to destroy the Russian ships from a distance with their long-range guns; the Russian guns could not reach their opponents. Nebogatov put an end to this target practice; he hoisted the white flag. In his ships were a crowd of people whom he had taken on board from other ships or pulled out of the water. By taking the responsibility for surrendering he saved about five thousand lives.

However, when he was tried after the end of the war he was found guilty and only pardoned three years later with Stössel. Roshestvensky was acquitted.

This acquittal took place under the pressure of public opinion, which regarded Roshestvensky as a victim of the incapable and decaying Tsarist régime. Everyone argued that the verdict had been given in the Sea of Japan and on the battlefields of Manchuria. 'The Japanese have not defeated Russia or even our army,' wrote Witte, 'but our system.' 'Not the Russian people, but the Russian aristocracy has suffered a shameful defeat,' said the leader of the Bolshevists, Lenin. 'Russia's disgrace will probably be the beginning of the end for the monarchy,' wrote Tikhomirov, a convinced monarchist.

PEACE

During the Russo-Japanese war the Americans were heart and soul on the side of Japan. Their friendly neutrality differed little from an alliance. Both in America and England the press praised Japan as the champion of the integrity of China and Korea.

Plehve's anti-Semitic policy not only provoked anti-Russian agitation in America, it also spurred Jewish high finance into activity. Jacob Schiff, president of the American banking firm of Kuhn, Loeb & Co., was decorated by King Edward VII for his collaboration with English banks in floating Japanese loans. The war had cost Japan about one thousand million dollars and more than half this sum had been lent by Great Britain and America.

Towards the end of the war the mood in America altered; people had no desire to see Japan master of the Far East in place of Russia. President Roosevelt began to have fears for the fate of the Philippines. After the Japanese had asked him to act as mediator (a fact which only became known twenty years later) Roosevelt took soundings in St Petersburg and then made a corresponding formal proposal to the two sides on 8 June 1905. Almost simultaneously a secret agreement was signed in Tokyo by which Japan renounced any claim to the Philippines and America in return recognized the Japanese protectorate over Korea. Once again a war for the integrity of Korea had ended in its complete dependence.

The composition of her peace delegation caused Japan no difficulties. The foreign minister, Komura, was appointed to lead it with the ambassador in Washington, Tokahira, as his colleague.

In Russia there was no argument about the identity of the second delegate – it was the Russian ambassador in Washington, Baron Rosen. But the question of the chief plenipotentiary caused rather more difficulty; competition for the post was not keen. After mature reflection two candidates reported that they were 'ill'. There was only one possibility left, the 'half Jew from Odessa', Witte.

So Witte set out on his way. He took a staff of first-class experts with him but he had to take all the important decisions himself, for in anything beyond matters of diplomatic routine Rosen was as naïve as a child – his memoirs bear eloquent testimony to that.

During the voyage Witte considered what his tactics should be. He decided to act 'as the representative of the greatest empire in the world, which had suffered a slight mishap', and not to seek peace at any price. He resolved to be particularly forthcoming to the press, 'to behave democratically', and to display no hostility to the Jews – an attitude which in any case corresponded to his own views.

The meeting with Roosevelt took place at the President's country house near New York. Roosevelt repeated again and again that if Russia did not accept the Japanese conditions she would lose Vladivostok and perhaps the whole of eastern Siberia as she had already lost Sakhalin, which in the meantime had been occupied by the Japanese. Witte replied in the words of the Tsar, 'not a copeck of indemnity, not an inch of Russian soil.'

The strained atmosphere of this conversation was only partly dissipated by lunch in Roosevelt's family circle. 'The food was not very digestible for a European,' wrote Witte, 'No wine at all, only iced water.'

The two delegations met on board the President's yacht, *Mayflower*. Every detail had been discussed beforehand with Rosen. It was a meeting of old acquaintances; Rosen knew all the Japanese well and Witte had met some of them in St Petersburg. But in the glances of the old acquaintances there was only 'iced water'. After the introductions they were all invited to lunch, which was taken standing to avoid questions of precedence. During lunch the President proposed a toast to the sovereigns and peoples represented by the two delegations. The toast had a historic significance; it was the first time that Japan was called a great power.

The conference was held in the little town of Portsmouth on the Atlantic coast. The popularity of the 'democrat' Witte rose as soon as the Japanese demands were published. Besides the recognition of their authority in Korea and the surrender of the leased territory of Liao-Tung, the Japanese demanded a huge indemnity and the island of Sakhalin; they also required the limitation of the Russian Far Eastern Fleet and the surrender of all vessels which had taken refuge in neutral ports.

The last two demands were obviously not justified either morally or legally. And what about the indemnity? Were the Japanese ready to prolong the bloodshed for money after they had attained all their war aims?

It became clear that the indemnity and Sakhalin were the most difficult points. Roosevelt exerted strong pressure on Witte, but he remained unyielding. On 23 August Roosevelt put his arguments to the Tsar personally through his ambassador, Lengerke von Meyer.

For two hours Meyer argued with the Tsar, but Nicholas always gave the same answer, 'Not an inch of territory, not a cent of indemnity'. He did remark at one point, speaking reflectively and more or less to himself, 'One might perhaps be able to think again about the southern part of Sakhalin.'

Roosevelt found himself in a difficult position. The collapse of the conference would be a terrible blow not only to himself personally, but also to the whole American policy in China, so he turned his efforts to Japan and recommended the Mikado to moderate his demands.

On 28 August Witte received orders from St Petersburg to break off the negotiations the next day if the Japanese did not give up their demand for an indemnity. At the same time Lamsdorff wired to him that if the worst came to the worst the Tsar was willing to cede the southern part of Sakhalin.

In situations like this the victor is usually the man with the stronger nerves, and Witte's nerves were in ribbons. American cooking did not suit him, he was suffering from pains in the stomach and his old laryngic trouble had become so much worse that he could only carry on with the aid of cocaine injections. Everyone was at a loss, his colleagues, the Japanese and Roosevelt, too. Witte alone, with gruel in his stomach, cocaine in his nose, and fear and despair in his heart, went on playing the gentleman 'who had suffered a slight mishap'.

He did not know that the completest of victories was already in his hands. On 27 August, after being informed of Witte's ultimatum, the Japanese cabinet and the council of elders under the presidency of the Mikado decided to abandon their demand for an indemnity and the whole of Sakhalin.

At the last moment, however, Witte's Portsmouth act was spoiled. The Tsar's reference to 'half Sakhalin' had been telegraphed to Roosevelt the same day by Meyer. The secret leaked out and a junior official in the Japanese foreign ministry in Tokyo, Kikujiro Ishii, who on 27 August dropped in to see a friend 'at a foreign embassy', learned from this friend that the Tsar had agreed to cede southern Sakhalin.

Ishii rushed off to the prime minister, Katsura. The cabinet was just having a break for lunch. The little official asked to see the prime minister immediately; he shouted and pleaded and at last the premier came out.

When he was alone with his visitor he learned what the Tsar had whispered four days before in the study of his palace.

Ishii was a determined young man; he knew the risk he was taking. That morning was the beginning of a dazzling career which he ended as a viscount and minister for foreign affairs.

The Japanese delegation at Portsmouth was at once ordered to ask Witte for twenty-four hours' grace and these twenty-four hours robbed Witte of a game he had already as good as won.

When the delegates met the next day Komura asked Witte if he could speak to him alone. Witte returned to the session after this conversation as pale as death but in complete control of himself. He read out the conditions on which he was prepared to sign a peace treaty. There was no reference to an indemnity but the cession of southern Sakhalin was mentioned. There was a long pause, then Komura rose and replied in a firm voice that the Japanese delegation accepted these conditions. Somewhere a gun began to boom.

Past a jubilant throng, amid the thunder of artillery salutes and the shrieking of sirens, the Russian delegation went to church. Strangers shook Witte by the hand and pushed presents into his pockets. A solemn thanksgiving and requiem were celebrated by an Episcopalian bishop assisted by seven Russian priests who had come from various cities in America. The music was provided by a huge choir.

The provisions of the peace treaty, which was signed on the 5 September 1905, were roughly as follows: Korea was relinquished to the exclusive influence of Japan; the Liao-Tung peninsula and part of the South Manchurian Railway, from Port Arthur to the modern town of Hsinking, were handed over to Japan, 'subject to the agreement of the Chinese government'; the rest of Manchuria was made accessible to all foreigners on the same conditions; and the southern half of Sakhalin was ceded to Japan. Russia also gave the Japanese the right to fish off the east coast of Siberia.

The treaty reflected the fact that Russia had lost the war, but contained nothing insulting. Russia had once again lost her position on the Pacific, as she had after the sale of Alaska; but she did not abandon the Far East and the whole world now saw that no power could drive her from there. She had lost Port Arthur and the South Manchurian branch line, but kept the East China Railway, which, with the Trans-Siberian Railway, formed the only link between the west of Asia and the East.

But the historical significance of wars cannot be measured in terms of the peace treaties that follow them. The chain reactions which they initiate cannot be foreseen by any politician. It only became evident later that the Russo-Japanese War was in reality the first world war, since in practice it was fought between Russia and a coalition of Japan, Great Britain and the United States. With it there began in the remotest corner of Asia a new epoch of world history, the age of world wars and social revolutions. The first result of the Russo-Japanese war was the Russian revolution of 1905. The political earthquake on the eastern frontier of Siberia shook the Russian empire and undermined the throne of the tsars; twelve years later this throne collapsed.

The revolution of 1905 was a beacon for all the countries of the East. The Russian revolution was followed by revolutions in Turkey and Persia, and afterwards in China. Then, five years after the proclamation of the Chinese republic Russia, too, became a republic – another example of the parallelism we find so often in history.

Japan's victory was regarded in the East as a defeat for the white race and western civilization. The Turkish, Persian and Chinese revolutions were all nationalistic revolutions. They gave a powerful impulse to the nationalist movement in India. The political and economic successes of Japan nourished this movement up to the Second World War; and at the end of the war India became independent. Great Britain herself had hastened the arrival of this moment by acting as godfather to Japanese imperialism at the beginning of the century.

At Portsmouth, Witte had won a diplomatic victory which can only be compared with Talleyrand's success at the Congress of Vienna. He showed the world that David had not struck Goliath down but only weakened him for a little while. The psychological effect was so powerful that the peace seemed like a defeat for Japan; when the Japanese plenipotentiaries returned home they were treated almost as traitors. There were anti-American demonstrations throughout Japan and soon afterwards Komura had to resign. Witte on the other hand was honoured wherever he went. In spite of his old antipathy even the Tsar was forced to show his gratitude and on his return Witte was made a count.

But the Tsar did not succeed, as he would have liked to, in getting rid of the Moor after he had requited his services. The revolution flared up and the ground under the throne quaked. At a moment of general helplessness, in autumn 1905, it was again Witte who pointed to the only way out. He was responsible for the famous manifesto of 17 October which was to turn the Tsar into a constitutional monarch. Witte was appointed chief minister, with the task of directing the activities of all the other ministers. This post had not existed before and it put more power into Witte's hands than anyone in Russia had ever possessed before.

He knew that to suppress the revolution money was needed as well as reforms. On the way back from Portsmouth he had made preparations in France for a loan which was concluded when he was chief minister. It was the biggest foreign loan in the history of international finance, two and a quarter thousand million gold franks.

Witte also began preparations for an agrarian reform, an idea which had occupied him for many years. It was not granted to him to put it into effect; his enemies had begun to attack him again with renewed vigour. He was accused of 'forcing' the October manifesto out of the Tsar in order to reduce the Tsar's power and thus increase his own. He was also accused of 'selling' half Sakhalin to the Japanese; in nationalistic newspapers he was called 'Count Halfsakhalinsky'. As soon as the revolutionary storm had subsided he was dismissed. That was in April 1906.

He spent the rest of his life as an 'internal enemy' hated by everyone and especially by the court. He delivered vain warnings against a war with Germany. People listened to him and then did the opposite. He died in St Petersburg in 1915.

In the wealth of official and unofficial records of the Portsmouth Conference many personal details about the participants have been preserved. Roosevelt liked Witte. He compares him with Kaiser Wilhelm and draws a lively comparison: both are 'energetic chaps, original, restless, blunt, forthright, but they both know how to pursue their aims'.

Roosevelt's testimony is sober and hard: 'I believe that Witte is the best man that Russia could have at the head of her affairs today, probably too good for the Grand Dukes.' But Roosevelt found his 'boasting and bluff . . . not only foolish but also shockingly vulgar'; moreover he 'horrified' the President because he struck him as 'a very egoistic man without any high ideals'.

Witte was cynical; he called things by their names, and he saw in the Russo-Japanese war not a conflict between civilization and 'egoistic expansion', but the struggle for the Pacific and Far Eastern markets. This shocked Roosevelt. However, the President understood neither the historical impulses behind Russia's Far Eastern policy nor Russia's rôle precisely from the point of view of civilization; even then it could be seen that by building the railway in Manchuria Russia had carried out a piece of first-class colonizing work and opened up a new region, the future key to the whole of eastern Asia. Witte's cynicism was also nearer the truth than Roosevelt's idealism in another respect. Here we must go back a little.

After the sale of Alaska the activities of the American fur traders and seal hunters had spread to the coast of Siberia. As a result of the lack of a coastguard service and the negligence of the government in St Petersburg, by the end of the century the Americans were making themselves at home on the Chukcha peninsula and monopolizing the whole fur trade.

About the same time the American railway king, E. H. Harriman, began to take an interest in the Far East. In 1899 he travelled to Alaska with his family and a whole geographical expedition. 'At Mrs Harriman's wish' the expedition also visited the Chukcha peninsula and even went ashore for a few hours.

A year later H. de Windt's Franco-American expedition visited the same peninsula to study the possibility of a railway linking New York and Paris by means of a tunnel under the Bering Strait. The man behind this fantastic plan was the French engineer Loicq de Lobel, who was in Alaska at that time.

L. de Lobel formed a company in France to obtain a concession, and when the Russian government refused to grant it he formed a syndicate in America, in whose name he repeated the proposal in 1905. Some of Harriman's closest collaborators belonged to this syndicate.

The syndicate offered to build a railway from Irkutsk to Cape Deshnev, whence a tunnel would lead to the American continent. The syndicate wanted a ninety-year free lease of a strip of territory sixteen miles wide in which 'all rights of the state' were to be transferred to the railway company. Furthermore, the syndicate wanted the right to acquire land, build branch lines and canals, mine ore, build factories, and form shipping companies – in short, to make eastern Siberia into an American colony.

After three refusals Lobel approached the Russian government for the fourth time in autumn 1905 and on this occasion was more successful: under pressure from the Grand Duke Nikolai Nikolayevich the council of ministers declared his proposals acceptable.

It was not until 1907 that the finance minister, Kokovtzev, was able to drop the project completely. This happened because the American proposers had decided on a change of front. It was well known that Harriman feared neither 'God nor Morgan', but even he had second thoughts about an undertaking whose Russian section alone required an expenditure of nearly five hundred million dollars. In the meantime the American ambassador in Tokyo, E. N. Conger, had suggested linking the two American transcontinental railways with the Chinese railway network by means of the shipping lines, and thus bringing into being a global transport system. This was more to Harriman's taste. He had helped Jacob Schiff to arrange the Japanese war loans, had travelled to Tokyo during the Portsmouth negotiations, and there had signed, in September 1905, a preliminary agreement for the sale to himself of half the shares in the South Manchurian Railway.

But when the foreign minister, Komura, returned from Portsmouth he vetoed the deal. Anti-American feeling was so strong in Japan that there could be no question of ratifying the agreement.

Harriman renewed his efforts four years later. Through his friend Jacob Schiff he approached the Russian government with the proposal that he should acquire the East China Railway. He intended to link it with the Chinese railway system and then to obtain control of the Trans-Siberian railway. The plan came to nothing because the Japanese government objected and the Russians rejected the proposal. A few months later Harriman died.

In all these negotiations and combinations, men very close to Roosevelt took part – members of his government, American ambassadors, consuls and bankers. The same Jacob Schiff who had been decorated during the war for his anti-Russian work wanted, with Harriman, the lion's share of the booty when it ended. It looks as if the cynical Witte was more truthful and honest than his idealistic critics.

THE END OF THE TSARIST RÉGIME

The Russo-Japanese war had shown that the great railway was not only the economic but also the political lifeline of Siberia. When a strike of the revolutionary workers interrupted the traffic in 1905, for all practical purposes Siberia was separated from Russia. Two military trains which Witte sent against the strikers from Harbin and Chelyabinsk restored the link, 'although not without sacrifices'; Siberian independence was at an end.

Siberia had suffered no damage in the Russo-Japanese war. The temporarily reduced colonization increased after the end of the war to an unprecedented rate: in 1906, 217,000 people crossed the Urals, in 1907 577,000 and in 1908, 759,000. That was the maximum figure reached; after that 'only' about 250,000–300,000 people migrated every year, that is, as many as in the twenty years before the construction of the railway. In 1913 the population of Siberia was 9,895,000 of whom more than eight million were Russians. In the last year before the Revolution the population was about ten million.

The railway gave a tremendous impulse to all branches of the Siberian economy. Even during the preliminary survey of the route, coal, gold, silver, copper, iron and lead had been found in many places. Siberia was now accessible to the outside world, and this attracted capital. The railway itself represented a huge outlay of Russian capital; foreign capital, too, now flowed to Siberia. As everywhere, it encouraged economic development. Where it led to exploitation and illegality, it was not its foreign origin that was to blame but Russian maladministration. The Americans could only strip the Chukcha peninsula of furs thanks to the St Petersburg connections of their straw men. The English Lena Goldfields Company, which had obtained control of the rich Lena-Vitim deposits, could only shoot down strikers pitilessly because its shareholders included a number of high-ranking Russians, including the Dowager Empress.

Where there is gold there is always bloodshed; to agriculture, on the other hand, which was incomparably more important to Siberia than gold, foreign capital brought nothing but gain. For example, butter production began to rise in western Siberia when Danish firms arrived with the railway, opened creameries and sold the farmers mechanical churns. Soon Siberian butter was going to Copenhagen, Hamburg, Rotterdam and London; in 1913 73,000 tons were exported. Butter was followed by other products. Before the First World War, Siberian butter was sold in Danish packings, German sausages sometimes had Siberian skins and Italian spaghetti was often made from Siberian wheat. Siberian furs went via Leipzig as German goods to all quarters of the world. Moscow textile firms started raising sheep in western Siberia and the export of wheat increased steadily.

The exploitation of mineral resources did not keep pace with the development of agriculture. First place was still held by gold;

before the First World War on an average 61,500 kilogrammes of gold were produced every year in Russia, 81 per cent of it in Siberia and two-thirds of this 81 per cent in the Lena and Amur basins. Coal was only mined in the neighbourhood of the railway, which was also the only customer for it. People now remembered the Kuznetsk coal, which had been reported by Pallas. These fields lay in royal property, and in 1913 W. F. Trepov, brother of the well-known reactionary general, obtained a concession to work them. He also obtained the right to build a railway from the southern Urals to Kuznetsk. After the Revolution the Bolshevists shot Trepov . . . and carried out his plans. The prosperity of Siberia was increasing visibly before the Revolution. It had been promised that the construction of the Trans-Siberian Railway would double or triple exports from European Russia to Siberia; in fact they increased fourfold. Siberia began to overtake European Russia swiftly. Farms there usually had twice as many agricultural machines as Russian farms. Every Siberian farmer's wife dreamed of a Singer sewing machine. The Siberian farmer drank five times as much tea and bought three times as much cotton material as his Russian counterpart. He could buy axes, scythes and saws cheaply in spite of the fact that the Trans-Siberian Railway had crippled his own iron industry; the primitive old works could not stand up to Russian competition.

Secondary schools had long ago been opened in all the Siberian towns and the University of Tomsk had already been joined by the Technical High School (College of Technology) in Omsk. The agricultural co-operative societies could point to tremendous successes; they took up half the butter production. Siberia worked, learned and became more and more prosperous.

Finally St Petersburg also remembered the northern sea route. In Witte's office in 1898 Admiral Makarov and the famous scholar, Mendelyev, argued about the best way to sail from the White Sea to the Bering Strait; Makarov suggested using the ice-breaker which he had built, the *Yermak*, and taking Nordenskiöld's route along the Siberian coast. Mendelyev took up Lomonosov's idea and offered to sail via the North Pole.

Neither project was carried out at the time, but they awoke fresh interest in the Arctic. In 1900, Baron E. Toll went for the third time to the New Siberian Islands to find the problematical 'Sannikov's land'. He explored the Taimyr peninsula and spent two years on the New Siberian Islands. From there he went with three companions to Bennett Island.

Another of Toll's colleagues, Lieutenant Kolchak, who had been left behind in the New Siberian Islands, tried to reach Bennett Island in the summer of 1902, but the pack ice barred his way. In the following year he sailed in a whaler from the mouth of the Lena to the New Siberian Islands and from there on to Bennett Island. After he had convinced himself that Toll had perished Kolchak returned to Siberia.

In spite of some failures the exploration of Arctic waters went on. Lieutenant Sedov's poorly prepared North Pole expedition ended in disaster in 1912; but the ice-breaker *Vaigach* reached Wrangel Island from the east and hoisted the Russian flag there in 1911. In 1913–14 the *Vaigach* and the *Taimyr*, under the command of B. A. Vilkitsky, made the trip from Vladivostok to Archangel.

Navigation of the Kara Sea was developed and the Duma, the new Russian Parliament, showed great interest in it. In Norway a company for trade with Siberia was founded; its scientific adviser was Fridtjof Nansen, but the chief shareholders were English firms. By the time war broke out the company had sent five expeditions to the mouth of the Yenisei. It was supported by the tsarist régime, for the Kara Sea and the Yenisei provided a water route to Mongolia.

Interest in Mongolia was not so much economic as political. The rapprochement with Japan favoured by Witte after the Russo-Japanese war had led in 1907 to the conclusion of an agreement by which northern Manchuria and Outer (or northern) Mongolia were recognized as Russian spheres of influence. The Russian government did not put much trust in this delimitation, and in the following year proceeded to build the missing section of the Trans-Siberian Railway from Chita to Khabarovsk along the Amur. This undertaking was not completed until 1916. However, the Russian government strengthened its influence in Mongolia when China became a republic (in 1912) and Mongolia declared itself independent; Russia recognized it and in 1913 forced China to do the same, although with reservations. Henceforth affairs concerning both Mongolia and China could not be settled except after consultations with Russia. A result of this political development in the heart of Asia was an intensification of traffic through the Kara Sea.

Political banishment, although considerably reduced in scale, did not stop. In the year of the occupation of Port Arthur a political agitator by the name of Ulyanov was sent across the Urals; the whole world came to know him later as Lenin. Trotsky and Stalin were repeatedly sent to Siberia, but were always able to escape again; when they attained power they guarded their prisoners rather more carefully. This underground Siberia was in constant touch with St Petersburg and Moscow, where revolutionary parties worked in secret. Siberia's old links with the throne took an absolutely fantastic form. The Tobolsk peasant Grigory Rasputin became the closest friend and adviser of the Tsar's family. This simple man, who could barely read and write, possessed an elemental vitality which the decadent royal family completely lacked; therein lies the secret of his influence. He was not stupid, nor does he seem to have been a bad man, but behind him a horde of intriguers and careerists streamed to the throne, and Badmayev turned up again, with all kinds of racketeers in the background. The eternal tragedy of a declining dynasty was repeated: for the German family on the throne Rasputin was a representative of Russian 'blood and soil'; to Russia he became the symbol of the corruption and degeneration of the tsarist régime. With him there appeared in the rooms of the palace not the new Siberia, which needed railways and agricultural machinery, but the old, wild, sinister Siberia of shamans and evil spirits.

During the First World War Russia was cut off from the West; the Bosporus was closed by Turkey and the railway to the Murman coast was not completed until 1917. For three years the only link with the outside world was the Trans-Siberian Railway. Siberia itself became a source of supplies; from there Russia now obtained wheat, butter, hides, Chinese tea, Mongolian wool and gold which was needed more than ever. Even the old iron works were put into action again. Health and strength streamed to Russia from the east; the Siberian divisions were among the best at the front.

The old practice of the seventeenth and eighteenth centuries was also renewed: Siberia began to fill up with prisoners of war and internees.

Like the rest of Russia, Siberia greeted the February Revolution with red flags, music and speeches. The exiles went to St Petersburg, 'to consolidate the revolution'. Stalin, with Kamenev and other comrades whom he later had shot, left his polar seclusion. The Trans-Siberian Railway, already known as the 'Transsib', was in full commission and Siberia remained quiet. It was only after the October revolution that local 'governments' began to spring up; they were soon incorporated in the Omsk 'provisional government', which proclaimed the independence of Siberia on 4 June 1918.

Siberia was at that time cordoned off from Bolshevist European Russia by the front set up by the Czechoslovak National Corps. It consisted of prisoners of war who in 1917 had obtained permission to proceed to Europe via Siberia in order to take part in the war. The Czechoslovak detachments succeeded in occupying a row of towns on the middle Volga and also in 'purging' the Transsib of Bolshevist elements. On the Volga a separate government had been formed at Samara. The front against the Red Army was held by the Czechs, the Siberian army and the Cossacks.

When the front began to draw back under the pressure of the Red Army the Siberian and Samara governments merged in the 'Directorate', which formed a new government in Omsk, with Admiral A. W. Kolchak as war and navy minister. Two months later, in the night of 18 November 1918, the Directorate was arrested, the government took over power itself and handed it to Kolchak, who was proclaimed supreme ruler.

This *coup d'état* was welcomed by the representatives of Great Britain, France and the United States at Omsk. The plan to move the Czechs to Europe was dropped and it was decided instead to build up a front against the Germans in Russia. The 'supreme ruler' was recognized by the allied governments.

Kolchak, now dictator of Siberia, was the polar explorer whom we have already met. He had also distinguished himself at the siege of Port Arthur. When the February Revolution broke out he was a vice-admiral and commander of the Black Sea fleet. He was probably the most talented of the Russian admirals and he impressed everyone he met – even the Bolsheviks who later tried and condemned him – as the very model of a proud and upright officer. But he was quite unsuited to the rôle of suppressor of the revolution, which demanded a Cromwell or a Napoleon. From what he said later before the Bolshevist commission of inquiry, it is clear that he did not possess the faintest understanding of political, social or economic questions. In comparison with his chief opponent,

Lenin, he seems like an elderly cadet. There was the further fact that his health was undermined; he paid for the polar nights and the siege of Port Arthur with rheumatism and recurring attacks of pneumonia.

Moreover, he was dictator only on paper, for the generals and *hetmeni* under his command did as they pleased. The commander of the East China Railway, General Horwarth, recognized Kolchak and was ready to support him; but he had to take account of the Japanese, who were hostile to Kolchak. Transbaikalia was controlled by the half-Buryat Semyonov, who was in the pay of the Japanese. Semyonov seized supplies intended for Kolchak, robbed the local population and had the just and the unjust shot indiscriminately.

The civil war was even wilder and fiercer in Siberia than in the rest of Russia. The Revolution revived the old Siberia, in which no one had ever spared his own or other people's lives. Both sides were equally bad, but the Reds were the first to resort to inhumanity. In the time of Kerensky's Provisional Government the Tsar, his little son and his four daughters had been taken to Tobolsk – Rasputin's native town! There they lived under guard but in reasonable conditions until the Bolshevists gained power in Tobolsk. After the Czech rising the Tsar and his family were transferred to Ekaterinburg (now Sverdlovsk) in the Urals and as the front approached they were brutally murdered in the night of 16–17 July 1918.

The exploration and colonization of Siberia cost the Russian people enormous sacrifices and suffering, but as a result Siberia became a Russian province. The first Russian tsar who was fully entitled to call it his own perished on the threshold of this Siberia where his subjects had perished for three and a half centuries.

Kolchak's dictatorship did not last long. He succeeded neither in building up a stable administration nor in organizing the economy. He could not even use Russian gold to make purchases abroad. At the beginning of the war the gold reserves of the imperial bank had been taken to Kazan, and from there the Czechs had taken them to Omsk. They consisted of 5,156 boxes and 1,678 sacks of gold and platinum and were altogether worth 1,151,500,000 roubles. All this wealth had been won in Siberia and now it returned there.

From the start the workers everywhere in Siberia had been

against the dictatorship, and now requisitions, call-ups and shootings alienated the peasants. When the Reds crossed the Urals in the summer of 1919 Red partisans began to appear in Siberia.

In November 1919 the Red Army captured Omsk and the government moved to Irkutsk. Kolchak and his prime minister, Pepelyaev, were with the army, but the Czechs were already abandoning him and the Siberian army was breaking up. In Irkutsk the local Soviet took over power and the rest of the government fled.

Kolchak's train, which was also carrying the gold, was stopped by rebellious workers, but was finally allowed to pass at the instance of the allied missions and the Czechs. Kolchak and Pepelyaev were taken to Irkutsk, guarded by the Allies and the Czechs, and there the allied representative, the French general Janin, entered into negotiations with the Soviet for safe conducts to Vladivostok for himself and the Czechs. There can be no doubt that in exchange for the gold he could have obtained a safe conduct for Kolchak as well had he not been more concerned about his own safety. But he handed over Kolchak and Pepelyaev straight away and with this treachery purchased safety for himself and the last Czech detachments. After a trial lasting nine days Kolchak and Pepelyaev were shot on 7 February 1920. Three weeks later the gold was handed over too.

What did the intervention of the great powers in Siberia, which has left such an ineradicable complex in the Soviet consciousness, really amount to? It is well known that Kolchak received almost no munitions, nor did the Allies send him any troops beyond guards for their missions. However, he was considerably assisted by the Allies' decision to keep the Czechoslovaks in Siberia. Even after they had left the front the Czechs protected the Transsib, without which Kolchak could not have lasted a month. The Allies wanted to set up a front against Germany and when this front became superfluous they dropped Kolchak; they were not thinking of any other advantage to themselves.

Japan behaved quite differently. The war had strengthened her position in the Far East considerably; the Russian Revolution made her mistress of Manchuria and China. This naturally brought up the question of the Russian Far Eastern territories. What at Portsmouth had been only an empty threat now became the plan of the general staff.

The Japanese had been the first to land at Vladivostok in April 1918 and in August they had sent fairly large forces there. Small American and British detachments arrived only later. The Japanese took possession of the Transsib as far as Lake Baikal and garrisoned all the strategic points. For all practical purposes the whole of eastern Siberia was in their power. They provided robber-*hetmeni* with gold, arms and advisers. At the same time they pumped raw materials out of the country, exported timber, took possession of Russian steamers and warehouses and acquired land from the *hetmeni*. The population hated them and the partisans made life difficult for them. When the Japanese garrison at Nikolayevsk was butchered by the local inhabitants, the Japanese occupied northern Sakhalin as a reprisal.

Getting rid of the Japanese was by now the main concern of the Soviet government. No country recognized it and no country would negotiate with it. It could not wage war against Japan because it was already fighting the Poles in the west.

Lenin found the solution. At his suggestion, but apparently on the initiative of the local Siberian Soviets, a buffer state was formed in 1920 out of the maritime region and Transbaikalia. It was known as the Democratic Far Eastern Republic. Its independence was recognized by the Soviet government and also *de facto* by Japan. At the same time the Japanese set up their own 'white' Russian government in Vladivostok.

The Far Eastern Republic succeeded in making an alliance with America, and when the Japanese tried to extort various privileges from it the American government replied with a public protest. America wanted to restore the balance of power in the Far East. It is true that she acted in her own interests, but in fact she defended the integrity of Russia. At the Washington Naval Conference in 1922 Japan was forced to renounce all her territorial acquisitions and other claims on Russia. In October 1922 Vladivostok and the whole Far Eastern region were evacuated by the Japanese and the four-year economic exploitation came to an end.

The Red Army occupied Vladivostok and the Far Eastern Republic announced its adhesion to the Russian, now Soviet, empire.

The Japanese remained in northern Sakhalin for another three years and only evacuated it in 1925 after obtaining exceptionally favourable concessions for the production of oil and coal.

This was a relatively low price to pay for the liberation of the Far East, and it was the U.S.A. which saved this territory for Russia.

As a matter of fact, another attempt at annexation was made in eastern Siberia about this time, but it was more private than official and it was not made by Americans. In 1912 a steamer called the *Karluk* belonging to a Canadian polar expedition was caught in the ice. It was later driven to Wrangel Island and there sank. The crew went ashore on the island and was not rescued until September 1914.

The sum total of this enterprise was the loss of eight good Arctic pioneers and the fact that the Union Jack had flown over the island for about six months. The same well-known polar explorer, Vilhjalmur Stefansson, who had organized the *Karluk* expedition sent out a fresh expedition in 1921 with the express task of confirming the rights of the British Empire to the island. Stefansson secured the support of the Canadian government; the Canadian prime minister, Arthur Meighen, informed him officially that he regarded Wrangel Island as a Canadian possession.

The Japanese were encamped in Vladivostok at this time and eastern Siberia was a no-man's-land. Stefansson did not bother about the fact that the Tsarist government had given notice of the island's incorporation in the Russian empire in 1916. He was obsessed with his own grandiose ideas, which few people understood at that time. He had already realized that flying not only meant a revolution in transport but in particular would draw the Arctic into world politics. Stefansson proceeded from the premise that the world was round and the Arctic did not correspond in reality to its appearance on an atlas. He pointed out that between America and Asia lay the 'Mediterranean of the north', over which intercontinental air routes led. Land bases would be needed for these Arctic air routes and one of these bases was Wrangel Island.

The steamer dispatched by Stefansson took five Canadians and an Eskimo woman (to do the cooking and sewing) to Wrangel Island, and sailed away after promising to return the following year. Meanwhile Stefansson himself went to London, conferred with various ministers and launched a press campaign. All this time the five people on Wrangel Island were waiting to be relieved. Relief did not come until 1923; only the Eskimo woman was still alive. Nevertheless another fourteen persons, mainly Eskimos, were landed on the island.

These 'islanders' lived there until August 1924, when a Soviet gunboat 'occupied' the island, hoisted the Red flag and took the residents to Vladivostok. In England the Labour party was now in power. His Majesty's government announced that it abandoned all claims to the distant island.

XII

RED SIBERIA

-------◀•••▶-------

NO FURTHER OBSTACLES

DURING THE few decades of the Soviet régime Siberia has experienced a more radical transformation than in the centuries of Tsarist rule. Its position in the world has also changed decisively.

After dealing with the 'white' adventure of the half-crazy Baron Ungern-Sternberg, the Soviet government succeeded in 1924 in re-establishing by virtue of a treaty with China a *de facto* protectorate over Outer Mongolia. It was also able to obtain recognition of its rights in the East China Railway. All this was possible because after the Washington conference in 1922 Japan adopted a passive, waiting attitude. However, she followed this development attentively and when the Manchurian dictator, Chang Tso-lin, began to limit Soviet influence the Japanese smiled to themselves. From this time onward the Soviet government received only half the revenues from the railway, and Russian employees were cheated and gradually forced out. In 1929 Chang Tso-lin tried to obtain complete control of the line. The U.S.S.R. frustrated this attempt by force of arms and the previous situation was restored. On this occasion, too, Japan remained neutral and preserved friendly relations with both sides; she already had her own plans.

Moscow knew this and the Soviet government simply tried to gain time. It was as accommodating as could be, observed the 1925 treaty to the letter, made no difficulties about the export of crude oil and coal from northern Sakhalin and did not prevent Japan extending her fishing operations off Kamchatka. Moscow saw that the Japanese were building strategic railways in Korea and southern Manchuria and also knew why, but was too weak to interfere.

Further developments showed that Japanese aggression was not just a turnip-ghost. Chiang Tso-lin, who tried to part company with the Japanese, was destroyed by them; in 1931 a Japanese army occupied Manchuria and set up the 'independent' empire of

Manchukuo, which in 1934 even obtained its own emperor. The East China Railway consequently lost all significance for the U.S.S.R. and in 1935 it was sold for 140 million yen – fifty-five million gold roubles at the current rate of exchange; it had once cost Russia five hundred million roubles. Inner Mongolia became a Japanese sphere of influence and the same fate obviously awaited Outer Mongolia. The Russian Far Eastern territories were being outflanked and could be cut off at any moment up to Lake Baikal.

The Soviet government had expected all this for a long time and had made preparations for war with Japan. It was clear above all that communications would have to be improved. But the Russo-Japanese war had shown that communications were not the only factor involved. The war potential of Siberia had to be increased to the point where the country could defend itself. The Far East was too remote to obtain all it needed from Russia.

The plan for a strong and economically independent Siberia fitted in with the general tendencies of the Soviet dictatorship, especially with its colonial policy. The 'liberation of peoples oppressed by the tsarist régime', especially Asiatic peoples, was to extend the revolution to Asia. This liberation had to raise the economic and cultural standards of the backward Asiatic peoples, above all by creating their own industries and their own proletariats for them. The industries subsequently became Soviet industries; a native proletariat did in fact come into being everywhere, although it was soon submerged in the flood of newly-arrived Russian workers.

It is well known that at the same time the Soviet government supported the nationalist movements in all the Asiatic countries by word and deed. In the middle of the 'twenties it had close links with the democratic revolutionary party of China, the Kuomintang. The leader of the Kuomintang, Dr Sun Yat-sen, even sent his young colleague, Chiang Kai-shek, to Moscow for 'ideological training'. Soviet instructors helped to train the Kuomintang army.

However, this alliance soon came to an end. Sun Yat-sen's successor, Chiang Kai-shek, declared war on the Chinese communists. But the Kremlin's policy remained unchanged; it simply withdrew its help from the Kuomintang and transferred it to the Chinese Communist Party. This policy only bore fruit after the Second World War.

Such were the political and ideological premises of the Soviet five-year plans in Siberia. But in judging the results obtained the following factors must be taken into account. The vision of a Siberia full of people and traffic had hovered before Witte's eyes, and, even earlier, before those of Muravyev-Amursky. The tsarist régime had begun to make this vision a reality by building the Trans-Siberian Railway, and it had been ready to continue working in the same direction. Plans for a Turkestan–Siberia and a South Siberian railway, and also for a host of other projects since executed by the Soviet régime, had already been worked out in tsarist times. The reason why the tsarist régime could not put these plans into effect with the speed of the Soviet government was that neither it nor Russia as a whole in those days possessed sufficient capital. Soviet Russia invested more in Siberia in a single year than tsarist Russia had in ten years. The talent of all dictatorships consists in their ability to find a source of capital in underpaid or completely unpaid labour. The hundreds of millions of hours of unpaid work put into the Siberian economy by the Soviets form a capital which even the American Federal Bank system cannot command.

No one knows precisely how much forced labour there is in Siberia at present nor how many workers have perished there. We only know that a great many have and still do, and that their numbers run to millions. The five or six thousand convicts who helped to build the Trans-Siberian Railway in tsarist times are a mere drop in the ocean in comparison.

The tsarist régime could not colonize Siberia by force and send streams of people into the *taiga* and tundra whenever it pleased. In those days colonization went on openly, and it was subject to the control of public opinion and the Duma. Even in Muravyev's time mistakes and blunders had caused a storm in the press, and his lack of success in the settling of the Amur region was still disturbing his rest twenty years later. Under the Soviet régime all these obstacles disappeared. In the morasses and wildernesses inside the Arctic circle towns with ten thousand inhabitants sprang up in the course of two or three years. It is difficult to believe that these people were all volunteers. But however that may be Siberia grew stronger than anyone could have possibly dreamed.

TREASURE-HOUSE

The job was done thoroughly. The Soviet leaders had a real interest in Siberia, which is not surprising seeing that they had all come to know it under the tsarist régime. Siberia was explored afresh. This work began immediately after the October Revolution; it was soon properly organized and put under government control through the Soviet (formerly Imperial) Academy of Sciences. Every year dozens of expeditions were dispatched to the most remote regions; permanent commissions were set up for the Taimyr peninsula, Kamchatka and so on. In 1926 an expedition under the leadership of S. W. Obruchev surveyed and described for the first time the vast mountainous area between the Yana and the Anadyr Mountains in eastern Siberia. The Severnaya Zemlya Islands, discovered in 1913, were thoroughly explored in 1930-2 by Ushakov and Urvantzev. Today there are special institutes at work on volcanoes in Kamchatka, the problem of permanently frozen ground, and every conceivable question of geography, climate and agriculture. As a result, the geographical blanks have disappeared from the map of Siberia.

Naturally it was not a matter only of geography. A further consequence was a tremendous enlargement of knowledge about the natural resources, especially the mineral resources, of Siberia. Of the many discoveries made, the most important concerned coal. The Kuznetsk coalfields turned out to be the biggest and best in the U.S.S.R.; their reserves are reckoned at 450,000,000,000 tons. To the east, near Minusinsk on the Yenisei, there are deposits of valuable bituminous coal; farther to the north-east, near Kansk, there is lignite. The lignite deposits near Irkutsk were also found to be much richer than had been supposed; they continue eastward on the other side of Lake Baikal. Enormous deposits of coal were discovered in the Yenisei basin, and fields of various sizes and quality on the Taimyr peninsula, on the Kolyma, on the Chukcha peninsula and in Kamchatka. Coal is also mined on the Bureya in the Amur valley, near Khabarovsk, near Vladivostok and on Sakhalin.

But coal alone was not enough. As we know, the development of Siberia was hindered by the lack of iron ore. Here was one of

379

the geographical and economic contrasts in which Eurasia is so rich. On the western border of Siberia are the Urals, where there are huge mineral deposits, including iron ore, but no coal; in the south-west of Siberia are the rich Kuznetsk coalfields, without any iron in the neighbourhood. The Soviet régime has linked these two regions in the so-called 'Ural-Kuznetsk complex'. The story of this complex, which was created in the 'thirties at a furious speed with tremendous sacrifices and no hope of a financial profit, forms one of the most fantastic chapters in economic history. The Kuznetsk coal was taken by rail over twelve hundred miles to the Urals, where at Magnitogorsk what is probably the greatest centre of iron and steel production in the world has been built up. Moreover, the Kuznetsk coalfields became the Ruhr of Siberia, for to prevent the trains returning empty from Magnitogorsk Kuznetsk was given its own iron and steel industry, together with rolling-mills, machine-tool factories, chemical works and many other things not mentioned in the Soviet press.

Meanwhile prospecting went on to find more coal for the Urals and more iron for Kuznetsk, and both were discovered. Today the two industrial areas are almost independent of each other. Coal for Magnitogorsk is provided by the new coal fields of Karaganda in the Kirghiz steppe, which are only half the distance from Magnitogorsk; naturally, heavy industry was built up at Karaganda as well, especially as iron and manganese ore were found in the neighbourhood. Kuznetsk now gets its iron ore from Gornaya Shoriya, mountains only a hundred and twenty miles away to the south.

Iron is also produced now in the Altai, near Ust-Kamenogorsk, on the Yenisei in the region of Minusinsk and Krasnoyarsk, farther to the east on the River Ilim, a tributary of the Angara, where the new town of Rudnogorsk ('Oretown') has arisen, in Transbaikalia and in the foothills of the Little Chingan, not far from Khabarovsk.

Besides these two basic raw materials, manganese was discovered near Krasnoyarsk, in Transbaikalia and in the Far East. Tin is produced in Transbaikalia, bauxite (aluminium ore) near Kuznetsk and nickel and cobalt on the lower Yenisei near Norilsk.

Siberia also contains silver, zinc, lead, wolfram, cadmium, gallium and probably uranium, too. As for gold, it is present everywhere, but production is now greatest in the east, in the Lena–Aldan basin and on the Kolyma. No figures are published, but it

is known that the U.S.S.R. is the second biggest producer of gold
in the world, ranking next to South Africa.

A NEW INDUSTRIAL POWER

All this wealth was not only discovered but also utilized at once.
Nothing hindered the Soviet régime in the choice of sites. The raw
materials were free and markets were created with the industries;
where there was no labour it was imported. People lived in forests
and marshes, in mud huts or quickly constructed wooden cabins,
and built up everything foreseen in the plan. In little more than
fifteen years industrial landscapes with forests of factory chimneys
sprang up all over Siberia; they were linked by a network of railways. The Urals, with vast numbers of iron and steel works, factories and chemical works, are already one of the world's great
industrial areas. Farther to the east and south-east runs another
line of industrial areas: Kazak, Novosibirsk, Kuznetsk, Transbaikalia and the Far Eastern area with its centres at Khabarovsk
and Komsomolsk.

All this was built up in the twelve years before the Second World
War, an amazingly short space of time. This war, which did so
much damage to European Russia, gave a colossal stimulus to
Siberia. At that time 455 big factories were moved to the Urals,
665 to Siberia and a large number to central Asia. A considerable
number of them stayed at their new sites. Siberia's share in the
total production of the Soviet Union was already increasing every
year even before the war and the war hastened the process. In
1913 Siberia had produced no pig iron at all, let alone steel. In
1937 it was delivering 10 per cent of the total Russian production.
During the war new blast furnaces with a total productive capacity
of 2·5 million tons of pig iron and the same quantity of steel were
built and by 1950 Siberia's share of total production had risen to
between 15 and 20 per cent. No detailed statistics of production
are published in the Soviet Union, so we can give only approximate
figures based on the laborious comparison of various sources and
on indications in the press, which usually confines itself to per-
centages and production curves. Total steel production in the
Soviet Union amounts today to about 35 million tons a year, of
which about 24·5 million tons come from the Urals, Siberia and

central Asia. As Siberia provides about a quarter of 'eastern' production it must be making about 6 million tons of steel a year. This is 50 per cent more than the whole of Russia was producing in 1913.

As for coal, Russia now produces about 300 million tons a year, and 90 million of these come from Siberia. The Kuznetsk fields alone produce sixty million tons, about twice as much as the whole of Russia produced in 1913.

Coal and iron are the two key raw materials, the bases of all other industries. It is hardly possible to name a branch of industry which is not represented in Siberia. It is not very surprising that in Novosibirsk there are huge machine-tool and textile factories, or that Kuznetsk produces iron, steel and chemicals. But when we find one of the biggest tractor factories in the Soviet Union at Rubzovsk in the Altai, and farther east, almost on the Mongolian frontier, the old Abakan works transformed into an ultra-modern iron and steel works, that is almost fantastic; at any rate, that was the feeling of American visitors during the war. No less fantastic are the locomotive, rolling stock and aircraft factories in Trans-baikalia and the chemical and ball-bearing works on the Amur. Today Siberia produces glass and plastic goods, lathes, radios, motor-cycles and paper. There are canning factories in Kamchatka and Sakhalin, sugar factories in western Siberia and textile and leather works in Transbaikalia.

Naturally electric power has not been forgotten, for according to Lenin, socialism consists of 'Soviet power plus electrification'. Already Siberia produces more electricity than the whole of Russia before the Revolution. There are coal-fired power stations in all the towns and efforts have been made to make the greatest possible use of the enormous reserves of power in the rivers. Apart from a number of small and middle-sized hydro-electric works a huge installation has been built on the Irtysh at Ust-Kamenogorsk and another giant is being constructed on the Angara near Irkutsk.

THE GREAT EXPANSION OF THE RAILWAYS

As an administrative region modern Siberia is smaller than might be supposed. The whole of the huge expanse of the Kazak steppe forms the Kazak Soviet Republic, one of the sixteen member republics of the Soviet Union. The Urals also form a separate administrative region.

All this has political and administrative significance, but no economic significance. Siberia, the Urals and Kazakstan form one geographical unity and the whole point of the Soviet Five Year plans consist in converting this geographical unity into an economic unity which did not exist before.

That was the goal of the whole communications policy in Siberia. It came into being under the pressure of the danger from Japan and thus served a strategic purpose. But the strategic ideas of the Bolshevists were more sweeping than those of the tsarist generals. Witte had already pointed out that every economically advantageous route is also useful from a strategic point of view. A few small branch lines may serve strategic ends alone. This conception was also the basis of Soviet thinking about communications. The policy began with the addition of a second track to the Transsib. As an insurance against air attack, the old bridges were not widened; new ones were built instead. At Novosibirsk two new bridges were built across the Irtysh. Heavy rail was now laid and all stations were equipped with the latest signalling devices. This was a long task and was only completed just before the Second World War.

Another railway that served both economic and strategic ends was the Turkestan–Siberia line, the 'Turksib', which links central Asia to western Siberia. This 900-mile line, which runs along the Russo-Chinese frontier, was built between 1927 and 1930. Its strategic importance hardly needs underlining, but it also takes wood, coal and corn from Siberia to Turkestan and cotton from Turkestan to Siberia. Just as important is the new railway which connects the Transsib to the Turksib via Karaganda and Lake Balkhash. It carries coal, iron, manganese, wheat and timber, but to the strategists it is a third route for reinforcements to central Asia.

The Transsib now ceased to be a thin steel wire with the dead weight of all Siberia hanging on it. It was more like a steel girder supporting a number of transverse girders.

For the new Siberia not even the double-track Transsib is sufficient; already a second, southern Transsib winds eastward. It has already crossed the Kirghiz steppe and been taken through the Abakan mountains to Minusinsk. From there it is to be continued – in fact this section may have already been built – to the station of Taishet on the old Transsib. The eastern section of the second Transsib had been started before the Second World War. It leads from Taishet round the north of Lake Baikal to the new town of Komsomolsk on the Amur. There were reports in the American press that the construction of this line had been halted and that it was to be replaced by a motorway. Later it was reported that the railway was being built after all. It may be taken for granted that the Soviet government will not abandon this project, for there is plenty of coal in Siberia, but not much oil, and in the climate of Siberia and over its enormous distances no motorway can replace the railway.

A REVOLUTION IN ECONOMIC GEOGRAPHY

From a historical point of view the Trans-Siberian Railway turned out to be a counterpart to the old silk routes, for it quickly became an important international trade route, speeding up and facilitating traffic between Europe, North China and even Japan. The Trans-Siberian line also showed its functional similarity to the silk routes by stimulating the flow of colonists from east to west as well as from west to east. The colonization of Manchuria by the Chinese and the surge of Chinese and Korean settlers into the Far Eastern territories and the whole of Siberia were a consequence of the construction of the Trans-Siberian Railway.

The Soviet government put the development of Siberia as well as its communications on a completely new basis. The old question of an east-west trade link through Siberia gradually broadened out into the problem of developing Siberia completely and making the whole country a link between east and west. The practical answer to this problem consisted in the addition by the Bolshevists of a third chain to the two previously connecting east and west (the silk route and the Trans-Siberian Railway). This third chain was the northern sea route.

Its development in the twentieth century was partly dictated by strategic considerations. In the Russo-Japanese war Admiral Makarov had pointed out its importance for the defence of the Far East and had emphatically recommended the use of heavy ice-breakers. In 1914–15 Vilkitsky did succeed in making the passage from east to west with two ice-breakers. The Soviets now adopted the old idea. They began with the 'Kara expeditions', which every year from the early 'twenties onward brought a number of freighters, most of them from Hamburg, through the Kara Sea to the mouths of the Ob and the Yenisei. Starting at three, the number of ships making this trip every year finally rose to fifty. The Commissar for foreign trade, Krassin, and Professor Otto Schmidt contributed a great deal to the success of this enterprise.

Gradually the voyages extended farther east and in 1932 the ice-breaker *Sibiryakov*, with Otto Schmidt on board, completed the trip from Archangel to Vladivostok in one season, a feat which no ship had achieved before. It had been suggested 407 years before by Gerasimov and first attempted by the English 379 years before.

At the end of the same year the Soviet 'Northern Sea Route Authority' was set up, which was headed for a long time by Professor Schmidt. This authority was given control of everything between the Arctic circle and the North Pole. The Arctic coast was explored again, every year new expeditions set sail from east and west and after several years and many setbacks regular traffic was eventually established.

Naturally this was only possible thanks to modern techniques which were not at the disposal of tsarist Russia. Today the authority owns the largest fleet of ice-breakers in the world, ships are assisted by meteorological and wireless stations with their own aircraft and a series of bases with food and coal has been set up along the route. The change of climate in the Arctic – it has been growing warmer since the 'twenties – has also contributed to the success of the enterprise.

In 1939 ten freighters sailed from Archangel to Vladivostok and dozens of steamers reached the estuaries of the great Siberian rivers. As a result of these improved communications there are now proper towns of ten and twenty thousand inhabitants inside the Arctic circle, with power stations, saw-mills, factories and private houses. The polar islands have been colonized and on both them and the mainland reindeer are reared and fur farms have been set up. On Wrangel Island children go to school on skis.

Like the Transsib, the northern sea route sends out branches in all directions, north to the polar islands and south to the navigable rivers, which are its natural 'branch lines'. Today there are two east-west links in Asia: the Trans-Siberian Railway (soon to be complemented by a second line) and the northern sea route.

The significance of this new factor needs no special explanation. Its truly revolutionary effect proceeds from the fact that the two latitudinal links are connected naturally by the northward-flowing Siberian rivers. There lies the real point of the revolution in communications in Siberia. Two traffic arteries, one of which cuts across the upper course of the rivers and the other of which runs along their mouths, form with the rivers a unified system of communications embracing the whole of Siberia. By the development of sea transport, the construction of harbours and bases at the mouths of the rivers and their main tributaries, and the combination of all these factors by the use of aeroplanes and wireless, the immemorial peace of the tundra and *taiga* has been shattered. The Soviet rulers shrank from no sacrifice to exploit the natural wealth of the land.

Convoys of freighters now traverse the Arctic waters as the caravans of camels laden with silk once traversed the deserts of central Asia. The northern sea route is the last ocean route of global importance to be opened and the only one which is controlled by a continental power. Moreover, the shortest air route from America to China and India is via the North Pole and Siberia. Bakunin had been right when he exclaimed a hundred years earlier, 'Siberia, land of the future!'

To carry out all these revolutionary changes the Soviet government naturally needed people, and it was never short of these. Hordes of emigrants and workers were packed off to Siberia. For example, the Soviet government set up the 'Autonomous Jewish Republic' of Birobidshan in a bend of the Amur to the west of Khabarovsk, where the Jews have to carry out pioneering work which would have been beyond even Siberian Cossacks. The heaviest tasks, with the most difficult conditions attached to them, were carried out by deportees who were transferred en masse, such as the Kulaks during the compulsory collectivization, and the hundreds of thousands of 'suspects' and 'unreliable persons' during and after the last war. The population of Siberia grew significantly faster than that of the rest of Russia. Between 1926 and 1939 the population of the Soviet Union as a whole increased by 16 per cent, but in the Novosibirsk region the increase was 53 per cent, in Transbaikalia 73 per cent and round Khabarovsk

136 per cent. The population of Siberia as a whole is unknown; estimates vary between forty and fifty million. The increase relates mainly to the towns, whose populations have grown enormously. In 1926 Novosibirsk had 126,000 inhabitants; in 1939 the figure was 400,000 and by 1944 700,000. In the same period the population of Omsk rose from 160,000 to 400,000. In the next ten years all the Siberian towns continued to grow at the same rate.

One is bound to wonder how all these people are fed, for most of them work in factories, forests and mines. Siberian agriculture is in the same state as that of the rest of the Soviet Union. All the conditions for its development are there: the area under cultivation has been increased and the collective farms are well provided with machinery and everything else necessary. Apparently the only thing lacking is zest for work in the collectivized peasants. Even in tsarist times Siberia could have fed itself, but the more remote regions went hungry because it was too difficult to transport food to them. This is much easier now. Considerable success has also been achieved in the north with crops which can stand frost. In the old Russia, sugar-beet was regarded as a monopoly of the Ukraine, which also contained all the sugar-beet factories; today sugar-beet thrives in western Siberia, just as special varieties of apple ripen in Yakutsk. Great efforts to develop agriculture have also been made in the Far Eastern region. Conditions there are unfavourable to the cultivation of wheat. The rice harvest is increasing, but the Russians are not very fond of rice. Another bottleneck is caused by the fact that this enormous area, whose diet is predominantly fish, has no salt of its own.

On the other hand, the industrialization of the Far East has produced results considered remarkable even in the U.S.S.R. As we know, the Far East has coal, iron and non-ferrous metals, and also oil. From an industrial point of view it is thus completely independent of the rest of the Soviet Union. Important iron and steel works have been built at Khabarovsk and at the new town of Komsomolsk, whose refineries receive their crude oil by pipeline from Sakhalin. A railway links Khabarovsk to Komsomolsk and to Soviet Harbour, where the Soviet Far Eastern fleet has first-class docks, yards and arsenals. Vladivostok is also an important naval base. In all these places and in Kamchatka, too, there are ultra-modern airfields.

All raw materials are converted into the finished article in the Far East. Rails, tubes, complicated tools and machines, loco-motives, cars, tractors, electronic apparatus, dyestuffs, explosives, chemical fertilizers, iron alloys, paper and glass are all made there, and probably many things of which we are not told as well.

The war potential of this Far Eastern bastion has only one weakness: it has no wheat of its own. However, this is to be found in neighbouring Manchuria. With Manchuria, the Soviet Far East forms an example of complete autarchy. But what is going on in Manchuria today?

THE 'NEW ORDER' IN ASIA

It was Russia that opened up Manchuria. At the beginning of the twentieth century her pioneering work and her capital created a new economic region and opened it up for Chinese colonization and further capital investment. This work was continued by the Japanese. At the beginning of the Second World War, Manchukuo was becoming a strong state with a population of forty million. As much coal was mined there as in the whole of the rest of China, its railway network was almost as good and its iron and steel production was twice that of China. There were huge Japanese armament factories in the country. Dairen (Dalny) had 600,000 inhabitants, Harbin 800,000 and Mukden more than a million.

This Japanese bastion lay opposite the Soviet one. From an economic point of view they were complementary and represented a potential unity. The question was, when would the unification take place and who would be the gainer?

The Soviet Union declared war on Japan on 8 August 1945, six days before the Japanese capitulation. The Red Army easily over-came the weak Japanese resistance and captured an army of 600,000 men. Its own losses were 8,000 killed and 22,000 wounded. All the aims outlined by Stalin at Yalta were thus achieved: the U.S.S.R.'s rights in the East China and South Manchurian rail-ways were restored, and the Soviet Union once again obtained control of the old leased territory on the Liao-Tung peninsula, with Port Arthur and Dairen, the Kuriles and southern Sakhalin. In this connection it is important to note that, under American pressure, Chiang Kai-shek's government, which was at that time the legal government of China and recognized by everyone, gave its agreement to these arrangements.

It is also worth pointing out that a year earlier, when the war with Germany was not yet over, the U.S.S.R. had announced the incorporation of the 'Republic of Tannu Tuva' in the Union. This country lies at the head waters of the Yenisei, between Siberia and Mongolia. Chiang Kai-shek did not protest on that occasion either.

The position which Russia had occupied in the Far East in 1913 was more than restored. Witte could have scarcely imagined this triumphal return.

When the Japanese capitulated, the war between Chiang Kai-shek and the Communists was in full swing. Since the Soviet government was not sure what the outcome of this war would be, it hastened to remove all the Japanese industries from Manchuria to the Soviet Union.

In return it was quite ready to help the Chinese Communists. They received all the Japanese war material in Manchuria, and Manchuria provided them with food. There was a genuine Chinese proletariat there which formed the kernel of the Communist army. Using Manchuria as a base the Communists defeated Chiang Kai-shek's armies.

So long as the Japanese controlled Manchuria and Korea they treated these two countries as one economic unit. North Korea delivered electricity and rice to Manchuria and received in return coal, iron and soya beans. The Russian Far East, too, needed the economic assistance of Manchuria, which in turn required technical help. All three regions were linked up by railway by the Japanese, and even before the time of the Japanese they were bound together by navigable rivers. From this magic triangle, called into life by Russia and developed by the Soviet Union and Japan, united Communist China went to war. It was thus understandable that an American-dominated South Korea was not acceptable to the Soviet Union and China. To them, an Americanized South Korea seemed considerably more dangerous than Formosa. The combined Sino-Soviet action against South Korea was an attempt to avert this danger.

On 14 February 1950 a treaty of friendship was signed between the Soviet Union and Communist China. In it the U.S.S.R. voluntarily renounced the rights conferred on her by Chiang Kai-shek; she promised to give back the whole of the Manchurian Railway and Port Arthur to China by the end of 1952. She also granted China a loan of three hundred million dollars. This and the Manchurian Railway certainly amounted to more than the value of the dismantled Japanese industries.

Thus in its Far Eastern policy the Soviet government did not follow tsarist methods. It did not confirm the expectations of the world press, which had reckoned on fresh open or concealed annexations in China. The agreement of 27 March 1950 on the joint exploitation of mineral resources in Sinkiang also testified to new methods and a fresh climate in Russo-Chinese relations. A combined Russo-Chinese company was to be set up for the production of oil, coal, gold and so on, and both partners were to have equal shares in its administration and profits. Both the Sinkiang agreement and the treaty of friendship were symbols of the Soviet policy in Asia, which, in comparison with Russian behaviour in the west, seemed remarkably moderate.

This attitude reflected not only community of outlook and solidarity in the cold war but also a precise estimate of the balance of power in Asia. In the seventeenth century Russia had to retreat in face of weak Chinese forces because she did not have at her disposal the human material for the settlement or defence of an unpopulated region. On the other hand, in the middle of the nineteenth century Russian colonization flowed right up to the Amur, whose left bank was still as empty as it had been 160 years before, and this made possible the 'conquest' of the Amur region, in which not a shot was fired.

This occupation was followed by the settlement of the Russian bank of the Amur, while the Manchurian vacuum opposite only filled up later, and only then under the influence of the gravitational pull from the Russian side.

Since then the balance of power has altered for the third time. The vacuum has been filled by Chinese settlers, a process made possible by the railway built by Witte! Today the population of Manchuria – about 50 million – is about the same as that of the whole of Siberia. In the foreseeable future it will be twice as big. The pressure comes this time from the Chinese side. In the last analysis, Russia is here going over from the offensive to the defensive.

The British geographer Halford J. Mackinder, who pointed fifty years ago to the importance of the Russo-Siberian region for the domination of the 'island of the Old World' recognized with amazing penetration the possibilities latent in the geography of Russia from a political point of view. Witte, too, recognized these possibilities. Both theoretical and practical preparations were made for the present Soviet power. But the most important preparation of all was the colonization and development of Siberia.

SELECTED BIBLIOGRAPHY

[R] *indicates works in Russian*

TREATIES

E. Adamov, *Collected Treaties 1856–1917* [R].

E. Grimm, *International Treaties relating to the Far East 1842–1925*, 1927 [R].

Martens, *Nouveau Recueil Général de Traités*, 1st series, Vol. XVI (1860) et seq., 2nd series, Vol. II (1869), Vol. IV (1878).

Treaties Between Russia and China 1689–1881, Petersburg, 1889 (texts in Russian, Latin, Manchurian, Mongolian and Chinese).

I–DRIVING FORCES

Afanasy Nikitin's Journey Across Three Seas, 1821, 1948 ed. [R].

D. Anuchin, *The Town and Region of Mangaseya*, 1903 [R].

—*Towards a History of the Knowledge of Siberia Before Yermak*, 1890 [R].

S. V. Bakhrushin, *Essays on the History of the Colonization of Siberia in the 16th and 17th Centuries*, 1927 [R].

—*Essays on the History of Towns and Commerce*, Collected Works I, 1952 [R].

W. Barthold, *12 Vorlesungen üb. d. Gesch. d. Türken*, 1935.

G. Fletcher, *The History of Russia or the Government of the Emperour of Muscovia*, 1657.

R. Grousset, *L'Empire des Steppes*, 1941.

R. Hakluyt, *Principal Navigations, Voyages, Traffiques and Discoveries of the English Nation, London 1589 and 1598–1600*, new ed. 1903.

H. Harrisse, *John Cabot and his son Sebastian*, 1896.

Histoire Généalogique des Tatars d'Abulghasi, Leyden, 1726.

N. Karamsin, *History of the Russian Empire, 1818–29*, IX [R].

V. O. Kluchevsky, *Russian History I*, 1904 [R].

P. Pierling, *L'Italie et la Russie au XVI Siècle*, 1892.

— *La Russie et le Saint-Siège, I*, 1896.

S. F. Platonov, *History of Russia's North*, 1924 [R].

— *Readings in Russian History*, 1917 [R].

G. B. Ramusio, *Discorso Sopra li Viaggi delle Spetierie*, from *Delle Navigationi e Viaggi*, 1550, 1563 ed.

B. Spuler, *Die Goldene Horde*, 1943.

N. Ustryalov, *The Noble Family of the Stroganovs*, 1842 [R].

V. Vladimirtsov, *Jenghiz Khan, 1922* [R].

393

II–FROM THE URALS TO THE PACIFIC

Anthology of Siberian History, Irkutsk, 1929 [R].

P. Avril, *Voyage en Divers Etats d'Europe et d'Asie*, 1692.

A. Baikalov, *Notes on the Origin of the Name 'Siberia'*, The Slavonic and East European Review, Dec. 1950.

L. S. Berg, *The Discovery of Kamchatka and the Bering Expedition*, 1924, new revised edition, 1946 [R].

M. Bodnarsky, *Essays on Russian Geography*, 1947 [R].

Correspondence Between Kuchum and Moscow, Collection of State Documents and Treaties, II, 1819 [R].

J. F. Fischer, *Sibirische Geschichte, I*, 1768.

F. A. Golder, *Russian Expansion on the Pacific*, 1914.

R. J. Kerner, *The Urge to the Sea; the Role of Rivers, Portages, Ostrogs, Monasteries and Furs*, 1946.

G. F. Müller, *Nachrichten von Seereisen und zur See gemachten Entdeckungen . . . etc.*, 1758

N. Spathari, *Travel Journal*, 1675, 1882 ed. [R].

S. Suslov, *Physical Geography of the U.S.S.R.: West and East Siberia, the Far East, Central Asia*, 1947 [R].

N. Yadrintsev, *Siberia as a Colony*, 1882 [R].

III–THE STRUGGLE AGAINST THE BLACK DRAGON

A. Andreyev, *Essays on Source Material for Siberia*, 1939 [R].

The Autobiography of the Archpriest Avakum, 1898 [R]. German trans. 1930.

J. F. Baddeley, *Russia, Mongolia, China*, 1919.

L. Bagrow, *Geschichte d. Kartographie*, 1951.

— *Die Priorität d. Entdeckungen des Amur, d. Tatarischen Strasse u. d. Insel Sachalin*, 1931.

N. N. Bantysch-Kamensky, *Diplomatic Documents relating to Russia and China*, 1792, 1882 ed. [R].

W. Barthold, *The Knowledge of the Orient in Europe and Russia*, 1925 [R].

G. Cahen, *Histoire des Relations de la Russie avec la Chine sous Pierre le Grand*, 1911.

—*Le Livre de Comptes de la Caravane Russe à Pékin en 1727–28*, 1911.

B. de Vaulx, *Hist. des Missions Catholiques Françaises*, 1951.

Du Halde, *Description Géographique, Historique, Chronologique, Politique et Physique de l'Empire de la Chine*, 1735, IV.

R. Grousset, *Histoire de la Chine*, 1942.

A. Hummel, *Eminent Chinese of the Ch'ing Period*, 1912.

Letters and Reports of the Jesuits concerning Russia, 1904 [R].

F. Michael, *The Origin of Manchu Rule in China*, 1942.

G. F. Müller, *Geschichte über die Länder am Flusse Amur gelegen*, 1757.

— *Reiseberichte, Instruktionen, etc.*, in the '*Akten*' and '*Ergänzungen*'.
— *Siberian Trade*, 1757 [R].
P. Pascal, *Avvakum et les Débuts du Raskol*, 1938.
M. N. Pavlovsky, *Chinese–Russian Relations*, 1949.
A. S. Rosso, *Apostolic Legations to China of the 18th Century*, 1948.
E. Silin, *Kyakhta in the 18th Century*, 1947 [R].
Spathari, *Die Beschreibung d. ersten Teils des Weltalls, genannt Asia, kirch.-slawisch*, 1910.

IV–THE LEAP ACROSS TO AMERICA
K. E. v. Baer, *The Advantages to Peter the Great of Geographical Discoveries*, 1849 [R].
V. Berkh, *The First Sea Voyage Undertaken by the Russians to Solve the Question of Whether Asia was Joined to America*, 1823 [R].
W. Coxe, *Travels into Poland, Russia, Sweden and Denmark, I*, 1784.
O. Franke, *Aus Kultur und Geschichte Chinas*, Peking, 1945.
J. G. Georgi, *Geogr.-physik. Beschreibung d. Russ. Reiches, I*, 1797.
J. G. Gmelin, *Erforscher Sibiriens, Ein Gedenkbuch*, 1911.
— *Reise durch Sibirien*, 4 vols. Göttingen 1751.
F. A. Golder, *Bering's Voyages, I*, 1922.
V. Guerrier, *Leibniz's Relations with Russia and with Peter the Great*, 1871 [R].
S. P. Krasheninikov, *Description of the Land of Kamchatka*, 1949 ed. [R].
P. Lauridsen, *Vitus Bering*, 1885.
P. N. Milyukov, *Main Lines of Russian Historical Thought*, 1898 [R].
— *Russian Political Economy in the First Quarter of the 18th Century*, 1892 [R].
Nachricht von Dr. D. G. Messerschmidts siebenjähriger Reise, Neue Nordische Beyträge, 1782.
A. Okladnikov, *Russian Arctic Explorers of the 17th Century on the Taimyr Coast*, 1948 [R].
L. Richter, *Leibniz u. sein Russlandbild*, 1946.
A. L. Schlözers öffentliches und Privatleben von ihm selbst beschrieben, 1802.
L. Srejneger, *G. W. Steller, The Pioneer of Alaskan Natural History*, 1936.
G. W. Steller, *Beschreibung von dem Lande Kamtschatka*, 1774.
— *Tagebuch seiner Seereise aus d. Petripauls Hafen bis an die westlichen Küsten von Amerika*, N. N. Beyträge 1793.
— *Topographische u. physikalische Beschreibung d. Beringinsel*, N. N. Beyträge, 1781.
S. Waxell, *The Second Kamchatka Expedition*, 1940 [R].

V—RUSSIAN AMERICA

A. Andreyev, *Russian Discoveries in the Pacific and North America in the 18th and 19th Centuries*, 1944 [R].
— *Russian Discoveries in the Pacific in the 18th Century*, 1948 [R].
H. H. Bancroft, *The History of Alaska, 1890*, Comp. Works Vol. XXXIII.
— *The History of British Columbia*, 1885–87.
— *The History of California*.
A. v. Chamisso, *Reise um die Welt . . . d. d. Brigg 'Rurik'*, 2 vols. 1836.
H. Chevigny, *Lord of Alaska*, 1942.
James Cook, *A Voyage to the Pacific Ocean . . . in 1776–80*, Vol. III (ed. J. King).
W. Coxe, *Account of the Russian Discoveries Between Asia and America*, 1780.
G. Davidov, *The Two Journeys to America of the Naval Officers Khvostov and Davidov*, 2 vols. 1810–12 [R].
Harriman Alaska Expedition, I, 1902.
Washington Irving, *Astoria, or Anecdotes of an Enterprise Beyond the Rocky Mountains*, 1836.
K. Khlebnikov, *The First Russian Settlements in America*, 1833 [R].
— *Life of Shelikhov*, 1838 [R].
O. v. Kotzebue, *Journey in the South Seas*, 2 vols, 1821–23 [R].
A. J. v. Krusenstern, *Voyage Round the World*, 3 vols. 1809–12; atlas 1814 [R].
G. v. Langsdorff, *Bemerkungen auf einer Reise um die Welt*, 2 vols., 1812–13.
J. Lisyansky, *Voyage Round the World*, 1812 [R].
J. R. Masterson and H. Brower, *Bering's Successors 1745–80* (Bibliography), *Pacific Northwest Quart.*, 1947, I and IV.
S. Okuny, *The Russian-American Company*, 1939 [R].
— *Treatise on the History of the Colonization of Kamchatka.*, 1935 [R].
V. Perevalov, *Lomonosov and the Arctic*, 1949 [R].
A. I. Radischchev, *Letters*, Comp. Works II, [R].
W. Robertson, *The History of America*, I, 1777.
G. Sarychev, *Journey in Northern Siberia, the North Sea and the Eastern Ocean, 1802*, 1952 ed. [R].
J. v. Stählin, *Das v. d. Russen 1765, 66 u. 67 entdeckte nördliche Insel-Meer zw. Kamtschatka u. Nordamerika*, 1774.
P. Tikhmenev, *Historical Survey of the Origins of the Russian-American Company*, 2 vols., 1861–63 [R].
S. Tompkins, *Alaska, Promyshlennik and Sourdough*, 1945.
Voyages et Mémoires de M. A. Comte de Benyovsky, 1791.
H. R. Wagner, *The Cartography of the Northwest Coast of America*, I, 1937.

Bibliography

VI–MURAVYEV TAKES THE AMUR

Bakunin's Letters to Herzen and Ogaryev, ed. by M. Dragomanov, 1906 [R].

I. Barsukov, *Count Muravyev-Amursky*, 2 vols. 1891 [R].

R. H. Fisher, *The Russian Fur Trade 1550–1700*, 1943.

E. Karnovich, *Notable Private Fortunes in Russia*, 1874 [R].

Khrapovitsky's Diary, in *Russkij Archiv*, 1901 [R].

M. Korff, *The Life of Count Speransky*, 1861 [R].

G. K. Kotoshikhin, *Russia in the Time of Tsar Alexei Mikhailovich*, 1840 [R].

P. Kropotkin, *Recollections of a Revolutionary*, 1906 [R].

G. V. Lantsev, *Siberia in the 17th Century*, 1943.

A. T. v. Middendorff, *Reise in d. äussersten Norden u. Osten Sibiriens*, 4 vols. 1847–75; atlas 1859.

E. G. Ravenstein, *The Russians on the Amur*, 1861.

V. Semevsky, *Labourers in the Siberian Goldmines, I*, 1898 [R].

S. Shashkov, *History of Slavery in Siberia*, Coll. Works II, 1898 [R].

V. Strandmann, *Memoirs*, in *Russkaya Starina*, 1879 [R].

M. Venyukov, *Russia and the East*, 1877 [R].

— *The Russian-Asian Borderlands*, Leipzig. 1874 [R].

VII–THE END OF RUSSIAN AMERICA

F. R. Dulles, *The Road to Teheran*, 1945.

W. Dunning, *Paying for Alaska, Pol. Science Quart.* Vol. 27, 1912.

V. Farrar, *The Background of the Purchase of Alaska, Wash. Hist. Quart.* Vol. 13, 1922.

F. Golder, *The Purchase of Alaska, Am. Hist. Rev.* Vol. 20, 1920.

P. Lyashtchenko, *History of Russian Political Economy, II*, 1948 [R].

H. Miller, *Russian Opinion on the Cession of Alaska, Am. Hist. Rev.* Vol. 48, 1943.

M. N. Pokrovsky, *Diplomacy and the Wars of Tsarist Russia*, 1923 [R].

F. W. Seward, *Reminiscences of a Wartime*, 1916.

B. P. Thomas, *Russo-American Relations 1815–67*, 1930.

VIII–THE MYSTERIOUS ISLAND OF SAKHALIN

W. Beasley, *Great Britain and the Opening of Japan*, 1951.

The Cambridge Modern History XI (The Far East) and XII (Japan).

Anton Chekhov, *The Island of Sakhalin*, 1895 [R].

V. Golovnin, *Notes on his Adventures as a Japanese Prisoner*, 2 vols. 1816 [R].

I. A. Goncharov, *The Frigate 'Pallada'*, 1858 [R].

A. Hyma, *The Dutch in the Far East*, 1942.

Journal historique du Voyage de M. de Lesseps, 1790.

Joshi S. Kuno, *Japan's Expansion on the Asiatic Continent, II,* 1940.
M. Mitchell, *The Maritime History of Russia,* 1949.
J. Murdoch, *A History of Japan, III,* 1926.
F. v. Siebold, *Urkundliche Darstellung d. Bestrebungen v. Niederlanden u. Russland zur Eröffnung Japans,* 1854.
Chitoshi Yanaga, *Japan Since Perry,* 1949.

IX–INTERLUDE AND GREAT ENDEAVOURS
P. Butzinsky, *The Colonization of Siberia,* 1889 [R].
H. Johnson, *The Life and Voyages of Joseph Wiggins,* 1907.
G. Kennan, *Siberia and the Exile System,* 2 vols., 1891.
Lettres de Nordenskiöld (to O. Dixon), 1880.
A. Mineyev, *Wrangel Island,* 1936 [R].
A. E. Nordenskiöld, *Sur la Possibilité de la Navigation Commerciale dans la Mer Glaciale de Sibérie,* 1879.
Y. Semyonov, *Die Eroberung Sibiriens,* 1937.
V. Shunkov, *History of Siberian Colonization in the 17th and early 18th Centuries,* 1946 [R].
Siberia and the Trans-Siberian Railway, published by the Russian Treasury Department, 1893 [R].
A. Sibiryakov, *Der Weg v. Jakutsk zum Ochotskischen Meer,* ed. Petermann 1902.
F. P. v. Wrangel, *Journey along the Northern Shores of Siberia,* 2 vols. 1841 [R].

X–THE RAILWAY SETS THE PACE
V. Avarin, *Imperialism in Manchuria,* 1934 [R].
V. Bérard, *La Révolte de l'Asie,* 1905.
A. Beveridge, *The Russian Advance,* 1903.
A. Colquhoun, *China in Transformation,* 1898.
G. Curzon, *Problems of the Far East,* 1896.
A. de Koulomzine, *Le Transsibérien,* 1904.
S. Dubrovsky, *Stolypin's Reform,* 1930 [R].
R. Ensor, *England 1870–1914, The Oxford History of England, XIV.*
O. Franke, *Die Grossmächte in Ost-Asien,* 1923.
N. G. Garin-Mikhailovsky, *Korea, Manchuria and Liao-Tung,* Comp. Works VII [R].
B. Glinsky, *The Prelude to the Russo-Japanese War,* 1916 [R].
A. Halperin, *The British-Japanese Alliance,* 1947 [R].
History of Diplomacy II, 1941 [R].
N. Karpov, *Stolypin's Agrarian Policy,* 1925 [R].
A. Kaufmann, *Resettlement and Colonization,* 1905 [R].
G. Kennan, *Tent Life in Siberia,* 1870.

V. Kokovtsev, *Out of my Past, I*, 1933 [R].
V. Korostovetz, *Graf Witte*, 1929.
G. Krahmer, *Sib. u. d. grosse Eisenbahn*, 1897.
P. Leroy-Beaulieu, *La Rénovation de l'Asie*, 1900.
T. Meadows, *The Chinese and their Rebellions*, 1856.
B. Romanov, *Essays on the Diplomatic History of the Russo-Japanese War*, 1947 [R].
— *Russia in Manchuria*, 1928 [R].
S. Sabler and I. Sosnovsky, *The Great Siberian Railway*, 1903 [R].
P. Sibiriaseff, *Exzellenz Witte*, 1904.
A. Suvorin, *Diaries*, 1923 [R].
S. J. Witte, *Memoirs*, 3 vols., Berlin, 1922 [R].

XI—THE FAR EASTERN DRAMA
V. Apushkin, *The Russo-Japanese War*, 1910 [R].
D. Dallin, *The Rise of Russia in Asia*, 1949.
T. Dennet, *Roosevelt and the Russo-Japanese War*, 1925.
H. de Windt, *Russia As I know It*, 1917.
A. Griswold, *The Far Eastern Policy of the U.S.*, 1938.
J. Hamilton, *A Staff Officer's Scrap Book*, 1908.
A. Ignatyev, *50 Jahre Militärdienst*, 1948.
K. Ishii, *Diplomatic Commentaries*, 1936.
A. Kantorovich, *America's Struggle for China*, 1935 [R].
H. Kohn, *Gesch. d. nationalen Bewegung im Orient*, 1928.
I. Korostovetz, *Von Tschingis-Khan zur Sowjet-Rep.*, 1926.
A. Kuropatkin, *The Russian Army and the Japanese War*, 1909.
H. Langer, *The Diplomacy of Imperialism*, 1935.
N. Levitsky, *The Russo-Japanese War*, 1938 [R].
A. Lobanov-Rostovsky, *Russia and Asia*, 1933.
I. Maisky, *Mongolia Today*, 1921 [R].
A. Novikov-Priboy, *Tsuschima*, 1936.
N. Oganovsky, *Siberian Political Economy*, 1915 [R].
T. Roosevelt, *Autobiography*, 1913.
R. Rosen, *Forty Years of Diplomacy*, 1922.
V. Semenikov, *The Policies of the Romanovs on the Eve of the Revolution*, 1926 [R].
V. Stefansson, *The Adventure of Wrangel Island*, 1925.
— *The Northward Course of Empire*, 1922.
V. Yakhontoff, *Russia and the Soviet Union in the Far East*, 1931.
E. Zabriskie, *American-Russian Rivalry in the Far East*, 1946.

XII—RED SIBERIA
N. Baransky, *Economic Geography of the Soviet Union*, 1951 ed. [R].

W. Barthold, *History of Turkestan*, 1922 [R].

V. Gurko-Kryashin, *The Main Lines of World History*, 1925 [R].

W. Kolarz, *Peoples of the Soviet Far East*, 1954.

W. Leimbach, *Die Sowjetunion*, 1950.

E. Lenguel, *Secret Siberia*, 1946.

H. J. Mackinder, *Democratic Ideals and Reality*, 1919.

O. v. Niedermayer and Y. Semyonov, *Die Sowjetunion*, 1934.

S. Prokopovicz, *Russlands Volkswirtschaft unter d. Sowjets*, 2 vols., 1944–48.

Aitchen K. Wu, *China and the Soviet Union*, 1950.

INDEX OF PROPER NAMES